Teatropace33
Roma

In the very heart of the historic centre of Rome, between Piazza Navona and the left bank of the Tiber, the Teatropace33 opened in May 2004. This charming three-star hotel with 23 rooms was a cardinal's residence during the papacy of "Urbano VIII". The building – painted the typical warm red of Roman palazzos and sunsets – is situated in a narrow street, Via del Teatro Pace, that runs behind Corso Vittorio from the small square with the statue where, during the night, Pasquino left his satirical verses criticizing those in power in the city.

The small door to the hotel, which could be taken for the door to a private house, stands unobtrusively among typical restaurants and craftsmen's workshops. Opposite is the fine building that housed the Teatro Pace in the eighteenth century. The performances took place in the open air on a wooden stage set up in the courtyard. The great playwright Goldoni trod the boards here on several occasions while on tour with his company.

Most of the art treasures of the seventeenth century are packed into this very small area of the still visible remains of Imperial Rome; Piazza Navona and the church of Sant'Agnese in Agone, the fountain of the four rivers, the Bramante's Cloister, Sant'Ivo alla Sapienza, Sant'Andrea della Valle, Palazzo Farnese (now the French Embassy). There are also some very important museums as the Museo Barracco with valuable Egyptian, Greek and Roman sculptures; Palazzo Braschi, which now houses the Museo di Roma; Palazzo Altemps with its collection of classical statues from the Altemps, Mattei and Ludovisi collections and, on the Lungotevere, the Museo Napoleonico.

Returning to the Teatropace33, on entering the main door you find yourself in a tiny hall with an imposing spiral stone staircase the steps of which are broad and shallow with a balustrade of small columns running alongside it. Dating from the late sixteenth century, it is the work of the architect Onorio Longhi (1568 - 1619). It rises in wide spirals to the three floors above and this is the only way to get to the rooms because the building has not a lift.

The twenty-three rooms, pleasantly and classically furnished, almost all have wooden-beamed ceilings and parquet floors. From the windows and the occasional balcony you can enjoy some of the most authentic views of Rome: the church domes, roofs, terraces with flowers, elegant old courtyards and lively streets. One of the jewels of this charming hotel is the Junior Suite with a terrace large enough for a table and chairs, which has a direct view of Sant'Agnese in Agone.

Wood is a dominant feature of the rooms: it has been used in the bedheads, in the comfortable desks with drawers, and in the wardrobes. Yellow and blue are the colours chosen for the bed covers and the nineteenth century upholstery with floral patterns on the comfortable padded armchairs. Prints by Piranesi decorate the walls. The bathrooms (most of which have windows) are in yellow Siena marble with shower cabins (three have bath tubs). The rooms have been fitted with every comfort: air conditioning, direct telephone line, satellite TV, minibar, safe, Internet Fast connection and a kettle for making tea or coffee at any time of the day or night in your own room.

Breakfast is served by an original room service: the waiters will rush your breakfast to you, expertly balancing on one hand a tray laden with frothy "cappuccino" and a fragrant cornetto. What more could you ask for to really experience what Rome is like?

Via del Teatro Pace, 33 - 00186 Roma
Tel. +39 06/6879075 - Fax +39 06/68192364
info@hotelteatropace.com - www.hotelteatropace.com

Something new in the heart of Rome…

the wonderful terraces of Hotel Alpi.

Extremely close to the main railway station and to the famous " Via Veneto ", Hotel Alpi always welcomes you in the most comfortable way.
48 rooms differently and carefully decorated in every detail. A romantic terrace offers you peaceful and relaxing moments.

Hotel Alpi
ROMA

AUTHENTIC

Rome

Touring Club Italiano
President and Chairman: *Roberto Ruozi*
General Manager: *Guido Venturini*

Touring Editore
Managing Director: *Alfieri Lorenzon*
Editorial Director: *Michele D'Innella*
Editorial coordination: *Cristiana Baietta*

International Department
Fabio Pittella
fabio.pittella@touringclub.it

Senior Editor: *Paola Pandiani*
Editor: *Monica Maraschi*
Writer and Researcher: *Pietro Ferrario*
with Banca Dati Turistica for Pratical info
Translation and page layout: *Studio Queens, Milan*
Maps: *Touring Club Italiano*
Design: *Studio Queens, Milan*
Cover photo: *A charming view of the Roman Forum
at sunset (M. Fraschetti)*
*We would like to thank Teresa Cremona for her help
in creating the Gastronomy route.*

Advertising Manager: *Claudio Bettinelli*
Local Advertising: *Progetto*
www.progettosrl.it - info@progettosrl.it

Printing and Binding: *CPM S.p.A., Casarile*

Distribution
USA/CAN – *Publishers Group West*
UK/Ireland – *Portfolio Books*

Touring Club Italiano, Corso Italia 10, 20122 Milano
www.touringclub.it
© 2007 Touring Editore, Milan

Code K8YOO
ISBN-13: 978 – 88365 – 4130 – 0
ISBN-10: 88 – 365 – 4130 – 5

Printed in January 2007

AUTHENTIC
Rome

TOURING CLUB
OF ITALY

SUMMARY

16   HERITAGE

Rome: a city with a unique character, where past, present and future live side-by-side, simply begging to be explored.

108   ITINERARIES

Rome: all the facts you need to explore the city and its province and discover their secrets for yourselves.

158   FOOD

Rome, once the center of the world, has a highly versatile cuisine. In fact, local specialties and international dishes often appear on the same menu. Where to eat and what to eat. Try some of the specialties from the Roman countryside.

180 SHOPPING

Rome is full of elegant shops and colorful street markets. Where to find sophisticated hand-made jewelry and ceramics, elegant boutiques and traditional tailor's shops. Choosing what to buy is no simple matter!

Art and crafts
Markets
Fashion

188 EVENTS

Rome: popular traditions and religious practices centuries old, rock concerts and sacred music. The backdrop of the local setting and the fact that this area has a very mild climate contribute in a major way to the success of events like these.

Music
Folklore

196 PRACTICAL INFO

The Practical Information is divided into sections on the hotels, restaurants, farm holidays and places of entertainment we recommend. The category of the hotels is indicated by the number of stars. In the case of restaurants we have awarded forks, taking into account the price of the meal, the level of comfort and service, and the ambience.

WHAT IS THE TOURING CLUB OF ITALY?

Long Tradition, Great Prestige

For over 110 years, the Touring Club of Italy (TCI) has offered travelers the most detailed and comprehensive source of travel information available on Italy. The Touring Club of Italy was founded in 1894 with the aim of developing the social and cultural values of tourism and promoting the conservation and enjoyment of the country's national heritage, landscape and environment.

Advantages of Membership

Today, TCI offers a wide rage of travel services to assist and support members with the highest level of convenience and quality. Now you can discover the unique charms of Italy with a distinct insider's advantage.

Enjoy exclusive money saving offers with a TCI membership. Use your membership card for discounts in thousands of restaurants, hotels, spas, campgrounds, museums, shops and markets.

These Hotel Chains offer preferred rates and discounts to TCI members!

How to Join

It's quick and easy to join.
Apply for your membership online at
www.touringclub.it
Your membership card will arrive within
three weeks and is valid for discounts
across Italy for the entire year.
Get your card before you go and start
saving as soon as you arrive.
Euro 25 annual membership fee
includes priority mail postage for
membership card and materials.
Just one use of the card will more than
cover the cost of membership.

Benefits

• Exclusive car rental rates with Hertz
• Discounts at select Esso gas stations
• 20% discount on TCI guidebooks
and maps purchased in TCI bookstores
or directly online at
www.touringclub.com
• Preferred rates and discounts available
at thousands of locations in Italy: Hotels -
B&B's - Villa Rentals - Campgrounds -TCI
Resorts - Spas - Restaurants - Wineries -
Museums - Cinemas - Theaters - Music
Festivals - Shops - Craft Markets - Ferries -
Cruises - Theme Parks - Botanical Gardens

ITALY: INSTRUCTIONS FOR USE

Italy is known throughout the world for the quantity and quality of its art treasures and for its natural beauty, but it is also famous for its inimitable lifestyle and fabulous cuisine and wines. Although it is a relatively small country, Italy boasts an extremely varied culture and multifarious traditions and customs. The information and suggestions in this brief section will help foreign tourists not only to understand certain aspects of Italian life, but also to solve the everyday difficulties and the problems of a practical nature that inevitably crop up during any trip.

This practical information is included in brief descriptions of various topics: public transport and how to purchase tickets; suggestions on how to drive in this country; the different types of rooms and accommodation in hotels; hints on how to use mobile phones and communication in general. This is followed by useful advice on how to meet your everyday needs and on shopping, as well as information concerning the cultural differences in the various regions. Lastly, there is a section describing the vast range of restaurants, bars, wine bars and pizza parlors.

TRANSPORTATION

From the airport to the city
Public transportation in major cities is easily accessible and simple to use. Both Malpensa Airport in Milan and Fiumicino Airport in Rome have trains and buses linking them to the city centers. At Malpensa, you can take a bus to the main train station or a train to Cadorna train station and subway stop.

Subways, buses, and trams
Access to the subways, buses, and trams requires a ticket (tickets are not sold on board but can be purchased at most newsstands and tobacco shops). The ticket is good for one ride and sometimes has a time limit (in the case of buses and trams). When you board a bus or tram, you are required to stamp your previously-acquired ticket in the time-stamping machine. Occasionally, a conductor will board the bus or tram and check everyone's ticket. If you haven't got one, or if it has not been time-stamped, you will have to pay a steep fine.

Trains
The Ferrovie dello Stato (Italian Railways) is among the best and most modern railway systems in Europe. Timetables and routes can be consulted and reservations can be made online at www.trenitalia.com. Many travel agents can also dispense tickets and help you plan your journey. Hard-copy schedules can be purchased at all newsstands and most bookstores.

A detail of the Colosseum.

Automated ticket machines, which include easy-to-use instructions in English, are available in nearly all stations. They can be used to check schedules, makes reservations, and purchase tickets.
There are different types of train, according to the requirements:
Eurostar Italia Trains **ES★** : Fast connections between Italy's most important cities. The ticket includes seat booking charge;
Intercity *IC* and **Espresso £** Trains: Local connections among Italy's towns and cities. Sometimes *IC* and **£** trains require seat booking. You can book your seat up to 3 hours before the train departure. The seat booking charge is of 3 Euro.
Interregionale Trains *iR* move beyond regional boundaries. Among the combined local-transport services, the *iR* Trains are the fastest ones with the fewest number of stops. No seat booking available.
Diretto *D* and **Regionale** *R* Trains can circulate both within the regions and their bordering regions. No seat booking available.

DO NOT FORGET: In Italy, you can only board a train if you have a valid ticket that has been time-stamped prior to boarding (each station has numerous time-stamping machines). You cannot buy or stamp tickets on the train.

If you don't have a ticket – or did not stamp before boarding – you will be liable to pay the full ticket price plus a 25 euro fine. If you produce a ticket that is not valid for the train or service you're using (i.e. one issued for a different train category at a different price, etc.) you will be asked to pay the difference with respect to the full ticket price, plus an 8 euro surcharge.

Taxis

Taxis are a convenient but expensive way to travel in Italian cities. There are taxi stands scattered throughout major cities. You cannot hail taxis on the street in Italy, but you can reserve taxis, in advance or immediately, by phone: consult the yellow pages for the number or ask your hotel reception desk or maitre d'hotel to call for you.

Taxi drivers have the right to charge you a supplementary fee for every piece of luggage they transport, as well as evening surcharges.

Driving

Especially when staying in the countryside, driving is a safe and convenient way to travel through Italy and its major cities. It is important to be aware of street signs and speed limits, and many cities have zones where only limited traffic is allowed in order to accommodate pedestrians.

Street parking is organized using road signs and different colored street markings. No line or a white line is for free parking, blue is for paid parking and yellow is for reserved parking (disabled, residents etc). There may be time limits for both free and paid parking. In this case, use your parking disc to indicate your time of arrival.

Although an international driver's license is not required in Italy, it is advisable. ACI and similar associations provide this service to members. The fuel distribution network is reasonably distributed all over the territory. All service stations have unleaded gasoline ("benzina verde") and diesel fuel ("gasolio"). Opening time is 7am to 12:30 and 15 to 19:30; on motorways the service is 24 hours a day.

Type of roads in Italy: The *Autostrada* (for example A14) is the main highway system in Italy and is similar to the Interstate highway system in the US and the motorway system in the UK. Shown on our Touring Club Italiano 1:200,000 road maps as black. The Autostrada are toll highways; you pay to use them. The *Strada Statale* (for example SS54) is a fast moving road that may have one or more lanes in each direction. Shown on our Touring Club Italiano 1:200,000 road maps as red. *Strada Provinciale* (for example SP358) can be narrow, slow and winding roads. They are usually one lane in each direction. Shown on our Touring Club Italiano 1:200,000 road maps as yellow. *Strada Comunale* (for example SC652) is a local road connecting the main town with its sorrounding. Note: In our guide you will sometime find an address of a place in the countryside listed, for example, as

"SS54 Km 25". This means that the you have to drive along the Strada Statale 54 until you reach the 25-km road sign.
Speed limits: 130 kmph on the Autostrada, 110 kmph on main highways, 90 kmph outside of towns, 50 kmph in towns.
The town streets are patrolled by the Polizia Municipale while the roads outside cities and the Autostrada are patrolled by the Carabinieri or the Polizia Stradale.
Do not forget:
• Wear your seat belt at all times;
• Do not use the cellular phone while driving;
• Have your headlights on at all times when driving outside of cities;
• The drunk driving laws are strict – do not drink and drive;
• In case of an accident you are not allowed to get out of your car unless you are wearing a special, high-visibility, reflective jacket.

ACCOMMODATION

Hotels

In Italy it is common practice for the reception desk to register your passport, and only registered guests are allowed to use the rooms. This is mere routine, done for security reasons, and there is no need for concern.
All hotels use the official star classification system, from 5-star luxury hotel to 1 star accommodation.
Room rates are based on whether they are for single ("camera singola") or double ("camera doppia") occupancy. In every room you will find a list of the hotel rates (generally on the back of the door). While 4- and 5-star hotels have double beds, most hotels have only single beds. Should you want a double bed, you have to ask for a "letto matrimoniale". All hotels have rooms with bathrooms; only 1-star establishments usually have only shared bathrooms.
Most hotel rates include breakfast ("prima colazione"), but you can request to do without it, thus reducing the rate.
Breakfast is generally served in a communal room and comprises a buffet with pastries, bread with butter and jam, cold cereals, fruit, yoghurt, coffee, and fruit juice. Some hotels regularly frequented by foreign tourists will also serve other items such as eggs for their American and British guests.
The hotels for families and in tourist localities also offer "mezza pensione", or half board, in which breakfast and dinner are included in the price.
It's always a good idea to check when a hotel's annual closing period is, especially if you are planning a holiday by the sea.

Farm stays

Located only in the countryside, and generally on a farm, "agriturismo" – a network of farm holiday establishments – is part of a growing trend in Italy to honor local gastronomic and wine traditions, as well as countryside traditions. These farms offer meals prepared with ingredients cultivated exclusively on site: garden-grown vegetables, homemade cheese and local recipes. Many of these places also provide lodging, one of the best ways to experience the "genuine" Italian lifestyle.

Bed & Breakfast

This form of accommodation provides bed and breakfast in a private house, and in the last few years has become much more widespread in Italy. There are over 5,000 b&bs, classified in 3 categories, and situated both in historic town centers, as well as in the outskirts and the countryside. Rooms for guests are always well-furnished, but not all of them have en suite bathrooms.
It is well-recommended to check the closing of the open-all-year accommodation services and restaurants, because they could have a short break during the year (usually no longer than a fortnight).

COMMUNICATIONS

Nearly everyone in Italy owns a cellular phone. Although public phones are still available, they seem to be ever fewer and farther between. If you wish to use public phones, you will find them in subway stops, bars, along the street, and phone centers generally located in the city center. Phone cards and pre-paid phone cards can be purchased at most newsstands and tobacco shops, and can also be acquired at automated tellers.
For European travelers, activating personal cellular coverage is relatively simple, as it is in most cases for American and Australian travelers as well. Contact your mobile service provider for details.

Cellular phones can also be rented in Italy from TIM, the Italian national phone company. For information, visit its website at www.tim.it. When traveling by car through the countryside, a cellular phone can really come in handy. Note that when dialing in Italy, you must always dial the prefix (e.g., 02 for Milan, 06 for Rome) even when making a local call. For cellular phones, however, the initial zero is always dropped. Freephone numbers always start with "800". For calls abroad from Italy, it's a good idea to buy a special pre-paid international phone card, which is used with a PIN code.

Internet access

Cyber cafés have sprung up all over Italy and you can find one on nearly every city block.

EATING AND DRINKING

The bar

The Italian "bar" is a multi-faceted, all-purpose establishment for drinking, eating and socializing, where you can order an espresso, have breakfast, and enjoy a quick sandwich for lunch or even a hot meal. You can often buy various items here (sometimes even stamps, cigarettes, phone cards, etc.). Bear in mind that table service ("servizio a tavola") includes a surcharge. At most bars, if you choose to sit, a waiter will take your order. Every bar should have a list of prices posted behind or near the counter; if the bar offers table service, the price list should also include the extra fee for this.

Lunch at bars will include, but is not limited to, "panini," sandwiches with crusty bread, usually with cured meats such as "prosciutto" (salt-cured ham), "prosciutto cotto" (cooked ham), and cheeses such as mozzarella topped with tomato and basil. Then there are "tramezzini" (finger sandwiches) with tuna, cheese, or vegetables, etc. Often the "panini" and other savory sandwiches (like stuffed flatbread or "focaccia") are heated before being served. Naturally, the menu at bars varies according to the region: in Bologna you will find "piadine" (flatbread similar to pita) with Swiss chard; in Palermo there are "arancini" (fried rice balls stuffed with

ground meat); in Genoa you will find that even the most unassuming bar serves some of the best "focaccia" in all Italy. Some bars also include a "tavola calda". If you see this sign in a bar window, it means that hot dishes like pasta and even entrées are served.

A brief comment on coffee and cappuccino: Italians never serve coffee with savory dishes or sandwiches, and they seldom drink cappuccino outside of breakfast (although they are happy to serve it at any time).

While English- and Irish-type pubs are frequented by beer lovers and young people in Italy, there are also American bars where long drinks and American cocktails are served.

Breakfast at the bar

Breakfast in Italy generally consists of some type of pastry, most commonly a "brioche" – a croissant either filled with cream or jam, or plain – and a cappuccino or espresso. Although most bars do not offer American coffee, you can ask for a "caffè lungo" or "caffè americano", both of which resemble the American coffee preferred by the British and Americans. Most bars have a juicer to make a "spremuta", freshly squeezed orange or grapefruit juice.

Lunch and Dinner

As with all daily rituals in Italy, food is prepared and meals are served according to local customs (e.g., in the North they prefer rice and butter, in South and Central Italy they favor pasta and olive oil). Wine is generally served at mealtime, and while finer restaurants have excellent wine lists (some including vintage wines), ordering the house table wine generally brings good results (a house Chianti to accompany your Florentine steak in Tuscany, a sparkling Prosecco paired with your creamed stockfish and polenta in Venice, a dry white wine with pasta dressed with sardines and wild fennel fronds in Sicily).

Mineral water is also commonly served at meals and can be "gassata" (sparkling) or "naturale" (still).

The most sublime culinary experience in Italy is achieved by matching the local foods with the appropriate local wines: wisdom dictates that a friendly waiter will be flattered by your request for his recommendation on what to eat and drink.

Whether at an "osteria" (a tavern), a "trattoria" (a home-style restaurant), or a "ristorante" (a proper restaurant), the service of lunch and dinner generally consists of – but is not limited to – the following: "antipasti" or appetizers; "primo piatto" or first course, i.e., pasta, rice, or soup; "secondo piatto" or main course, i.e., meat or seafood; "contorno" or side-dish, served with the main course, i.e., vegetables or salad; "formaggi", "frutta", and "dolci", i.e., cheeses, fruit, and dessert; caffè or espresso coffee, perhaps spiked with a shot of grappa.

The pizzeria

The pizzeria is in general one of the most economical, democratic, and satisfying culinary experiences in Italy. Everyone eats at the pizzeria: young people, families, couples, locals and tourists alike. Generally, each person orders her/his own pizza, and while the styles of crust and toppings will vary from region to region (some of the best pizzas are served in Naples and Rome), the acid test of any pizzeria is the Margherita, topped simply with cheese and tomato sauce.

Beer, sparkling or still water, and Coca Cola are the beverages commonly served with pizza. Some restaurants include a pizza menu, but most establishments do not serve pizza at lunchtime.

The wine bar (enoteca)

More than one English-speaking tourist in Italy has wondered why the wine bar is called an enoteca in other countries and the English term is used in Italy: the answer lies somewhere in the mutual fondness that Italians and English speakers have for one another. Wine bars have become popular in recent years in the major cities (especially in Rome, where you can find some of the best). The wine bar is a great place to sample different local wines and eat a light, tapas-style dinner.

CULTURAL DIVERSITY

Whenever you travel, not only are you a guest of your host country, but you are also a representative of your home country. As a general rule, courtesy, consideration, and respect are always appreciated by guests and their hosts alike. Italians are famous for their hospitality and experience will verify this felicitous stereotype: perhaps nowhere else in Europe are tourists and visitors received more warmly. Italy is a relatively "new" country. Its borders, as we know them today, were established only in 1861 when it became a monarchy under the House of Savoy. After WWII, Italy became a Republic and now it is one of the member states of the European Union. One of the most fascinating aspects of Italian culture is that, even as a unified country, local tradition still prevails over a universally Italian national identity. Some jokingly say that the only time that Venetians, Milanese, Florentines, Neapolitans, and Sicilians feel like Italians is when the national football team plays in international competitions. From their highly localized dialects to the foods they eat, from their religious celebration to their politics, Italians proudly maintain their local heritage. This is one of the reasons why the Piedmontese continue to prefer their beloved Barolo wine and their white truffles, the Umbrians their rich Sagrantino wine and black truffles, the Milanese their risotto and panettone, the Venetians their stockfish and polenta, the Bolognese their lasagne and pumpkin ravioli, the Florentines their bread soups and steaks cooked rare, the Abruzzese their excellent fish broth and seafood, the Neapolitans their mozzarella, basil, pizza, and pasta. As a result of its rich cultural diversity, the country's population also varies greatly in its customs from region to region, city to city, town to town. As you visit different cities and regions throughout Italy, you will see how the local personality and character of the Italians change as rapidly as the landscape does. Having lived for millennia with their great diversity and rich, highly heterogeneous culture, the Italians have taught us many things, foremost among them the age-old expression, "When in Rome, do as the Romans do."

NATIONAL HOLIDAYS

New Year's Day (1st January), Epiphany (6th January), Easter Monday (day after Easter Sunday), Liberation Day (25th April), Labour Day (1st May), Italian Republic Day (2nd June), Assumption (15th August), All Saints' Day (1st November), Immaculate Conception (8th December), Christmas Day and Boxing Day (25th-26th December).
In addition to these holidays, each city also has a holiday to celebrate its patron saint's feast day, usually with lively, local celebrations. Shops and services in large cities close on national holidays and for the week of the 15th of August.

EVERYDAY NEEDS

State tobacco shops and pharmacies
Tobacco is available in Italy only at state licensed tobacco shops. These vendors ("tabaccheria"), often incorporated in a bar, also sell stamps.
Since January 2005 smoking is forbidden in all so-called public places – unless a separately ventilated space is constructed – meaning over 90% of the country's restaurants and bars.
Medicines can be purchased only in pharmacies ("farmacia") in Italy. Pharmacists are very knowledgeable about common ailments and can generally prescribe a treatment for you on the spot. Opening time is 8:30-12:30 and 15:30-19:30 but in any case there is always a pharmacy open 24 hours and during holidays.

Shopping
Every locality in Italy offers tourists characteristic shops, markets with good bargains, and even boutiques featuring leading Italian fashion designers. Opening hours vary from region to region and from season to season. In general, shops are open from 9 to 13 and from 15/16 to 19/20, but in large cities they usually have no lunchtime break.

Tax Free
Non-EU citizens can obtain a reimbursement for IVA (goods and services tax) paid on purchases over €155, for goods which are exported within 90 days, in shops which display the relevant sign. IVA is always automatically included in the price of any purchase, and ranges from 20% to 4% depending on the item. The shop issues a reimbursement voucher to present when you leave the country (at a frontier or airport). For purchases in shops affiliated to 'Tax Free Shopping', IVA may be reimbursed directly at international airports.

Banks and post offices
Italian banks are open Monday to Friday, from 8:30 to 13:30 and then from 15 to 16. However, the afternoon business hours may vary.
Post offices are open from Monday to Saturday, from 8:30 to 13:30 (12:30 on Saturday). In the larger towns there are also some offices open in the afternoon.

Currency
As in many other European Union countries, the Euros is the Italian currency. Coins are in denominations of 1, 2, 5, 10, 20 and 50 cents and 1 and 2 euros; banknotes are in denominations of 5, 10, 20, 50, 100, 200 and 500 euros, each with a different color.

Credit cards
All the main credit cards are generally accepted, but some smaller enterprises (arts and crafts shops, small hotels, bed & breakfasts, or farm stays) do not provide this service. Foreign tourists can obtain cash using credit cards at automatic teller machines.

Time
All Italy is in the same time zone, which is six hours ahead of Eastern Standard Time in the USA. Daylight saving time is used from March to October, when watches and clocks are set an hour ahead of standard time.

Passports and vaccinations
Citizens of EU countries can enter Italy without frontier checks. Citizens of Australia, Canada, New Zealand, and the United States can enter Italy with a valid passport and need not have a visa for a stay of less than 90 days.
No vaccinations are necessary.

Payment and tipping
When you sit down at a restaurant you are generally charged a "coperto" or cover charge ranging from 1.5 to 3 euros, for service and the bread. Tipping is not customary in Italy. Beware of unscrupulous restaurateurs who add a space on their clients' credit card receipt for a tip, while it has already been included in the cover charge.

USEFUL ADDRESSES

Foreign Embassies in Italy

Australia
Via A. Bosio, 5 - 00161 Rome
Tel. +39 06 852721
Fax +39 06 85272300
www.italy.embassy.gov.au.
info-rome@dfat.gov.au

Canada
Via Salaria, 243 - 00199 Rome
Tel. +39 06 854441
Fax +39 06 85444 3915
www.canada.it
rome@dfait-maeci.gc.ca

Great Britain
Via XX Settembre, 80 -
00187 Rome
Tel. +39 06 42200001
Fax +39 06 42202334
www.britian.it
consularenquiries@rome.
mail.fco.gov.uk

Ireland
Piazza di Campitelli, 3 -
00186 Rome
Tel. +39 06 6979121
Fax +39 06 6792354
irish.embassy@esteri.it

New Zealand
Via Zara, 28 - 00198 Rome
Tel. +39 06 4417171
Fax +39 06 4402984

South Africa
Via Tanaro, 14 - 00198 Rome
Tel. +39 06 852541
Fax +39 06 85254300
www.sudafrica.it

United States of America
Via Vittorio Veneto, 121 -
00187 Rome
Tel. +39 06 46741
Fax +39 06 4882672
www.usis.it

Foreign Consulates in Italy

Australia
Via Borgogna, 2
20122 Milan
Tel. +39 02 77704217
Fax +39 02 77704242

Canada
Via Vittor Pisani, 19
20124 Milan
Tel. +39 02 67581
Fax +39 02 67583900
milan@international.gc.ca

Great Britain
Via S. Paolo, 7
20121 Milan
Tel. +39 02 723001
Fax +39 02 86465081
ConsularMilan@fco.gov.uk

Lungarno Corsini, 2
50123 Florence
Tel. +39 055 284133
Consular.Florence@fco.gov.uk

Via dei Mille, 40
80121 Naples
Tel. +39 081 4238911
Fax +39 081 422434
Info.Naples@fco.gov.uk

Ireland
Piazza San Pietro in Gessate, 2 -
20122 Milan
Tel. +39 02 55187569/62 55187641
Fax +39 02 55187570

New Zealand
Via Guido d'Arezzo, 6
20145 Milan
Tel. +39 02 48012544
Fax +39 02 48012577

South Africa
Vicolo San Giovanni
sul Muro, 4
20121 Milan
Tel. +39 02 8858581
Fax +39 02 72011063
saconsulate@iol.it

United States of America
Via Principe Amedeo, 2/10
20121 Milan
Tel. +39 02 290351
Fax +39 02 29001165

Lungarno Vespucci, 38
50123 Florence
Tel. +39 055 266951
Fax +39 055 284088

Piazza della Repubblica
80122 Naples
Tel. +39 081 5838111
Fax +39 081 7611869

Italian Embassies and Consulates Around the World

Australia
12, Grey Street - Deakin, A.C.T.
2600 - Canberra
Tel. 02 62733333, 62733398,
62733198
Fax 02 62734223
www.ambcanberra.esteri.it
Consulates at: Brisbane, Glynde,
Melbourne, Perth , Sydney

Canada
275, Slater Street, 21st floor -
Ottawa (Ontario) K1P 5H9
Tel. (613) 232 2401/2/3
Fax (613) 233 1484 234 8424
www.ambottawa.esteri.it
ambital@italyincanada.com
Consulates at: Edmonton,
Montreal, Toronto, Vancouver,

Great Britain
14, Three Kings Yard, London
W1K 4EH
Tel. 020 73122200
Fax 020 73122230
www.amblondra.esteri.it
ambasciata.londra@esteri.it
Consulates at: London, Bedford,
Edinburgh, Manchester

Ireland
63/65, Northumberland Road -
Dublin 4
Tel. 01 6601744
Fax 01 6682759
www.ambdublino.esteri.it
info@italianembassy.ie

New Zealand
34-38 Grant Road, Thorndon,
(PO Box 463, Wellington)
Tel. 04 473 5339

Fax 04 472 7255
www.ambwellington.esteri.it

South Africa
796 George Avenue, 0083 Arcadia
Tel. 012 4305541/2/3
Fax 012 4305547
www.ambpretoria.esteri.it
Consulates at: Johannesburg,
Capetown, Durban

United States of America
3000 Whitehaven Street, NW
Washington DC 20008
Tel. (202) 612-4400
Fax (202) 518-2154
www.ambwashingtondc.esteri.it
Consulates at: Boston, MA -
Chicago, IL - Detroit, MI - Houston,
TX - Los Angeles, CA - Miami, FL -
Newark, NJ - New York, NY -
Philadelphia, PA - San Francisco, CA

ENIT (Italian State Tourism Board)

Australia
Level 4, 46 Market Street
NSW 2000 Sidney
PO Box Q802 - QVB NSW 1230
Tel. 00612 92 621666
Fax 00612 92 621677
italia@italiantourism.com.au

Canada
175 Bloor Street E. Suite 907 –
South Tower
M4W3R8 Toronto (Ontario)
Tel. (416) 925 4882
Fax (416) 925 4799
www.italiantourism.com
enit.canada@on.aibn.com

Great Britain
1, Princes Street
W1B 2AY London
Tel. 020 7408 1254
Tel. 800 00482542 FREE from
United Kingdom and Ireland
italy@italiantouristboard.co.uk

United States of America
500, North Michigan Avenue
Suite 2240
60611 Chicago 1, Illinois
Tel. (312) 644 0996 /644 0990
Fax (312) 644 3019
www.italiantourism.com
enitch@italiantourism.com

12400, Wilshire Blvd. – Suite 550
CA 90025 Los Angeles
Tel. (310) 820 1898 - 820 9807
Fax (310) 820 6357
www.italiantourism.com
enitla@italiantourism.com

630, Fifth Avenue – Suite 1565
NY – 10111 New York
Tel. (212) 245 4822 – 245 5618
Fax (212) 586 9249
www.italiantourism.com
enitny@italiantourism.com

15

In Rome, art, history and centuries-old monuments combine to form a backdrop for its colorful popular traditions and the everyday life of the metropolis, pervaded by an atmosphere where past, present and future co-exist. A crossroads of the world for more than 2,000 years, over the centuries, the city has generated and received all kinds of different influences which were absorbed into the fertile sub-soil of the local culture. To understand Rome, you mustn't forget that it was once *caput mundi* (head of all the world), the mightiest city of the Mediterranean, which, for centuries, dominated much of the known world of that time, and then became the center of Christianity.

Cathedral	→ Duomo	Fountain	→ Fontana
Chapel	→ Cappella	Hall	→ Sala
Castle	→ Castello	Museum	→ Museo
Church	→ Chiesa	Temple	→ Tempio
Doorway	→ Porta	Sanctuary	→ Santuario

Here you can feel the powerful aura of the places which were the cradle of Western civilisation. Paying the respect and attention you would give to a wise old man, let the spirit of the Holy City speak to you through the gold in St Peter's, its statues and its buildings.

Heritage

Highlights

- The majestic sight of Piazza S. Pietro enclosed by Bernini's colonnade.
- The Colosseum, symbol of Rome.
- The Roman Forum and Imperial Fora, the civic and economic fulcrum of the Roman Empire.
- Its streets and squares, bridges and palazzi: an open-air museum of art and history.

Bold, stars and italics are used in the text to emphasize the importance of places and art-works:
bold type ** → **not to be missed**
bold type * → **very important**
bold type → **important**
italic type → **interesting**

Inside

Today, the sheer size of Rome and its truly unique urban landscape never fail to astonish visitors and tourists. Rome, the Eternal City, is pervaded by a magical, special atmosphere. Once the capital of the world's largest and longest-lasting empire, today, it is a metropolis where one can 'live' a truly extraordinary cultural experience. At every turn, visitors are struck by the incredible layers of architecture, culture and traditions that make Rome unique across the world. The uninterrupted sequence of archeological and Roman Imperial remains and early-Christian, Romanesque, Gothic, Renaissance, Baroque and modern buildings conjure up an overall image of this City of a Hundred Churches, the outward sign of the continuity of a city which, for almost three millennia, has developed basically on the same area of land. The ancient harbors, filled in centuries ago and given the name Fiumicino, where Roman galleys used to moor, are now a port of call for the larger, faster vehicles of air travel. But things have not changed so very much with the passing of the centuries and millennia. You still find the letters S.P.Q.R. (an acronym of the Latin phrase *Senatus Populusque*

ROUTE 1

THE HOLY CITY

Il Gesù ❶

Reaction to the Reformation demanded a new model for places of worship, because the new liturgical requirements prescribed settings where the attention of the worshippers focused on the high altar. The prototype was the church of the Santissimo Nome di Gesù, begun in 1568 and based on a design by Vignola. Another architect, Giacomo Della Porta, was entrusted with the facade (1571-77), which also became a model, and it was he who completed the church, consecrated in 1584. Inside, the long nave leading to the presbytery and the apse is crossed by a transept of equal width, dominated by a semi-spherical dome resting on a drum. The triumphal architectural language of late Baroque decorates the interior (1672-85). The fresco by Baciccia (1679), the **Triumph of the Name of Jesus***, uses an unusual aerial perspective technique which seems to ignore the limitations of the dome. Andrea Pozzo designed the **chapel of S. Ignatius Loyola** (in the left transept), where the remains of the Jesuit saint are buried.

Area Sacra dell'Argentina ❷

It is very probable that it was here, on the Ides of March of the year 44 BC, that Julius Caesar was murdered, since *Pompey's Curia*, where the crime was committed, was also discovered here during excavations in 1926-29. This is the largest archeological complex dating from the Republican period. The remains of four temples were discovered on the site (not open to the public). The round temple in the center is called *Temple B* and some scholars believe it is the "Aedes Fortunae Huisce Diei" built in 101 BC. Above

Romanus – the Roman Senate and People) imprinted on the seats of the public transport buses and the man-hole covers! This is Rome, a place where time has, in many ways, stood still.

Visitors to Rome have many treats in store. Here you can tread in the footsteps of the Caesars, you can kneel before the Pope, you can stroll in places where history was made. Lovers can hold hands in its romantic streets and splendid gardens. The streets are full of music day and night, making the atmosphere in the squares and around its fountains even more delightful. Rome is one of Italy's greenest cities. The climate means that winters are mild and, in spring, a gentle breeze wafts among the domes and the tree-tops. Life here has an unexpectedly human dimension. There are quiet areas where the air still smells of the countryside and *osterie* where you can still eat cheaply and sample the very tasty, genuine local cuisine. In Rome, you can feel at home, in a truly majestic setting.

ROME
IN OTHER COLORS...

ITINERARIES: pages 113, 128
FOOD: page 163
SHOPPING: page 183
EVENTS: pages 190, 194
PRACTICAL INFO: page 198

Temple A, built in the 3rd century BC and restored during Domitian's reign, to the right of the previous one, stands the *little church of S. Nicola de Calcarariis*, dating from the 8th century. To the left of the round temple are the remains of *Temple C*, the oldest of the four (early 3C BC). Finally, the road now conceals most of the remains of *Temple D* (early 2C BC), which was rebuilt in the late Republican period.

were the object of fierce rivalry between two painters, Giovanni Lanfranco (*Glory of Paradise* 1625-28) and Domenichino (**Scenes from the Life of St Andrew** and the *Six Virtues*). Together, they form one of the finest examples of Baroque decoration in Rome, together with the gigantic frescoes in the tribune by Mattia Preti (especially the *Crucifixion*).

Palazzo Massimo "alle Colonne" ❹

The location of this building, which was Baldassarre Peruzzi's last work, on the corner with Via del Paradiso, highlights the *chiaroscuro* effect of the colonnade on the ground floor. The convex rusticated facade follows the line of the Odeon of Domitian which once stood here. The building has a fine horizontal entablature over the **doorway**. The building is still occupied by members of the original family, who have lived in Rome since the late 10th century and whose founder was none other than Quintus Fabius Maximus the Hesitant, depicted in the frieze in the entrance-hall.

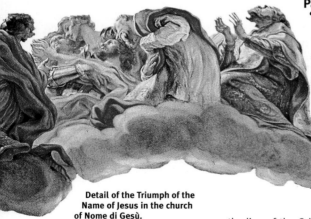

Detail of the Triumph of the Name of Jesus in the church of Nome di Gesù.

S. Andrea della Valle ❸

Rome's tallest dome after that of St Peter's was designed in 1622 by Carlo Maderno, while the travertine facade was designed by Carlo Rainaldi and Carlo Fontana (1656-65). Olivieri was responsible for the luxuriantly decorated, light-filled interior in the shape of a Latin cross, like the Gesù. The *frescoes* in the dome and the apse

Museo Barracco ⑤

The purpose of the collection is to provide an overview of ancient sculpture through works that are representative of their culture. All the most important schools of ancient sculpture are represented (Egypt, the Assyrian Empire, Etruria, Phoenicia, Greece, Rome), with particular emphasis on Egyptian sculpture. In fact, *Egyptian art* makes up the lion's share (the sculptures date from between 3000 and 30 BC), but the smaller *Etruscan section* has some fine cippi from Chiusi from the 5th century BC. Many of the sculptures in the *Greek section* are copies of the originals, from the late 6th century BC to the late 3rd century BC. *Roman art* is represented by sculptures made on the Italian peninsula, as well as from provinces of the Roman Empire.

The Holy City

Inside the Museo Barracco.

Palazzo Farnese ⑥

Standing on the same square, where the twin *fountains* are attributed to Girolamo Rainaldi, this splendid building, commissioned by Cardinal Alessandro Farnese (afterwards Paul III), was begun in 1517 by Antonio da Sangallo the Younger. On his death, supervision of the building work passed to Michelangelo (1546-49) and Vignola (1569-73), but it was under Giacomo Della Porta (1589) that the work was completed. Vignola and Della Porta were responsible for the rear facade, whereas Sangallo designed the facades overlooking the side-roads and the square. However, the **cornice** and the loggia with the Farnese crest above it,

together with part of the second floor and the upper floor of the courtyard are attributed to Michelangelo. Sangallo also designed the magnificent **atrium**, divided into three aisles, which lead through the building to the **courtyard**. This is surrounded by an arched portico resting on pilasters faced with Doric engaged columns. The famous gallery was frescoed in 1597-1604 by Annibale Carracci and Domenichino. The frescoes, which depict the **Triumph of Love over the Universe**, represent the transition from the Mannerist to the Baroque style.

Galleria Spada ⑦

Galleria Spada has retained the typical appearance of private collections of the 17th century. The works are displayed in one or two rows, according to purely decorative criteria. The works, almost all by Italian artists working in the 16th and 17th centuries, are displayed in four large frescoed rooms furnished with antique furniture and marbles. The most interesting works include *Boreas abducting Oreithytia* by Francesco Solimena, the *Death of Dido* by Guercino, *Anthony and Cleopatra* by Francesco Trevisani and a sketch for the frescoes in the church of the Gesù by Baciccia. Look out for the *Pietà* by Orazio

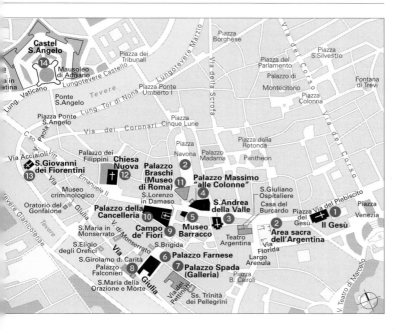

Borgianni and *Masaniello's Revolt in Naples* by Michelangelo Cerquozzi. The Gallery and the Council of State are housed in **Palazzo Spada**, built in the mid-16th century by Giulio Merisi, Girolamo da Carpi and Giulio Mazzoni. Mazzoni was responsible for the fine decoration on the outside of the palazzo and the stuccoes in the courtyard. Here you can see Francesco Borromini's ingenius *trompe l'oeil* **gallery**, which looks much longer than it actually is (in fact it is only 9m long). This has been achieved by accentuating the perspective by depicting the floor sloping upwards and the ceiling sloping downwards between converging walls.

Via Giulia ⑧

The long straight road designed in the early 16th century by Bramante was commissioned by Julius II, who imagined it as the setting for the most important buildings of the Holy See. His plan was never fulfilled, but the street has become one of the most noble and beautiful in Rome. This is partly because of the elegant residences on either side, the numerous churches, often linked to the nationalities present in Rome since time immemorial, and its exclusive antiques shops. Like all the historic streets in the capital, the numbers of the houses and shops gradually increase on the left-hand side and decrease on the right-hand side.

Campo de' Fiori ⑨

Giordano Bruno, commemorated in the *statue* (1887) in the center of the square, was burnt at the stake on February 17, 1600 and was one of many condemned men to be executed here. Although, traditionally, it is thought that the name of the square comes from Flora,

The main hall of Galleria Spada.

Pompey's beloved, the square, which has been a market-place since 1869, probably acquired its name in the late 14th century, when it was abandoned and became a meadow.

Palazzo della Cancelleria ⑩

To be sure of having a residence worthy of his rank, Cardinal Raffaele Riario summoned Bramante, who worked mainly on the splendid courtyard. Possibly in the hope that the popes might forget that the Roman Republic of 1849 was proclaimed from this very building, in the Lateran Treaties of 1929 it was declared an exclave of the Vatican, not subject to Italian sovereignty. It still houses the Papal Chancellery and the pope also established the seat of the Tribunal of the Roman Rota here. The most striking feature of the facade is its length, and the fact that it is completely faced in travertine.

An elegant **balcony** adorns the curved part of the facade facing Campo de' Fiori and Via del Pellegrino. Inside the building (not open to the public), the **courtyard** mentioned above has three orders of arcades, typical of palazzi in the Urbino area. The first two orders rest on granite columns with Tuscan capitals with rosettes and marble strips with reliefs between series of medallions; the third order consists of a brick wall with alternating pilaster strips and windows.

Fresco by Pietro da Cortona in the Chiesa Nuova.

Museo di Roma ⑪

The museum was founded to illustrate the history and life of the city from the Renaissance to the present day through a highly diverse range of exhibits. Sedan chairs used for carrying popes are found alongside works by Baciccia, Pierre Subleyras, Francesco Mochi, Antonio Canova, *Roman views* by *vedutisti* of the Flemish School, *tapestries* from Gobelins, *costumes* dating from the 17th-19th centuries and the famous collection of **watercolors** by Ettore Roesler Franz depicting views of the Eternal City.

The *Gabinetto delle Stampe* is a valuable collection of prints and drawings showing how the city and the surrounding territory has changed over the centuries. The *Gipsoteca Tenerani* is a collection of plaster-casts of works by the sculptor.

Chiesa Nuova ⑫

Until 1924, the strange *fountain of the Terrina* which stands in front of the church stood in Campo de' Fiori. When the church was rebuilt, it was based on the church of the Gesù, which was under construction at that time. However, this church differs in many ways from the Gesù prototype. Not so much in terms of the facade (1594-1606) as its interior, where the dome does not stand above the intersection of the transepts, and the side-chapels are connected by a passageway, effectively adding two side-aisles to the single-nave plan. The Baroque decoration of the interior also outstrips in sheer flamboyance that of the church on which it was based. Pietro da Cortona painted the **frescoes** on the ceiling and designed the stuccoes which frame them. The presbytery contains several *masterpieces* by Peter Paul Rubens, painted during his time in Rome (1606-1608). To the left of the presbytery, an extraordinary range of precious marbles adorns the chapel of San Filippo Neri, 1600-1604, where the saint is buried, while the chapel in the **left transept** contains a *Presentation of the Virgin in the Temple* by Federico Barocci. In the sacristy, the ceiling *frescoes* by Pietro da Cortona date from 1633-34.

S. Giovanni dei Fiorentini ⑬

Leo X consulted all the important architects of the time to work on a design for this church. Antonio da Sangallo the Younger, Baldassarre Peruzzi, Michelangelo and Raphael all competed for the design, but it was Jacopo Sansovino who began to work on the church in 1519. Carlo Maderno (1602-1620) designed the dome and the transept and Alessandro Galilei (1734) the facade. An imposing row of pillars divides the nave from the side-aisles, and there are five side-chapels on each side. The presbytery is flooded with light from an invisible source. A *Baptism of Christ* by Antonio Raggi occupies the center of the huge *altar* by Francesco Borromini, who was buried in this very church, as a memorial stone on the third pillar on the left testifies.

Castel S. Angelo ⑭

Castel Sant'Angelo began as a grand mausoleum (known as the *Hadrianeum*). It was built at the wishes of the Emperor Hadrian who wanted his remains to be buried there, along with those of his family. Begun in about 123, the mausoleum may have been designed by the emperor himself. He had the *Pons Aelius*, subsequently called **Ponte S. Angelo**** (133-134), built across the Tiber to provide access. The finishing touches to the bridge were added by Gian Lorenzo Bernini and his school (in the 17th century, Bernini designed the statues and decided how they should be arranged). The mausoleum was completed by Antoninus Pius. It began as a round building on a square base, on top of which was another smaller round tower. Inside, three great superimposed halls, which you can still see, were built to house the Imperial tombs, with a double spiral ramp, part of which has survived.

The Archangel Michael on the top of Castel S. Angelo.

Aurelian transformed the mausoleum into a fortified stronghold, surrounding it with defensive walls and towers. It continued its defensive role, and was also used as a prison, in the following centuries. During the revolt of 1379, the Romans occupied it with the intention of razing it to the ground and the popes transferred their most secret archives there, along with the treasury of the Church. The outward appearance of the complex is the result of restoration work carried out in the late 19th century and in 1933-34. Note the four large corner towers set into the square defensive walls, added by Nicholas V and Alexander VI. If you stand at the end of Ponte S. Angelo, the tower on the right is that of San Giovanni and the one on the left is that of San Matteo. On the far side, the two corresponding corner towers are those of San Luca and San Marco. The curtain wall between the towers of San Giovanni and San Luca contains the reconstructed entrance to the castle.

Inside, the old round base of the castle, with the square tower above, stands next to the papal apartments built in the Renaissance, facing the Tiber River. Up on the terrace stands the statue of the Archangel Michael sheathing his sword. The **Museo Nazionale di Castel S. Angelo**** certainly contains interesting collections of ceramics, ancient weapons, furnishings and Renaissance paintings. But the most fascinating aspect of the museum (rather like participating live in a virtual game) is that you are walking about in buildings which, in some cases, are more than 2,000 years old. One minute you are

Castel S. Angelo, and the bridge with the same name on the Tiber.

in a room of Roman Imperial date and the next you find yourself in one that was frescoed in the 16th century in the Mannerist style. Just beyond the entrance is the **ambulatory** which Boniface IX had built between the rounded wall of the castle and the square defensive walls. But, in no time, you are taken back at least ten centuries, when, at the gateway opposite Ponte S. Angelo, a flight of steps leads down to the **dromos**, on the same level as the *Hadrianeum*. A scale model shows which are the oldest parts of the building. Another very early feature is the **spiral ramp** which leads up to the right to the **straight passageway**. Beyond the **sepulchral cella** where the urns containing the Imperial ashes were kept, you come to the **Cortile d'Onore** or

dell'Angelo and the statue of the Archangel Michael created by Raffaello da Montelupo in 1544. To the right is the **Armeria Antica (Museum of Arms and Armor)**, while, on the left, the **Rooms of Clement VIII** and the **Hall of Apollo** are decorated with grotesques. From here, you can also access the **Hall of Justice**, which is the second of the three rooms above the *Hadrianeum*. The **Rooms of Clement VII**, next to the Hall of Apollo, house a small art gallery, including paintings by Niccolò di Liberatore, Carlo Crivelli, Luca Signorelli and Marcello Fogolino. From the **Cortile del Pozzo**, where there is a charming 15th-century *well*, a narrow flight of stairs leads up to the beautifully decorated **bathroom of Clement VII**. Another doorway marks the entrance to the **historical prisons**, and a

 TCI HIGHLIGHTS

VIEWS OF ROME

If you look through the keyhole of the gate of No.3 Piazza dei Cavalieri di Malta, you will see one of the most unusual views of the capital, perfectly framing the dome of St Peter's. But the city of views *par excellence* always has more surprises in store. From the portico of the Monument to Victor Emmanuel II, perhaps the best viewpoint in the old part of the city, you have good views of the sequence of Piazza Venezia, Via del Corso and Porta del Popolo, but also of the bend of the Tiber, with views out to the Janiculum and the Vatican, and, from the opposite side, of the whole archeological area of the Fori Romani and the Palatine Hill, with the Celian Hill, the Colosseum and the Esquiline Hill in the background. There are plenty of other, more traditional viewpoints in the city, which have become tourist venues in their own right: the terrace beside Palazzo Senatorio, on the Capitoline Hill has lovely views over the ruins of the Fori Romani and the verdant Palatine Hill. The views from Piazzale Napoleone in the park of

the Pincio should not be missed. The *passeggiata* on the Janiculum, the ridge above the Tiber covered with parks and gardens, has splendid views - especially from the terraces near the beacon and the monument to Garibaldi – and you can almost count the churches in the city center. The Basilica of St Peter's itself rewards the effort of climbing the last more than 300 steps, with views that extend as far as

General view of Michelangelo's dome on St Peter's.

the sea and the mountains of the Central Apennines. From the top of Monte Mario, the highest hill in Rome, the views stretch for miles in every direction. And for those who enjoy taking a step back in time, don't miss the walk along the Aurelian walls between the gates of Porta S. Sebastiano and the Porta Ardeatina, where you can stroll with the villas and gardens of this part of Rome on one side, and ancient walls on the other.

Castel S. Angelo and Hadrian's mausoleum

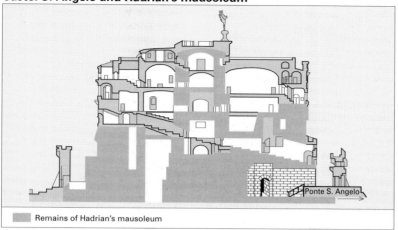

Ponte S. Angelo

Remains of Hadrian's mausoleum

staircase descends to the castle's **provisions stores**, with 84 oil jars and 5 round grain silos. Stairs lead up from the courtyard to the elegant **Loggia of Paul III**, decorated with grotesques (1543). This is possibly the best place to observe the pentagonal outer defensive walls, with their bastions, and the castle moat. The **Giretto of Pius IV** (**views**) lead to the **Loggia of Julius II**, attributed to Giuliano da Sangallo and facing Ponte S. Angelo, the entrance to the elegant rooms of the **Apartments of Paul III*** which were frescoed in 1542-49. Beyond the **Hall of the Library**, where dignitaries were received, the **Room of the mausoleum of Hadrian** was named after the frieze showing an idealistic depiction of the mausoleum in 1545. Nearby, the **Room of the Festoons** leads to the **Cagliostra**, formerly the loggia of the apartment of Paul II. In the **Room of the Treasury**, which is accessed from the Hall of the Library and which corresponds to the third room of the Roman mausoleum, the secret papal archives were kept in the walnut-wood cabinets set into the walls. The last part of the Imperial monument is the **Round Hall**, which can be reached by an ancient staircase. At the top is the large terrace situated below the bronze statue of the *Archangel Michael*, placed here in 1752 to replace the marble statue by Raffaello da Montelupo. To the left, the *Campana della Misericordia* used to be rung to announce the execution of capital sentences. The **views**** from the terrace are breathtaking.

S. Pietro ⑮

Many say that **Via della Conciliazione***, the broad, straight, monumental approach to St Peter's, is the most beautiful street in Rome. It leads symbolically into Piazza S. Pietro, and the heart of the Eternal City.
Piazza San Pietro** (St. Peter's Square) is one of the places where the Pope appears in public, a huge area enclosed by the double *colonnade* designed by Gian Lorenzo Bernini. Occupied by churches and oratories at the time of the old basilica, the oval square was laid out in 1656-67. Each of the two colonnades has a quadruple row of columns (there are 284 of them, and 88 pillars), arranged converging on a central point so that anyone standing there sees only one row of columns, so perfectly are they aligned. Many of the wax models for the 140 *statues of saints* crowning the portico also bear Bernini's signature. Enormous efforts were required when, on the orders of Sixtus V, the great **Obelisk** was placed in the center of the square. Domenico Fontana was put in charge of the operation. Ordinary ropes were used for lifting the obelisk into place and, once the spectators had been silenced, work began. Caligula had brought it to Rome from Alexandria in 37 AD, to adorn the Circus of Nero. The crowd should have remained silent until the operation was completed, but a sailor called Bresca, who realized that some of the ropes were about to give way, interrupted, shouting "*acqua alle funi*" (put water on the ropes), thus

preventing the huge stone from falling. The Pope rewarded him by granting his family the privilege of supplying the Vatican with palms for Palm Sunday. The bronze *lions* are by Prospero Antichi. The *fountain* on the right of the obelisk is by Carlo Maderno (1613) and the one on the left by Carlo Fontana (1677).

The **Basilica of S. Pietro ****, the revered heart of the Papacy and all Christianity, is the first and most important church of the city known as the "City of a Hundred Churches". A few figures may help the visitor to comprehend its awesome proportions. It covers a total area of 22,067m², making it the largest church in the world. From the ground to the top of the cross above Michelangelo's dome, it is 136m high, and the diameter of the dome is 42m. The historical events which, over the centuries, led to the church we see today, date back to the beginnings of Christianity. The first basilica, built during the reign of Emperor Constantine, was begun in about 320 and, having been consecrated by Pope Sylvester I in 326, was completed in 349.

In the mid-15th century, Nicholas V entrusted Bernardo Rossellino (1452) with the radical rebuilding of the church. But it was Julius II who, in 1506, launched the building work in earnest. He summoned Bramante, and other architects who opted alternately for a new church built on a Greek-cross (Bramante himself, Baldassarre Peruzzi and Michelangelo) or a Latin-cross plan (Raphael and Antonio da Sangallo the Younger). It was Paul V who eventually decided in favor of the Latin-cross plan. The job of extending the basilica was given to Carlo Maderno, who completed it in 1614. On November 18, 1626, on the 1,300th anniversary of its first consecration, it was officially opened for worship by Urban VIII. Gian Lorenzo Bernini, who succeeded Maderno, would have liked to add two bell towers to the facade, but various problems made this impossible. As far as the **exterior** of the church is concerned, Gian Lorenzo Bernini designed the broad, triple **flight of steps**. At either side stand the two large *statues of St Peter* and *St Paul*. Carlo Maderno's **facade** is crowned in the middle by a tympanum and spanned by eight columns with pillars at the sides. A portico forms the lower part of the facade, with archways at each end (the left archway leads into the Vatican City).

Worshippers await a papal audience in St Peter's Square.

General view of Michelangelo's dome on St Peter's.

The upper part of the facade is decorated by a balustrade with 13 statues of the Redeemer, St John the Baptist and eleven of the Apostles, except St Peter, and has nine large windows with balconies. The name of the newly elected Pope is announced from the central balcony and is where the new Pope gives his blessing (it is known as the *Loggia delle Benedizioni*). Michelangelo never saw his **dome**** finished. When he died, only the drum had been completed. The double shell of the dome, divided by trusses into 16 sections, was

completed by Giacomo Della Porta and Domenico Fontana (1588-89). Vignola added the two side-domes, which are purely decorative. In the **portico**, beyond the door on the far right which leads into the Vestibule of the Scala Regia, you can see the equestrian *statue of Constantine* (Bernini, 1670). The original inscription with the papal seal of Boniface VIII proclaiming the first Jubilee, or Holy Year, (1300) can be seen above the *Porta Santa*, which is only opened in Holy Years. The bronze **doors** in the central doorway, decorated by Filarete (1439-45), are from Constantine's basilica. Above the central doorway of the portico is the *mosaic of the Navicella*, executed by Giotto in 1298 but completely reworked in the 17th century. **Inside** the basilica, the artistic masterpieces and the places associated with particular historical events are part and parcel of the fabric of the building.

On Christmas night in the year 800, Charlemagne knelt on the large porphyry *disk* in the **nave** to receive official approval and the Imperial crown from Leo III. The bronze **statue of St Peter** sits below the huge **dome***. Four pentagonal piers sustain the massive arches supporting the drum. The pilaster strips between the 16 windows support a cornice at the base of the top of the dome which is divided into 16 segments. The six orders of mosaic decoration and the *statues* at the base of the piers are of extraordinary workmanship. Above

Pentagonal piers
supporting the
huge dome

Michelangelo's dome

Drum

Vignola'
dom

Gilded bronze canopy by Gian
Lorenzo Bernini

+ TV ES PETRVS ET SVPER HAN

Papal altar

Confession and the crypt
containing St Peter's tomb

Side chapels

THRONE BY BERNINI
(1658-66)

Wooden Chair of
St Peter, a gift
made by Charles
the Bald to the
Pope in 875

St Peter's Basilica

In the year 1506, having decided that it was time to build a new church to replace Constantine's basilica, Pope Julius II entrusted Bramante with the design. The great architect designed a domed church on a Greek-cross plan and, in 1506, set to work. At his death, the work was continued by Raphael who, with the aid of Fra' Giocondo and Giuliano da Sangallo, proposed a new design based on a Latin-cross plan - then by Baldassarre Peruzzi, who had supported the Greek-cross idea, and then by Antonio da Sangallo, who went back to the plan favored by his nephew and Raphael. Finally, in 1546, Michelangelo developed Bramante's initial idea, and designed the dome which was to become the symbol of Rome. He actually only succeeded in overseeing the building work as far as the drum, but the work was subsequently completed by Giacomo della Porta and Carlo Fontana. In the early 17th century, Carlo Maderno broadened the basilica and designed a new facade, following the orders usually employed for the facades of private buildings rather than churches. Finally, the Baroque master Gian Lorenzo Bernini was summoned to complete the church. He designed an oval square enclosed by a colonnade four columns wide, joined to the church by two slightly diverging arms stretching towards the facade of St Peter's. The square gradually, solemnly draws the visitor towards the magnificent basilica, reinstating the rapport with Michelangelo's dome which had been erased by Maderno's facade.

Facade by Carlo Maderno

Atrium

Colonnade by Gian Lorenzo Bernini

them, four balconies by Bernini contain the church's most precious relics.

"*Quod non fecerunt barbari, fecerunt Barberini*" (What the Barbarians didn't achieve was achieved by Barberini). This gibe refers to the fact that Urban VIII Barberini removed the bronzes from the pronaos of the Pantheon and had them melted down to construct the imposing **canopy** (29m high) above the high altar of St Peter's. Bernini was assisted in this task (1624-33) by Duquesnoy, Giuliano Finelli and, for the architectural part of the project, Francesco Borromini. Among the vine-tendril decoration of the spiral columns are the bees of the Barberini family (the sun and bees are the symbols of the Barberini family, to which Urban VIII belonged). 99 eternal flames illuminate the "tomb of Peter" in the **confession** below. In the first chapel of the **right aisle**, decorated like many others and like the transept with 18th-century

St Peter's Basilica

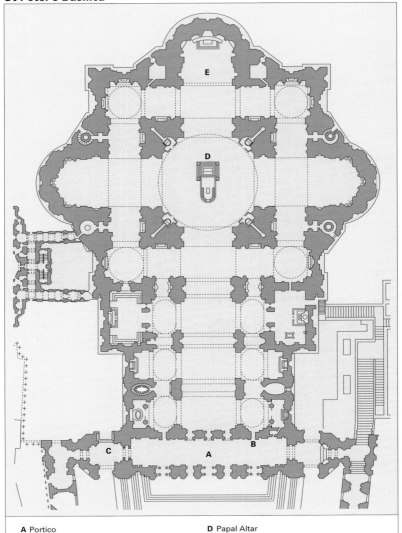

A Portico
B Holy Door
C Arch of the Bells

D Papal Altar
E Tribune

Bernini's canopy in St Peter's, cast with bronze from the Pantheon.

mosaics, a glass screen protects the **Pietà****, the white marble sculpture (1498-99) considered to be one of Michelangelo's finest works, carved when he was only 25. Under the first arch of the right aisle, below the *statue of Leo XII* (1836), is Bernini's *chapel of the Reliquaries*, also called the chapel of the Crucifix because of the beautiful wooden crucifix attributed to Pietro Cavallini. To the left is the *funerary monument to Queen Christina of Sweden* by Carlo Fontana. The second chapel contains the *monument to Pius XII*, while, under the arch of the aisle, the *tomb of Innocent XII* is situated opposite the *monument to Countess Matilda of Canossa*, designed by Bernini. The Neapolitan artist is also responsible for the gilded bronze *ciborium* (1674) in the large chapel of the Blessed Sacrament, decorated by gilded stuccoes and barred by a *gate* (by Borromini). On the right, under the third arch of the aisle is the *monument to Gregory XIII* (1720-23); on the left, the *tomb of Gregory XIV*. The four chapels below a dome mark the corners of the **ambulatory** in the style of Michelangelo, which winds its way around the piers supporting it. The **monument to Clement XIII** (1784-92) is one of Antonio

Canova's best works. To complete the symbolic and dramatic effect of the canopy, Bernini placed the **Chair of St Peter*** in the **apse** (or tribune). This enormous gilded bronze throne is supported at the corners by *statues of the Fathers of the Church*, and a gilded stucco gloria draws attention to the symbol of the Holy Spirit. It encloses an old wooden chair which may have been the throne of Charles II the Bald (9C). Bernini also executed the **monument to Urban VIII** (1627-47), while the **statue of Paul III** (1551-75) is by Guglielmo Della Porta. A marble *altar-piece* stands above the altar with relics of Pope Leo the Great. The *sacristy* leads into the **Sacristy of the Canonici,** next to a chapel with a painting by Giulio Romano of the *Madonna and Child and St John the Baptist* by Giulio Romano. Would you expect to find a work by a Protestant artist in St Peter's? Believe it or not, the *tomb of Pius VII* (1823) in the *Clementine chapel* is by the Danish sculptor Bertel Thorvaldsen. There is a copy of Raphael's *Transfiguration* on the pillar of the dome on the corner of the **left-hand aisle**. The dome of the *chapel of the choir* by Carlo Maderno is richly decorated with gilded stuccoes. The chapel contains the gilded bronze **tomb**

Detail of Michelangelo's Pietà.

31

of Innocent VIII. The upside-down porphyry lid of an old sarcophagus, which was probably used for the tomb of Hadrian and then that of Otto II, forms the *font* of the baptistery. Although visitors to St Peter's should not miss the **Museo Storico Artistico-Tesoro di S. Pietro* (Treasury)**, it was seriously depleted by the raids of the Saracens in 846, the Sack of Rome in 1527 and the treaty concluded with Napoleon in 1797. It contains the *Colonna Santa*, once thought to be the column against which Christ leaned in the Temple of Solomon (actually dates from the 4C); the so-called *dalmatic of Charlemagne*, which is actually Byzantine; the famous *Crux Vaticana*, a gift from the Emperor Justinian II of the Eastern Empire to Rome (6C); the **monument to Sixtus IV*** signed by Pollaiolo (1493); the **sarcophagus of Junius Bassus**, Prefect of Rome in 359. It was the excavations of the **Sacred Vatican Grottoes**** which threw light on the foundation of the first basilica. Traditionally it was thought that the first church had been built above the ruins of the Circus of Nero, where Peter was martyred, but the excavations conducted by Pius XII found no trace of the circus but necropolises dating from the 1st to 4th centuries. However, it is the chapel of St Peter, built above the Apostle's tomb, that forms the nucleus of the **New Grottoes**, created when the floor of the church was raised to build the new church and arranged in a semi-circle around St Peter's tomb. Extensions from a later period lead to the oratories situated at the base of the piers supporting the dome and the five *chapels*. The **Old Grottoes** date from 1606 and consist of three corridors with low ceilings supported by massive pillars, which extend for about 50m below the nave of the church. In the right-hand aisle, a small, round chapel contains the tomb of Pope John XXIII, next to those of Queen Christina of Sweden and Queen Charlotte of Cyprus; at the end of the same aisle are the *tombs of Boniface VIII* and *Nicholas III*, who was laid to rest in an early-Christian sarcophagus. The central aisle contains a *monument to Pius VI* (1821-22). Visitors wishing to make the **ascent to St Peter's dome**** may either climb the stairs or take advantage of the lift to the terrace, which has **views** over St Peter's Square and the city beyond. From here, 330 steps lead up to the round corridor inside the dome where you can almost touch the mosaics. A steeper spiral staircase leads up to the loggia at the top of the lantern, where there are marvelous **views**** over Rome and, on a clear day, to the Apennines and the sea.

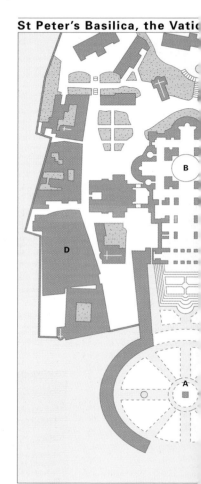

St Peter's Basilica, the Vatic

Città del Vaticano/Vatican City ⑯

This city of museums is proof of the fact that the popes were some of the most prodigious patrons of Italian art. The **Cortile della Pigna** is named after the huge bronze **fir-cone** which now stands in front of the niche designed by Bramante on a floor of the double staircase. Dating from Roman times, it is mentioned in Dante Alighieri's "Divine Comedy". The courtyard, in the center of which is a contemporary sculpture called *Sphere within a Sphere*, is part of the much larger *Cortile del Belvedere*, designed by Bramante to connect the palace of Innocent VIII to the Vatican Palace. The courtyard was divided in 1587-88 when Domenico Fontana built a

paintings include the *Last Judgement* (11-12C) and the *Legend of St Stephen* by Bernardo Daddi; paintings by Giotto and his School are represented by the famous **Stefaneschi polyptych***, painted by Giotto for the Basilica of St Peter, along with works by Pietro Lorenzetti, Simone Martini, Gentile da Fabriano and Sassetta. The Tuscan painters Filippo Lippi, Benozzo Gozzoli and Beato

...ces, seat of the Vatican Museums, and the Vatican City

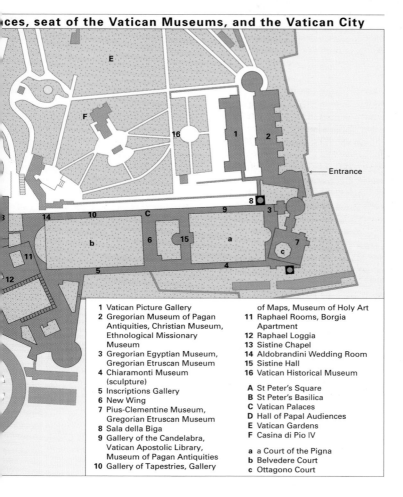

← Entrance

1 Vatican Picture Gallery
2 Gregorian Museum of Pagan Antiquities, Christian Museum, Ethnological Missionary Museum
3 Gregorian Egyptian Museum, Gregorian Etruscan Museum
4 Chiaramonti Museum (sculpture)
5 Inscriptions Gallery
6 New Wing
7 Pius-Clementine Museum, Gregorian Etruscan Museum
8 Sala della Biga
9 Gallery of the Candelabra, Vatican Apostolic Library, Museum of Pagan Antiquities
10 Gallery of Tapestries, Gallery

of Maps, Museum of Holy Art
11 Raphael Rooms, Borgia Apartment
12 Raphael Loggia
13 Sistine Chapel
14 Aldobrandini Wedding Room
15 Sistine Hall
16 Vatican Historical Museum

A St Peter's Square
B St Peter's Basilica
C Vatican Palaces
D Hall of Papal Audiences
E Vatican Gardens
F Casina di Pio IV

a a Court of the Pigna
b Belvedere Court
c Ottagono Court

new wing for the library. The first of the papal art collections is in the **Pinacoteca Vaticana****, the gallery opened by Pius VI in 1816. It contains paintings with mainly religious themes from the various papal palaces, which are now arranged chronologically and according to the various schools of painting. Early

Angelico precede masterpieces by Melozzo da Forlì, Ercole de' Roberti, Lucas Cranach the Elder and a group of *polyptychs* and *works* by the 15th-century Umbrian School. Visitors to the gallery tend to cluster around Raphael's masterpieces: the 10 **tapestries*** commissioned from him by Leo X for the

TCI HIGHLIGHTS

THE RIGHT "LOOK" FOR THE VATICAN

In an age when people can circulate freely within the European Union, the State of the Vatican City requires no identification of any kind (passport or identity card) to visit the Basilica of St Peter or the Vatican Museums. However, there are some restrictions governing access to this "foreign" state which are rigorously applied by the Swiss Guards on duty at the entrance to the basilica and outside the Arco delle Campane. No-one wearing shorts, bermudas, mini-skirts or sleeve-less tops may visit St Peter's Tomb or participate in a guided tour of the Vatican City. And, for those wishing to attend one of the Wednesday audiences, being decently dressed means long trousers with a jacket and tie for men, preferably black; women may also wear white – never red – but the outfit must be long, with a high neckline and preferably long sleeves.

Sistine Chapel (1515-16); the **Transfiguration****, his splendid **Madonna of Foligno***, painted in 1512-13, and his **Coronation of the Virgin** (1503). Leonardo da Vinci's **St Jerome** (c. 1480) precedes works executed in the 16th century. 17th-century works include Caravaggio's **Deposition*** (1602-1604), Domenichino's *Communion of St Jerome* and Guido Reni's *Crucifixion of St Peter*, an expression of the Baroque style which was to permeate many 18th-century works, such as the paintings by Giuseppe Maria Crespi and Francesco Mancini. When ancient finds began to emerge from excavations conducted throughout the Papal States, there was a veritable stampede on the part of the popes to claim them. Much of the Greek and Roman material displayed in the five sections of the **Museo Gregoriano Profano*** comes from this source. Greek originals in the collection include the Attic **stele by Palestritos*** (mid-5C BC), **fragments of sculptures from the Parthenon** and a **head of Athena** in the style of Magno Graecia (mid-5C BC). Perhaps the most important example of copies and re-stylings of Greek originals is the **Chiaramonti Niobid**. Roman sculpture of the 1st and 2nd centuries is represented by a relief depicting personifications of the Etruscan cities of *Tarquinia*, *Vulci* and *Vetulonia*, as well as the relief of the **altar of Vicomagistri** (c. 30-40) and the 39 **fragments** from the sepulchral monument of the Haterii. The **Museo Pio Cristiano** contains other interesting architectural features, sculptures and mosaics. The **Museo Gregoriano Egizio*** puts the exhibits into context by relating them to the dynasties which succeeded each other on the throne, with inscriptions ranging from 2600 BC to the 6th century. There are numerous sculptures, sarcophagi and funerary steles, documents and other finds associated with funeral rituals and many works from the Roman period inspired by Egyptian art. The **Museo Chiaramonti**, which occupies about half of the gallery (300m long) designed by Bramante, contains Roman copies of Greek originals as well as original works. The **Galleria Lapidaria** comprises about 4,000 pagan and Christian inscriptions collected by Clement XIV, Pius VI and Pius VII. The **Braccio Nuovo (New Wing)**, the floor of which incorporates some 2nd-century **mosaics**, contains the most interesting works, nearly all of which are copies of original Greek sculptures: the **statue of Augustus of Prima Porta***, a copy of a bronze original, the *Wounded Amazon*, a Roman copy of a Greek original, **The Nile**, a statue dating from the 1st century, and the **Doryphoros**, a Roman copy of a Greek original by Polikleitus. The **Museo Pio-Clementino*** has some remarkable Greek and Roman sculptures including the famous **Apoxyomenos***, a Roman replica of a bronze original by Lysippos (4C). From the room behind the statue, you can see **Bramante's spiral staircase**. In the Octagonal Courtyard, the recesses at the four corners of the portico contain some fine statues: the **Apollo Belvedere****, created in the Roman Imperial period and based on an original dating from the 4th century BC, attributed to Leochares, the famous **Laocoön****, a 1st-century

Greek marble copy of a Hellenistic original, a **Hermes**, and a **Perseus** by Canova. The Galleria delle Statue contains more ancient statues, including the **Apollo Sauroctonos**, a Roman copy of a bronze by Praxiteles; the **Barberini candelabra** (2C) are a splendid pair. Portraits of Roman emperors and divinities crowd the Sala dei Busti (Gallery of Busts). The Gabinetto delle Maschere (Mask Room) has 2nd-century polychrome *mosaics* of theatrical masks in the floor, as well as the beautiful **Venus of Cnidos**, a fine replica of a work by Praxiteles. Another masterpiece in these museums is the famous **Belvedere Torso*** (1C BC). It was discovered in the early 15th century and influenced many Renaissance artists, especially Michelangelo, who used it as a model for his frescoes of decorative nude figures (the *Ignudi*) in the Sistine Chapel. Other exhibits worth noting are the **Jupiter of Otricoli**, a 1st-century copy of a 4th-century BC Greek original and the two large, 4th-century red-porphyry **sarcophagi of Costantina** (Constantine's daughter) and **St Helena**, Constantine's mother. Few other museums in the world illustrate so completely the mysterious culture of the Etruscans. The finds displayed in the **Museo Gregoriano**

Etrusco*, come mainly from tombs and other graves found in the north of Lazio (19C). And, completing the cultural overview of the period between the Early Iron Age Etruscan finds from Lazio (9-8C BC) and the Hellenistic period, is a fine collection of Greek and Italiot vases. Some of the pieces are unique: the famous **Mars of Todi***, a late-5th-century BC bronze statue, the **Guglielmi collection** of Etruscan and Greek bronzes and vases, and about 800 pieces dating from the Villanova culture and the Hellenistic period, as well as the **black-figure amphora** of Exekias. The collections in the **Galleria degli Arazzi** and the **Galleria delle Carte Geografiche**, which precede the Raphael Rooms, are named after the exhibits they contain. The first has tapestries made in Brussels in the 16th century. The second gallery was frescoed in 1580-83 with maps which provide interesting insight into geographical knowledge in the late 16th century and Rome's role as the geographical center of the whole Italian peninsula. The **Stanze di Raffaello** (Raphael Rooms)** are one of the things you must see in the Vatican Museums since they represent one of the most important phases of Italian painting. In 1508, Julius II commissioned

Raphael's School of Athens in the Stanza della Segnatura.

the young Raphael to decorate this part of the Vatican. After his death, his assistants continued the work until 1525. The painter from Urbino left drawings and instructions for the decoration of the **Sala di Costantino** for Giulio Romano,

Sistine Chapel, detail of the Creation of Adam.

Raffaellino del Colle and Giovanni Francesco Penni. Beyond the **Sala dei Palafrenieri**, the room after the Sala di Costantino, and the **chapel of Nicholas V**, where there are **frescoes** by Beato Angelico, is the first room frescoed by Raphael himself (1512-14). This is the **Stanza di Eliodoro**, where the **subject-matter of the painting**, which glorifies the Church, was probably suggested by Julius II. The **Stanza della Segnatura** was also entirely decorated by Raphael (1509-11), except for some of the ceiling decoration which was executed by Il Sodoma and Bramantino. The **frescoes**, in which the Humanist ideas associated with the Classical tradition converge with 15th-century probings into perspective, are among his finest masterpieces.
In the **Stanza dell'Incendio**, completed during the pontificate of Leo X, Raphael's assistants based the wall **frescoes** on the cartoons and drawings of their master. The paintings on the ceiling are by Perugino. When Sixtus IV decided to build the **Sistine Chapel**** (1475-81), he could not have imagined that this rectangular space with a low ceiling would become the setting for one of the finest expressions of Renaissance painting. Having commissioned Mino da Fiesole, Andrea Bregno and Giovanni Dalmata to make the *rood screen* and the *balustrade* of the chancel, the Pope summoned (1481-83) some of the most skilful masters of the time (Sandro Botticelli, Luca Signorelli, Piero di Cosimo, Perugino, Domenico Ghirlandaio and Pinturicchio) to paint the frescoes on the side-walls and opposite the altar. In 1506, Julius II took over the project,

entrusting its completion to Michelangelo who, between 1508 and 1512, frescoed the ceiling and, under the pontificate of Paul III, the back wall of the chapel. The bottom of the side-walls and the wall opposite the altar are decorated with *fake drapes*. The tapestries by Raphael, now in the Pinacoteca of the Vatican Museums, used to hang above them. The middle part of the side-walls are decorated with *Scenes from the Life of Moses* (right) and *Scenes from the Life of Christ* (left). Between the windows, the top of the side-walls and the wall opposite the altar are decorated with 24 *portraits of popes*. A vast painting cycle covers the ceiling, an extraordinary fusion of architectural and sculptural features, emphasized by the brilliant use of color.
The composition is organized into three superimposed registers. The central part of the ceiling illustrates nine of the **Stories of Genesis***. Starting at the panel above the altar: *The Separation of Light from Darkness, the Creation of the Sun, the Moon and the Planets, the Separation of the Land and the Sea and the Creation of the Fishes and the Birds*, the magnificent **Creation of Adam***, *the Creation of Eve, Temptation and Expulsion from Paradise, the Sacrifice of Noah, the Flood* and *the Drunkenness of Noah*. Between the panels, framed by a marble structure, are decorative male figures (called **Ignudi***) holding medallions. On the lower, curved part of the vault are the powerful *figures of Sybils and Prophets* enthroned. Other *Biblical scenes* are depicted in the triangular spaces at the corners of the ceiling of the lower register, while the *forerunners of Christ* are depicted in the vaults and lunettes above the windows.

A majestic composition moving within a space without limitations: this is how Michelangelo painted the frescoes on the back wall in 1536-41. In his magnificent and awesome **Last Judgement****, he exceeded every iconographic ideal and every concept of perspective of Renaissance art. The composition is dominated by the majestic figure of **Christ the Supreme Judge**, next to the *Virgin Mary* surrounded by the *Saints*, *Patriarchs* and *Martyrs* who throng Paradise; on the right, the *Elect ascend into Heaven*, while, on the left, the *Damned are cast into Hell where Charon and Minos await them*. In the lower part of the composition: on the left, the *Resurrection of the Dead*, in the center, *Angels blowing the Trumpets of Judgement*, and, above, in the lunettes, *Angels with the Symbols of the Passion*. (The nude figures were covered in 1564 by Daniele da Volterra at the wishes of Pius IV, who found their nudity distasteful). It is also interesting to visit the **Biblioteca Apostolica Vaticana (Vatican Library)**. The richly decorated **Salone Sistino*** contains 75,000 manuscripts, 70,000 documents from the archives, 100,000 separate autographs, and more than 800,000 volumes. These form the basis of the library created by Sixtus IV in 1475.

TCI HIGHLIGHTS

A FOREIGN STATE IN THE HEART OF THE CAPITAL

Perhaps not everyone is aware that, when you step into Bernini's St Peter's Square or the Vatican Museums, you are actually entering a foreign country. There is no visible frontier and you do not need to show documents of any kind, but, at an international level it certainly exists, because every country diplomatically represented in Italy also has an ambassador to the Holy See. The fact that it is a *de facto* state is demonstrated not only by the Swiss Guards (*in the photo*) who man the few points of access, but also by the way you must go about visiting the Vatican City. Visits can only be arranged through the Ufficio Informazioni Pellegrini e Turisti in St Peter's Square, on the left side of the square in front of the basilica. And even that is on foreign soil. The most famous building to see in the Vatican City, and the one which receives most visitors, is the hall where the papal audiences are held. This daring modern structure in the shape of a shell was designed by Pier Luigi Nervi in 1971. It has a seating capacity of 12,000, but this is often not enough to accommodate all the people who want to participate in the Wednesday audience or other ceremonies. As a result, such ceremonies are often held in St Peter's Square. The **Vatican Gardens**, the green lung of the Vatican City, are still laid out in the Italian style and, in many places, look exactly as they did in the 16th century. They are the setting for the country's most famous monument: the **Casina of Pius IV**, built by Pirro Ligorio in 1558-61. It comprises two separate buildings with side pavilions. The smaller of the two buildings is preceded by a fountain.

The ground floor is decorated with mosaics, with a loggia above. The larger building is decorated with stuccoes on the outside and, inside, with frescoes by Federico Barocci, Santi di Tito and Federico Zuccari.

S. Maria sopra Minerva ❶

In 1280, the church was rebuilt on Gothic lines, although it has been altered many times since. In the 17th century, the original Gothic facade was replaced with one with three doorways. The interior (a nave and two side-aisles with cross-vaulting, a transept and two chapels at either side of the presbytery) is the result of work done in 1848-1855.

The **furnishings** are some of the richest in Rome and reflect the development of art in the city from the late 13th century to the turn of the 17th century. In the right transept, the archway over the entrance to the **Carafa chapel** and the **fresco decoration** by Filippino Lippi (1488-93) are quite remarkable. The **statue of the Resurrected Christ*** (1519-21) by the left-hand pillar of the presbytery is by Michelangelo, near the choir are the **funerary monuments of Clement VII** and **Leo X**, by Antonio da Sangallo the Younger in 1536-41.

The Pantheon ❷

This remarkable building is one of the most famous ancient monuments in the world and the best-preserved in Rome. It constitutes a brilliant example of building technique, an ingenious combination of the domed rotunda often used in Roman bath-complexes, and the traditional pronaos with a tympanum often used to front classical temples. It was built by Marcus Vipsanius Agrippa, the son-in-law of Augustus, in 27 BC, but was later rebuilt by Hadrian in 118-125. With the fall of the Roman Empire, the temple was abandoned until 608, when Boniface IV decided to dedicate it to the Madonna and all the Martyrs. Subsequently it was used as a fortress. In 1625, Urban VIII Barberini removed the bronze from the beams of the portico to make 80 canons for Castel Sant'Angelo and the 4 twisted columns supporting the canopy in St Peter's. When Rome became capital of Italy, it was designated as the burial place of Italy's sovereigns. The 16 monolithic columns of the pronaos are of gray and

Around Via del Corso

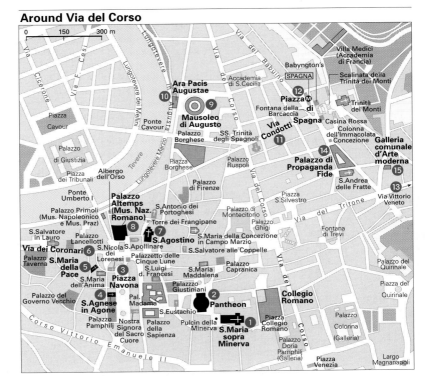

The Pantheon

1 Annunciation attributed to Melozzo da Forlì
2 Tomb of Victor Emmanuel II
3 Tomb of Raphael
4 Tombs of Umberto I and Margherita di Savoia
5 Chapel of the "Virtuosi del Pantheon"

pink granite. Beyond them is the doorway (the bronze *doors* were repaired by Pius IV in the 16C) and two niches which probably contained statues of Augustus and Agrippa. Inside, there are seven rectangular and semi-circular recesses, preceded by pairs of grooved columns of *giallo antico* and *pavonazzetto* marble, and interspersed with shrines; an eighth recess preceded by an archway stands opposite the entrance. The concrete ceiling is decorated by five orders of

coffers, the bronze-rimmed oculus being the only source of daylight in the building. Most of the marble *floor*, with its square and circular motifs, is original. The church contains the *tombs of Victor Emmanuel II* (last king of Sardinia, first king of Italy) and *Raphael*, a re-use of a Greek marble sarcophagus. It was Raphael himself who commissioned Lorenzetto to carve the statue of the **Madonna del Sasso** to his own design.

Piazza Navona ❸

If you view it from above or look at a plan of this famous square, so dear to the heart of Italian and American movie directors, who have used it for many scenes in their movies, you can see what it was originally. In fact, it stands above the *stadium of Domitian*, built in about 86 AD, with a seating capacity of about 30,000. From roughly the 13th century onwards, small houses and fortified buildings were erected here, and were subsequently joined by churches and palaces. In 1477, the market previously held on the Capitoline Hill was moved here. Its name probably derives from the athletic games once held here, the *Agoni Capitolini*: *agone*, meaning competition, was transformed into *nagone* and then *navone*. However, it is also possible that it comes from the shape of the square, which vaguely resembles a ship (*nave*) and the fact that, in the 17th-19th centuries, its concave floor used to be flooded for the processions of the retinues of prelates and princes in August. The tradition of selling sweets and toys between December and Epiphany is still alive today. One of the square's most famous features is the famous **Fountain of the Four Rivers****. The proverbial rivalry between Gian Lorenzo Bernini and Francesco Borromini gave rise to the saying that the allegorical figures of the great rivers at the corners of Bernini's fountain (the *Nile*, the *Ganges*, the *Danube* and the *Rio de la Plata*) look appalled at the sight of Borromini's church

Inside the Pantheon, the mausoleums of the sovereigns of Italy.

Piazza Navona, which occupies the site of Domitian's ancient stadium.

of S. Agnese in Agone. Set on a rock, (1651) the obelisk brought to Rome under Domitian was originally located in the Circus of Maxentius. Bernini also designed the *Fountain of the Moor*, named after the central figure, an Ethiopian, who is wrestling with a dolphin. Giacomo Della Porta (1576) designed the *Fountain of Neptune*, to which decorative sculptures were added in 1878.

S. Agnese in Agone ④

According to the legend, when the saint was exposed to public ridicule on this spot, her hair miraculously fell down, covering her body. The church was reputedly built on the site of the miracle between the 8th century and 1123. However, the present church was begun in 1652 by Girolamo and Carlo Rainaldi, and was completed in 1653-57 by Francesco Borromini. He gave it a concave facade with a single order of pillars and columns, a dome and twin bell towers. Baciccia worked on the *pendentives* (1665) and Ciro Ferri frescoed the inside of the *dome* in 1689. The monument above the entrance is dedicated to Innocent X, who is buried, along with other members of the Pamphilj family, in a crypt to the left of

the *high altar* (1730). Below the church you can see some remains of Domitian's stadium, a Roman mosaic floor, a marble relief by Alessandro Algardi depicting the miracle of St Agnes and some medieval frescoes.

S. Maria della Pace ⑤

This little church with its beautiful facade is situated in a corner of Rome that many tourists tend to miss. Pietro da Cortona designed this corner in the Baroque style, using the convex facade of the church as a sort of theatrical backdrop so that the church blends with the nearby houses. At the same time, an indissoluble link is established between the actual square, into which the semi-circular pronaos of the church protrudes, and the interior of the church. The interior has retained its late 15th-century appearance: a short nave with two bays with cross-vaults, and a tribune with a dome. The nave is decorated with *works* by Raphael, Baldassarre Peruzzi, Antonio da Sangallo the Younger, Simone Mosca, Giuliano da Sangallo, Pietro da Cortona, Carlo Maratta and Carlo Maderno. The **cloister***, Donato Bramante's first project in Rome (1500-1504), is surrounded by a portico with arches resting on pillars with pilaster strips in the Ionic style, supporting an entablature with a long, heavily indented frieze.

Via dei Coronari ❻

The name of the street derives from the merchants who sold sacred images and crowns (in Italian *corone*) to pilgrims here until the 19th century. Antique shops have taken their place. This fact, and the small squares added in 1939, are the only changes in this street, which has otherwise retained its Renaissance and Baroque appearance.

S. Agostino ❼

The facade of this church, founded in 1420 and enlarged in 1479-83, is typical of the early Renaissance. It has two orders of pilaster strips joined by volutes, dividing it into three parts, with three doorways. The interior was renovated by Luigi Vanvitelli (1756-61), who replaced the semi-spherical dome with a bowl-shaped vault. Pietro Gagliardi (1856) painted the frescoes of the *Prophets* on the pillars, except the one on the 3rd pillar on the left (**Isaiah**), which is by Raphael (1512). Below, the **Madonna and Child with St Anne** is by Andrea Sansovino (1512). On the high altar (1627), designed by Gian Lorenzo Bernini, is a Byzantine *Madonna*. In the first chapel on the left, the altar-piece of the **Madonna di Loreto** was painted by Caravaggio in 1603-1604. The much revered statue of the **Madonna del Parto** (1521), to the left of the central doorway, is by Jacopo Sansovino.

Palazzo Altemps ❽

It is hard to say whether the success of the annex of the Museo Nazionale Romano is due more to the building or its contents (Renaissance sculptures, including the famous Ludovisi collection). The residence of the Altemps family was built in 1471 over the foundations of medieval houses and other buildings, around a **courtyard** with two loggias, in the typical Renaissance style. Inside the palazzo, the **Sala della Piattaia**

The statue of Mars in Palazzo Altemps.

was painted in about 1477. The **painted Loggia** or **gallery** reflects the vogue for magnificence and the exotic sparked off by the discovery of the New World. Some **examples of ancient sculpture** are exhibited here, including the famous **Ludovisi throne*** (5C BC) and the **Galatian's suicide***.

Mausoleo di Augusto ❾

The tomb of Octavian, begun in 27 BC, was originally built as a tomb for the emperor and members of his family. It fell into ruin in Late Antiquity but was restored when Piazza Augusto Imperatore was laid out in 1936-38. Little remains of it today. Outside, the massive tumulus was once planted with cypresses. It had obelisks on either side of the entrance, now in Piazza dell'Esquilino and Piazza del Quirinale respectively, and a bronze statue on the top. Inside, the cella once contained the tomb of Augustus, while the most important members of the Julia-Claudia family and the Emperor Nerva were buried around the central pillar.

Ara Pacis Augustae ❿

Today, this monument, the name of which means Altar of Peace, dedicated by the Emperor Augustus in 13 BC, is one of the most significant to survive from that period. He had it built in the heart of Campus Martius, where Palazzo Fiano stands today. Parts of it were rediscovered in the 16th century, but, in the 1930s, they were transferred to the present site on the river, where the altar was reconstructed. Now it is enclosed within a glass pavilion resting on a plinth. The side facing Via di Ripetta bears the inscription *Res Gestae Divi Augusti* (a gesture of the Emperor). The actual altar is inside the rectangular enclosure, the right side of which is decorated on the outside with marvelous reliefs depicting Augustus, Agrippa, Julia and Tiberius. The carving throughout is of an exceptionally high standard.

Azaleas adorn the Spanish Steps below the church of Trinità dei Monti.

Via dei Condotti ⑪

This street, which is named after the conduits of Acqua Vergine and was laid out in the 16th century, contains many of Rome's most fashionable shops. Tucked among its noble residences, dating mainly from the 16th and 17th centuries, is the *church of the Santissima Trinità degli Spagnoli*, built in 1741-46. Further along, *Caffè Greco* is a historic venue and was once the haunt of famous artists, writers and composers (including Goethe and Stendhal).

Piazza di Spagna ⑫

Many movies of the 1950s included at least one scene shot in this extraordinary, typically Roman setting. The famous **Boat Fountain**** was designed by Pietro Bernini, assisted by his son, Gian Lorenzo, in the form of a leaking boat, set slightly below ground level. It stands at the foot of the "Spanish Steps" which lead up to the church of Trinità dei Monti. The cunning design overcame the problem of low water pressure in the piazza. Urban VIII commissioned the fountain in 1629 to commemorate the flood of 1598. The spectacular **Scalinata della Trinità dei Monti**** (known in English as the Spanish Steps was commissioned by Innocent XIII from Francesco De Sanctis, 1723-26). De Sanctis succeeded in solving the problem of the difference in height between Piazza di Spagna and

the church of Trinità dei Monti by building a monumental staircase with a succession of gently curving and converging flights of steps. To make the staircase look more theatrical, he also designed the buildings at each side. The English poet, John Keats, lived and died in the *red house* on the right which, since the early 20th century, has been a museum, the *Keats-Shelley Memorial House*. The building on the opposite side of the steps houses the famous *Babington's* tea-rooms, the first to be opened in Rome and very popular with artists. The square is named after Palazzo di Spagna, residence of the Spanish ambassador to the Vatican since 1622. For once, **Trinità dei Monti*** is a church that was not founded by a pope. In fact it was a French king, Louis XII, who began work on the church in 1502. Pope Sixtus V consecrated it in 1585 and another French king, Louis XVIII, restored it in 1816. As if to highlight the exception to the rule, the pope who commissioned the church asked Domenico Fontana (1587) to design a double staircase in front of it, and a facade with a single order of pilaster strips and a large central semicircular window at the top. Inside, the single nave is divided by a grille in line with the third chapel. It has late Gothic features in the triumphal arch, the presbytery and the transept and some good *paintings*. Behind the church, **Villa Medici** has spectacular views over the Pincian Hill. On the facade **overlooking** the garden, the two wings protrude slightly from the main building, which has a central portico with a serliana motif. The whole facade is richly decorated with stuccoes, festoons, low reliefs and statues, reflecting the Roman vogue for Antiquity in the late 16th century. The **garden*** has retained its original layout of straight avenues and beautifully kept hedges.

Via Veneto ⑬
Via Vittorio Veneto has retained its distinctive charm. A place where Romans like to stroll, this is where the most elegant shops are located, together with interesting venues like the famous Caffè Doney and exclusive hotels built by the town-planners of the late 19th century for a well-heeled clientele. On the corner with Piazza Barberini is Bernini's *Fontana delle Api*, dedicated to the Barberini family (1644), bees being one of the family symbols.

Palazzo di Propaganda Fide ⑭
This building, built in 1586, bears the signature of the two greatest architects working in Rome in the 17th century (Gian Lorenzo Bernini and Francesco Borromini). In 1626, it became a college for training young missionaries, founded by Gregory XV. In 1644, Bernini worked on the formal brick facade, spanned by

pilaster strips, with travertine string-courses and rustication at the sides. Borromini built the wings overlooking Via di Capo le Case and Via di Propaganda (the latter is a very bold **facade**). The *Column of the Immaculate Conception*, found in 1777 among the ruins of the convent of S. Maria della Concezione in Campo Marzio, was put up in Piazza di Spagna, in front of Palazzo di Propaganda Fide, to commemorate the proclamation of the dogma of the Immaculate Conception of the Virgin Mary by Pius IX.

Galleria Comunale d'Arte Moderna e Contemporanea ⑮
This gallery, founded in 1883, is a must for anyone interested in 19th- and 20th-century Italian art. It contains about 200 *works* by artists such as Giulio Aristide Sartorio, Giacomo Balla, Armando Spadini, Felice Carena, Fortunato Depero, Giorgio Morandi, Scipione, Achille Funi, Felice Casorati, Giorgio De Chirico, Carlo Carrà and Renato Guttuso.

ROUTE 3
VIA DEL CORSO
Palazzo Doria Pamphilj ①
The descendants of this Roman noble family still live in the palazzo, which was built in various phases between

The Casino di Allegrezze in the park of Villa Doria Pamphilj.

Via del Corso

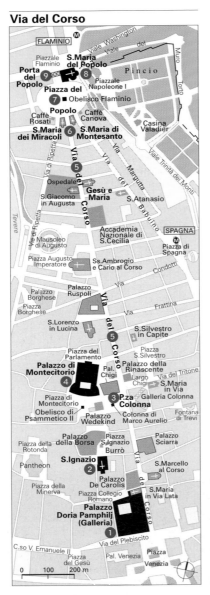

which can also be reached from the doors at either end of the facade. As you approach the heart of the **Galleria Doria Pamphilj****, the richness of the decor of the reception rooms seems to announce the splendor of the more than 400 paintings in the collection. The paintings are arranged according to criteria established by a document published in the 18th century, mainly according to symmetry, and occasionally according to type and style. The four wings which house the paintings contain *works* by Guercino, Paris Bordon, Correggio, Lorenzo Lotto, Guido Reni, Giovanni Bellini and his workshop, Jan Brueghel the Elder, and there is a *bust of Innocent X* by Alessandro Algardi. A small room is reserved for the famous **portrait of Innocent X***, by Diego Velázquez (1650), and another bust of Innocent X by Gian Lorenzo Bernini. Four small rooms house groups of paintings arranged according to the century in which they were painted. Here you will find masterpieces such as Caravaggio's **Flight into Egypt***. The Salone Aldobrandini contains a collection of archeological finds from Villa Doria Pamphilj on the Janiculum and some paintings.

S. Ignazio ❷

When Ignatius Loyola, founder of the Jesuits, was canonized in 1622, Gregory XV decided to dedicate this church to him. Work on the church began in 1626. The church of the Gesù was used both as a model for the facade and for the interior. In fact, it has a single nave with three chapels on either side, linked by a passageway. In addition to interesting *works* by Alessandro Algardi, Pierre Legros the Younger and Camillo Rusconi, in the center of the nave is a yellow marble disk. From here you can see the amazing perspective of the vaulting and the *trompe l'oeil* "dome" depicted in the **Triumph of the Saint**. Andrea Pozzo used this technique instead of the planned dome, which was never built. The simulation of depth and light on canvas is quite extraordinary. The three small palazzi with theatrical Rococo facades opposite the facade of the church are called **Burrò**.

the mid-15th and early 18th centuries. The **facade** overlooking Via del Corso dates from the 18th century. The ground and mezzanine floors have unusual cornices above the windows. On either side of the main entrance, the capitals of the columns are decorated with lilies (the heraldic emblem of the family) rather than the usual acanthus leaves. Inside, a monumental staircase (1748-49) leads up to the private apartments,

The Baroque interior of the church of S. Ignazio.

Piazza Colonna ❸

In the 19th century, this square was one of the hubs of Roman life. Many cafés were opened und often hosted concerts. The 1873 plan to widen Via del Corso led to the demolition of Palazzo Boncompagni Piombino. Galleria Colonna was built in its place in 1915-22, drawing on similar galleries built in Milan and Naples in the 19th century. In the middle of the square stands the **column of Marcus Aurelius****. Incursions by various Germanic tribes revealed the considerable strategic ability of Marcus Aurelius who, after three years of fighting (172-175), succeeded in driving them back beyond the Danube. To commemorate this victorious campaign, his son Commodus (180-193) erected this column in Luni marble. The spiral frieze depicts the various stages of the conflict. There used to be a statue of Marcus Aurelius on the top, but it

was lost in the Middle Ages and replaced by a bronze *statue of St Paul* in 1588-1589, under Sixtus V. The restoration of some of the figures in the central and upper parts of the frieze dates from the same period.

Palazzo di Montecitorio ❹

Most Italians are familiar with this building. Since 1871, it has housed the Italian Chamber of Deputies (parliament). Gian Lorenzo Bernini was commissioned to build it in 1653 by Innocent X and he designed the convex facade with its Baroque ornamental decoration. In the late 17th century, it was converted into courtrooms by Carlo Fontana. The brick and travertine facade overlooking Piazza del Parlamento, on the other side of the palazzo, and the *parliamentary chamber* (paneled in oak carved with floral motifs) is by Ernesto Basile (1903-1927). Here you can see works by Ottone Rosai, Carlo Carrà, Giorgio De Chirico, Lorenzo Viani, Giovanni Boldini and Massimo Campigli. In front of the palazzo stands the *obelisk of Psammetichus II* (early 6C BC), brought home from Egypt by Augustus, and erected here in 1792.

Via del Corso ❺

The name of the long, straight Via del Corso comes from the races that used to be organized here during Carnival and were moved here from the Testaccio area in the late 15th century. It has been a main thoroughfare since Roman times and follows the line of the old Via Flaminia within the Aurelian walls. It used to cross **Campus Martius**, a vast public area which once comprised the mausoleum of Augustus, the Ara Pacis, the Pantheon and the column of Marcus Aurelius. Some of the oldest early-Christian churches were built on this road, which maintained its role of providing access to the city from the north even after the fall of the Roman Empire.

In the 16th century, the popes of the time transformed the houses into palaces and

The Roman wars with Germanic tribes depicted on a column.

REMEMBERING THE FLOODS

In several places in Rome, inscriptions or plaques on the walls record the times when the Tiber has burst its banks. The first is on the facade of the church of S. Maria sopra Minerva, where plaques near the right-hand corner record the floods between 1422 and 1870. The second is at Castel S. Angelo, near the site of a bridge (called the Neronianus) which was destroyed by the might of the river in full spate. The third is at the Porto di Ripa Grande, again not far from the point where a bridge was destroyed by the force of the water. The fourth is hidden in the hospital of S. Spirito in Sassia, where, on the fourth-last pillar of the portico, an inscription gives an idea of the water-level in 1598. But the oldest inscription recording the flooding of the Tiber is on the Arco dei Banchi, at the corner of the homonymous street and Via Paola, not far from Corso Vittorio.

built churches. In the 18th century, Via del Corso became the hub of the intellectual, political and artistic sphere, members of which haunted the numerous cafés (especially Caffè Aragno). In the mid-19th century, the street began to attract commercial buildings. In the early 20th century, it was renamed after King Umberto I, and only regained its original name in 1947.

S. Maria di Montesanto and S. Maria dei Miracoli ⑥

They may look like identical twins, but they're not. For a start, there are 13 years between them. The first church was built in 1662 and completed in 1679. Bernini oversaw the work, indeed he designed it, and executed the *statues of saints* which grace its balustrade. The *bell tower* was finished

in 1761. Work on the second church began in 1675 and it was completed in 1681. Its balustrade is also decorated with statues in a style similar to that of Bernini, while the elegant 18th-century *bell tower* is by Theodoli.

Piazza del Popolo ⑦

Dino Risi's famous movie "Il Sorpasso" (Overtaking), made in 1963, a masterpiece of Italian comedy, is just one of many movies incorporating scenes filmed in this theatrical square, formerly the setting for fairs, games and other popular events.

To the north of the square stands Porta del Popolo, and, dominated from the east by the Pincian Hill, in the center of the square, is the **Flaminian obelisk**, the oldest and the second-tallest (25m) in Rome, after the one erected near the Lateran Palace. This granite monolith was erected in Heliopolis in Egypt in about 1200 BC. It was brought to Rome by Augustus, who placed it in the Circus

One of the fountains in Piazza del Popolo.

Maximus. It was moved here in 1589 under the orders of Sixtus V. The semi-circles on each side of the square contain two *fountains* in travertine by Valadier (1818-21), with basins in the shape of huge shells, crowned with statues. Valadier also designed the buildings (1818-24) on the side of the Tridente (the name given to the point where three long, straight roads penetrate the city, forming a trident), which house the famous Caffè Rosati and Caffè Canova. A footpath, also designed by Valadier (1834) and decorated with niches and statues in the Neoclassical style, winds up the Pincian Hill from Piazza del Popolo, ending below the *Casina Valadier*. The large terrace nearby, which overlooks Piazza del Popolo, has incredible **views**** of the city, dominated by the dome of St Peter's.

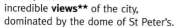

Caravaggio's Conversion of St Paul.

responsible for the **marble altar** (1473) in the sacristy. Behind the *high altar* (1627) are **monuments to Cardinal Ascanio Sforza*** (1505, on the left) and **Cardinal Girolamo Basso Della Rovere*** (1507, on the right) by Andrea Sansovino. The **stained glass windows*** in the choir were made by Guillaume de Marcillat in 1509, whereas the beautiful **frescoes** on the ceiling are by Pinturicchio (1508-1510). In the first chapel of the left transept, on either side of the *Assumption* by Annibale Carracci (1601), there are two masterpieces by Caravaggio (1600-1601): the **Conversion of St Paul*** (right) and the **Crucifixion of St Peter*** (left). The banker Agostino Chigi built the **Chigi chapel** (second chapel, left-hand aisle) as a family mausoleum. There is a marked contrast between the chapel's plain outside and the richly decorated interior. Begun in 1513-14 by Lorenzetto, it was completed by Bernini in 1652-56. Raphael prepared the cartoons for the *mosaics* in the dome, executed in 1516.

S. Maria del Popolo ⑧

The splendid artworks inside this church add to its appeal. It was built in 1475-77 in the Lombard religious architectural style, on the site of a small chapel erected during the pontificate of Paschal II, with funds raised by the local people (hence its name). In the 16th century, it was altered (Bramante rebuilt the choir and the apse and the Chigi chapel was rebuilt according to a design by Raphael). In the following century, the facade and the interior were decorated in the Baroque style, under the supervision of Gian Lorenzo Bernini, and the Cybo chapel by Carlo Fontana was added. The Della Rovere chapel (first chapel, right-hand aisle) contains the *tombs of Cardinals Cristoforo and Domenico Della Rovere* by Bregno and a *Nativity* by Pinturicchio. Bregno was also

Porta del Popolo ⑨

This gate began as Porta Flaminia, one of the gates in the Aurelian walls. The external facade was renovated in 1561-62 by Nanni di Baccio Bigio, who based his design on the Arch of Titus. Alexander VII decided to rebuild the internal facade and entrusted the work to Gian Lorenzo Bernini. The facade is decorated with festoons, oak leaves and ears of wheat, and bears the inscription *Felici faustoque ingressui* (Fortune and happiness to all who enter here). The gate was altered again in 1877-79, when the towers added by Sixtus IV in the 15th century were demolished in order to make the side-entrances.

FROM TORRE DELLE MILIZIE TO THE TREVI FOUNTAIN

Torre delle Milizie ❶

A leaning tower in Rome! The tower acquired an obvious lean in 1348, when a violent earthquake (which also caused the third floor to collapse) caused subsidence. Its history dates back to the lengthy conflicts between the great noble families of the papacy. Built by the Conti in the early 13th century, the tower was acquired by Boniface VIII, who fortified it against the Colonna. Having been restored and consolidated by Antonio Muñoz in 1914, it was joined to Trajan's markets in 1927. Above the base, built of tufa blocks, there are two floors with brick outer walls and merlons on the top.

Palazzo Colonna ❷

The lines of the present facade date back to 1730, when the building was renovated. There are pavilions with a loggia and large windows at each side (the one accessed from Piazza Ss. Apostoli houses the *Museo delle Cere* - Wax Museum). The same style prevails in the courtyard where the palace proper begins. It was built in 1484 at the wishes of Cardinal Giuliano Della Rovere and now houses the famous **Galleria Colonna***. Together with that of Palazzo Doria Pamphilj, it can be regarded as the most important private collection in Rome. The red marble *column being* watched from the wall by the *Venus, Cupid and Satyr* by Bronzino and the *Narcissus* by Tintoretto is the symbol of the Colonna

family. The spectacular decoration of the **Great Hall** alone justifies a visit: stuccoes, frescoes, and large Venetian mirrors provide the setting for *pictures* by Guercino, Niccolò di Liberatore, Giovanni Lanfranco and Francesco Albani. The *Room of the Apotheosis of Martin V* is named after the subject of the fresco in the center of the ceiling by Benedetto Luti. Also look out for the famous *Peasant Eating Beans* by Annibale Carracci. Close by, the basilica of **Ss. Apostoli** contains some fine 15th-century **frescoes**.

Museo Nazionale Romano ❸

This museum will take you on a fascinating journey through the most important aspects of the artistic culture of Imperial Rome. Not surprisingly, this is regarded as one of the world's most important archeological collections. The museum is housed in *Palazzo Massimo alle Terme*, built in the late 19th century in the style of Roman early Baroque residences.

The journey begins with the iconography representing the difficult phase of transition between the late Republican period and the period of Augustus: portraits, inscriptions, and coins from the Republican period gradually give way to works which represent the ideological and political plans of the founder of the Empire. The **statue** found in Via Labicana of **Augustus as Pontefex Maximus*** is one of the finest depictions of the emperor. There are *original Greek* statues in the *Gardens of Sallust*. The exhibits reflect the development of Roman taste from the 1st to 4th centuries with some of the sculptural decoration from the Imperial

From Torre delle Milizie to the Trevi Fountain

villas, aristocratic residences and gardens. Masterpieces of the collection include the **Discus-thrower from the Lancellotti** collection (from the Antonine period but restored in the 18ᵗʰ century) and another from **Castel Porziano** (1C BC), both copies of the famous sculpture by Myron, the **Apollo found in the Tiber** (copy of a prototype attributed to Pheidias) and the **Chigi Apollo**. A large section of the museum is devoted to official portraits.
One room contains the bronzes from the **ships** once moored in Lake Nemi in front of the Caligula's villa (1C BC) which overlooked the lake. Other important finds include the *Portonaccio sarcophagus*, where the battle scenes of Romans fighting Barbarians resemble the reliefs of the Antonine Column, the **sarcophagus of Acilia** with a relief depicting the procession to name the new consul (second half of the 3C), the *sarcophagus*

The Lancellotti discus-thrower.

of Claudianus depicting scenes from the Old and New Testaments (c. 330 AD) and a huge **crater** decorated with one of the earliest images of the Virgin and Child.
The next part of the museum contains wall-paintings and mosaic decoration dating from the 1ˢᵗ century to the late Imperial period. There are splendid **frescoes** (late 1C BC) **from the villa at Gallinas Albas**** at Prima Porta depicting an orchard and flower garden, there are **stuccoes** and **frescoes from Villa della Farnesina****, depicting charming architectural landscapes framed by elegant candelabra, festoons and plants, and the **frescoes** from the villa at Castel di Guido. The basement contains a coin collection and jewelry.

Mura Serviane ❹
When King Servius Tullius decided to build the first set of defensive walls around the town, the future capital of the world was little more than a village. Reinforced by an earth embankment (*agger*), they were about 11km long, almost 10m high and an average of 4m wide. A section of the walls was discovered at Piazza dei Cinquecento when the foundations for the first Termini station were being dug (1869-70). It comprised 17 rows of tufa blocks about 94m long and 10m high.

Porta Pia (off map) ❺
To begin with, this breach in the **Aurelian Walls** had no external facade. The main facade, commissioned by Pius IV as a background for Strada Pia, faced inwards towards the city. It was designed by Michelangelo (1561-64). The decoration was possibly inspired by the pope's family (the five de' Medici balls, the pateras with hanging ribbons and the square block of marble in the center are associated with the barber's trade because the first de' Medici were barbers). The rooms inside the gate house the *Museo Storico dei Bersaglieri* (Museum of the Bersaglieri, a light-infantry regiment). Not far away is a *commemorative column* crowned with a statue of *Victory*.

Terme di Diocleziano ❻
The Emperor Diocletian was from Dalmatia and he made no secret of the fact that he was not keen on the luxury and intrigues of Rome. In fact, he only visited the city sporadically. However, since he wanted to be remembered in a good light, he gave the Romans this bath complex. It was begun in 298 and finished in 305-306, and was eventually the grandest in Rome (it covered an area

of 136,000m²). It could accommodate about 3,000 people, and the main part of the complex, surrounded by gardens with nymphaeums, exedras and blocks of rooms, was based on the Trajan's Baths. In an extraordinary example of the re-use of building material, part of the complex was converted into the Basilica of S. Maria degli Angeli and another was converted into the building which now houses the Museo Nazionale Romano. What's more, two of the rotundas of the outside walls and the main exedra were incorporated into the buildings erected by Gaetano Koch in Piazza della Repubblica. Long the seat of the Museo Nazionale Romano, a section of the Baths of Diocletian is reserved for the **Inscriptions Department** and the museum's collection of inscriptions.

S. Maria degli Angeli ➐

Shortly after he acceded to the Imperial throne (284) Diocletian began a period of severe repression of the already sizeable Christian community. According

Basilica of S. Maria degli Angeli in the Baths of Diocletian

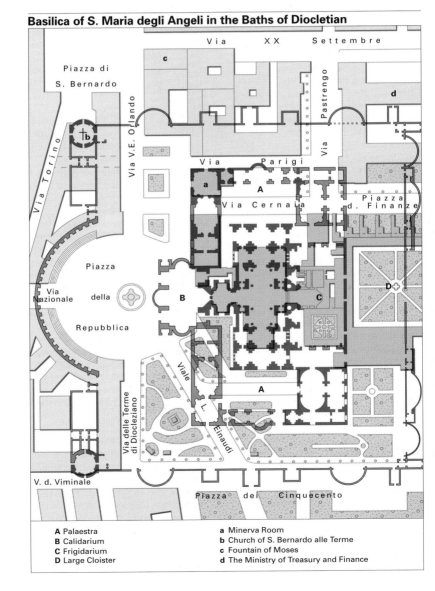

A Palaestra	**a** Minerva Room
B Calidarium	**b** Church of S. Bernardo alle Terme
C Frigidarium	**c** Fountain of Moses
D Large Cloister	**d** The Ministry of Treasury and Finance

to tradition, hundreds of people died building his baths on account of the appalling working conditions. The idea of building a church within part of the bath complex to commemorate those who died emerged in the early 16th century, but not until 1561 did the plan receive the papal seal of approval from Pius IV. The design for it was assigned to Michelangelo, who incorporated the *tepidarium*, the four rooms next to it and those running across it in a complex with a shape similar to a Greek cross with three doors. At the same time, the Carthusian monks, to whom the pope had entrusted the building work, built the adjoining monastery. The complex changed again in the 18th century when a chapel was built dedicated to St Bruno, founder of the Carthusian order. However, its present appearance dates from the Holy Year of 1750, when Luigi Vanvitelli renovated the exterior. Those interested in funerary monuments will find plenty to look at in the *shrines* of the internal vestibule and the *sculptures* in the passageway. Note the **Sala della Minerva** or **Aula Ottagona**, which contains some fine statuary, including two bronzes of a **Hellenistic Prince** (2C BC) and a **Boxer Resting** (1C BC), where the wounds have been created with inlay work. Not far from the church are two interesting 19th-century palaces. **Palazzo delle Esposizioni**, preceded by a formal flight of steps, is one of the city's most important cultural centers, and is used for exhibitions and other events. The building, designed by Pio Piacentini, is unusual because of the complete lack of windows on the walls and the 12 *statues of famous artists* on the top. The **Palazzo della Banca d'Italia** is one of the most successful expressions of the Neoclassical style of Gaetano Koch. Opposite it is the fine Art-Nouveau exterior of *Teatro Eliseo*.

Palazzo Barberini ⑧

Overlooking **Piazza Barberini** and Gian Lorenzo Bernini's **Triton Fountain** (1642-43), richly decorated with allegorical figures, Palazzo Barberini is an ingenius combination of a patrician city palazzo and a villa with a garden. The most prestigious names of the period worked on this building. It was designed by Carlo Maderno, while Gian

Sculptural decoration at Palazzo Barberini.

Lorenzo Bernini designed the loggia-window and the famous *staircase with a square* well which starts at the left-hand side of the portico. On the opposite side of the portico, Borromini designed a *spiral staircase* with pairs of columns. The *mithraeum* in the back garden has an ancient Roman fresco depicting *Mithras in the act of killing the bull* (in the center) and *scenes of myths associated with the god*. The palazzo houses the **Galleria Nazionale d'Arte Antica****, the exhibits of which, dating from the 14th and 18th centuries, trace the development of all the artistic trends: the Giottoesque artists of Rimini, the Mannerists of Rome, painters (some foreign) who imitated the style of Caravaggio and 18th-century painters from the Veneto and Naples. The ground floor of the north wing is devoted to paintings up to the 16th-century, the first floor to the 17th century, the second floor to the 18th century, the library of Cardinal Francesco Barberini to the cartoons on which the tapestries of the Barberini family are based, the nearby store-rooms to the **decorative** arts, and the ground floor of the south wing to temporary exhibitions. The rooms where the paintings are displayed are beautifully decorated. Highlights include works from the north of Italy and Tuscany of the 16th century, works by Raphael and his workshop (including Raphael's famous

One of the niches at the crossroads of Quattro Fontane.

a masterpiece by Gian Lorenzo Bernini (1644-52). Opposite the church is the **Fountain of Moses***, an imposing work by Domenico Fontana (1587), made in the form of a nymphaeum to celebrate the building of the Acqua Felice aqueduct.

Quirinale ⑩

This theatrical setting of papal Rome, **Piazza del Quirinale*** includes the **Fountain of Monte Cavallo**, whose name comes from the Dioscuri (Castor and Pollux). The statues of the gods, depicted standing by their horses, are Imperial Roman copies of 5th-century BC Greek originals found at the Baths of Constantine. Another ancient relic is the obelisk towering above the granite basin (1818), which previously stood at the Mausoleum of Augustus. **Palazzo del Quirinale*** was conceived as a summer residence for the pope but, between 1870 and 1945, was occupied by the Royal House of Savoy. An impressive list of artists contributed to the building of this beautiful palazzo, now the official residence of the Italian President. It was begun by Martino Longhi the Elder in 1573. He was succeeded by Ottaviano Mascherino (who designed the *smaller building* at the far end of the courtyard), Domenico Fontana, Flaminio Ponzio (who designed the *Grand Staircase* and the *chapel of the Annunciata*), Carlo Maderno (who designed the doorway and the *chapel of Paolina*) and, finally,

portrait, **Fornarina***), the *sketches* by El Greco, two important works by Caravaggio (**Judith and Holofernes** and **Narcissus**), and other works by Guido Reni, Guercino, Hans Holbein the Younger and Bernini.

S. Carlo alle Quattro Fontane ⑨

The creative skills of Francesco Borromini, who spent 29 years working on this church, are easily recognizable in the facade, the characteristic bell tower and the interior. Four elegant fountains *with statues of the Tiber, the Arno, Diana and Juno* (1588-93) have given the name to the **crossroads of the Quattro Fontane**, laid out under Sixtus V, where Strada Pia intersects with Strada Felice. Further along *Via XX Settembre* are the churches of **S. Susanna**, *S. Bernardo alle Terme* and **S. Maria della Vittoria**. The last church is famous for the **statue of Ecstasy of St Theresa***,

Palazzo del Quirinale, with the Manica Lunga (left) and the great tower (right).

The Trevi Fountain, a must on the itinerary of any visit to Rome.

Gian Lorenzo Bernini, who designed the *tower* on the left-hand side of the facade (1626) and the *Loggia delle Benedizioni* (1638). Restoration work has given the palazzo its original 18th-century colors. The right-hand side of the palace (known as the *Manica Lunga*, referring to a long corridor inside) has an unusual facade overlooking Via del Quirinale. The palazzo contains many fine *artworks*: the paintings by Guido Reni in the chapel of the Annunciata and by Giovanni Lanfranco and Agostino Tassi (fresco frieze, 1616) in the Sala Regia. The *gardens* (only open to the public on June 2, the Festa della Repubblica, in memory of the referendum of 1946 when Italians voted in favor of the Republic), are laid out in the style of the 16th century and contain a *Coffee House*, created by Ferdinando Fuga for Benedict XIV. Near the Quirinal Hill is the **church of S. Andrea al Quirinale***, commissioned by Cardinal Camillo Pamphilj (1658) from Gian Lorenzo Bernini, then at the height of his artistic career. The great architect designed an unusual elliptical plan for the church, with the main axis on the shorter side, and a dome with an innovative lantern that would enhance the position of the **altar** of his own design. The church is a masterpiece of religious Baroque architecture. *Paintings* by Baciccia and Carlo Maratta add to the interest of the interior.

Fontana di Trevi ⑪

Anita Ekberg's bath in the Trevi Fountain in the movie "La Dolce Vita" made the whole world familiar with this wonderfully theatrical Baroque composition. The fountain, based on the theme of the sea, took 30 years (1732-62) to complete. The style of decoration imitates that of Bernini. At the top of it is a balustrade with allegorical figures, and the crest of Clement XII who commissioned the work. The great *statue of the Ocean* (1759-62) stands in the central niche (on a chariot in the shape of a shell pulled by sea-horses led by tritons), with the personification of *Health* on one side (and another statue above of the *Virgin Mary*, pointing to the spring) and *Abundance* on the other, both works by Filippo Della Valle. As they admire this splendid Baroque blend of sculpture and architecture, visitors to Rome should not forget that, according to tradition, if they want to return to Rome, they should throw a coin into the water. Beyond the fountain, **Piazza di Trevi***, named after the meeting of three roads (*tre vie*) in Piazza dei Crociferi, is also enhanced by the colonnade of the 17th-century *church of Ss. Vincenzo e Anastasio*.

ROUTE 5

THE HISTORIC HEART OF ROME

Palazzo di Venezia ❶

This massive building with its merloned facade was built in 1455-64 by Cardinal Pietro Barbo as his private residence. It was extended by adding the "viridarium" (later Palazzetto Venezia) after he was elected pope (Paul II). This palazzo established the Renaissance model of Leon Battista Alberti in Rome, with a rectangular plan and porticoes and loggias overlooking the central courtyard (only part of this remains). Legacies, donations and groups of exhibits from the former Museo Kircheriano and Museo Artistico-industriale now form the collection of the **Museo di Arti Applicate del Palazzo di Venezia****. The extreme diversity of its exhibits is one of the museum's main attractions.

An impressive group of paintings from the 13th to 16th centuries from the Veneto, Emilia-Romagna, Lazio, Umbria, the Marches and Tuscany is displayed, region by region. Sala Altoviti contains *ivories* and *jewelry*. Pastels illustrate the popularity of this particular art form in France in the late 18th and mid-19th centuries. The porcelain collection provides an overview of the production of the main European manufacturers from the early 18th to early 20th centuries and there is also a remarkable ceramics collection dating from the 15th to 18th centuries. There are about 800 pieces of silver (17C-19C), 150 items of glassware, and more than 400 pieces of Chinese and Japanese porcelain dating from the 17th to 19th centuries. There are also some interesting bronzes and *terracotta models*.

The historic heart of Rome

The "heart" of Rome: the Roman Forum and the Imperial Fora, the Palatine Hill and the Colosseum.

Basilica di S. Marco ❷

Much of the building material used to construct the facade of the church came from the Colosseum and the Theater of Marcello. Again, the three-arched doorway is influenced by Leon Battista Alberti. In the second half of the 15th century, this church, founded in 336 and rebuilt for the first time in 792 (but the Romanesque *bell tower* is 12C), became the palatine chapel of Palazzo di Venezia.

Despite alterations during the Baroque period, the coffered ceiling has been preserved. This, along with that of S. Maria Maggiore, is the only 15th-century **ceiling** in Rome to have survived. The **mosaics** of Gregory IV in the apse dated 827-844 belong to the first reconstruction phase, while the *tomb of Leonardo Pesaro* in the right-hand aisle is by Antonio Canova (1796). Note the interesting *reliefs* on the altar in the sacristy (1474). The "viridarium" (1464), designed by Alberti as a garden surrounded by a portico, was enlarged in 1466-68 by adding an upper loggia. By blocking up some of the arches, it was converted into **Palazzetto Venezia**, and then, in 1911-13, it was moved to the left of Palazzo di Venezia, following the construction of the Monument to Victor Emmanuel II. In the center of the beautiful **courtyard** is a *well-head* by Antonio da Brescia.

The Vittoriano ❸

Building the *monument to Victor Emmanuel II*, first king of Italy, took 50 years. However, it was completed in time for the centenary celebrations for the Unification of Italy. The **Altare della Patria** was opened in 1925 to mark the Grave of the Unknown Soldier (1921). The *quadriga* was placed on the top in 1927. Inside the monument is the *Sacrario delle Bandiere delle Forze Armate*, a collection of standards of the various branches of the Italian Armed Forces.

S. Maria in Aracoeli ❹

The church acquired its present name after the reconstruction of 1285-87. In 1348 Cola di Rienzo inaugurated the staircase built to honor the image of the *Madonna and Child* (10-11C) which adorns the altar. Behind the simple, 13th-century brick facade, the church is a treasure-trove. Below the *coffered ceiling* (1572-75), the interior was decorated by many artists, including Andrea Bregno (*funerary monument to Cardinal Ludovico d'Albrecht*, back of the facade), Donatello (*tombstone of Giovanni Crivelli*, back of the facade), Pinturicchio (**Stories from the Life of St Bernardino**, first chapel on the right), Michelangelo (design for the *tomb of Cecchino Bracci*) and Arnolfo di Cambio (*tomb of Luca Savelli*, right transept).

The archeological site of the Roman Forum and the Palatine Hill: a stroll through history ❺

Rome, "*caput mundi*" (head of all the world), the city that became the largest metropolis in the Mediterranean and then dominated much of the ancient world for centuries. It was here that the principles of civilized living, on which modern constitutions are still based, were conceived. Rome was, firstly, the capital of the Roman Empire. In the West, it was the first great unifying power that succeeded in creating a proper state. The Romans advanced thousands of kilometers, colonizing foreign lands and leaving behind them a rich legacy, not only of knowledge but of laws, infrastructures and rules for social organization. Europe today is based on Rome's legacy, despite the fact that its history has a darker side to it, involving the persecution of Christians and slavery. However, throughout its history, many great men have been fascinated by the "dream of Rome": Charlemagne, Dante Alighieri, Machiavelli, to name but a few. For the first time, a Western people had organized themselves into a complex social system that was a moral and political entity above particular interests. They left much. All over Europe, we drive along roads that were originally laid by the Romans.
The saying that all roads lead to Rome is no coincidence.
This, one of the world's most important archeological sites, has a powerful, fascinating charm which stems from the fact that it was the cradle of our civilization.
Our tour begins with **Trajan's Column****, which is almost 40m high. After the conquest of the Dacians (from modern Romania) Trajan's empire was at its height. To celebrate, the events of the wars of 101-103 and 107-108 were depicted on the low-relief frieze which now surrounds the column. The base is decorated with trophies of war taken from the enemy. A spiral staircase inside climbs to the top, where, in 1587, the statue of the emperor was replaced by one of *St Peter*.
The majestic complex of the **Forum** and **Trajan's Markets****, designed by Apollodorus of Damascus, was begun in 107 and completed under Hadrian. The tour begins at the **markets**, where business was conducted in the great *hall* overlooking Via IV Novembre. Architectural fragments and statues are displayed in the six *tabernae* (shops) off the hall. From here, a staircase descends to *Via Biberatica*, the *semi-circular* area where the markets were held, which has spectacular views over the whole area. A passageway leads under Via Alessandrina to the **forum**, site of the Greek and Roman libraries, the huge Trajan's temple (the surviving column drums and capitals give you an idea of its size) and the *Basilica Ulpia*, the largest and most sumptuous in Rome. You can still see the columns in the center of the area that has been excavated.
The **Forum of Augustus**** (part of the Imperial Fora), next to Trajan's Markets,

The Roman Forum at sunset.

was laid out at the wishes of Rome's first emperor, and part of it was excavated in 1924-32. The rest of the site is still under excavation. In the center of the forum, opened in the year 2 BC, stood the *Temple of Mars Ultor*, surrounded by eight columns on each side (three of the ones on the right side survive). The **Casa dei Cavalieri di Rodi***, built in the 15th century above the left-hand exedra of the forum, was constructed at the wishes of Cardinal Pietro Barbo, and subsequently became the seat of the Order of the Knights of St John of Jerusalem (later of Rhodes and then of Malta, changes reflecting Turkish expansion into the

Mediterranean). In the atrium with its portico you can still see the travertine pillars of the Augustan structure, whereas the *chapel of S. Giovanni Battista* is a 20th-century adaptation of part of the covered structures. On the upper floor is a great *hall* dominated by a tribune (possibly the hall where the knights convened) and an elegant arched loggia (**view**).

The **Forum of Nerva**** was laid out in the narrow space between the Subura and the Roman Forum and contained the *Temple of Minerva* (hence its other name, "Forum Minervae" or "Palladium"). You can still see part of the base of the temple and the so-called *Colonnacce* (enormous Corinthian columns) which formed the portico and supported the frieze with low reliefs. Recent excavations have revealed fragments of another frieze depicting a female figure.

The **Colosseum****, or Flavian Amphitheater (its proper name), is universally regarded as the symbol of Rome, one of the world's most famous monuments. Built at the wishes of Vespasian (dedicated in the year 79 AD) in the area occupied by the artificial lake near the Domus Aurea, it was inaugurated in 80 AD by Titus with games lasting 100 days. Completed by Domitian and restored by Alexander Severus, in the late empire it was used as a hunting ground. Today, visitors are still amazed by the Colosseum's size and the functional way it was built. It is one of the Roman Empire's great feats of engineering, along with countless bridges and kilometers of aqueducts. The Colosseum is a worthy symbol of the huge size of Imperial Rome and the incredible ability of its architects and engineers.

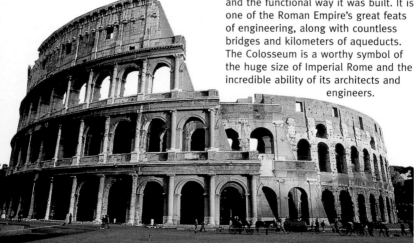

The Colosseum, scene of bloody but popular events in Antiquity.

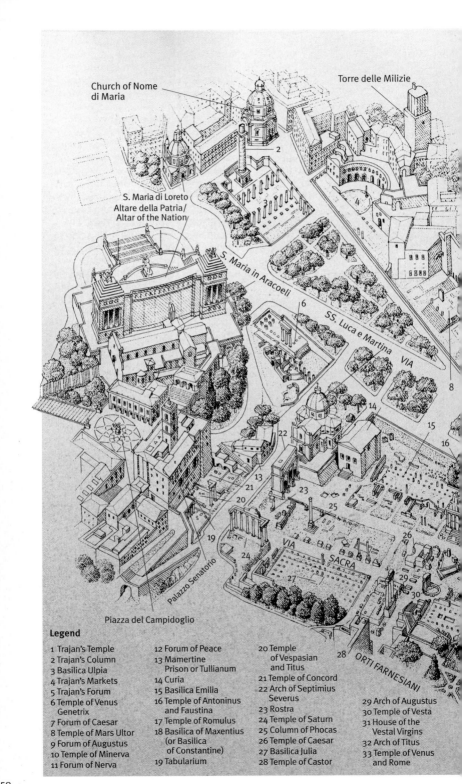

Church of Nome di Maria

Torre delle Milizie

2

S. Maria di Loreto
Altare della Patria/
Altar of the Nation

S. Maria in Aracoeli

4

6

SS. Luca e Martina VIA

8

14

15

16

22

13
21
23
20

25

26

19
24

VIA SACRA

27

29

30

Palazzo Senatorio

28 ORTI FARNESIANI

Piazza del Campidoglio

Legend

1 Trajan's Temple
2 Trajan's Column
3 Basilica Ulpia
4 Trajan's Markets
5 Trajan's Forum
6 Temple of Venus
  Genetrix
7 Forum of Caesar
8 Temple of Mars Ultor
9 Forum of Augustus
10 Temple of Minerva
11 Forum of Nerva

12 Forum of Peace
13 Mamertine
   Prison or Tullianum
14 Curia
15 Basilica Emilia
16 Temple of Antoninus
   and Faustina
17 Temple of Romulus
18 Basilica of Maxentius
   (or Basilica
   of Constantine)
19 Tabularium

20 Temple
   of Vespasian
   and Titus
21 Temple of Concord
22 Arch of Septimius
   Severus
23 Rostra
24 Temple of Saturn
25 Column of Phocas
26 Temple of Caesar
27 Basilica Julia
28 Temple of Castor

29 Arch of Augustus
30 Temple of Vesta
31 House of the
   Vestal Virgins
32 Arch of Titus
33 Temple of Venus
   and Rome

The Roman Forum and the Imperial Fora

As the civic and economic fulcrum of the Roman city, the Forum was the public meeting-place par excellence. This was where justice was meted out, where people came to trade and where people met for religious purposes. The Imperial Fora were not merely an extension of the old Forum but a whole new city plan for the heart of what had become the "capital of the world". It was built in various stages, first by Julius Caesar, and then by Augustus, Vespasian, Nerva and, finally, Trajan – who gradually expropriated and demolished the many houses which occupied this area - to build a grand, monumental complex. It was arranged in an area stretching between the Capitoline and the Quirinal Hills, and the vanishing point was the unforgettable sight of Trajan's Column, one of the few monuments to have survived from this period, together with the remains of the Basilica Ulpia, Trajan's Markets and the Temple of Mars Ultor. The rest was swept away in unscrupulous demolition work carried out in the Fascist era to make way for the building of the broad avenue named after the Imperial Fora.

Reconstruction of the plan of the Roman Forum, below, and, above, the Imperial Fora.

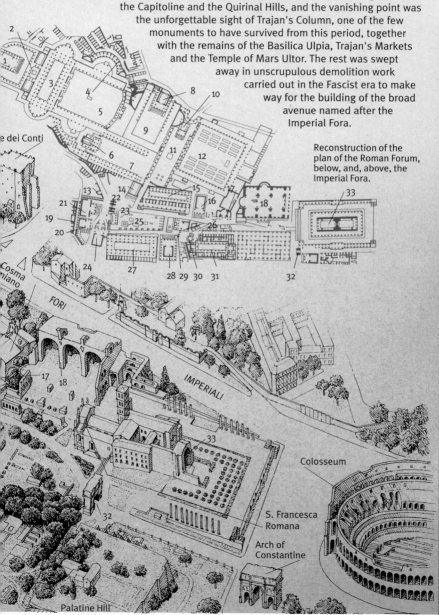

Colosseum

S. Francesca Romana

Arch of Constantine

Palatine Hill

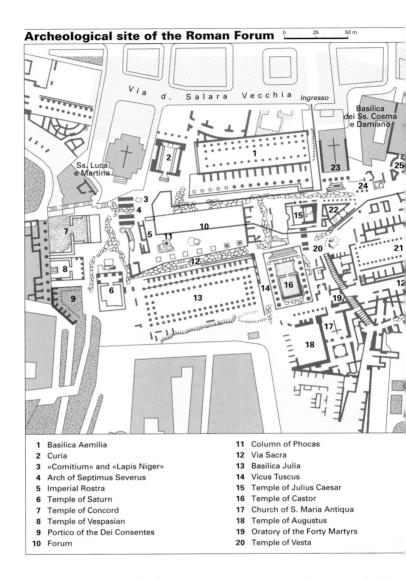

Archeological site of the Roman Forum

0 25 50 m

V i a d. S a l a r a V e c c h i a Ingresso

Basilica dei Ss. Cosma e Damiano

Ss. Luca e Martina

1 Basilica Aemilia	11 Column of Phocas
2 Curia	12 Via Sacra
3 «Comitium» and «Lapis Niger»	13 Basilica Julia
4 Arch of Septimus Severus	14 Vicus Tuscus
5 Imperial Rostra	15 Temple of Julius Caesar
6 Temple of Saturn	16 Temple of Castor
7 Temple of Concord	17 Church of S. Maria Antiqua
8 Temple of Vespasian	18 Temple of Augustus
9 Portico of the Dei Consentes	19 Oratory of the Forty Martyrs
10 Forum	20 Temple of Vesta

The arena was the scene of bloody spectacles which, at the time, were regarded as entertainment. Even today, as you enter the Colosseum, you can almost hear the crowd cheering the gladiators, the cries of the men and the roaring of the animals. In the Middle Ages, the period to which it owes its current name, it was converted into a fortress. In 1312 it passed into the hands of the Roman Senate, and was then consecrated to the Passion of Jesus by Benedict XIV, who put a stop to the devastation and pilfering of the monuments, which had by then become a source of building material. The facade has three orders of arches and is about 50m high. The elliptical arena, which measures 86x54m, was separated from the *cavea* (rows of seating) by a podium decorated with niches containing statues, reserved for members of the imperial family and other dignitaries. It had a seating capacity of 50,000. The spectators entered the arena through vaulted corridors which led up to the various floors to the seats (the highest seats were reserved for women). A *velarium*, or sail, provided shade from the sun.

26

27

S. Francesca
Romana

28

House of the Vestal Virgins
Imperial Palace
Temple of Antoninus and Faustina
(church of S. Lorenzo in Miranda)
Necropolis
Temple of Romulus
Basilica of Maxentius
Museum
Arch of Titus

Areas being excavated

above the cornice and those under the central arch), others from the reign of Hadrian (the medallions above the smaller arches) and others again from the reign of Aurelian (the reliefs above the cornice at either side of the inscription). Other reliefs, made specially for the arch, depict allegorical and historical motifs. It is the largest and best-preserved triumphal arch in Rome, despite having been incorporated into the fortifications of the Colosseum at one time. The arch was restored in 1804.

Retracing our steps, near the *Forum of Peace*, almost at the end of the slope which runs down from Largo Romolo e Remo to the Roman Forum (the buildings on the left belong to the Temple of Antoninus and Faustina), stands the **Basilica Aemilia**, which dates from 179 BC. Its name comes from the Gens Aemilia who, in the 1st century BC, restored the decoration of the basilica. What you see today, partly destroyed by fire, dates from the restoration carried out by Augustus. At that time, the Senators of Rome met in the **Curia** (senate). You can see its plain brick facade and, nearby, the remains of the base of the round *shrine of Venus Cloacina*. This dates from the reconstruction phase under Diocletian after 283 AD, although its foundation is usually attributed to Tullus Hostilius. Inside the Curia, on either side, you can still see the three broad, marble-clad steps on which the 300 members sat. The president's tribune is marked by the figure of a Roman in a toga, which has replaced a statue of Victory. The **Plutei of Trajan** are exhibited here: two finely carved balustrades with reliefs depicting the animals used at *public sacrifices* (a pig, a sheep and a

Below the arena, as well as lifts, there were tunnels where the wild animals used in the performances and the "stage scenery" were kept.

The decoration of the **Arch of Constantine**** is a fine example of material recycled from other buildings. This was possibly due to the state of the public finances which, after the emperor's victory over Maxentius in 312, could not afford entirely new decor for the triumphal arch built to mark the occasion. Some of the reliefs date from the Trajan period (the captured Barbarians, the lateral frieze

The Arch of Constantine at night.

bull), *food being distributed by the emperor and the burning of registers of outstanding taxes.*

The **church of Ss. Luca e Martina*** is an architectural masterpiece by Pietro da Cortona. It has a striking facade with vertical features and is built on a Greek-cross plan with a dome and a lantern. Although there is no historical evidence that the Apostle Peter was imprisoned in the ancient "Tullianum", in 1726 the **Mamertine Prison*** was consecrated to S. Pietro in Carcere. The travertine facade, dating from 40 BC and preceded by a portico, conceals an earlier facade made of tufa, the same material used inside, dating from the 2nd century BC. Prisoners condemned to death were thrown through a trap-door into a round chamber where they were strangled.

The **Arch of Septimius Severus**** was built to celebrate the tenth anniversary of the emperor's accession to the imperial throne. The inscriptions on the faces of the upper part of the arch refer to the victories over the Parthians, Arabs and Adiabenians. The reliefs above the two smaller arches also refer to the *wars fought by Septimius Severus against the Parthians*, while the frieze below depicts a *triumphal procession*.

The iron beaks (*rostra*) of the ships captured at the battle of Antium in 338 BC were placed on the orator's tribune, which has been called the *Rostra* ever since. Caesar moved it from the center of the Comitium to the left-hand side of the Arch of Septimius Severus. The eight granite columns which stand behind the Rostra and the arch belong to the **Temple of Saturn** (497 BC), one of the most revered monuments in Republican Rome. Nearby is a round platform which once supported the Umbilicus Urbis (the symbolic center of Rome) and site of the Miliarum Aureum, a column from which all the distances in the Roman Empire were measured.

The forum stretches out before the Rostra, but, of the many monuments which once stood here, only the *Column of Phocas*, dedicated to the Emperor of the Eastern Empire in 608, has survived. You can still walk along the original polygonal stone paving of

1 Temple of Magna Mater
2 «House of Romulus»
3 House of Livia
4 House of Augustus

the *Via Sacra*, so-called because of the many sanctuaries on either side of it. The street separates the forum from the *Basilica Julia*. This basilica, erected by Caesar and completed by Augustus, comprises a central hall surrounded by a gallery supported by pillars. The street nearby was named *Vicus Tuscus* because an Etruscan community lived between the forum and the Tiber River.

The **Temple of Caesar** was built by Augustus in 29 BC, where the body of the first Julius was cremated. The terrace in front of the pronaos used to be decorated by the *rostra* of the Egyptian ships captured by Octavian during the battle of Antium (31 BC). The nearby **Temple of Castor*** or Temple of the Dioscuri was built in 484 BC. The three surviving grooved

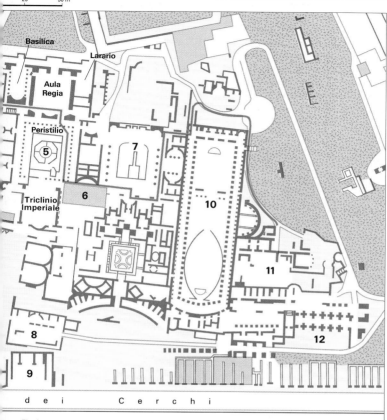

25   50 m

Basilica

Larario

Aula
Regia

Peristilio

5

7

Triclinio
Imperiale

6

10

11

8

12

9

d   e   i   C   e   r   c   h   i

mus Flavia

tiquarium of the Palatine Hill

mus Augustana

aedagogium»

9   Domus Praeconum
10   Palatine Stadium
11   Baths of Septimius Severus
12   House of Septimius Severus

columns date from the temple built by
Tiberius. The oldest Christian building
in the forum, **S. Maria Antiqua**, was
once part of the Imperial Palace. The
church, dedicated to the Virgin Mary in
the 6th century, was embellished by
various popes and abandoned after
a series of earthquakes. It has an
extraordinary collection of murals:
a fresco in the right aisle depicts the
*Virgin Enthroned with Angels and
Saints*. Hadrian I, who commissioned
the work, is depicted with a square
halo. The left aisle also has interesting
frescoes. Those in the chapel left of the
apse date from the period of Pope
Zachary (8C). There is a **Crucifixion** in
the rectangular niche. On one side of
the church stands the so-called *Temple
of Augustus* where excavations have

unearthed commercial buildings dating
from the 1st century BC. On the other,
the *Oratory of the 40 Martyrs* was
founded over a building from the Trajan
period, to which an apse was added
(the frescoes date from the 8C and 9C).
Only the round base and a few
architectural fragments are left of the
Temple of Vesta* where the symbols
of the perpetuity of Rome were kept.
According to tradition, King Numa
Pompilius built the *House of the Vestal
Virgins* for the priestesses who kept the
sacred fire alight. After a fire in 64 AD, it
was rebuilt by Nero and restored and
extended several times. The cells of the
priestesses were arranged around a
large rectangular courtyard with a
double portico, and other rooms were
possibly used as store-rooms and for

sacred furnishings. The **Temple of Antoninus and Faustina*** is another ancient ruin that adds to the Roman Forum's theatrical splendor. To begin with, the temple was dedicated to the emperor's wife, and, after his death, when he became a god, to Antoninus Pius himself. You can still see the *cipollina* marble columns of the pronaos and the base. The steps were rebuilt during restoration work, while the internal chamber was converted into the *church of S. Lorenzo in Miranda* in the 7th-8th century. The grassy areas right of the church mark the edge of the *necropolis* discovered in 1902, attributed to the first inhabitants of the Palatine Hill, who settled there in the late 10th to 8th centuries BC. The lock on the door of the facade of the **Temple of Romulus** is one of the oldest in the world. The temple was begun by Maxentius in honor of his son and completed by Constantine. The huge **Basilica of Maxentius** (also known as the Basilica of Constantine) had a similar fate. You can see the interior with three aisles, and the apse added by Constantine by the new entrance off the Via Sacra (the original one faced the Colosseum).

Titus's seizure of Jerusalem, culminating in the sack of the city (70 AD) marked the beginning of the Jewish diaspora. To commemorate his achievements, Domitian built the **Arch of Titus****, a single, marble-faced archway with grooved columns. During the Middle Ages, it was incorporated into the fortifications built by Frangipane, and was only restored in 1821. Note the reliefs under the arch, depicting the *triumphal procession preceded by the emperor* (right) and *the imperial quadriga carrying Titus*

The Arch of Titus at the end of the Via Sacra.

(left). In the middle of the coffered ceiling is the *Apotheosis of Titus*.

The **Farnese gardens** were created in the mid-16th century by Vignola, Jacopo Del Duca and Girolamo Rainaldi. In 1625, they became host to one of the world's first botanical gardens. Today, not much is left of the gardens on the Palatine, except the *birdcages* on the upper terrace, but there are splendid views over the archeological site.

The **"House of Romulus"** lies in a part of the site that is thick with ancient remains. Nearby are the remains of the *Temple of Victory*, built in 294 BC and restored in the 1st century BC, and the three **Iron-Age** huts which form the first nucleus of the future city of Rome.

The **House of Livia*** is famous for its elegant wall paintings. The *triclinium* has *trompe l'oeil windows* and views, another room has *mythological scenes* in the Pompeian style and, on the right, *Mercury rescuing Io from the clutches of Argos*. The decoration is so luxurious that, for a long time, it was thought to be the **House of Augustus***. However, the latter has been identified as a residence on two levels, part of a complex built in 36 BC. Here the Room of the Masks (theatrical motifs), the Room of Perspectives and the Study are decorated with splendid paintings in the Pompeian style.

The **Domus Flavia** is only the first part of the many *imperial palaces* which occupy the top of the Palatine Hill. But it was effectively the Imperial Palace, since it was here that most of the state functions were held. In the three-aisled *basilica*, the emperor listened to legal cases being discussed. Below it, Caligula consecrated the *Aula of Isis* to the god and decorated it with magnificent wall paintings. The *Aula Regia* was reserved for imperial audiences. The *Lararium* was the emperor's private chapel (the *Casa dei Grifi* below it dates from the 2C BC). A large peristyle separates the three large halls from the imperial banqueting hall where dignitaries were entertained. Note the splendid marble floor. Below this level is the *Domus Transitoria*, where Nero lived.

With regard to the **Palatine Antiquarium,** the Villa Stati Mattei (built above the ruins of the Flavian palace in the 16th century and enlarged by Virginio Vespignani in 1855) was demolished, except for the so-called *Loggetta Mattei*, which has frescoes attributed to Baldassarre Peruzzi or his workshop, and the 19th-century building which now houses the museum. It contains finds relating to the first settlement on the Palatine, sculptures found between 1870 and the present day and a series of stuccoes and frescoes. The finest examples of statuary are the *head of Meleager* (4C BC), and the **Palladium Palatinum*** (an original of the late 6C BC). The **Campana slabs** (36-28 BC) come from the Temple of Apollo on the hill. The **paintings** in the second Pompeian style (second half of the 1C BC) come from the House of Augustus. The **marble-inlay** wall decoration comes from the Domus Tiberiana and the Domus Transitoria. The **Domus Augustana**, next to the Domus Flavia, was part of the imperial residence. From here, if you look down at the slope of the hill facing Circus Maximus, you can see the *Paedagogium*, built under Domitian to house the school of imperial pages, and the remains of the *Domus Praeconum*, an annex of the imperial palace. The **Palatine Stadium** was built by Domitian, the last of the Flavian emperors, although much restoration was carried out under Septimius Severus. Inside, it had a double portico with the imperial box in the middle of the east side. The oval exterior was possibly built in the early Middle Ages by Theodoric, king of the Ostrogoths, who reigned over Italy between 493 and 526.

S. Clemente ⑥

The Basilica of S. Clemente is a real treasure-trove of surprises, an extraordinary conglomeration of superimposed structures which began as a private house in the 2nd century. In the courtyard of the house was a mithraeum which, shortly afterwards, was converted into a place for Christian worship. Having been damaged by the fire started by the Normans in 1084, it was rebuilt on the same lines by Paschal II, and acquired its present appearance in 1713-1719. The interior of the **upper basilica** has preserved its early 12th-century structure, with a nave and two side-aisles with apses separated by columns, and a Cosmatesque **floor**. The **choirstalls** in

The Basilica of S. Clemente, the nave and the apse with the altar in the center.

the center of the nave date from the same period, as do the fine Cosmatesque *ciborium* in the presbytery and the *bishop's throne* in the apse. The mosaic in the bowl of the apse, a **Triumph of the Cross** of the Roman school, dates from the first half of the 12th century. In the right aisle there are two 15th-century *funerary monuments* worthy of note, beside the presbytery. In the left aisle, the chapel of St Catherine contains **frescoes*** painted by Masolino da Panicale (1428-31), possibly with the assistance of Masaccio. A staircase decorated with architectural fragments from the 4th-century church and the mithraeum leads down to the **lower basilica**. A fresco in the nave depicts the **Legend of Sisinius**: the orders and the names included in the scene are vitally important for scholars of the earliest "vulgar" form of Italian. More frescoes (9C-12C) adorn the walls of the nave and the narthex. A staircase at the end

of the left aisle leads down to buildings of Roman date and the 3rd-century *mithraeum*. On the way out, try to spot the *face of the Madonna* dating from the 9th-11th centuries and the early-Christian *baptistery*.

S. Stefano Rotondo ❼

You have to really look for this church, hidden away behind the arches of **Nero's aqueduct**. Rome's oldest church (5C), built on a circular plan, is still quite visible, despite the addition of the 12th-century portico and the elimination of the colonnade and three arms of the Greek cross in the mid-15th century. Note the lovely *frescoes* on the perimeter wall.

S. Maria in Domnica ❽

Paschal I built a church over the site of an earlier place of worship (called a *dominicum*). When the church was rebuilt in the 16th century, the 9th-century basilica form of the

---

 TCI HIGHLIGHTS

THE PALACE OF THE "GOD" NERO

The **Domus Aurea****, the pleasure palace built by Nero on the area devastated by the fire of 64 AD, was opened to the public on June 25,1999. A unique place, it occupied  almost a square quarter of a mile of land, and included gardens, an impenetrable forest where wild and domesticated animals lived side by side, and an artificial lake surrounded by porticoes, simulating a town by the sea. This wondrous creation was short-lived, since Trajan and other emperors destroyed much of it after Nero's death, after which it fell into oblivion. Until the Renaissance, when several famous painters used ropes to descend into the underground "grottoes" of the Oppian Hill by torchlight and discovered the richness and variety of the wall-paintings, especially the decoration known as grotesque (from the word "grotto"), in which dolphins, griffons, chimeras and other imaginary animals intertwine with plant motifs. This discovery was to provide endless inspiration for the new Renaissance taste. The palace itself was to remain undiscovered for much longer. Worse still, its frescoes deteriorated as a result of the crystallization of mineral-salts. However, as a result of the recent restoration project, some of the rooms are now accessible: the *Nymphaeum of Ulysses and Polyphemus*, with a barrel vault ceiling decorated with pumice and sponge-like stones to simulate stalactites; the Room of the *Golden Ceiling*, thought to have been Nero's throne-room; the *Octagonal Room*, possibly the center of the palace; the two twin *rooms of Achilles in Sciro*, the *Room of Stuccoes* or the *Room of Hector and Andromache* (*in the photo, a detail*); the *Room of the Little Birds*. The author of these masterpieces was called Fabullus, who is said to have always worn a toga, even when he was up on the scaffolding painting.

interior, with a nave and two side-aisles separated by gray granite columns, was preserved. The coffered ceiling dates from the 16th century. Below it is a frieze by Perin del Vaga based on a design by Giulio Romano. The **mosaics** in the apse and the triumphal arch both date from the original building.

Parco del Celio ⑨

Given its proximity to the Palatine, this precious public garden opened in the early 19th century was certain to contain vestiges from the classical period. One of them is the Temple of Claudius, built by Agrippina in 54 AD but converted by her son Nero into a nymphaeum for the nearby Domus Aurea. Inside the park is **Villa Celimontana,** formerly a *casino,* built in the first half of the 19th century by Gaspare Salvi. It contains a selection of material from the former City Antiquarium, including the famous sarcophagus of Crepereia Tryphaena, containing a splendid ivory doll with hinged joints and wearing bracelets.

S. Saba ⑩

The church dedicated to founder of an eastern order of monks stands on the top of the "little Aventine" hill. Historical sources confirm that there was an early-Christian church here as early as 768. The relief of the *knight with the falcon* (8C) is the most significant of the archeological remains displayed on the portico and in the gallery (both date from 1463) on the facade of the church. A marble *doorway* with mosaic decoration (1205) leads into the bare interior: a nave with two side-aisles separated by 14 Classical columns. The Cosmatesque *floor* dates from the 13th century, while the frescoes in the apse were executed for the Jubilee of 1575. The *Crucifixion* above the bishop's throne dates from the 14th century, although it has obviously been repainted several times.

A Roman ruin in the garden of Villa Celimontana.

S. Sabina ⑪

There was already a *titulus* here when Peter of Illyria built his basilica on this site (5C). In 824, Eugenius II added an iconostasis, the ambones and the ciborium. The bell tower and the cloister date from the 13th century. The **wooden doors*** of the main doorway leading into the atrium are from the first basilica. The 18 panels, framed by tendrils, depict *scenes from the Old and New Testaments.* The interior of the church, divided into a nave and two side-aisles, clearly echoes the style of the basilicas in Ravenna. Above the door, a fragment of mosaic bears an *inscription* in gold lettering on a blue background with the names of the founder, Pope Celestine I and depicting the Ecumenical Council held at Ephesus in 431. The *frieze* of red and green mirrors in the spandrels of the arches of the nave date from the 5th or 6th centuries. The *choirstalls* have been reconstructed with fragments dating from the 5th to 9th centuries, like the bishop's throne in the apse. Finally, the Elci chapel contains a *Madonna of the Rosary* by Sassoferrato.

Portico di Ottavia ⑫

In 23 BC, Augustus dedicated the renovation of the portico, built in 146 BC by Quintus Cecilius Metellus, to his sister, Octavia. Originally it enclosed two temples but it was rebuilt in 203 by Septimius Severus and Caracalla and later became a fish market, a role which lasted from the Middle Ages until the wall of the Jewish ghetto was demolished. An inscription refers to a curious privilege granted to the Conservatori (city magistrates), who had rights over the heads of the largest fish. Not surprisingly, the *church* built behind the portico in the mid-8th century was given the name of *S. Angelo in Pescheria.* The medieval facade of the nearby *House of Vallati* is mainly the result of restoration carried out since 1927.

In Piazza del Campidoglio, the centrifugal pavement design is by Michelangelo.

S. Maria in Campitelli ⑬

This church was built as a votive offering to give thanks for deliverance from the plague of 1656. It was begun in 1662 to house the miraculous image of *S. Maria in Portico Campitelli* (11C) above the *high altar*. This and, indeed, the rest of the church, decorated in the late-Baroque style, is the work of Carlo Rainaldi. The facade in travertine is decorated with columns and cornices. Inside, the architect has reached a cunning compromise between a central and a longitudinal plan. The chapel of the Reliquaries contains a delightful *portable altar* dating from the 12th century, said to have belonged to St Gregory Nazianzenus.

Piazza del Campidoglio ⑭

The square at the top of the Capitoline Hill is pervaded by the genius of Michelangelo. From the outset, he had the idea of turning attention (and, consequently, the symbolic point of reference for town-planning) away from the Roman Forum, the ancient center of the city, and directing it towards the Vatican, the "new" heart of Rome. From this ensued the idea of enclosing the square with three buildings, leaving the side facing St Peter's open, apart from the balustrade bedecked with statues. And finally he imagined the plinth supporting the equestrian statue of Marcus Aurelius as the fulcrum of a pavement with a centrifugal design. The design of the stepped ramp (known as the "Cordonata") leading up to the square is also Michelangelo's. Paul III, the pope who decided to reorganize the area, approved the whole plan, but Michelangelo was only ever able to see it on paper in his preparatory designs. Indeed, other architects built Palazzo Senatorio, Palazzo dei Conservatori and Palazzo Nuovo, paved the square and arranged the *statues* on the balustrade. There is nothing left now to suggest that **Palazzo Senatorio** (not open to the public) was once a medieval fortress. After the rebuilding of 1582-1605, the only part of the building conforming to Michelangelo's original plan was the external staircase. The rear facade of the palazzo incorporates 11 arches of the Roman **Tabularium** (included in the tour of the Musei Capitolini), the depository of the state archives of Ancient Rome, built in about 78 BC and used in the Middle Ages as a prison

the facade, the portico overlooking the courtyard and the staircase. Roman remains decorate the internal courtyard including the famous gigantic *head of Constantine*, part of a monument to which the fragments of an arm, a leg, a hand and the feet also belong. In 1655, on the opposite side of the square, Girolamo and Carlo Rainaldi built *Palazzo Nuovo*, again following Michelangelo's design.

The Sistine Chapel in the Vatican Museums is proof that Sixtus IV was a patron of the arts. But Rome can also thank this pope, with a passion for painting, for one of the world's most important institutions, the collections known as the **Musei Capitolini**** (Capitoline Museums). Sixtus IV donated the bronzes from the Lateran Palace, the symbols of the power of Ancient Rome. Leo X (1515), Pius V (1566) and, in 1733, Cardinal Albani imitated his example. After that, works discovered during excavations prior to the construction of new buildings after the Unification of Italy increased the collection so that it became one of the most extensive and complete collections of classical sculptures in Europe. This "museum city" comprises the Appartamento dei Conservatori, the Museum of Palazzo dei Conservatori, the Pinacoteca Capitolina (art gallery) and the Museo Capitolino. The first three are housed in Palazzo dei Conservatori, while the last occupies the whole of Palazzo Nuovo (since 1997, some of the sculptures from these museums are on display at the converted Montemartini Power Plant).

and warehouse. Behind the great portico were various vaulted rooms organized in several layers to overcome the difference in height between the Capitoline Hill and the Roman Forum. There is an unparalleled view over the fora from the terrace behind the right-hand side of Palazzo Senatorio.

Musei Capitolini ⑮

In 1563, it was Michelangelo himself who laid the first stone of **Palazzo dei Conservatori**. But he was able to do little else, except leave his designs so that his successors could complete

Part of the **Appartamento dei Conservatori*** belongs to the Comune di Roma (Rome City Council), which uses it for public ceremonies. In addition to the numerous, splendid **artworks** displayed in its beautiful **rooms**, the museum houses

The Tiber below Palazzo Senatorio.

the symbol of the Eternal City: the bronze statue of the **Lupa Capitolina**, or she-wolf of Rome, cast in the early 5th century BC (the twins Romulus and Remus were added in the 15th century); the fragments of the Fasti *Consulares et Trionfales* (records of Roman magistrates and of the great captains of Rome in 13 BC-12 AD) on the walls opposite the windows are all that remain of the Arch of Augustus, which once stood in the Roman Forum. In the center of the adjacent Sala delle Oche is the famous *Head of Medusa* by Bernini (1630) and the magnificent *mastiff* in green spotted serpentina marble (from a Greek 4C BC original). The **Sala delle Guerre Puniche** is the best-preserved, in terms of the original 16th-century decoration of the palace. The **Museo del Palazzo dei Conservatori** contains many fine exhibits, including a **bust of Commodus**, depicting the emperor with the attributes of Hercules (2C), the **Esquiline Venus** (1C BC) and the **crater of Aristonothos** (late 7C BC). The **Pinacoteca Capitolina*** is a result of Benedetto XIV's passion for Italian and European art from the Middle Ages to the 18th century. A passion which embraced all the schools of painting: from the school of Ferrara to the Venetian school, which, throughout the 15th and 16th centuries produced great

Musei Capitolini, a hand from the massive statue of Constantine.

masterpieces, but also works by foreign painters, such as Rubens and Van Dyck. A valuable porcelain collection shares a room with Caravaggio's *St John the Baptist*, while the huge gilded bronze statue of *Hercules* is a Roman copy of a 2nd-century BC original. Italian 17th-century painting is represented by works by Pietro da Cortona, Giovanni Lanfranco, Domenichino, Guido Reni and Ludovico Carracci, as well as the **Burial and Glory of St Petronilla**, one of Guercino's most famous works (1623). The two exhibits in the courtyard denote the importance of the collections of the **Museo Capitolino***. In the exedra at the far end of the courtyard is a 1st-century fountain with the colossal figure of a river-god called *Marforio*, one of Rome's "talking statues". The second is the **equestrian statue of Marcus Aurelius*** which graces the right-hand side of the courtyard. This splendid bronze statue depicts the emperor in the act of talking to the people. The raised foreleg of the horse originally rested on the head of a prisoner. According to tradition, when the gilding that originally covered the emperor and his steed returns (only a few traces are left), the tuft of hair between the horse's ears will move, announcing the Last Judgement. During the Imperial period, the eastern cults of Mithras, Isis and Serapis were very popular and widespread. Finds associated with these **cults** (statues, reliefs and inscriptions) are displayed in the rooms on the ground floor. *Hellenistic sculptures* alternate with *Roman copies* of Greek originals in the gallery on the first floor. The Sala delle Colombe has a fine *mosaic* and a child's

The Dying Gaul in the Museo Capitolino.

sarcophagus depicting the *myth of Prometheus* (3C) and the *Tavola Iliaca*, or Trojan Tablet, with reliefs representing the Trojan cycle (1C). The nearby Gabinetto della Venere is named after the **Capitoline Venus**, a Roman replica of the Greek original from Cnidos. The 65 *busts of Roman emperors* form a fairly complete "family album" of the emperors, while 79 other *busts depict Greek and Roman philosophers, poets, doctors and writers*, some of whom have yet to be identified. However, some of the most interesting works are exhibited in the great hall on the first floor. They include the famous **Wounded Amazon**, an excellent copy of the 5th-century BC Greek original, and the **Dying Gaul***, regarded as two of the most eloquent expressions of ancient sculpture.

ROUTE 6

TOWARDS THE LATERAN PALACE...

S. Pietro in Vincoli ❶

The name of the church commemorates the miracle of the chains which bound the Apostle Peter when he was a prisoner in Jerusalem. When they were laid next to those used during Peter's imprisonment in Rome, they were miraculously joined. They are now kept in the reliquary below the altar. The church was begun in 439, on the site of a church that was dedicated to the Apostles in the 4th century but which dated from at least a century earlier. The church was restored in the 15th century, when the beautiful colonnaded *portico* with arches supported by octagonal stone pillars was added. The marble *doorway* dates from the same period. Inside, the bases of the 20 classical marble columns are an 18th-century addition. When Leo X released him from his commitment, Michelangelo had already worked for three years (1513-16) on the **mausoleum of Julius II**, which stands unfinished in the right transept. He executed the statue of **Moses**, seated, and some of the *figures* in the

niches, which were later completed by Raffaello da Montelupo (1542-45). Note the *low reliefs* of the gilded bronze doors in the altar of the Confessio; also the gilded bronze *tabernacle* (1856) containing the presumed chain associated with the saint. A *Byzantine mosaic* (c. 680) adorns the second altar of the left aisle.

S. Prassede ❷

Paschal I (817-824) gave orders that the church must be rebuilt. It dates from at least 489 (the remains of the colonnade in the courtyard in front of the facade belong to the early-Christian church). The pope also commissioned the **chapel of St Zeno***, the most important Byzantine monument in Rome. The polychrome marble *floor* is a splendid example of *opus sectile*, a mosaic made with pieces of marble of various shapes and color. Although they have been restored, the **mosaics** in the vault, the right-hand lunette, the lunette below it and the niche of the altar are all very interesting. Paschal I also commissioned the **mosaics** on the triumphal arch and possibly also those in the apse.

S. Maria Maggiore ❸

The patriarchal basilica of the Esquiline has three names: S. Maria Maggiore, S. Maria ad Nives or S. Maria Liberiana. According to the legend, it was built by Pope Liberius on the site of a miraculous snowstorm which occurred on August 3, 356, but, in actual fact, not before the

S. Prassede, mosaics in the dome of the chapel of St Zeno.

papacy of Sixtus III, who dedicated it to the Motherhood of Mary, defined in 431 by the Ecumenical Council of Ephesus. At that time, the church had a nave, two side-aisles and a central apse. The apse

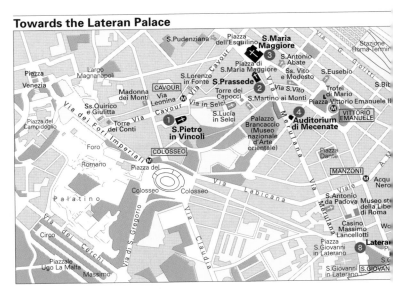

was moved further back during the papacy of Nicholas IV to permit the addition of a transept. The chapels date from the 16th century. Paul V built the palazzo to the right of the facade (1605). Clement XI began the one to the left of it, which was completed by Ferdinando Fuga. It was this architect who, in 1741-43, added a new facade. You can see the Romanesque bell tower behind it. Above the portico, Fuga added a loggia with three arches. Behind the arches you can still see two series of the 13th-century mosaics which adorned the original facade. Fuga also contributed to the interior (1746-50), limiting himself to discreetly rearranging various features and making the church more symmetrical. This is the only one of Rome's patriarchal church interiors that has retained

its original appearance. 36 stone columns support the entablature decorated with a 5th-century mosaic frieze. The beautiful coffered ceiling is supposed to have been gilded with the first gold brought from America. Along the side-walls of the nave, above the entablature, the 36 mosaic panels dating from the time of Sixtus III, but restored in 1593, are a rare example of art of the late Roman Empire. The mosaic of the triumphal arch dates from the same period. The splendid mosaic in the apse is the work of Jacopo Torriti (1295). In 1931, the transept from the time of Nicholas IV was partially restored, unveiling frescoes of the prophets attributed to Pietro Cavallini, Cimabue or the young Giotto. The paintings in the vault of the chapel of Sts Michael and

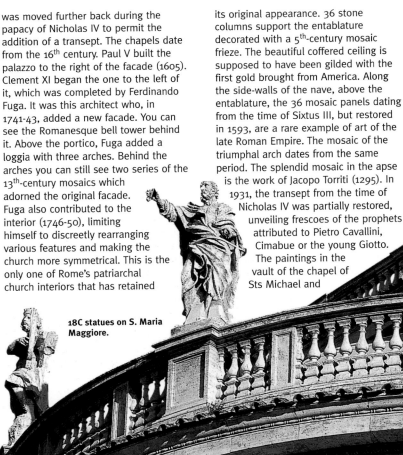

18C statues on S. Maria Maggiore.

Porta Maggiore ⑥

The gate, formed by re-using two arches of the aqueducts carrying the *Acqua Claudia* and the *Anio Novus*, was begun by Caligula in 38 AD and completed by Claudius in 52. The gate in the Aurelian walls marked the beginning of *Via Prenestina* and *Via Casilina*. It has two arches, three niches, and a large attic with inscriptions on the side facing Piazzale Labicano commemorating the achievements of Claudius and the restoration of the aqueduct carried out by Vespasian (71) and Titus (81). In 1838, a late-Republican funerary monument in travertine was discovered behind the central niche of Porta Maggiore. The frieze on it depicts scenes in a bakery, leaving no doubt as to the trade of its owner, **Eurisace**.

S. Croce in Gerusalemme ⑦

The legalization of the Christian religion did not come about until the reign of Helena's son, Constantine, but it is possible that Helena had already built a small church in her villa. It was rebuilt by Lucius II (1144-45) in the form of a basilica and, having been altered again in the 15th and 16th centuries, was renovated in 1743 by Domenico Gregorini and Pietro Passalacqua. The facade, which owes much to Borromini's influence, is one of the finest expressions of Roman Baroque and its curve almost seems to announce the elliptical form of the atrium behind it. The interior is divided into a nave and two side-aisles by huge granite columns (partly incorporated into the pillars added in the 18th century) and has a fine Cosmatesque *floor*. Note the *tomb* in the apse and the *fresco* in the bowl of the apse. Stairs lead down from the right of the apse to the chapel of St Helena, which has a fine **mosaic** ceiling. Under the floor of the chapel, according to tradition, is the earth from Calvary and the relics of Christ's Passion, brought to Rome from the Holy Land by St Helena. This legend is the reason for the name of the church.

The Laterano ⑧

Piazza di S. Giovanni in Laterano** was another project entrusted by Sixtus V to his favorite architect, Domenico Fontana. Memories of the beginnings of the

Peter in Chains, accessed through the baptistery from the right aisle, are thought to be by Piero della Francesca. But, in this part of the basilica, the eye is drawn to the Sistine Chapel or chapel of the Blessed Sacrement (1584-87). It was Domenico Fontana, commissioned by Sixtus V, who designed the chapel on a Greek-cross plan, with a dome decorated with ancient marbles. A staircase leads down from the ciborium to the oratory of the Presepio, an old chapel renovated by Arnolfo di Cambio (c. 1290). The Paolina or Borghese chapel (1605-1611), situated at the beginning of the left aisle, is very fine. Michelangelo designed the Sforza chapel just beyond it, between 1564 and 1573.

Auditorium di Mecenate ④

The Auditorium of Mecenate was probably a summer nymphaeum, in one of the *horti* (gardens) owned by one of Octavia's councilors. Discovered in 1874, the vast rectangular hall has fragments of wall paintings from the 1st century.

Tempio di Minerva Medica ⑤

The Temple of Minerva Medica, which served as a model for both Renaissance and Baroque architecture, is a large ten-sided hall with niches set below arched windows. It is named after the statue of Minerva with a serpent found nearby (now at the Vatican Museums).

The papal altar in S. Giovanni in Laterano.

Church here were still very vivid. The
Emperor Constantine's second wife
(of the Gens Laterani) gave the Villa dei
Laterani to Pope Melchiades
(or Miltiades). This led to the building
of a basilica (313-318) and, subsequently,
the Palace of the Popes. In 1585-89,
Fontana, who was aware of the early
history of the site, opened up straight
roads leading towards the Basilica of
S. Maria Maggiore, the Colosseum and
the Appian Way. He raised an obelisk at
the confluence of the three roads and
added the Palazzo Lateranense, the
Loggia delle Benedizioni and the building
which houses the Scala Santa. In the
18th century, the facade of the basilica
was renovated along with the Triclinium
of Leo III, which was the state
banqueting hall. In the middle of the
square, which is often used for concerts,
not to mention the very popular festival
of the patron saints of Rome, stands the
Lateran obelisk (47m high including the
plinth). It was first erected in Thebes in
the 15th century BC and brought to Rome
in 357 AD by Constantinus II. Initially, it
was placed in the Circus Maximus but it
toppled over during an earthquake and
was only rediscovered in 1587.
The Lateran Treaties signed in **Palazzo
Lateranense**** (Lateran Palace) on
February 11, 1929 put end to more than
50 years of squabbling between the

Italian Government and the Holy See.
It resulted in the creation of the State
of the Vatican City and, at the time,
the Lateran Palace was included in the
papal property, with the privileges of
an exclave. In his plan for Sixtus V,
in 1586-89, Domenico Fontana imagined
the palace as having a representative
role. The palace re-acquired this role to
some extent in 1967 (having been used
as a hospital, an archive and a museum
in the interim), when it became the
offices of the Cardinal Vicar of Rome.
In 1987, the **Museo Storico Vaticano**
opened its doors. In the *Papal
Apartments*, the late-Mannerist frescoes
in the chapel glorify Sixtus V, while those
in the other rooms provide a summary of
Imperial Roman and Christian history.
The actual *Museo Storico* has a section
devoted to iconography of the popes
and another to papal ceremonial.
A balustrade with *twin bell towers* (13C)
decorates the top of the *Loggia delle
Benedizioni*. To the right of it,
S. Giovanni in Fonte, better known as the
Lateran Baptistery, dates from the same
period as the basilica and was altered by
Sixtus III, who added an atrium. The
baptistery is built on an octagonal plan,
with eight columns supporting an
architrave and the drum encircling the
basalt font. The **church of S. Giovanni in
Laterano**** (St John Lateran) is dedicated

to St John the Baptist, St John the Evangelist and the Redeemer, and is the cathedral of Rome. It is the descendant of the basilica founded in 313-318 by Constantine, and has been rebuilt and restored many times. The facade dates from the restoration of 1732-1735, conducted by Alessandro Galilei. It has a single order of pilaster strips and semi-columns supporting an entablature with a tympanum. Above the balustrade are 15 *statues of Christ, St John the Baptist, St John the Evangelist* and *the Fathers of the Church*. Almost a century before, in 1660, the bronze **doors** of the Curia in the Roman Forum were placed in the central doorway of the church. To the right of it is the *Porta Santa*, which is only ever opened in Jubilee or Holy

Worshippers ascending the Scala Santa on their knees.

Years. Francesco Borromini altered the nave and four aisles twice (1646-50 and 1656-57) but preserved the 16th-century wooden ceiling and the Cosmatesque floor. Before 1718, he made 12 niches in the piers of the **nave** to house huge *statues of the Apostles*. Giovanni di Stefano was responsible for the Gothic *papal altar* (1367) at the end of the nave; the *frescoes* on the outer panels were later altered by Antoniazzo Romano and Fiorenzo di Lorenzo. Until 1963, only the pope could officiate at the *high altar*. It incorporates the original wooden altar

before which the first popes celebrated mass. The confessio below the high altar contains the *tomb of Martin V* (Simone Ghini, 1443). In the **far right-hand aisle**, between the 2nd and 3rd statue, is a *small statue of St James* by Andrea Bregno (1492); beyond it is the *tomb of Cardinal Antonio Martino De Chaves* (1447). The **inner right-hand aisle** contains the *tomb of Cardinal Ranuccio Farnese*, designed by Vignola; note the **fragment of a fresco** by Giotto on the first pillar. In the **far left-hand aisle**, the Corsini chapel by Alessandro Galilei contains the tomb and the columns of the *monument Clement XII* from the atrium of the Pantheon. The last pillar of the **inner left-hand aisle** contains the *tomb of Elena Savelli* by Jacopo Del Duca (1570). The right arm of the **transept**, which was renovated architecturally and repainted in 1597-1601, leads into the *museum* of the church, which contains some 15th-century jewelry and the *Cross of Constantine* (12C-13C). When Francesco Vespignani altered the **apse** in the 19th century, the **mosaic** of the previous late 13th-century structure was preserved. The **cloister***, built in 1215-32, is a masterpiece of Cosmatesque art. The arches are supported by small smooth or spiral columns, some of which are decorated with mosaic. The *well-head* in the courtyard dates from the 9th century. Sculptures, architectural fragments and tombstones line the walls of the cloister (note the remains of the **tomb of Riccardo degli Annibaldi** by Arnolfo di Cambio) together with Roman and early-Christian artifacts.

Close by is the **Scala Santa**** (Holy Staircase), believed to be the actual steps that Jesus climbed the day he was sentenced to death. Formerly the Monumental Staircase of the Patriarch, it was re-used in the building erected by Sixtus V (1589) for the private chapel of the popes (the *Sancta Sanctorum*), situated on the first floor of Constantine's palace. Since then, the Scala Santa, which may only be ascended by worshippers on their knees, has lead to the chapel of St Lawrence, where the entrance to the "Sancta Sanctorum" is located. The current appearance of the interior (only visible through a grille) dates from the rebuilding of 1278.

ROUTE 7:

FROM ISOLA TIBERINA TO THE JANICULUM

S. Carlo ai Catinari ❶

The domed church, dedicated to
San Carlo Borromeo, is named after the
many shops in the vicinity which once
sold basins (*catini*). It was built in
1612-20 by Rosato Rosati. The
travertine facade was completed by
G.B. Soria (1638). The inside of the
church is richly decorated with *works*
by 17th-century painters.

Isola Tiberina ❷

If it were really a ship, which is what it
seems at first glance, it would be a
hospital ship. In fact, according to
tradition, during the plague of 293 BC,
the serpent consecrated to Aesculapius
jumped onto the island from the boat
which had brought it here from
Epidaurus in Greece, indicating the site
where a temple should be dedicated to

The dome of S. Carlo ai Catinari.

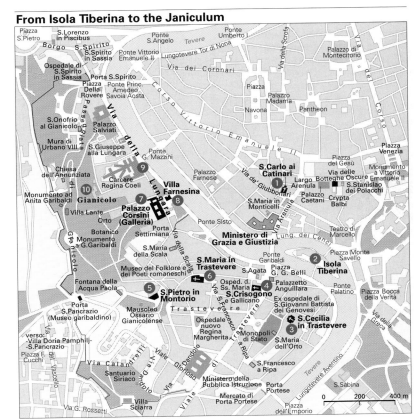

From Isola Tiberina to the Janiculum

the god. To commemorate this legend, there is still a *carving of Aesculapius* on the eastern bank, *with the serpent entwined around a stick and a bull's head*. The first nucleus of the *Fatebenefratelli hospital* dates from the 16th century and the healing vocation of the island was confirmed during the plague of 1656, when it was used as a lazzaretto or hospice. It is linked to Lungotevere degli Anguillara by *Ponte Cestio*, a late 19th-century reconstruction of the bridge built in 46 BC by Lucius Cestius, of which only the central arch survives. The **church of S. Bartolomeo all'Isola*** was built above the ruins of the Temple of Aesculapius. It was rebuilt in 1583-85 after the flood of 1557 and altered again in 1623-24. The top of the facade incorporates a *mosaic* fragment from the time of Alexander III (1180) and the *bell tower* dates from the first restoration of the church (1113). The interior is divided into a nave and two side-aisles by columns which probably belonged to the

medieval fortress. The bridge has two other names: Ponte dei Quattro Capi and Pons Judaeorum because it was used by Jews crossing the Tiber to the ghetto from Trastevere. The bridge, built in 62 BC, seems to have survived the passage of time remarkably well. It was restored once, in the 2nd century, when the original travertine facing was replaced with bricks. The **bridges** of Rome deserve a special mention. They are all wide and monumental and it's hard to decide which is the most beautiful.

S. Cecilia in Trastevere ❸

A vast garden courtyard lies before the church which, having begun as the *titulus Caeciliae* before the 5th century, was rebuilt as a basilica in the early 9th century under Paschal I. The bell tower and the cloister were added between the 10th and 13th centuries, but, in the 18th century, the church underwent a radical transformation which especially affected the *interior*: the *Apotheosis of*

The interior of S. Cecilia in Trastevere with the ciborium by Arnolfo di Cambio.

Temple of Aesculapius. The marble *well-head* in the courtyard may belong to a well which was reputed to contain water with miracle-working powers.
The *Torre Caetani*, which controls access to the **Ponte Fabricio***, was part of a

St Cecilia by Sebastiano Conca (c. 1727) which adorns the vault above the nave gives an idea of the lively nature of the decoration applied to the church in the 18th century. A frescoed corridor leads from the right aisle to a room identified

The ceiling of S. Maria in Trastevere.

St Chrysogonus was built, restored by G.B. Soria in 1620-26. At that time, inside the church, the stucco decoration, the coffered ceiling above the nave and the transept were added, along with the barrel vaults above the side-aisles and the canopy in the presbytery, a re-use of the four alabaster columns of the old ciborium. The 11th-century Cosmatesque *pavement* dates from the 13th-century church. The *chapel of the Blessed Sacrament* at the end of the right aisle is attributed to Gian Lorenzo Bernini. Below the present church lie the remains of the early-Christian and early medieval basilica, where, between the fragments of 11th-century *mosaics* are earlier mosaics dating from the 8th and 9th centuries.

S. Pietro in Montorio ❺

The old name of the Janiculum ("Mons Aureus", Hill of Gold) is preserved in the name of this church, which was possibly founded in the 9th century but rebuilt in the late 15th century. Its chapels contain many interesting *artworks*. According to tradition (although there is no historical evidence), the cross on which St Peter was martyred once stood on the present site of **Bramante's Tempietto**** (1502-1507), the most eloquent expression of a Renaissance building with a central plan. This monument, placed in the middle of the cloister to the right of the church, consists of a round chamber surrounded by an ambulatory with 16 Tuscan granite columns. It has an elegant, segmented dome supported by a drum with shell-shaped niches. As well as providing a benchmark for early 16th-century Roman architecture, the Tempietto is also remarkable for the use of classical features (for the first time in this building Doric and Tuscan styles are correctly employed together) and the skilful harmony of sculptural decoration and space.

S. Maria in Trastevere ❻

The material used to construct the basilica (1138-48) was plundered from the Baths of Caracalla. It was built on the site of an early-Christian building (c. mid-4C). Although, in 1702, the facade of the church was altered and the portico rebuilt, the main structure of the

as the *calidarium* where St Cecilia was left for three days and was supposed to be scalded to death but miraculously survived. The *Beheading of the Saint* above the altar is by Guido Reni. Arnolfo di Cambio (1293) made the famous **ciborium** in the center of the presbytery; below the altar, the statue of **St Cecilia** by Stefano Maderno (1600) depicts the body of the saint as it appeared when her tomb was opened in 1599. Some of the decoration of the original church survives, such as the **mosaic** (c. 820) in the bowl of the apse. But the masterpiece of the basilica is in the Nuns' Choir: the remains of the fresco of the **Last Judgement** painted by Pietro Cavallini in 1289-93. This is an exceptional example of Roman painting before Giotto arrived in Rome. The *frescoes* beside the entrance and on the opposite wall are part of the same cycle.

S. Crisogono ❹

The fairly simple facade of this church does not do justice to its more than 1,000 years of history. The first record of a basilica here dates from the 5th century, but it was not until 1123 that the first church dedicated to church has not changed significantly. The 13th-century *mosaic* depicting two processions of *female figures* still adorns the facade. In the 18th century, marbles, reliefs and inscriptions previously kept in the basilica or the catacombs were used to decorate the portico. The frames of the three doorways date from the Roman Imperial period. The 22 columns which separate the interior into a nave and two side-aisles also date from the Classical period. This is one of the finest buildings to survive from the 12th century. The *ceiling* was designed by Domenichino, while the marble *tabernacle* at the beginning of the nave is by Mino da Fiesole. However, all of this is of minor importance compared to what we find in the presbytery and the apse. The presbytery contains the *fons olei*, which marks the spot where, in 38 AD, a miraculous fountain of oil is supposed to have flowed, forcing Callistus I (217-222) to found what was the first official church in Rome. The apse has splendid **mosaics** in the bowl,

Palazzo Corsini ❼

It was in this remarkable setting that the Arcadia literary movement, supported by Queen Christina of Sweden, came into being. The movement, whose aim was to eliminate bad literary taste and purify Italian poetry, was very influential in the first half of the 18th century. The memory of the academic life is still kept alive today by the many institutions which have offices there. The palazzo was built in 1510-1512 but rebuilt by Ferdinando Fuga (the architectural features on the facade verge towards the Neoclassical style). The palazzo houses the **Galleria Corsini***, the only 18th-century art collection in Rome which is still intact. It was begun in the 18th century by Cardinal Neri Maria Corsini, nephew of Clement XII. The paintings, especially those of the Italian schools of the 16th and 17th century, but also a considerable number of paintings by foreign artists, illustrate the first classical trends,

Piazza di S. Maria in Trastevere (with the church in the background).

on the arch, and by the windows. The marble *throne* with a rounded back dates from the 12th century. Notice the *Altemps chapel*, to the left of the apse, where the altar is decorated by a **Madonna della Clemenza**, an encaustic painting of the 6th or 7th century. Sculptural decoration adorns the *Avila chapel* (1680), in the left aisle, with a lovely dome.

steering away from the Baroque style. The Italian part of the collection begins with works by early painters and continues with *portraits*, especially the one of **Bernardo Clesio** by Joos van Cleve, and *bronze figurines*. Caravaggio's **St John the Baptist** introduces works in the style of Caravaggio while, among the landscapes, note the **Tancred and**

Inside the Botanical garden.

scenes in the Sala del Fregio are by Baldassarre Peruzzi, as is the ceiling of the **Sala di Galatea****, where Raphael had painted the fresco depicting the sea-nymph on the main wall (1513-14).
The *Polyphemus* by Sebastiano del Piombo (1512-13) is a typical expression of the Venetian school of painting. Peruzzi painted the frescoes in the Salone delle Prospettive.

Erminia by Gaspard Dughet. The room dedicated to Queen Christina of Sweden contains *still life paintings* by Christian Berentz. Other works in the gallery include those by Carlo Maratta, Nicolas Poussin, G.B. Piazzetta and Rosalba Carriera. Note the *Judas and Tamar* by Giovanni Lanfranco, **Salomè with the Head of John the Baptist** by Guido Reni and *Ecce Homo* by Guercino, which precede works by Neapolitan painters, represented by Marco De Caro, Spagnoletto, Domenico Gargiulo and Luca Giordano.
Since 1883, the gardens have been host to a **Botanical Garden**, which has partially retained the layout of the original palace garden. A small artificial lake contains aquatic plants, and the 19th-century glasshouses contain orchids and succulents.

Villa Farnesina ⑧

The architectural design of the villa incorporates the principles of balance, harmony and proportion typical of the vogue of Roman Classicism of the early 16th century and contains one of Raphael's most important frescoes. The building is one of the first examples of a villa comprising a central block and a loggia with five arches. The loggia is currently closed because the frescoes are being restored. They depict the *story of Psyche* and were painted in 1517, over Raphael's cartoons, by his pupils Giulio Romano, Giovanni da Udine, Giovanni Francesco Penni and Raffaellino del Colle. The mythological

Via della Lungara ⑨

On this street designed by Bramante stands the *Porta Settimiana*, commissioned by Alexander VI, the Borgia pope, to replace a postern gate in the Aurelian walls.
According to tradition, the *house* to the right of the gate once belonged to "La Fornarina", the beautiful Roman woman whose portrait Raphael painted.

Passeggiata del Gianicolo ⑩

Laid out in 1880-84 on the Janiculum Hill, along with the Pincian Hill, this footpath above the battlements of the walls built by Urban VIII has some of the most beautiful views of Rome. The path meanders up and down through the *Parco Gianicolense* (Janiculum Park), dotted with busts of followers of Garibaldi. A *lighthouse* marks one of the highest points. The *equestrian monument to Anita Garibaldi* stands in front of both the splendid **Villa Lante**, built by Giulio Romano (1518-27) and the *equestrian monument to Giuseppe Garibaldi* (1895). The large square in front of the villa has possibly the farthest-ranging views over Rome. Not far away, **Villa Doria Pamphilj** is Rome's largest public park. It is decorated with the beautiful *Fountains of the Snail* and *the Lily*, and the **Casino di Allegrezze** (an elegant building used by the Italian Government for formal occasions), also known as the Villa del Bel Respiro. Its lovely facade is decorated with ancient marbles and there is a secret garden dotted with statues and low reliefs. Part of the *aqueduct* built by Paul V in 1609-1612 runs through the park.

ROUTE 8
ROME'S, GREEN DIMENSION

Villa Borghese ❶

Rome's most famous public park was created in the 17th century by Cardinal Scipione Borghese as a park for the Casino Borghese, but, in the following century, was transformed into a picturesque Neoclassical garden.

In 1827, Luigi Canina extended it and created the *Roman Arch*, the *Greek* and *Egyptian monumental gateways*, and the *Fountain of Esculapius*. Cardinal Scipione planned the **Casino Borghese*** as the center of his suburban residence, a setting in which to display his art collections. This is what he had in mind when he entrusted Flaminio Ponzio with the project. In his design (1608-1613), the architect imagined a facade decorated with statues, a fitting introduction to the Classical works inside, preceded by a double staircase. The portico connects the two symmetrical apartments to the central hall, built to reflect the new Neoclassical lines of the late 18th century. The **Museo and Galleria Borghese**** certainly deserves the definition of "queen of the world's private collections" accorded to the Borghese family's passion for collecting fine things. They loved ancient statuary and the masterpieces of Renaissance and Baroque art, but also the sculptures and paintings of the 16th to 19th centuries. Cardinal Scipione began the collection in 1608. Much of his collection of marbles and sculptures, along with those given to him by Paul V, originating from the old church of St Peter's, was sold

to Napoleon Bonaparte by Prince Camillo Borghese in the early 19th century. The collection was re-formed with the contents of the Casino, Palazzo Borghese and the Borghese villas outside Rome. The collection of paintings was more fortunate: the Cardinal brought together works of the great masters, including works from other collections, in particular, that of Olimpia Aldobrandini. In the **Museo Borghese***, the ancient statues, busts and sculptures are still arranged in the early 18th-century manner, which attempted to place them in a suitable background. They are displayed with a "modern" sculpture, often placed in the center of the room, by the Borghese's favorite sculptor, Gian Lorenzo Bernini. The same combination is found in the portico and in the **great hall**, where the niches contain the busts of 12 Roman Emperors (the huge bust of *Hadrian* is one of the best depictions of the emperor). The floor incorporates fragments of a 4th-century mosaic. The display of masterpieces begins in the former Sala del Vaso: they include the famous **Venus Victrix**** by Antonio Canova, the dramatic sculpture of

HERITAGE

The park behind Casino Borghese.

Rome's green dimension

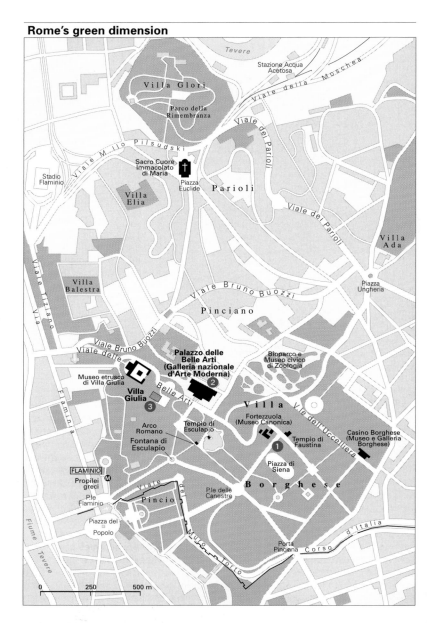

Apollo and Daphne* by Gian Lorenzo Bernini (1624), the **Boy with Basket of Fruit*** (c. 1593-95) and the **Madonna dei Palafrenieri*** (1605), two masterpieces by Caravaggio. The **Galleria Borghese*** provides an overview of Italian painting from the 15ᵗʰ to 17ᵗʰ centuries. To call the collection exhaustive is almost an understatement. The rooms where the collection is displayed, many of which are frescoed, contain an uninterrupted sequence of paintings by Italy's greatest masters and foreign painters. Raphael's undisputed talent can be seen in his **Deposition***, but all the paintings in this marvelous collection are wonderful. To mention just a few examples, Correggio's **Danaë***, **Portrait of a Man*** by Antonello da Messina and Titian's **Sacred and Prophane Love***, a triumphal celebration of Venetian Renaissance painting.

Correggio's Danaë, one of the masterpieces in the Galleria Borghese collection.

Galleria Nazionale d'Arte Moderna ❷

The style of the building that houses this gallery, *Palazzo delle Belle Arti*, designed for the International Exhibition of 1911, introduces its visitors to the main subject of the collection. In fact, behind that solemn, Classical-style facade, decorated with Art-Nouveau motifs and friezes, is Italy's finest collection of 19th- and 20th-century art. The gallery was supposed to house artworks representative of Italian culture and art, but, as a result of additions to the collection, and Italy's increasing ties with other countries, the collection also includes works by foreign artists. The gallery, which now owns an enormous number of works, is currently in the process of reorganizing its collection, part of which has been moved to the new premises in Via Guido Reni. (When the work begun there in 2003 is finished, it will open its doors as the new Museum of 21st-century Art.) The collection includes works from the Neoclassical and Romantic periods, by the Tuscan artists known as the *Macchiaioli*, and exponents of the Neapolitan school, Social Realism and Divisionism. 19th-century works by Rodin, Courbet, Degas, Monet and Van Gogh precede masterpieces by foreign artists of the 20th century, such as Klimt and Cézanne. Further on, there are works by Futurist and Cubist artists, works of Metaphysical Painting by Carrà and Morandi, the "*non oggettivo*" movement of Mondrian and the Dadaism of Duchamp. There is quite an extensive collection of works executed between the two World Wars, while the Novecento movement is represented by Casorati and Campigli and works of the Second Futurist movement by Balla, Fillia and Dottori. Works by Antonietta Raphael, Mario Mafai and Scipione were painted in reaction to the principles of the Novecento movement. Leoncillo, Basaldella and Scilian represent the Roman school. The Six from Turin and the Milanese Corrente group, including Guttuso, were opposed to the Novecento movement. After WWII, surrealism was accompanied by more informal artistic trends associated with the expressiveness of materials, color and signs. Foreign trends represented include Jackson Pollock's American action painting and others by the Cobra group, while movements on a global scale include the kinetic art of Munari and Albers, the pop art of Kounellis and Schifano, arte povera and the Conceptual Art of Piero Manzoni.

Villa Giulia ❸

What a contrast there is between the formal facade of the villa, decorated only by the rusticated doorway with its Doric columns, and the splendid loggia on three sides of the internal courtyard! The **loggia** was designed by Bartolomeo Ammannati, who was commissioned to design the building (1551-55) by Julius III, together with Giorgio Vasari (who designed the elegant **nymphaeum**) and Vignola. Prospero Fontana and Taddeo Zuccari were responsible for decorating the interior of the villa. The **Museo Nazionale Etrusco di Villa Giulia*** was created about a century ago to house the finds from the archeological site of *Falerii Veteres*. Today, that small nucleus of archeological material has grown into the largest museum of Etruscan antiquities in the world, with finds from excavations conducted in southern Etruria, including an important group of Greek finds. The reconstruction of Etruscan history begins with finds from the necropolis and the settlement at Vulci with grave-goods from the Villanovan period (9-8C BC). The site has produced the earliest pottery imported from Greece, a chariot burial marking the transition from the late Villanovan period to the Oriental period (c. 680 BC) and the bronze weapons from the **Tomb of the Warrior**, dated to the 6th century BC. The polychrome terracotta **statues** of **Hercules fighting Apollo for the Sacred Hind** and the goddess Latoma holding Apollo as a child, decorations from the acroterion of the sanctuary of Portonaccio at Veii (late 6C BC), show Greek and Oriental influences. A large number of Greek vases dating

An Etruscan artifact in the Museo di Villa Giulia.

from the 7th and 6th centuries BC were found at Cervèteri, as well as the splendid polychrome terracotta sarcophagus of a husband and wife reclining on a couch, known as the **Sarcofago degli Sposi*** (c. 530 BC). The **Chigi Vase** (640-625 BC) is one of the most important late proto-Corinthian artifacts from Veio. The **shafts** (530-520 BC) of a chariot from a tomb at Castro reflect Ionic influences on Etruscan craftsmanship. The excavations at Pyrgi, the Etruscan port of Cervèteri, have produced some of the most prolific finds, including the **gold tablets*** with an inscription in two languages (Etruscan and Phoenician) referring to the dedication of the sanctuary to the Phoenician divinity Astarte and the Etruscan Uni. A large amount of space is devoted to the towns in the territory around the *Ager Faliscus*, the area between Lake Bracciano and the Tiber, and the area around Capena, culminating in the reconstruction of the terracotta decoration from the **sanctuaries of Falerii Veteres****, built between 480 BC and the late 4th-early 3rd century BC. The architectural terracotta decoration, acroterial friezes and other decorative features are evidence of the extraordinary level of communication between this area of central Italy, Greece and Magno Graecia. The fabulous grave-goods from **tombs** of the Oriental period from the **Barberini** and **Bernardini** collections come from another corner of central Italy. They were discovered at ancient Praeneste (now Palestrina), and comprise fine objects made of precious metals, ivory and bronze dating from the mid-7th century BC. The **Cista Ficoroni**, a beautiful toilet box, made in Rome in the late 4th century BC, comes from the same site. An inscription on the handle in Archaic Latin reads *Novios Plautios med Romai fecid, Dindia Malconia fileai dedid*: Novio Plauzio made me in Rome, Dindia Malconia gave me to her daughter.

HERITAGE

DAY TRIPS

ALBANO LAZIALE [24 km]

The original settlement, built above the ruins of Domitian's villa and the military camp (the *Castra Albana*) established here by Septimius Severus, was half destroyed during the Barbarian invasions. It came under the Holy See in the late 17th century. Today this residential town is also well-known for its wine-production and is much visited by people from Rome on account of its rich cultural heritage. The main street is *Corso Matteotti* which, together with its extension (*Borgo Garibaldi*), corresponds to the route of the Appian Way through the town. The **Duomo** ❶, the basilica of S. Pancrazio, was founded under Constantine, and you can still see some of the ancient columns. Rebuilt several times over the centuries, its current Baroque style blends well with the buildings surrounding it. From nearby Piazza Mazzini there are lovely views of the Roman Campagna.

Not far away is the **church of S. Maria della Rotonda*** ❷. The name of the church refers to its shape, and it is round because it was built above the nymphaeum of Domitian's villa. It has a portico at the front, a dome, and the bell tower dates from the 13th century. The icon of the Madonna inside dates from 475 and, according to tradition, was brought to Albano by nuns from Greece. The **Cisternone*** ❸, an enormous underground cistern with a capacity of approximately 10,000 m³, dates from the 2nd century. It was dug out of the rock for military purposes and is still in use today. It has five aisles supported by pillars and a barrel-vaulted ceiling. Nearby stands the *church of S. Paolo*, situated at the apex of the triangle formed by Via Saffi and Via Murialdo. Behind it you can see the remains of the outer wall of the Roman *amphitheater* (mid-3C), built to entertain the Roman legionaries, with a seating capacity of 15,000. **Porta Pretoria*** ❹ was the main entrance to the "Castra Albana". This gate with three arches and a tower on either side re-appeared along with the other Roman ruins you can see on Via Saffi following the air raids of 1944. The Roman ruins also

incorporate the **church of S. Pietro*** ❺, erected in the 6th century. You can still discern parts of the baths, despite the fact that the church has been altered many times, and there are fragments of Roman marble in the side door, and in the bell tower with its two-light windows. Inside, there are Roman *marble friezes* along the edge of the presbytery, and a 3rd-century *sarcophagus* has been re-used as an altar in the left wall. There

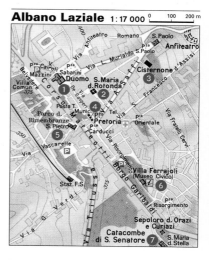

Albano Laziale 1:17 000

are 13th-century frescoes on the right-hand wall and a *painting* by Gherardo delle Notti. **Villa Ferrajoli** ❻, built in the 19th century and surrounded by a lovely garden, now houses the *Museo Civico*. Its exhibits range in date from prehistory to the late-Roman period, and it has an Archeological Park attached. Nearby is another Roman monument: the *tomb of the Horatii and the Curatii*. It consists of a rectangular base of stone with a cornice and a frieze, surmounted by two truncated cones, also in stone. Hidden below the late 16th-century *church of S. Maria della Stella*, the cemetery complex known as the **Catacombe di S. Senatore** ❼ probably dates from the 3rd century. The central chamber is decorated with frescoes from the 5th and 9th centuries.

Not far from the town, **Lake Albano** occupies two small secondary craters of an ancient volcano, separated by a ridge at a depth of about 70m. The bowl of the crater is wooded (oak and chestnut) and, in some places, the land drops vertically down to the lake. The artificial emissary of the lake, which is still functioning, is an ingenious feat of Roman engineering. According to tradition, it was built in a year (398-397 BC) because an oracle had predicted that the Romans would defeat the Etruscan Veii only if the water in the lake could reach the sea without overflowing from the crater. The underground channel, on the southwest side of the lake, begins at a maneuvering chamber built of blocks of peperino marble with perforated bulkheads. It is 1,350m long, between 1m and 1.8m wide and is situated 128m below the edge of the crater. In the Imperial period, numerous patrician villas were built around the lake. At Domitian's villa, you can still see the nymphaeum known as the *Bagni di Diana*, whereas the *nymphaeum in the Doric style* is a small temple built during the Republican period. At Palazzolo, in the garden of the English boarding-school, there is a *monument* thought to be that of *Lucius Cornelius Scipio* (176 BC), dug out of the rock, with carvings of 12 lictorian fasces and the curule chair, symbols of the post of consul. The *monastery of S. Maria in Palazzolo* stands on a hill overlooking the shores of the lake and has many

features dating from the Roman period. In the early 13th century, a group of hermits lived here. Later it came under the power of the *church of S. Anastasio* and the *Abbey of the Tre Fontane*, both in Rome, and, in about 1240, Pope Gregory IX decided to use it as a summer retreat for the monks of Rome.

ANZIO [57 km]

The town is now one of the departure points for ferries heading for the islands of the Pontine Archipelago, however, its vocation as a port dates from the Imperial period, when Nero built the original harbor, northwest of the present one. The new harbor was built in the last years of the 17th century by Innocent XII, who had the old harbor filled in. The entrance to the town from the sea-front, which follows the line of the Imperial Via Severiana, passes the ruins of the **Villa of Nero** ❶, now surmounted by an arch. The villa had several rooms, including an exedra where the Apollo Belvedere, now in the Vatican Museums, was found. The so-called *grottoes of Nero* are actually the remains of warehouses associated with the nearby Roman port.
Despite its 19th-century facade, the **Castle** ❷ has medieval origins. Another Roman villa was found near *Villa*

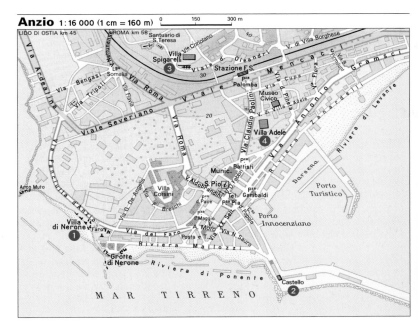

Anzio 1: 16 000 (1 cm = 160 m)

Baths of Caracalla

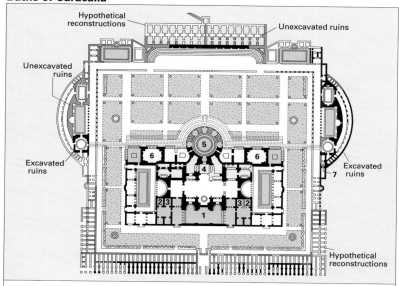

1 Frigidarium
2 Oil massage room
3 Sand treatment room
4 Tepidarium

5 Calidarium
6 Exercise area
7 Mithraeum

Spigarelli ❸, which stands on the site of the acropolis of Anzio. **Villa Adele** ❹, built in 1615 by Cardinal Bartolomeo Cesi, now houses the *Museo Civico Archeologico* and the *Museo dello Sbarco e della Battaglia di Anzio*, a museum illustrating the events associated with the Allied Landings here in 1944.

On the coast a few kilometers north of Anzio lies the **Riserva Naturale Regionale Tor Caldara**, 44 hectares of Mediterranean forest with Roman ruins.

APPIAN WAY

The Appian Way, the *"regina viarum"* (queen of roads) and famous the world over, was built in 312 BC by Appius Claudius Ciecus. Because of the extraordinary number of monuments and the pleasant landscape which still lines much of the route, a walk along this, the most important of the Roman consular roads, is an opportunity to admire its archeological heritage and enjoy the leafier parts of the route. The original basalt lava paving adds extra charm to this ancient road. By walking along the walls near the suburban part of the road, you can see what Rome must have looked like until 1870.

Until the Baths of Diocletian were opened, the huge **Terme di Caracalla**✱✱ ❶ (Baths of Caracalla) was the largest bath complex in Rome. Begun in 212 and opened in 217, they were completed by Alexander Severus and restored by Aurelian (270-275). They continued to function until the period of the Gothic

An opera staged at the Baths of Caracalla.

invasions, when the troops of Vitige, who were laying siege to the city, destroyed a section of the Antonine aqueduct which supplied the complex. The main entrance to the baths lay on the Via Nova (parallel to the Appian Way). The baths were organized according to the planning criteria of the 2nd century, with a *frigidarium*, with rooms on either side for the oil and salt treatments. This led into the *tepidarium* and a large, circular *calidarium*, which overlooked an outdoor area for exercising. Then there were gyms, exedras, a school for gymnasts, a stadium, two libraries and a vast network of underground service tunnels, one of which was used as a large, elaborately decorated mithraeum. The first records of the **church of Ss. Nereo e Achìlleo** ❷ date from the 4th century, but the current building dates from the 9th century and the facade from 1475. Although little remains of the original exterior, inside the church, unusual masonry pillars separate the space into a nave and two side-aisles, all decorated with *frescoes*. There are some very old mosaics in the arch over the apse, whereas the Cosmatesque high altar, part of the *balustrade* of the presbytery (12C) and the *bishop's throne* are medieval. **Via di Porta S. Sebastiano** and Viale delle Terme di Caracalla lie over the urban section of the Roman Appian Way. Walking along these two streets, we can imagine what the Eternal City looked like before it became the capital. Luxuriant weeds grow out of the walls on either side of the road.

In the late 16th century, the church of *S. Cesareo in Palatio* ❸ was built above the ruins of an older building. Under the

church, you can still see a 2nd-century mosaic *floor*. The nearby *house of Cardinal Bessarione* dates from the 15th century. The size of the **Tomb of the Scipios*** reflects the status of the family. The tomb remained in use from the early 3rd century to 139 BC. It was erected in the 3rd century BC over the hypogeum of a *house*. You can still see traces of the old mosaic floor and fragments of wall-paintings. At the nearby *Colombarium of Pomponius Hylas* there are still some quite good mosaics in a shrine and in the cella. Built in 211-216, the *Arch of Drusus* spans the Appian Way. It is not a triumphal arch but served to carry the aqueduct of the *Acqua Antoniniana*, a branch of the Acqua Marcia, to supply the Baths of Caracalla. **Porta S. Sebastiano*** ❹ is the place where the Appian Way emerges from the Aurelian walls. It was rebuilt by Honorius in the 5th century. It stands opposite the Arch of Drusus. The galleries and towers of the gate now house the *Museo delle Mura di Roma* (Museum of the Walls) which illustrates the history of Rome's fortifications.

Starting at the museum, it is pleasant to walk along the **Aurelian walls**, built in 271 and named after the emperor who erected them, to the new *Porta Ardeatina*. The walls were virtually complete in 275, when the emperor died, but, almost immediately, it proved necessary to strengthen them, a task which lasted not only throughout the Byzantine period, but also the period of the pontificate. The walls are 6m high and there was a tower with an upper chamber every 30m. The four brick arches in the new Porta Ardeatina were built in 1939 at the top of Via Imperiale,

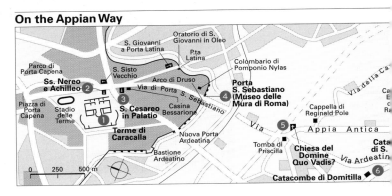

On the Appian Way

The Tomb of Cecilia Metella, the most famous Roman monument on the Appian Way.

whereas the **Bastione Ardeatino** was built by Antonio da Sangallo the Younger. As the Apostle Peter was fleeing from Rome to escape the persecution of Nero, he met Jesus and asked him, "Domine, quo vadis?" (Master, where are you going?) Christ answered, "I'm going to Rome to be crucified again". This encounter is supposed to have taken place just after the middle of the 1st century, but the **church of Domine Quo Vadis?** ❺ was founded in the 9th century and its current appearance dates from the 16th and 17th centuries.
Via Ardeatina, which leaves the Appian Way just beyond the ancient *tomb of Priscilla*, used to connect Rome to Àrdea. On it are the **Catacombe di Domitilla*** ❻, the largest catacombs in Rome. In the

4th century, the *Basilica of Ss. Nereo e Achìlleo* was built above the catacombs. One column of the ciborium bears a rare depiction of a *martyr being beheaded*. The memory of the tragedy of the **Fosse Ardeatine** ❼, which took place on March 24, 1944, is still very much alive. As a reprisal for the killing of German soldiers in Via Rasella by partisans, 335 civilians were shot by the Nazis and buried in these mass graves. Behind the mausoleum is the *Museo delle Fosse Ardeatine*, with documents and testimonials about the Nazi occupation of Rome (September 10, 1943 – June 4, 1944). It is well worth visiting the **Catacombe di S. Callisto*** ❽ (Catacombs of St Calixtus). They comprise 20km of tunnels scattered on five levels, over an area of 15 hectares. These figures give

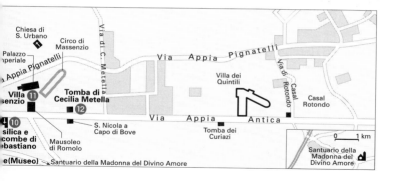

89

you an idea of the size of the necropolis, designated by Pope Calixtus as the official burial place of the Roman Church. They contain the remains of about 50 martyrs and 16 popes. The oldest parts of the catacombs are the Papal Crypt and the Cubiculum of St Cecilia (late 2C), whereas the cubicles of St Gaius and St Eusebius date from the late 3rd century, and the "Occidentale" and "Liberiana" regions of the catacombs from the 4th century. The *Papal Crypt*, where the remains of nine popes are buried, and the adjoining tomb of St Cecilia, which contains some remarkable 9th-century *frescoes*, are the most important parts of the catacombs.

St Sebastian was a victim of the persecution of Christians by Diocletian. When he had been martyred, he was buried in the place where the Apostles Peter and Paul had been inhumed. A necropolis grew up around these relics and the **Basilica of S. Sebastiano** ⑨ was erected nearby. This church was replaced in the 17th century by a new building commissioned by Cardinal Scipione Borghese, completed in 1613. Inside, note the early 17th-century wooden **ceiling**. The Relic Chapel (first on the right) contains one of the arrows from St Sebastian's martyrdom, the columns to which he was bound and the imprints supposedly left by Christ's feet during the "Domine Quo Vadis?" episode. The large *Albani chapel* dates from 1706-12, and has a painting of *St Sebastian Baptizing Philip the Arab* to the right of the altar. The *chapel of St Sebastian* (first on the left), built above the saint's grave, contains a *statue* of the martyr dating from 1671-72, based on a design by Bernini. Some of the first Christian martyrs were buried in the **Catacombe di S. Sebastiano*** ⑩ (Catacombs of St Sebastian). The parts open to the public today are located in the second of the four levels into which the catacombs are divided. One cubicle contains paintings of the *Story of Jonah* (4C). The *bust* in the Crypt of St Sebastian is attributed to Bernini. Overlooking the so-called "piazzuola" are three mausoleums built in the second half of the 2nd century and then re-used by Christians. From here you can climb up to the room used for funerary banquets, where you can see graffiti (3rd-4th century) depicting worshippers invoking the protection of the Apostles. The **Villa of Maxentius**** ⑪ is set in a beautiful area of the Roman Campagna: it has a circus and a mausoleum dating from the Imperial period which is one of the most scenic ruins on the Appian Way. The central *spina* of the *Circus of Maxentius*, which had a seating capacity of approximately 10,000, was decorated

---

 BANDIERA ARANCIONE

THE QUALITY LABEL FOR TOURISM AND ENVIRONMENT IN ITALY'S INLAND AREAS

The BANDIERA ARANCIONE (ORANGE FLAG) is a label of quality for the development of tourism in Italy's inland areas. Municipalities with less than 15,000 inhabitants may be awarded it if selected criteria are achieved and maintained: cultural heritage, respect for the environment, hospitality, information and services, and quality local production. The ORANGE FLAG program is run by the Touring Club of Italy. The World Tourism Organisation has chosen the ORANGE FLAG PROGRAM as a success in the sphere of environmental tourism. For more information: www.touringclub.it/bandierearancioni

NEMI
Perched on a rocky spur above the lake of the same name, Nemi is one of the most charming towns in the Castelli Romani. Its beautiful natural setting enhances the historical and artistic heritage of the town, including the Roman ship Museum, the baronial palace, the castle and the lovely fountains dotted around old center.

TREVIGNANO ROMANO
Overlooking Lake Bracciano, Trevignano Romano is worth visiting for the picturesque buildings that grace its old town center, the considerable artistic heritage in the church dedicated to the Assumption and the romantic Rocca degli Orsini. It also has a small, but very good Museo Civico.

by the obelisk which Gian Lorenzo Bernini later erected in Piazza Navona. The circus was connected to the *imperial palace*, which has not yet been excavated. However, it is interesting to visit the **mausoleum of Romulus**, built by the emperor in honor of his son when he died prematurely. The tomb, which also contains the remains of other family members, is round with burial niches around the central pillar and the walls. Two great military men were connected with the woman buried in the **Tomb of Cecilia Metella**** ⑫: in fact she was the daughter of Metellus, conqueror of Crete, and the wife of Crassus, Caesar's general in Gaul. The tomb, a circular tower on a square base built in about 50 BC, is faced with travertine and still contains the internal burial chamber. The frieze carved in relief surrounding the upper art has a bucrania motif, hence Capo di Bove, the name given to one of the most beautiful stretches of the Appian Way. The Ghibelline merlons on the top date from the early 13th century, when the Caetani transformed the tomb into a keep for their castle. Across the road, the little *church of S. Nicola a Capo di Bove* is an example of Roman Gothic architecture.
The **ancient part of the Appian Way** lies between the third and ninth milestones and is bordered by a continuous succession of tombs, many reduced to a few fragments, and dotted with pine-trees and cypresses.
Beyond the tomb of Cecilia Metella, the small hill on the right is supposed to contain the *tomb of the Curiatii*, who fought the Horatii here. However, the remains found in the tombs date from the late Republican period. The reign of Commodus was a very tempestuous one, as the owners of the **Villa Quintili** found out to their cost. These brothers were put to death for the sake of their possessions, including their villa on the Appian Way. You can gain some idea of its size just by looking at the arches of the aqueduct which supplied the villa complex. It comprised large halls and smaller rooms and a nymphaeum.
The largest tomb on the Appian Way is *Casal Rotondo*, a round tomb dating from the Augustan period, formerly faced with travertine, and buried under a mound.

FRASCATI [21 km]

This town stands in an area famous for its high-quality wine-production. Its reputation as a holiday destination because of its healthy air dates from the Renaissance, when some of the most important villas outside Rome were built here. The tradition continued until the 19th century, when Frascati was the first town of the Holy See to have a railway connection to the capital (the line was

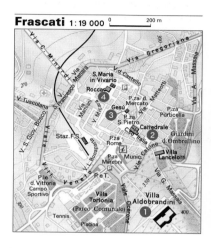

Frascati 1:19 000

opened in 1857). **Villa Aldobrandini*** ① is the most famous noble residence of the area known as the Castelli Romani, a wonderful example of the various types of Mannerist architecture used for building stately homes. The park is scattered with statues and fountains with water features, and the land slopes gracefully down from the villa to the town by means of elegant terraces. The villa was begun in 1598 for Cardinal Pietro Aldobrandini and finished in 1604, although the monumental entrance and some of the stuccoes were added more than a century later. It contains splendid early 16th-century **frescoes** which are a remarkable example of the transition from late Mannerism to the Baroque, and a bronze *bust of Clement VIII*. In the **park**, note particularly the Teatro delle Acque (Fontana designed the hydraulic system), a large, semi-circular nymphaeum decorated with niches containing water features and statues.
The **Museo delle Scuderie Aldobrandini** has been created in the former stables of the villa, including the *Museo*

Frascati: the entrance to Villa Aldobrandini.

Tuscolano on the ground floor, which has an archeological section with finds dating from proto-history to the medieval period. The *Auditorium* on the first floor and two other large rooms are used for exhibitions. The tall, richly decorated facade (1698-1700) of the **Cathedral** ❷ has two orders of half-columns, niches containing statues and a *relief* above the main doorway. The interior, built on a Greek-cross plan, dates from the 16th century. There is a 12th-century wooden *Crucifix* in the second chapel on the right, a *Madonna* by Domenichino (third chapel on the right) and a *Madonna del Gonfalone* by the 14th-century Roman school (2nd chapel on the left). The elegant travertine facade of the 17th-century **church of Gesù** ❸ overlooks the square of the same name. Inside, a white marble line leads to the black circle on the floor at the point where the fake **dome** can best be admired. Another fake dome is painted above the presbytery, while the walls behind the side-altars and the high altar are frescoed by ingeniously-painted architectural features.

The **Rocca** ❹, now the bishop's palace, was the turreted fort of the town in the Middle Ages and has a 15th-century porticoed courtyard. Many of the rooms are frescoed, those on the ground floor in the Pompeian style. Next to the Rocca is the little *church of S. Maria in Vivario*. Its bell tower, with three orders of three-light windows (1305), used to belong to the earlier church on this site, dedicated to St Roch.

From Frascati, a panoramic road leads to **Tùscolo**, 5km away. The ancient Latin town of Tusculum was a popular holiday resort, as you can see from the ruins of villas in the surrounding hills. Remains of the Roman town include *Via dei Sepolcri*, a shady road with pine-trees and cypresses, a Roman *amphitheater* and, on a piece of flat ground, the *forum* and the Roman *theater*, still well preserved. The remains of the town of the Counts of Tùscolo, razed to the ground by papal troops in 1119, are still visible at the top of the hill. There are marvelous **views** over all the Castelli as far as Rome from the Croce di Tùscolo. Near the cross are the ruins of the *wall* of the ancient acropolis and, close by, a *cistern* (6th-5th century BC).

PALESTRINA [37 km]

This town of medieval appearance was founded in a strategic position on the site of an ancient cult. The surviving structures of this grand and ancient sanctuary dedicated to Fortuna Primigenia, which was used throughout the 4th century and fell into disuse when Theodosius banned the pagan cult, have shaped the town that grew up around it. Cyclopean walls, dating from the 6th century BC, some of which have survived, once linked the settlements (now separated) of ancient Praeneste and the acropolis of Castel San Pietro Romano. The **Duomo** ❶, built above the ruins of an earlier tufa building of Roman date (you can see parts of it in the facade, the side-wall and the crypt),

was enlarged in the 12th century.
The church has been altered many times since and, today, only the facade with its tympanum and the lower part of the bell tower remain from the Romanesque period. Inside, in the left aisle, is a copy of the *Pietà di Palestrina* attributed to Michelangelo. **Piazza Regina Margherita** ② is thought to have been the ancient forum of Praeneste. The side of the cathedral overlooks the square, together with a building several storeys high with four Corinthian half-columns. In the basement is the *Aerarium*, or Treasury, which has been dated from an inscription, visibile at the far end of it, to the 2nd century AD. From the square, a doorway to the left of the Seminary leads into the *Area Sacra*, a vast area carved out of the hillside, built on a basilica, plan with four aisles. On the right, at the end of the Area Sacra, is a rectangular *Sala Absidata*, the walls of which are decorated with columns and pilaster strips. The so-called *Antro delle Sorti*, on the left-hand side of the Area Sacra, is the extension of a natural cave. In ancient times it probably also had a nymphaeum. You can still see fragments of a 1st-century mosaic depicting the

bottom of the sea. The remains of the **Sanctuary*** ③, one of the most important cult sites to survive from Antiquity, are built on artificial terraces and date from the 2nd-1st century BC. The site can be accessed from Piazza della Cortina, in front of the museum, and extends down the hill to a wall built of polygonal blocks of stone, just above Via del Borgo. From here, two long flights of steps lead up to the *Terrazza degli Emicicli*, named after the two exedras with columns which stood in the center of the two wings with porticoes (the one on the right still has its coffered ceiling and Corinthian columns). Above this level is the *Terrazza dei Fornici*, named after the motif on the far wall. The highest terrace is the *Terrazza della Cortina*, a large courtyard with porticoes around the edge and, at the end of it, a large cavea with a semi-circular portico, beyond which was a small round temple. **Palazzo Barberini** ④ was built on the highest part of the site of the sanctuary, with an unusual layout which takes advantage of and incorporates the semi-circular portico of the hemicycle. The palazzo was destroyed several times during the wars between the Colonna

Palestrina 1 : 8 000 (1 cm = 80 m)

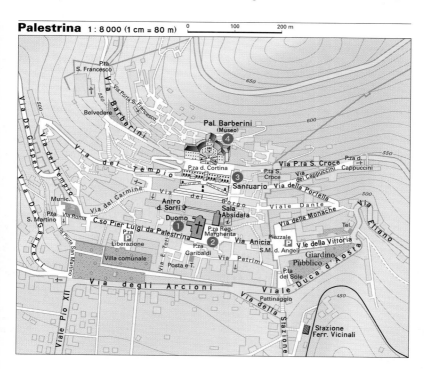

Palestrina: Palazzo Barberini, now the Museo Archeologico Prenestino.

and the papacy and rebuilt in 1640 by the Barberini. It now houses the **Museo Archeologico Prenestino***. Many of the rooms still contain elegant frescoes. At the entrance is a 4th-century relief depicting the *Triumph of Constantine*. The first rooms contain *statues* and *honorary inscriptions* from the town and the sanctuary, *grave goods* from the necropolises of Praeneste, *funerary altars* and *cippi* in the form of a pine-cone. In Room III is a large fragment of a *statue* in gray stone (1C BC), found in the sanctuary, thought to depict Fortuna Primigenia. In the following rooms: *antefixes*, numerous *friezes* and terracotta *figurines* (7C-2C BC), *busts* and *portraits* dating from the 2nd century BC to the 1st century AD. In Room X, there is a model of the sanctuary of Fortuna Primigenia. Room XIV contains various *architectural* features in *terracotta* and a bronze facing of the 4th century BC. However the main exhibit here is the famous **Nile mosaic**, a true masterpiece of Roman mosaic art (probably dating from the 1st century BC). Next to Palazzo Barberini stands the *church of S. Rosalia*, built in 1656-60 and decorated inside with polychrome marble. 4km north of Palestrina is **Castel San Pietro Romano**, situated below the ancient acropolis of Praeneste. The town is clustered around the remains of the

Colonna *castle*, which stands above pre-Roman and Roman buildings, and was rebuilt several times. The castle has great **views** over Rome, the Alban Hills, and the Lepini Mts. Up in the Predestini Mts, above Castel San Pietro, is **Caprànica Prenestina**. The 16th-century *parish church* has interesting Baroque stuccoes and a broad dome inspired by Bramante. In Palazzo Barberini, the *Museo Naturalistico dei Monti Prenestini* has exhibitions on various themes relevant to the area.

SCAVI DI OSTIA ANTICA/ EXCAVATIONS OF OSTIA ANTICA [10 km]

A disasterous flooding of the Tiber in 1557 put an end to Ostia's long history. The town was founded between the end of the 5th and the beginning of the 4th century BC as the base for the Roman fleet (today it lies about 2km from the coast). It had a population of approximately 50,000, and enjoyed prosperity under Emperor Hadrian. In the 19th century, Pius VII began to excavate the site. After WWII, greater priority was given to restoration, although many parts of the site are still being excavated. The description of the site begins with the buildings on the right-hand side of the Decumanus Maximus and then, turning back towards the entrance, the buildings on the other side. The **Decumanus Maximus** is the continuation, within the city walls, of the Via Ostiense (the Roman road between Rome and Ostia), and ends at the *Porta Romana*, marked by two square towers. The *statue of Minerva Victoria* dating from the reign of Domitian, which once stood beside the road, now stands in Piazzale della Vittoria. To the right of the road, a brick portico stands in front of the **Baths of Neptune**, of the same date as the Caserma dei *Vigiles* (Firemen's Barracks), which used to house about 400 men. You can reach it from Via dei Vigili, decorated by a mosaic from the Claudian period, depicting the *symbols of the winds and the various provinces which supplied Rome*. The **theater** was built by Agrippa but rebuilt in brick in 196. The corridors at the sides of the orchestra emerge in the **Piazzale delle Corporazioni**, the name of which comes from the mosaics of the guilds (*collegia*) depicted in the floor of the portico which surrounds the square. Between the 2nd and 3rd century AD, Iranian cults were very popular in Ostia, as shown by the presence of 17 sanctuaries. One of the best preserved is the *Mithraeum*, connected to the square by a street to the left of the House of Apuleius. The commercial business of the town was conducted mainly around the **horrea**, or warehouses, which can be reached by turning right, off the Decumanus Maximus into Via dei Molini. This large brick building dates from the time of Commodus. Via della Casa di

Diana leads to the **thermopolium**, a 3rd-century inn, with a counter where wine was served and a fresco depicting food and drink. Nearby is the *House of Jupiter and Ganymede*, part of a large complex known as the Casa dei Dipinti. It contains frescoes and, in the garden, is a fine *mosaic depicting the months* of the year (4C). The **Museo Ostiense*** is housed in a 16th-century building once used as offices associated with the extraction of salt. It contains fine exhibits from the site. In addition to finds associated with everyday life, there are marble and terracotta reliefs, sculptures inspired by Oriental cults, Roman copies of Greek and Hellenistic originals, and a fine collection of busts of emperors and other figures, *sarcophagi*, and wall-paintings. The *Galleria Lapidaria* contains inscriptions and clay seals. During Hadrian's reign, when Ostia's prosperity was at its height, the town underwent radical changes. These culminated in the rearrangement of its political center, the **forum**, the meeting-point of the Decumanus Maximus and the Cardo Maximus. There was already a *Temple of Rome and Augustus*, dating from the reign of Tiberius, and a *Basilica*, or law courts, erected under Domitian or Trajan. The new town plan involved the building of the **Capitolium**, the town's largest temple (traces of an earlier temple are visible by the front steps), the *Casa dei Triclini*, which was possibly once an inn, and, under Septimius Severus, the headquarters of the builders' guild. Situated behind the forum, the *Forum Baths* were built under Antoninus Pius.

Ostia Antica: the Forum with the "Capitolium".

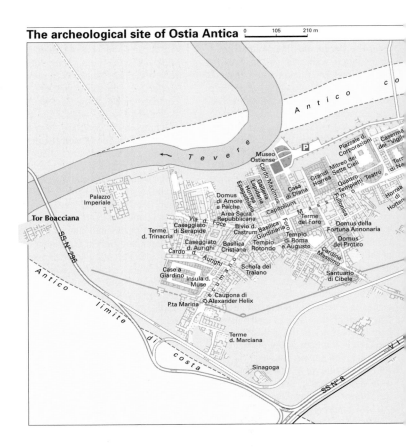

The archeological site of Ostia Antica

Near the forum, overlooking the next section of the Decumanus Maximus, is the *Tempio Rotondo*, dedicated to the cult of the emperors. It has a pronaos with 10 columns and a *cella* with seven niches for statues. Beyond is the *Casa del Lario*, which was once a market with houses above the shops.

Via della Foce, which heads off to the right at the *castrum*, or camp, leads to the **sacred area** of the Republican temples, which was used from the 3rd century BC. Here, note the *Temple of Hercules* (late 2C BC). Nearby, the *House of Cupid and Psyche* is a fine example of a richly decorated 4th-century house. Further on, on the opposite side of the street, is the *House of Serapis*, named after a stucco statue of the god found in an aedicule in the courtyard. From here, a doorway with stucco bucrania leads into the *Terme dei Sette Sapienti* (Baths of the Seven Sages, 126-140), which have fine wall-paintings. The **Casa delle Muse***, which can be reached by turning

right into the Cardo degli Aurighi and then left into Via delle Volte Dipinte, is a large house dating from the time of Hadrian. You can still see the hall leading into a fine porticoed courtyard, and exceptional *paintings of Apollo and the Nine Muses*. The nearby complex of four houses built around a garden, known as the *Case a Giardino* was built in 128 (with an incredibly rational, modern layout). Just before **Porta Marina** is the *Caupona* (wine-shop) of *Alexander Helix* (the erotic mosaics date from the 3C). The gate marks the point where the *Decumanus Maximus* leaves the town. Once it used to continue down to the shore. By following Via di Cartilio Publicola down to the left, you come to the *Baths of Marciana* (or Baths of Porta Marina), which were used until the 6th century. You can still see the ruins of an ancient **Synagogue**, an unusual phenomenon in the Western Mediterranean during the Classical period. It was built in two stages, in the

Ostia Antica

Castello
di Giulio II

del Tevere Ostiense

Via Ostiense

Ingresso

P.ta
Romana *i*

STAZ. OSTIA
ANTICA FS

SS N° 8 bis

least the 1st century BC and restored until the 5th century AD. Under the portico overlooking the street are two **fish-shops** with mosaics depicting marine motifs. The **Sanctuary of Cybele**, accessed from Via del Pomerio and the Cardo Maximus, also known as Campo della Magna Mater, dates from the reign of Hadrian or Antoninus Pius. It comprises the *Temple of Cybele* and the *Temple of Bellona* (the warrior goddess associated with Cybele), the *Schola degli Hastiferes* (the lance-bearers who protected the cult of the goddess) and the *Sanctuary of Attis*, son and lover of Cybele, whose annual resurrection referred to the reawakening of the earth in spring. The **main fullonica** (where wool was fulled) of Ostia is located on *Via degli Augustali* (named after the priesthood instituted by Augustus for the cult of the emperor), perpendicular to the Decumanus Maximus (on the right). Built during the reign of Antoninus Pius, it comprises four large basins surrounded by a portico, where 35 large terracotta receptacles built into the floor were used for trampling and stiffening cloth. The last monument on the Decumanus, beyond the theater, is the *horrea of Hortensius*, possibly the oldest warehouses in the town (from the Julius-Claudian period). As far as **medieval Ostia Antica*** is concerned, the floods of 1557 also affected the fortified citadel which had been built above the ruins of Gregoriopolis, built by Gregory IV in the first half of the 9th century as a commercial and customs center. When these facilities and the port were transferred to Fiumicino (1613), the town was abandoned. Today, all that is left is the Rocca, and a little

1st and 4th centuries. Turning back now from Porta Marina towards the forum, the Decumanus Maximus passes the *Schola del Traiano*, probably the headquarters of the shipbuilders' guild, and, opposite, the *Christian Basilica*, built in the late 4th century, with two aisles divided by columns and ending in apses. At the crossroads with Via del Pomerio stands the *macellum*, a meat market dating from at

The castle built by Pope Julius II at Ostia Antica.

town with 15th-century buildings where the most important monuments are located. The bodies of St Aurea, a Christian martyr of the 3rd century, and St Monica, mother of St Augustine, who died here in 387, used to be kept in the 5th-century **church of S. Aurea**, as the *Easter candle* to the left of the high altar confirms.

Behind the church, *Palazzo Episcopale* (1472) has a fine cycle of **frescoes** (1508-1513). The splendid **castle*** was built for **Julius II** when he was still Cardinal Giuliano Della Rovere. Built on a triangular plan with an internal courtyard, it incorporates typical defensive criteria of the period as well as innovative features: the two round towers and the large pentagonal tower for extra defense herald features (curtain walls between the towers, casemates connected by galleries) which became widely used in the 16th century. From a distance, you can see the church of **S. Paolo fuori le Mura*** because of its white bell tower. According to tradition, the church was built on the spot where St Paul was buried, and was consecrated by Sylvester I in 324. Nothing remains of the first church, which was first rebuilt in 395. Then, because of a fire which, on July 15 and 16, 1823 spared only the transept, the sacred arch and part of the facade (this was subsequently demolished), it was rebuilt again according to the original design (1825-33). In 1854, Pus IX reconsecrated the new basilica. Then, in 1890-92, the quadriporticus was added and a narthex with 10 huge stone columns. In the center is a 19th-century *statue of St Paul*. The church is the second-largest in Rome after St Peter's. This is obvious not only from looking at the facade, the top of which is decorated with a mosaic dating from 1854-74, but also the interior, divided into a nave and four aisles (65m wide, 131.66m long, 30m high) and

The cloister of S. Paolo fuori le Mura.

decorated with a mosaic frieze depicting all the popes in the long history of the Church. The *triumphal arch* is decorated with a mosaic based on an original from the time of St Leo the Great (5C). At the high altar is a precious Gothic **ciborium** (1284) by Arnolfo di Cambio, possibly helped by Cavallini. Notice also the **candlestick holder for the Easter candle** to the right of it. The huge mosaic in the apse dates from the time of Honorius III (he is depicted at the feet of *Christ making the sign of the blessing, with St Peter and St Andrew* on the right and *St Paul and St Luke* on the left). The two chapels at each side of the apse were designed by Carlo Maderno. The one on the left (called the Cappella del Santissimo) contains a wooden **Crucifix** attributed to Cavallini (who is buried here) and a mosaic of the **Virgin Mary** dating from the 12th century. At the altar of the chapel on the right of the apse (chapel of St Lawrence) is a marble *triptych* by the school of Andrea Bregno (1494). The altars faced with malachite and lapis lazuli at each end of the transept were a gift from the Tsar Nicholas I of Russia. The *pinacoteca* can be accessed from the right transept. It contains precious paintings by the Umbrian school of the 16th century, as well as works by Bramantino, Cigoli and a beautiful *Madonna and Child with Saints*. The *cloister* is one of the masterpieces of Vassalletto. The **Centrale Montemartini**** at Via Ostiense 106, formerly a power station, was opened in 1911-13 to provide the capital with electricity. It has now been transformed into a museum, its dark gray turbines and slender pillars providing an unusual setting for number of exhibits from the Musei Capitolini and other works which once belonged to the former Antiquarium Comunale. They include a splendid set of acroteria depicting **Hercules being presented to Mt. Olympus** (mid-6C BC) from the shrine of St Homobonus, a fresco fragment depicting battle **scenes of the wars** with the Samnites (first half of the 3C BC) and the **pediment** of the Temple of Apollo Sosiano, from a temple of a Greek cult (mid-5C BC) re-used in Rome on the orders of Augustus. The demands of Rome's traffic – and the fighting which took place here in September 1943, events which are commemorated on a plaque – have isolated **Porta S. Paolo*** from the Aurelian walls of which it was once part. Only the two arches on the internal facade of the gate remind us that this was not only where the Via Ostiense began, but also the old Via Laurentina. Inside the two massive semi-circular towers of the gate, the *Museo della Via Ostiense* is devoted to the first of the two. It contains models and plaster casts from the archeological site of Ostia, the ports of Claudius and Trajan, milestones and drawings. It took only 330 days – so the inscription on the facade facing Piazzale Ostiense informs us – to build the **Pyramid of Caius Cestius*** who died in 12 BC. It is about 36m high with a base of 30m² and it is still not known where the original entrance was. During the Romantic period, the nearby *Protestant cemetery* became a compulsory stop for travelers and artists visiting the capital. It was created in about 1738 and, amongst others, contains the graves of the poets John Keats and Percy Bysshe Shelley. Now, the name of **Piazza di Porta Capena** is all that is left to remind us that the gate in the Servian walls that once stood here was the beginning of the Appian Way. The seating capacity of the **Circus Maximus** alone (300,000) – never equaled by any other sports stadium – gives us some idea of the popularity of horse-racing in ancient

Rome. The atmosphere of such a stadium was superbly recreated, albeit with the slight exaggeration typical of Hollywood, in the classic movie "Ben Hur". The first circus was built in the large valley between the Aventine and Palatine Hills under Tarquinius Priscus. This masonry structure was altered by Julius Caesar (46 BC), and Augustus added an imperial box and the obelisk of Rameses II, now in Piazza del Popolo. It was rebuilt by Trajan (100-104), extended by Caracalla and restored again by Constantine, who erected the obelisk of Tutmes III that was later moved to Piazza di S. Giovanni in Laterano. It remained in use until 549. Today you can only see the vague outline of the race-track in the area now designated as a public park.

Piazza della Bocca della Verità, quite close to the Forum and not far from the Isola Tiberina, where the ancient cattle market used to be held, is named after the marble disk on the left side of the portico of the church of S. Maria in Cosmedin. Two buildings in the square date from the 2nd and 1st centuries BC and are still well preserved. One is the **Temple of Fortuna Virile**, obvious from its rectangular plan, which, in 872, was converted into the *church of S. Maria Egiziaca*. The small round building known as the **Temple of Vesta** was probably dedicated to Hercules Victor, and is the oldest marble building in Rome (late 2C BC). In the 12th century it was converted into the church of S. Stefano, also called S. Maria del Sole from the 16th century onwards, after a miraculous ray was seen to emerge from an image found in the Tiber. The church of **S. Maria in Cosmedin*** was named after the Greek word *kosmidion*, meaning decoration, because of the splendid decorations which once adorned *S. Maria in Schola Graeca*. It was erected

Statue of St Paul.

above a 3rd-century chapel and, in the 6th century, was incorporated into a building which was extended by Hadrian I in 782 and restored after the Sack of Rome by Robert Guiscard (1082). The famous **Bocca della Verità*** (Mouth of Truth) is the large marble disk depicting the mask of a river-god (probably an ancient manhole cover). According to tradition, if someone told a lie with his hand in the mouth of the sculpture, it would be bitten off. For centuries it was situated in the outside wall of the church but, in 1632, it was placed under the portico of the facade, with its fine Romanesque *bell tower* (12C). Pillars and 18 ancient Roman columns with ancient and medieval capitals divide the interior into a nave and two side-aisles. The fine Gothic *canopy* is by Deodato di Cosma the Younger (1294), the *floor* dates from the 8th century and the frescoes in the wall of the apse date from the 11th century. The fragment of mosaic in the sacristy from the early basilica of St Peter's is also from the 8th century.

The **Arch of Janus** stands in the middle of *Via del Velabro*. Its four piers support a cross-vault and the attic is missing. Next to it is the *church of S. Giorgio in Velabro*. It dates from the 5th and 6th centuries, but was rebuilt by Gregory IV in the first half of the 9th century. Its 5-storey Romanesque *bell tower* dates from the 11th and 12th centuries. The *fresco* cycle in the bowl of the apse is attributed to Pietro Cavallini, but was altered in the 16th century. To the left of S. Giorgio in Velabro stands the **Arco degli Argentari**, erected by the guild of money-changers in 204 in honor of the imperial family. On the arch you can see Septimius Severus depicted with his wife, Julia Domna, and their children Caracalla and Geta. Geta's portrait and name were erased after he was killed by his brother. Two pillars faced with marble and travertine support a marble architrave decorated mainly with plant motifs. The nearby **Casa dei Crescenzi***, a rare example of a medieval building, was erected in 1040-65, incorporating parts of Classical buildings.

The **church of S. Nicola in Carcere**, where the Forum Holitorium, the vegetable and oil market of Ancient Rome once stood, was rebuilt in 1128 above a 9th-century building (or possibly

The Temple of Apollo Sosiano at the archeological site next to the Teatro di Marcello.

7C) and restored in 1808. Even at a first glance you can see features from the temples which once stood here. In 1599, two columns of the *Temple of Juno Sospita* (197 BC) were re-used for the facade, whereas six columns from the *Temple of Janus* and eight from the *Temple of Spes* (Hope), erected after the First Punic war, are incorporated in the side-walls of the church. The remains of the temples can best be admired under the church, the right aisle of which has an interesting *fresco* fragment. Augustus never missed a chance to dedicate (in 13 or 11 BC) buildings to his beloved nephew (and son-in-law), who died before he reached the age of twenty.

The **Teatro di Marcello**** was begun by Julius Caesar, and was one of the largest places of entertainment in Ancient Rome. It had a seating capacity of c. 15,000 and a cavea with a diameter of almost 130m. 41 arches supported each of the three orders that can be seen on the facade. The theater was abandoned in the 5th century, but, in 1523-27, Baldassarre Peruzzi based his design for Palazzo Orsini, the splendid residence of the Savelli family, on the twelve surviving arches, and used the ancient site as a source of building material. The adjacent *archeological site* is also very interesting.

SUBIACO [73 km]

The medieval town, surrounded by wooded mountains, is situated high in the Aniene Valley. The name comes from the Latin *Sublaqueum*, a term referring to Nero's large villa which overlooked an artificial lake. Today, on the right bank of the river (at the town entrance), you can see the remains of the baths and, on the left bank, the scant ruins of a nymphaeum, both of which were associated with Nero's villa. Subiaco has become a pilgrimage site thanks to St Benedict of Norcia and his monks. At the end of the 5th century, the young Benedict retreated here to the cave known today as the Sacro Speco. After three years he was persuaded by his twin sister Scolastica to leave his hermitage, after which he dictated the fundamental rules of the Benedictine order. The convent of Scolastica and the monastery of S. Benedetto at Subiaco are southeast of the town, amid dramatic mountain scenery. The town is dominated by the *Rocca abbaziale*, a medieval fortress that was converted in the 18th century and is now a center of Benedictine studies. It contains interesting frescoes. Not far away, in *Piazzetta della Pietra Sprecata*, is the Neoclassical *church of S. Maria della Valle*. Above the altar is a much revered 15th-century painting. The *Cathedral of*

S. Andrea in the square of the same name is a Neoclassical building erected between 1766 and 1789. In the apse is a fine 16th-century wooden *crucifix* and, on the wall at the end of the right transept, a lovely painting of the *Miracle of the Fishes*. At the beginning of Corso Cesare Battisti stands the *Arch of Pius VI* (1798). A 14th-century hump-backed *bridge* leads across the Aniene River to the *convent of S. Francesco*, hidden deep in a chestnut forest. The church (1327) has a fine *triptych* (1467) above the high altar. In the apse are wooden *choir-stalls* from the early 16th century and, in the 3rd chapel on the left, some frescoes and an altar-piece by Pinturicchio. The **Monastery of S. Scolastica*** is the only surviving convent of the 13 founded in the area by St Benedict. For centuries, it has been an important center of culture and spiritual evangelism. The buildings are around three cloisters. The first, in the form of a garden, is from 1580-1689. The second, in the Gothic style (late 13C – early 14C), with a flamboyant arch on the entrance side and a well in the middle (the two columns next to it are from Nero's villa), is overlooked by the *church of S. Scolastica*. Its 14th-century facade has a fine Romanesque bell tower (1052) with three-light windows, a Gothic doorway and frescoes from the 14th and 15th centuries. The interior is

Monastery of St Benedict, at Subiaco

1 Upper church   2 Lower church

The bridge over Aniene in Subiaco.

Neoclassical. The sacristy leads down to the *chapel of the Angels*, with 15th-century frescoes, and to other early chapels dug in the rock. The **Library** is off the second cloister. It contains illuminated codices and incunabula, including the first book printed in Italy (1465). In 1464, two German pupils of John Gutenberg (Sweynheym and Pannartz) set up the first Italian printing-press here. From the second cloister, a Gothic archway leads into the *third cloister*, decorated with Cosmati work (early 13C), with slender marble columns and elegant capitals. The **Monastery of S. Benedetto****, built daringly into the hillside and supported by mighty arches and buttresses, was begun in the 11th century, incorporating the very first hermitage of St Benedict. Also known as the Sacro Speco, today, this sanctuary is open for worship and contains some fine frescoes, especially from the late-Medieval period. From the gate, a corridor with frescoes (14C and 15C) leads past several rooms to the **upper church***, which is divided into two bays. The first contains 14th-century frescoes of the Sienese school and a 13th-century *pulpit*. The second, the back part of which is dug into the rock, has frescoes from about 1430. A double staircase in front of the altar leads to the **lower church****, which consists of a number of chapels dug out of the rock at various levels. Most of the walls are frescoed, with paintings from about 1280 and the 14th century. The chapel of St Gregory the Great has frescoes of the Roman Byzantine school and a **rare portrait of St Francis of Assisi** (possibly the only one made during his life; note the absence of the halo), painted when the saint visited Subiaco in 1223.

Steps lead down from the lower church to the **Sacro Speco**, the cave where Benedict spent the first three years of his monastic life before founding the monastery at Montecassino (the *statue of the saint* - 1657 - is by Antonio Raggi). From the lower church, you can also access the frescoed *scala santa*, the Gothic *chapel of the Madonna* and the *Shepherds' Cave*, with the earliest rock paintings in the monastery (8C).

Near the monastery is the **Parco Naturale Regionale dei Monti Simbruini**. This area, inhabited since prehistoric times, covers seven municipalities and several ski resorts. Besides beech, sycamore, yew, mountain ash and Norway spruce, there are typically Mediterranean trees (holm oak, terebinth, strawberry tree) and hazel-nut and chestnut groves. The undergrowth contains raspberries, strawberries and edible mushrooms; orchids, violets, daffodils, gentians and colombines. Mammals in the park include the wolf, Marsican brown bear, wild boar and fox; there are also many small carnivores, such as martens, badgers and weasels. Resident bird species include the buzzard, jay, falcon, woodpecker and kestrel, while the migratory birds include the redstart, hoopoe and thrush. Golden eagles nest high in the mountains. **Jenne** is a holiday resort high on Monte Pratiglio, on the park's southern edge. Buildings of interest include the *church of the Madonna della Rocca*, with 16th-century frescoes, and the ruins of a *castle* (11C). The *municipal mill* (early 20C) is an example of industrial archeology. By traveling northeast for about 14km, you come to **Vallepietra**, at the head of a wooded valley in the heart of the park. From here, a road leads to the isolated *Sanctuary of the SS. Trinità*. Perched high on a rocky outcrop, it contains 12th-century frescoes.

TIVOLI [32 km]

Tivoli overlooks the Roman Campagna from a low hill in the Monti Tiburtini where the Aniene River forms a broad loop, creating the famous waterfalls which have captured the imagination of travelers and illustrators for centuries. This little town, founded by the Sabines, fell into Roman hands in 338 BC. You can still see the ruins of some of the temples and part of the first set of fortifications from that period. The mild climate and beautiful setting have attracted visitors ever since. Roman artists and influential politicians first transformed the town into a sort of health resort. It became a residential town again in the Middle Ages. The church of S. Lorenzo, now the cathedral, was built in the 5th century on the site of the Roman Forum. (In the mid-12C, a second set of walls was built, inside which Tivoli continued to grow, until the Renaissance.) Having been involved in the struggles between the Goths and the Byzantines, between the Papacy and the Holy Roman Empire and the period of the communes, the town finally submitted to the Pope in the

16th century. As a result, sumptuous patrician villas were built here with amazing water features, grottoes, belvederes, terraces and sculptures. The most recent (Villa Gregoriana) was built in 1835 following a disastrous flood of the Aniene, which forced Gregory XVI to dig the tunnel and thus create the famous waterfall. A beautiful doorway with the family crest adorns the entrance to **Villa d'Este**** ❶, built for Cardinal Ippolito II d'Este, son of Lucrezia Borgia and Alfonso I d'Este, in the late 16th century. It was formerly a Benedictine monastery. In the 17th century, the next owners, Cardinals Luigi and Alessandro d'Este, added to the villa. It then became the property of the Habsburgs until 1918, when it was acquired by the Italian state. The *villa* has formal lines and several of the rooms are decorated with

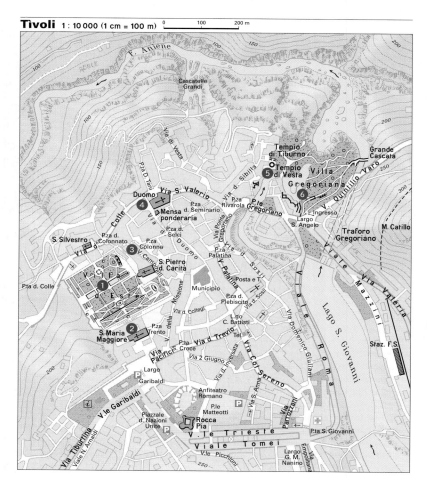

Tivoli 1 : 10 000 (1 cm = 100 m)

16th-century frescoes. From the loggia there is a beautiful view of the **garden****, which slopes down from the villa in a series of symmetrical terraces, connected by steps and paths, and decorated with fountains and spectacular water features. A double staircase leads down from the loggia in the garden.

From the *Fontana del Bicchierone*, you enter the charming Viale delle Cento Fontane, with a series of water jets and sculptures on either side. On the far right-hand side of the avenue is the **Fontana di Tivoli**, also called the *Fontana dell'Ovato* because of its egg-shape. It represents the Tivoli waterfall, the surrounding mountains and the Aniene and Erculaneo Rivers, symbolized by statues. On the far left of the avenue is the *Fontana di Roma* or *Rometta*, a reproduction in miniature of Ancient Rome. By continuing along the central avenue, you can get down to the *Fontana dei Draghi* and, from there, to the three fish-ponds. On the right, at the far end, is the monumental **Fontana dell'Organo**, begun in 1568 and finished in 1611. The water once drove a completely automatic hydraulic organ, one of the wonders of the villa. As it fell, the water compressed air which filled the bellows, then, passing into the organ pipes, produced sounds controlled by a cylinder activated by another water jet. The central avenue ends at the *Rotonda dei Cipressi*, surrounded by ancient cypresses. Other further-flung features of the garden are the *Fontana di Arianna*, the *Fontana di Pegaso*, the *Fontana della Sfinge* and the *Fontana della Natura*.

The church of **S. Maria Maggiore** ② is 13th century but was rebuilt in the 16th. Above the doorway of the facade is a late-Gothic rose-window (15C). Inside, the floor contains sections of Cosmatesque paving and there are various *art works*. Not far away is the Rocca Pia, a castle built for Pius II. It is rectangular in shape with round merloned towers at the corners. The popes of the late 15th and 16th centuries used to spend part of the summer here. There is an *amphitheater* from the Imperial period outside the castle walls.

Via Campitelli ③ is one of the most picturesque streets in the town because of the many charming palazzi and the *church of S. Pietro alla Carità*. The re-

used ancient columns in the church point to its 5th-century origins. You can see Roman columns being re-used again in nearby Piazza del Colonnato, site of the Romanesque *church of S. Silvestro*, with frescoes from the late 12th century. The only Romanesque feature of the **Duomo** ④ to survive is the bell tower. The church was rebuilt in the 18th century, as you can see from the interior. It contains a 13th-century wooden *sculpture of the Deposition* (last chapel, right) and a 12th-century **triptych** in a silver 15th-century case (third chapel, left). To the right of the church is the *mensa ponderaria*, used as a public weigh-bridge in Roman times. You can still see the tables with the capacity measures used. From the **Temple of Vesta*** ⑤ you can see the waterfall and great tunnel built to regulate the flow of water. The temple was used in the Republican period and, after restoration

Tivoli, Villa d'Este: a vieus of the garden.

in the 1st century BC, it was turned into a Christian church. It was restored to its original form in the 19th century. The Roman ruins nearby are from the *Temple of Tiburnus*, dedicated to the town's mythical founder, but also known as the Temple of the Sybil.

Villa Gregoriana ⑥ is actually a large park. Its lush vegetation covers a series of terraces, tunnels and gardens to the edge of the Aniene Gorge. It contains the remains of Roman buildings, mostly brought there as a result of flooding. From the park terraces – laid out in 1832-35 – and especially from the *Ferro di Cavallo* (horse-shoe) terrace, there are marvelous views of the **Grande Cascata**: the water plunges about 120m out of the underground tunnel built during the papacy of Gregory XVI. Not far away, and worth visiting, is the spa of **Bagni di Tivoli**. Famous since Antiquity, the white water of Tivoli, of the earthy alkaline bicarbonate sulphate type, with a constant temperature of 23°C/73°F, is used for various treatments (mud therapy, inhalations, aerosols, hydro-massage, baths) in the modern spa resorts. The water, which surfaces in nearby *Lake Regina* or *Lake Solfatara*, a narrow lake, giving the area a sulfurous smell, is tinged with shades of blue. You can see the ruins of the Roman *baths*, built during the Augustan period.

VILLA ADRIANA [40 km]

It was Publius Aelius Hadrianus himself, the great emperor and son of a Roman family in Spain, who designed this imposing complex, his favorite residence. It was begun in 118 and completed almost 20 years later. Despite the fact that many buildings have yet to be excavated, it is the largest villa built in Antiquity (it is thought to have occupied about 300 hectares). The vastness of the buildings was equaled by the splendor of the decoration, reproducing buildings and styles of decoration typical of the eastern provinces of the Empire, which Hadrian had visited and where he stayed many times. The villa's charming position and the abundance of water attracted Hadrian's successors, from Antoninus Pius to Diocletian, who used it as a luxurious holiday home. After Constantine, who began to remove some of the furnishings, it was plundered many times, by the Huns, then the Lombards and, later on, the Saracens. After that, for centuries, the local inhabitants and even people from Rome continued to remove building material, doorways, statues, capitals, and columns, often transforming them into lime. The villa was rediscovered in 1450, and, after the 16th century, the excavations ordered by the pope uncovered new parts of the site. Although this helped to re-establish the importance of the site in the public eye, it also increased the risk of plunder. In fact, more material was removed from the site and this continued well into the 19th century. Some of the statues and the finds which survived are now in the

Temple of Venus.

collections of the Museo Nazionale Romano in Rome. The *Museum* (currently closed) contains a large number of drawings of the ruins of the imperial villa, most of which were made in the 18th century. The vast quadriporticus of the **Pecile*** ❶ (232m x 97m), used, according to some scholars, as a gymnasium and, according to others, as a gestatio (that is, the gentle walk taken after dinner), has a fish-pond in the middle. At the west side of the quadriporticus is a substructure with three rows of small chambers on several levels, called the *Cento camerelle*, used as store-rooms or as slaves' quarters. The large, circular building known as the **Teatro Marittimo** ❷, accessed from the *Sala dei Filosofi*, has a diameter of about 43m and an Ionic peristyle which surrounds a circular moat spanned once by drawbridges. In the middle is a small round island. The long, narrow shape of the **Nymphaeum** ❸, with its pools, peristyles and polychrome mosaics, has been identified as a cult site. The huge **Baths*** ❹ complex is divided into two separate parts, connected by a *vestibule*. The *Small Thermae*, possibly reserved for female members of public, are situated to the west of the curve of the nymphaeum. You can still see the typical layout of a Roman bath complex (with *calidarium*, *tepidarium* and *frigidarium*, the latter with a dome more than 10m high). The facade had a loggia with an inlaid polychrome marble floor. The *Great Thermae* consist of three large rooms, two of which are square and one round,

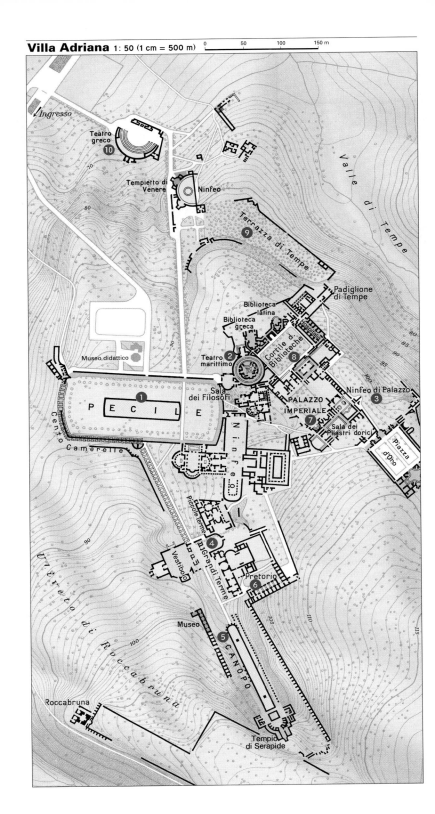

Villa Adriana 1: 50 (1 cm = 500 m)

0   50   100   150 m

Ingresso

Teatro greco **10**

Tempietto di Venere   Ninfeo

Terrazza di Tempe   **9**

Valle di Tempe

Padiglione di Tempe

Biblioteca latina
Biblioteca greca

Museo didattico

Teatro marittimo **2**

Contile di Biblioteche **8**

Sala dei Filosofi

Ninfeo di Palazzo **3**

PALAZZO IMPERIALE

7 Sala dei Pilastri dorici

P E C I L E **1**

N i n f e o

Piazza d'Oro

Cento Camerelle

Piccole terme

Vestibolo   Grandi Terme **4**

Pretorio **6**

Uliveto di Roccabruna

Museo **5**

C A N O P O

Roccabruna

Tempio di Serapide

106

Hadrian's Villa: a view of the Canopus, restored in the last century.

surrounded by smaller rooms used for massage, toilets and special treatments. They had very high ceilings, and you can imagine the splendor of the decoration from the few fragments that have been found. The **Canopus*** ⑤ is another of Hadrian's architectural caprices inspired by his travels in the Eastern Empire. Canopus was a place of leisure near Alexandria, west of the Nile delta. The emperor wanted to recreate the atmosphere of Egypt in this green valley. He dug out a hollow measuring 119x18m which is supposed to represent the canal linking Canopus to Alexandria. At each side of the canal there were marble steps (now are plaster casts of statues and columns, with a line of caryatids and sileni halfway up the pool) as well as benches, pavilions and other buildings imitating the houses and luxurious venues of Alessandria. On the southeast side of the pool is the *Temple of Serapis*, a nymphaeum preceded by a semi-circular hall. It is said to have been dedicated to the memory of Antinous, the emperor's favorite, whom he drowned in the Nile out of jealousy at Canopus. The nearby *Museum* contains material found during excavations, particularly from the area of the Canopus. The sculptures here include the four *caryatids* (2m high) which originally graced the Canopus, along with the two sileni; *copies of the Wounded Amazon* by Pheidias and by *Polikleitus*, the mutilated *copy of the Venus of Cnidos* by Praxiteles, and the statues of the *Nile* and the *Tiber* (which seems to be protecting the mythical founders of Rome

and the she-wolf). The **Praetorium** ⑥, a series of tall, narrow arcades with three storeys of rooms, was not the residence of the emperor's personal guards but was used as for storing goods. In winter, Hadrian lived in the **Imperial Palace*** ⑦, a complex with three sets of living accommodation and reception rooms. Covering an area of 50,000m², it was arranged around three peristyles which were kept warm by a complicated heating system. The broad *Piazza d'Oro* was named after the extraordinary number of rich finds made here. The square is surrounded by an octagonal peristyle with concave and convex sides, the latter of which were used as nymphaeums. In line with the square is the so-called semi-circular *Nymphaeum*, possibly used as a triclinium. West of it is the *Sala dei Pilastri Dorici*. The **Cortile delle Biblioteche** ⑧ (Courtyard of the Libraries) stands between the heart of the villa and the other parts of the complex. It is overlooked by the *Greek and Latin Libraries*, buildings several floors high which may have been used as *triclinia*. The **Terrazza di Tempe** ⑨ is another tribute to Greece, in particular, to the Valley of Thessaly dear to the god Apollo. It was represented here by digging out the tufa and placing a *pavilion* on the top. Beyond the *Temple of Venus*, an elegant circular building surrounded by Doric columns with a reproduction of the *Venus of Cnidos* in the middle, and the 8th-century *Casino Fede* lies the **Greek Theater** ⑩. It is overgrown, but you can still make out parts of the cavea and stage.

Rome, with its unique environmental heritage, has plenty to offer hikers. The city wears a mantle with a thousand folds, and every fold contains a secret. By exploring these folds, you can uncover the better- or lesser-known facets of the city. The more you walk, the more you discover. Ancient voices thousands of years old whisper through the passages of the underground city, the breeze caressing the bridges spanning the Tiber, Audrey Hepburn's smile mingling with the traffic of Piazza Venezia, and the sharpness of Pasquino's tongue are just a few of Rome's hidden delights, and which we recommend

Itineraries

you discover for yourself. In fact, the city has an enormous number and variety of pursuits to offer if you are wondering about spending a few days here. Pamper yourself at one of its wellness centers, relax in one of its beautiful parks, and enjoy the delights of the Roman table.

Highlights

- Discover the fascinating secrets of the underground city.
- Admire the water features and the stunning decoration of Rome's many fountains.
- Enjoy unusual views of the city by taking a boat-trip on the Tiber.
- Beware! Even the statues talk in Rome!

Inside

BIOPARCO

PIAZZALE DEL GIARDINO ZOOLOGICO 1,
VILLA BORGHESE, ROMA
TEL. 063608211 -
CALL CENTER 063614015

WEB: WWW.BIOPARCO.IT

OPEN: FROM JANUARY TO SEPTEMBER

OPENING TIMES: EVERY DAY FROM JANUARY
TO MARCH FROM 9.30AM TO 5PM.
EVERY DAY FROM MARCH TO SEPTEMBER
FROM 9.30AM TO 6PM. EXTENDED OPENING:
FROM APRIL TO SEPTEMBER, SATURDAYS,
SUNDAYS AND BANK HOLIDAYS
FROM 9.30AM TO 7PM. TICKET OFFICE
CLOSES 1 HOUR BEFORE CLOSING TIME.
OPEN AT NIGHTS FOR EXHIBITIONS
AND SPECIAL OCCASIONS.

ADMISSION: FULL-PRICE € 8.50;
REDUCED (CHILDREN FROM 3 TO 12,
PARENTS, INVALID AND DISABLED
HELPERS, EXCEPT WEDNESDAYS,
GROUPS OF 15 ADULTS AND OVER) € 6.50;
FREE ADMISSION FOR CHILDREN UNDER 3,
INVALIDS AND DISABLED PEOPLE,
OVER 60S WEDNESDAYS ONLY.
TICKET PRICE INCLUDES ORGANISED
ACTIVITIES ON SATURDAYS
AND SUNDAYS, VISIT TO THE
LIPU WILDLIFE CENTRE
AND CHILDREN'S ACTIVITIES.

GETTING THERE

BY TRAM: "BIOPARCO" STOP TRAMS Nº 3
AND 19

BY BUS: Nº 52, 53, 926, 217, 360, 910

BY METRO: RED A LINE, FLAMINIO
AND SPAGNA STATIONS

 **Centro
di Conservazione
e di Educazione
Ambientale**

The Biopark is the modern version
of the Rome Zoo which was founded
in 1911. Today its aim is to promote
wildlife conservation through special
programmes to protect endangered
species and raise public awareness
through specific campaigns.
The strategically central Villa Borghese
site within one of Rome's most historic
parks, hosts roughly 1000 animals
belonging to almost 200 species
of mammals, birds and reptiles, many
of whom are now in risk of extinction
in their native lands, thanks to
environmental change, poaching and
the encroachment of man.

The park is home to a wide assortment
of animals from all over the world,
including the black lemur, the pygmy
hippopotamus, the hyena-dog, the
mandrill and the gila monster as well as
brown bears, pythons, crocodiles,
chimpanzees, storks, giraffes, zebras,
ostriches, lynx, tigers, orangoutangs
and leopards. There is also a petting
farm with cows, pigs, sheep, goats,
hens, turkeys and donkeys where
children can enjoy coming into direct
contact with familiar farm animals.
A few examples of the animals' housing
arrangements: the Chimps' Village,

the Giraffe House (with info panels,
scenes and animations), Bear Valley,
the Butterfly Garden, the Birds'
Restaurant, with special feedtrays and
the Lake Oasis for migrating birds with
ducks, geese, terrapins, carp and
goldfish. There is also a Reptile House,
a large Aviary and a Mediterranean
wetlands area with flamingoes, badgers
and porcupines. Right by the Lake
Oasis is the historic Mascagni
restaurant (built in 1926), which has
recently been extensively renovated.
There is also a nature trail exploring
Mediterranean flora and exotic
plants. The park is well-equipped
with recreational facilities, including
a café, a lakeside picnic area,
a children's area with toys and
educational games, a play area,
a welcome and info centre, carpark,
lecture room, auditorium and
mini-theatre (The Penguins' Theatre).

HYDROMANIA

Casal Lumbroso, vicolo Casale Lumbroso 200, Roma
Tel. 0666183183 - 0661816

Web: www.hydromania.it

Open: end of May to mid-September

Opening times: Monday-Friday 9.30am-6.30pm; Saturday, Sunday and Bank Holidays 9.30am-7.30pm.

Admission: Monday-Friday full-price € 14.50; reduced (children under 12 and under 1.50 m tall) € 10; Saturday, Sunday and Bank Holidays full-price € 16; reduced € 11.50.

GETTING THERE

By bus: N° 88, 906

By car: Exit 33 (Lumbroso - Pescaccio) of the Roman ring road (GRA)

Hydromania is a large water park and sports centre on the outskirts of Rome. The complex is carefully laid out in activity zones that are linked by shady paths, with five-a-side football pitches, tennis courts, dance floors and a semi-Olympic swimming pool. A chalet houses the restaurant, services and amenities. Visitors can relax and get into shape in the well-being centre with its techno-pool, hydromassage, acquagym and watersports equipment, while a children's lagoon with slides and toys, and a multi-plunge pool will keep younger visitors amused. Another area houses the wavepool, and a series of four connecting pools where the centre's feature slides arrive: an impressive array of 3 Kamikazis, a Twister, a 6-in-a-row multislide and 2 toboggan slides. Another favourite for the adventurous is the Black hole slide complex with its 160 metre ride on two-seater rubber dinghies, one of the longest water slides in Europe. Apart from the children's lagoon, younger guests can also use the baby-club with its toys, 2 curving slides and a baby-kamikaze slide, but one of the favourite attractions for hours of fun is the foam cannon, an unusual feature in Italian water parks.

THE ZOOLOGY MUSEUM/ MUSEO CIVICO DI ZOOLOGIA

Via Ulisse Aldrovandi 18, Roma (access also from Bioparco).
Tel. 0667109270

Web: www.museodizoologia.it

Opening times: every day except Monday, from 9am to 5pm.

Admission: full-price € 4.50; reduced (students, groups of more than 50 people, go-card holders) € 2.50; no charge for children and young people under 18 and adults over 65, and university students studying natural sciences or biology.

GETTING THERE

By tram: n° 19, 30B

By bus: N° 52, 53, 95, 217, 490, 495, 910

By metro: red A line, Flaminio and Spagna Stations

The Zoology Museum at Villa Borghese used to be part of the zoo. It is a modern museum housing over 5 million exhibits and with a mission in conservation, research, teaching and spreading science. The exhibition revolves around the biodiversity project and explains the difference between living organisms through a tour that includes multisensorial and interactive stations, and 3D reconstructions, such as the room dedicated to coral reefs. The Myosotis cooperative (tel. 0632609200) organises guided tours and labwork sessions to explain courting rituals in the animal world, survival strategies for animals living in hostile environments like deserts or on icecaps and show how animals move around and find food. There is a well-stocked bookshop with a good range of publications on natural science. There is lift access for people with reduced mobility but no suitable toilet facilities.

PERONI BEER-MUSEUM
MUSEO BIRRA PERONI

GENERAL INFORMATION:
VIA RENATO BIROLLI 8, ROMA, TEL. 06225441
WWW.PERONI.IT

HOW TO GET THERE:
BY CAR. FROM THE GRA (GRANDE RACCORDO
ANULARE), THE ROME RING ROAD, TAKE EXIT
15 (LA RUSTICA), AND THE VIA COLLATINA
TOWARDS ROME UNTIL YOU COME TO THE
MUSEUM SIGNPOST. BY PUBLIC TRANSPORT.
METRO B TO REBIBBIA; BUS 447;
OR THE ROME-TÌVOLI URBAN RAILWAY
TO TOR SAPIENZA.

OPENING HOURS:
WEEKDAYS, BY APPOINTMENT.
FREE ENTRY.

How the museum began

The Peroni Beer
Museum is the outcome
of a complex project
designed to preserve
the Peroni legacy. It was
begun in 1996 to mark
the company's 150th
anniversary and,
following the publication
of a historical monograph
and the cataloguing of
the archive material, it
was decided to create a
place that would
showcase the company
and its past, and
illustrate its influence on
Italian lifestyle and
society. The Peroni
Brewery was originally created in 1846
in the northern Italian town of Vigevano,
but almost twenty years later, in 1864,
the brewery moved to Rome. The early
years of the 20th century, when it
relocated to the capital's Porta Pia
district, saw rapid growth that in the ten
years that also witnessed the first world
war between 1910 and 1920, turned it
into one of Italy's leading beer makers.
Following a series of takeovers of other
smaller breweries, Peroni expanded its
production across the country to cover
other areas of the Italy.

What's inside

The museum tells the story of the
company using original objects,
images, films and documents. The first
section is dedicated to the history of
the Peroni brewery from the early
20th century to the 1950s, and has
equipment and installations from
offices and divisions whose activities
were discontinued, an interesting
example of industrial archaeology.
The Peroni beer-brewing tradition is
told through a presentation of raw
materials and the numerous quality
awards the beer has received in Italy
and abroad. The 'hands-on' experience
gives visitors a clear idea of the nature
of the product, its feel and its smell.
The company's commercial trading
past is covered in section two, through
using pictures and exhibits that show
the development of packaging
and promotional material
supplied to retail
outlets from the late
19th century onwards.
The exhibition offers
insights into the evolution
of lifestyles, leisure time
and eating and drinking
habits, especially
in economic and
social terms.
Section three focuses
more closely on the
advertising of Peroni,
one of the biggest italian
beer firms, with an all
Italian capital.

Aims

The Peroni Museum
presents the past and present of the
Società Birra Peroni, offering
an interpretation of its industrial,
commercial and advertising success.
The picture that emerges is one
of a quite extraordinary entrepreneurial
venture that has 'tapped into' Italy's
tradition of high quality beer
production, passed down through the
generations, without foregoing an
ability to innovate and be modern.

Activities

Guided tours in Italian and English,
visits to the production plant, tasting
of a selection of Peroni products
(on request), explanations of the
brewing process, and of how glasses
of draught beer are 'pulled' at the bar.

Rome and its passion for water features

The Romans have always felt strongly about the public water supply, as the ancient aqueducts and public baths we can still see today show. Fountains are part of Rome's artistic and cultural heritage and have always been a fascinating characteristic of the city. Many have become famous, thanks to their creators who embellished them with stone, travertine and marble.

Since ancient Roman times, the authorities and those in power have used these forms of urban decoration to ensure that their names would be remembered. But although, in ancient times, the water they provided was used for the daily needs of the population, it was not until the period of the architect Maderno and the Renaissance that the role of fountains became mainly decorative. In fact, during this period, water began to be used as a form of entertainment and fountains were increasingly built as decorative features. The capital has an enormous number of them: monumental fountains, faucets, ornamental fountains, some standing in the elegant courtyards of beautiful palazzi, others dotted about in the gardens of historic noble villas, in streets and squares, or in city parks: an endless succession of jets, sprays and gushing water that has no equal anywhere. The English poet, Shelley, who was a great admirer of Rome's abundant supply of water, said that the fountains alone justified a visit to Rome. There follows a description of just a few of the hundreds of fountains which adorn the city. The route winds its way past the alleyways, warehouses, shops and magnificent views of Rome.

In Piazza S. Giovanni in Laterano, at the foot of the great Roman obelisk, is a fountain built by Domenico Fontana in 1586, adorned with the crests of important noble families. If we proceed along the shady Via Merulana we come to Via Machiavelli which leads into Piazza Vittorio Emanuele II. Here, we can see the commemorative **Fontana dei Trofei di Mario**, (celebrating the

Fontana delle Naiadi in Piazza della Repubblica.

victories of Marius) from the 2nd century. Now we retrace our steps to Via Merulana as far as the church of S. Maria Maggiore, and walk along Via Torino to Piazza della Repubblica, where we find the **Fontana delle Naidi**, built in 1885. The basin was designed by the architect Guerrieri whereas the naiads (water-nymphs) are attributed to Mario Rutelli. Completed in 1901, it was "inaugurated by the people". The beautiful nude water-nymphs, which, at that time, were regarded as being too daring and inappropriate for the demure eyes of the period, were covered with drapes for the opening ceremony, but the crowd who had assembled to watch pulled off the coverings so that they could see the statues. If we continue along Via Vittorio Emanuele Orlando to Piazza San Bernardo, we then follow Via del Quirinale to Piazza del Quirinale. Here stands the imposing Fontana di Piazza del Quirinale (the circumference of the bowl

alone measures 24 m). It is also known as the **Fontana dei Dioscuri** because of the two gigantic equestrian statues of Castor and Pollux. They have adorned the fountain since 1588, when on the orders of Pope Sixtus V Peretti (1585-1590), Domenico Fontana designed the fountain, placing an octagonal basin in front of the statues. The fountain now below the obelisk dates from 1818, when Pope Pius VII Chiaramonti (1800-1823) replaced the previous fountain, which has been lost, with the splendid granite basin we see today. If we climb the Spanish Steps up to the church of the Trinità dei Monti, we come to Villa Medici. In 1587, the **Fontana della Palla di Cannone** was built in front of it (there is another cannon-ball fountain on one side of Castel Sant'Angelo). They say that the sphere which now forms part of it was a real cannon-ball, fired at the orders of Queen Christina of Sweden, to attract the attention of French painter Charles Errand, who lived here at that time. We now climb back down the steps and turn left into the narrow Via S. Sebastianello towards Piazza Trinità dei Monti. On the way down we pass a fountain made out of a Roman sarcophagus decorated with an 18th-century architrave. This is one of the 18 fountains (the project was never completed) commissioned to celebrate the restoration of the Acqua Vergine aqueduct, according to a design by the architect Giacomo Della Porta. The famous Via Margutta contains the **Fontana degli Artisti**, created in 1927 by the architect Pietro Lombardi, depicting symbols associated with artists. Two painters' easels sit on a triangular base with two masks expressing sadness and joy, emphasizing the fluctuating nature of artists' fortunes. Also in Via Margutta, level with No. 53/A, is the **Fontana del Cortile**: a terracotta amphora tipped over, pouring water into a square white-marble basin, dating from the Roman period. Not far away, in the broad, spacious Piazza del Popolo, there are five fountains. The **Fontana dell'Obelisco** (1823) in the center of the square is the largest. It was designed by Valadier, a founder of the Roman Classicism movement. Set around

the obelisk are four white-marble lions in the Egyptian style. Water gushes from their mouths into four round travertine basins set on a square base with five steps. On the side of the square by the Pincio Hill, also designed by Valadier in 1823, is the **fountain dedicated to Rome**. In this marble sculpture executed by Giovanni Ceccarini, Rome is represented as a goddess wearing a helmet and armed with a spear. Around her are the reclining statues of the Tiber and the Aniene rivers and the she-wolf suckling Romulus and Remus. A broad, shell-shaped travertine basin collects the water flowing from a small basin at the base of the monument. Opposite is Neptune with two tritons. At each side of the gate leading into the square are two more fountains made out of sarcophaghi. Near the mausoleum of Augustus is the small, delightful Fontanella ("little fountain"), also known as the **Fontana della Botte** (*botte* means barrel) or Botticella di Ripetta, again in reference to the small barrel. The figure pouring the water out of the barrel is one of the city's talking statues (see page 156). The fountain was put there in the second half of the 18th century by the guild of innkeepers and boatmen. In 1704, Pope Clement XI Albani

TCI HIGHLIGHTS

THE MYTHS OF ANCIENT GREECE IN ROME

In Piazza del Quirinale, near the fountain of the same name, stand the huge statues of the Dioscuri Castor and Pollux, the great heroes of Sparta. The legend of the birth of the Dioscuri twins is as follows: Zeus, king of all the gods, appeared to Leda, wife of Tyndareus, king of Lacedaemon, and made love to her in the form of a swan, so that she later gave birth to two eggs. The eggs hatched near Sparta, one producing Pollux (or Polydeuces) and Helen (who was later to be the cause of the Trojan war), and the other produced Castor and Clytemnestra. However, the latter were the children of Tyndareus, who had made love to Leda after her union with Zeus. As a result, Pollux, who was the son of a god, was immortal, unlike his brother Castor. Pollux is described as being an invincible fighter, while his brother was a fearless warrior. The story of Clytemnestra is also fascinating. Having been betrothed to Agamemnon, king of Mycaenae and Argos, Clytemnestra's feelings for her husband turned to hate on his departure for Troy, when he sacrificed their daughter Iphigenia so as to have favorable winds. The queen's affections turned to Aegisthus, Agamemnon's cousin, who, like Clytemnestra, feared Agamemnon's return. When the war was over, Agamemnon did return, accompanied by the slave Cassandra, princess of Troy, but, when he reached the palace, was killed by Aegisthus and Clytemnestra. The importance of Clytemnestra in Greek mythology is determined by the tragic poets, who were struck by her fate and her jealousy.

had the **Fontana dei Navigatori** built on the bank of the Tiber, near the small harbor of Ripetta, so that the stevedores who unloaded firewood and wine from the boats could slake their thirst. The man who designed it, Alessandro Specchi, created an oval basin with a rock at one end, crowned with a shell with a dolphin on either side. The water flows from the top of the rock (which bears the Albani family crest) and the mouths of the dolphins into the basin below. In the mid-18th century, a lantern was placed on top of the rock so that boats returning at night could locate the harbor easily. Near the prestigious Via del Corso is the elegant **Fontana di Piazza Colonna**, built at the wishes of Pope Gregory XIII Boncompagni (1572-1585). It was designed by Giacomo Della Porta and executed by the sculptor Rocco De Rossi. It was placed here in 1577. When it was restored in 1830, several new features were added: two groups of dolphins with their tails intertwined and 16 lion's heads. At that time the upper basin was also replaced by a smaller one, from which the single central cascade flows into the basin below. In 1575, Giacomo Della Porta received a commission from Pope Gregory XIII Boncompagni to design the elegant **fountain** for the square in front of the **Pantheon**. Leonardo Sormani created the fountain which consists of a basin standing on three travertine steps, with four dolphins and masks with a smaller basin in the center containing jets of water. In 1711, on the orders of Pope Clement XI Albani, the architect Filippo Barigoni replaced the basin with a rock which supports the obelisk of Rameses II, 6 meters high, and decorated the base with four dolphins executed by the sculptor Vincenzo Felici. When the fountain was restored in 1804, the four 16th-century masks were replaced by copies executed by Luigi Amici. Piazzetta S. Marco has a fountain by Pietro Lombardi (1927), known as the **Fontana della Pigna** (pine-cone, the symbol of the district.) The water falls into small basins surrounded by four small columns. The **fountain in Piazza**

Sant'Andrea della Valle, based on a design by Carlo Maderno, is decorated with classical motifs. It consists of an elegant multi-form bowl on a base of the same shape. In the center of the basin, which is supported by a base decorated with dragons and eagles (the symbols of the Borghese family), is a smaller concrete basin which has replaced the original marble one, now lost. A jet of water rises from the top basin and falls into the larger basin below, where four more jets of water rise up from the level of the water. At the end of Via del Corso, close to the bottom of the monument to Vittorio Emanuele II, are two fountains dating from 1911 which represent the Tyrrhenian Sea (on the right) and the Adriatic (on the left). In Piazza del Campidoglio, in front of Palazzo Senatorio, the **Fontana della Dea Roma** depicting the city as a goddess is also known as the Fontana della Scala

Fontana delle Tartarughe in Piazza Mattei.

Senatoria and the Fontana di Pallade Rapita (Rape of Pallas Athena). Above it is the she-wolf. Michelangelo designed it in about 1536, not as a fountain (water came to the Capitoline Hill about 50 years later) but as a splendid ornament for his square. In the large niche half-way up the steps is the statue of the goddess Rome triumphant. The statue, resting on three supports, has a white marble face and arms, while her robes are made of porphyry. Next to the large niche, below the flights of steps on either side, Michelangelo arranged two enormous reclining statues of Roman date depicting the Nile and the Tiber, which originally decorated the Baths of Constantine on the Quirinal Hill. In 1562, two Egyptian lions made of black Numidian basalt were placed at the foot of the steps leading up to Piazza del Campidoglio. Previously they decorated the entrance to the church of S. Stefano del Cacco. In 1587, when the Acqua Felice aqueduct was extended to the Capitoline Hill, which had been left without water when the supply of water from the Marcian aqueduct was interrupted, the two lions were altered and converted into fountains. In 1588, the sculptor Francesco Scardua made two basins to collect the water spouting from tubes in the lions' mouths. On at least two occasions, when Pope Innocent X Pamphili (1644-1655) and Pope Clement X

Altieri (1670- 1676) were elected, white and red wine spouted from the pipes of the **lion fountains** instead of water. Towards the end of the 16th century, in 1589, during the papacy of Sixtus V Peretti (1585-1590), Giacomo della Porta created the lovely **fountain in Piazza d'Aracoeli**. Four cherubs on the top of the fountain stand back to back pouring water out of the amphoras. When the fountain situated at the bottom of the Capitoline Hill was restored in the 19th century, the original large, oval-shaped basin was replaced by the round one we see today. In Piazza Farnese (where Palazzo Farnese, now the French

TCI HIGHLIGHTS

THE LEGEND OF THE SHE-WOLF

The legend of the she-wolf, the symbol of Rome, associates the founding of the city with the family of Aeneas, the hero of Troy who, having fled from the ashes of the vanquished city, after wandering far and wide throughout the Mediterranean, landed on the shores of Latium (modern Lazio). After 30 years, Ascanius, the son of Aeneas, founded a new city, Alba Longa, over which his descendants ruled until the time of King Numitor. He was deposed from power by his evil brother, Amulius, who held him prisoner and killed his male heirs, forcing the only surviving daughter, Rhea Silvia, to become a Vestal Virgin and obliging her to make a vow of celibacy. But the girl, who was a beautiful and innocent child, made the fatal error of falling asleep on a riverbank. Her beauty had not passed unnoticed by the gods and, in fact, shortly afterwards, Mars took advantage of her. From this union, twin boys, Romulus and Remus, were born. King Amulius ordered them to be

 killed, but the servant charged with carrying out the order lacked the courage to see it through, put them in a basket and entrusted them to the Tiber River. The basket containing the twins was washed up on the riverbank near a marsh between the Palatine and Capitoline Hills. Here, the crying of the boys was heard by a she-wolf which, having carried the basket to her den, suckled them. Subsequently, the brothers were found by a shepherd called Faustulus who took them home and reared them as if they were his own sons. Romulus

and Remus grew up among the shepherds, distinguishing themselves for their strength and courage (after all, they were the sons of the god of war) but, when they discovered their true origins, they returned to Alba Longa, killed Amulius and restored their grandfather Numitor to the throne. The twins then decided to found a new city in the place where they had grown up. But Romulus wanted to build it on the Palatine Hill whereas Remus favored the Aventine Hill. To resolve the dispute, they decided to resort to augury, a very common practice in ancient times, which invlolved observing the flight of birds from the respective hills in order to decide how to proceed. Romulus, having seen more eagles than his brother, dug a trench to mark the line of the walls of the new city, which no-one could cross without his permission. His brother Remus, challenging him, leaped across the trench and Romulus killed him with his sword. According to the myth, this is how the Eternal City was founded in 753 BC and how Romulus became the first king of Rome.

Embassy, is situated) there are two fountains which were once supplied by the Acqua Paola (one of the many aqueducts dating from Roman times which supplied the city with water), the basins of which come from the Baths of Caracalla. The fountains, which date from 1626, are decorated with lilies, symbols both of the Farnese family and of France. The elegant **fountain in Piazza Campitelli** was designed by the architect Giacomo della Porta in 1589 (and executed by the sculptor Pompilio De Benedetti). Originally the fountain was situated in the center of the square, but in 1679, when the church of S. Maria in Campitelli was enlarged, it was moved to its present position. The monument is made of travertine and has an octagonal base. The longer sides alternate with concave sides and the top octagonal basin is decorated with the crests of the four most important families of the area (the Albertoni, the Capizucchi, the Muti and the Ricci), who paid for the fountain to be built, and two masks from which the water gushes out. Above the basin, surrounded by a marble cup-shaped balustrade, is another round basin with a central water spout. The **fountain in Piazza delle Cinque Scole**, regarded as one of Giacomo della Porta's most successful designs, has a base with two steps, a long, white marble basin of irregular shape, in the center of which a balustrade supports a round basin with a central water-spout. From here, the water falls into the basin below from the open mouths of four masks resembling Gorgon's heads (with snakes for hair). The charming little square of Piazza Mattei is surrounded by 16th-century buildings and contains the **Fontana delle Tartarughe** (1584). Four youths support a basin on which the four tortoises (copies of the originals after which the fountain is named) stand facing each other. Now we are near the Jewish Ghetto where, in Piazza Giudea, there is another beautiful fountain. Before Ponte Sisto, overlooking the lovely Via Giulia, with its many Baroque buildings, is the famous **Fontana del Mascherone**, in Piazza S. Pietro d'Illiria, one of Rome's most charming and best-kept secrets. In 1970, during the celebrations held to mark the election of the Grand Master of the Knights of St John of Malta, wine flowed from this

fountain. On the other side of Ponte Sisto, on the far side of the Tiber, in Trastevere, one of Rome's most famous districts, Piazza Trilussa, named afer one of the greatest singers of Roman popular songs, is the large **Fontana di Ponte Sisto**, which stands in line with the bridge. Made of travertine, it dates from 1613 and was executed by Giovanni Vasanzio (the local name for the Flemish sculptor, Van Zanten) for Paul V Borghese (1605-1621). Ionic columns stand at either side of a large niche with a barrel-vaulted ceiling which supports an architrave. Above is a commemorative inscription and, on the top, the Borghese family crest. Water pours down from an opening in one side of the niche into a basin before continuing noisily down to the basin at street level. Jets of water also pour into the basin below from the two dragons carved on the bottom of the columns and two lion's heads. Six small red granite columns connected by an iron structure surround the fountain which,

Fontana del Mascherone at Santa Sabina.

having been moved in 1879 when it was decided to widen the bed of the Tiber, was reconstructed in the late 19th century. At that time it was raised on a base of 15 steps to road level to make it visible from Ponte Sisto. Another famous square in the district contains the **Fontana di Piazza S. Maria in Trastevere**, thought to be the oldest in Rome. The church of S. Maria in Trastevere was once known as *Sancta Maria in fontibus* (St Mary of the Fountains) and it is therefore thought that the fountain, which stands in the middle of a polygonal basin above two superimposed basins with a balustrade, replaced a much earlier fountain (possibly dating from the 1st century). The inscription in couplets on the stone at one corner of the fountain dates from

Fontana della Botte.

restoration work carried out by Cardinal Lopez in the late 15th century. The functioning of the fountain was dogged by the lack of a decent water supply until the papacy of Pope Alexander VII Chigi (1655-1667), when it began to receive 36 ounces of water (instead of 5) and was moved to the middle of the square. The work was entrusted to Bernini (1659). The top of the monument remained as it was, but the lower part of the fountain, namely the octagonal basin, was raised up onto a base of octagonal steps. Four double shells, the emblem of the Chigi family, were added, together with inscriptions commemorating the restoration. But only about 30 years later (1692) Pope Innocent XII had to carry out radical restoration and cleaning, during which the size of the basin was probably increased and the double shells were turned down towards the basin almost as if protecting it. Finally, in 1873, Rome City Council rebuilt the fountain completely, based exactly on the 1692 model, using bardiglio marble rather than travertine. At the corner of Via della Cisterna and Via San Francesco a Ripa under a travertine arch, stands the famous **Fontana della Botte** (1927), created by the architect Pietro Lombardi in honor of the wines served in Roman *osterie*. The barrel, which stands vertically on its flat base, is the typical

caratello (the barrel once used to transport the wines of the Castelli Romani). Water gushes out of a hole in the center of the barrel and is collected in the half-vat below. At the sides of the barrel are two wine measures, like the ones they still use in Roman *osterie* today, from which water gushes out into the basins below. At the crossroads of Via L. Manara and Via Mameli stands the **Fontana della Prigione**, by Domenico Fontana. The fountain has a large niche, edged by two pilaster strips with a richly decorated pediment and a lion's head in the middle where water gushes out into a basin below surrounded by six small columns. The statue of the prisoner which gave the fountain its name has been lost. On Via Garibaldi, near one of the entrances to the lovely park of the Janiculum Hill, is the majestic **Fontana di Acqua Paola**, also known as the Fontanone del Gianicolo, built to celebrate the re-opening of Trajan's aqueduct. It was commissioned by Pope Paul V Borghese (1605-1621), designed by Giovanni Fontana and Flaminio Ponzio and completed by Carlo Fontana. The monumental fountain has a large white-marble basin, and three wide niches (with two smaller niches on either side). The water comes from Lake Bracciano. The large inscription above the niches, the papal crest and the figures on either side are by Ippolito Buzio. In 1690, Pope Alexander VIII Ottoboni (1689-91) had the five basins below the water jets replaced by one large basin, according to a design by Carlo Fontana. He also opened a space in the central arcade towards the botanic gardens at the rear, and had the square behind it built, which has beautiful views

Fontana dell'Acqua Paola.

over the capital. Gian Lorenzo Bernini designed the famous colonnade in St Peter's Square and moved Maderno's fountain, which formerly occupied a position which was asymmetrical to the facade of the basilica and the obelisk. To match it, he built another fountain which was inaugurated in 1677. The older of the two has the crest of Pope Paul V Borghese, who had the fountain restored, while the other bears the six-starred crest of Clement X, since the work was completed during his rule. One of the most recent fountains, which is no less interesting for that reason, is located not far from Villa Ada. The **Fontana delle Rane** was built in Piazza Mincio in 1924 according to a design by the architect Gino Coppedè. Above a round basin not much higher than the level of the street, four couples of figures each support a

from the deck of the little ship, set on a base decorated with the crests of Pope Leo X, and falls into the oval travertine basin below. In 1613, Pope Paul Borghese had a simple fountain built in the open countryside on the right bank of the Tiber at a place called Tor di Quinto, where there was a mineral water spring that was regarded as being "beneficial for the kidneys, stomach, liver, spleen and a thousand other ailments".
But it was the pope with a penchant for town-planning, Alexander VII Chigi (1655-1667), who was responsible for having the nymphaeum of Acqua Acetosa designed and erected in the form we see it today. For a long time, the design of this delightful work, worthy of the finest private garden, was attributed to Bernini, but it seems to have been designed by a painter, Andrea

ITINERARIES

TCI HIGHLIGHTS

DRINKING-FOUNTAINS

Romans call the approximately 2,000 free drinking-fountains dotted around all over the city "nasoni" (big noses). The name comes from the typical curved iron tap, the shape of which vaguely resembles a large nose. These fountains, which are a common feature in Rome, were first installed in the 1860s. Today, the model is the same: a round cast-iron object with a hole at the top for drinking from. However, if you look at them closely, they are not all the same. Over the years, the words "Acqua Marcia" inscribed on the original fountains (because the water once came from the Marcian aqueduct) have disappeared. (some have survived, for example at the corner of Via Duse and Via Belotti-Bon). Some fountains have been personalized, or rather "sponsored" (for example the fountains in the Foro Italico, which bear the emblem of CONI – the Italian National Olympic Committee). But quite apart from these details, it is important to understand the Romans' affection for these objects, which is why they are still there.
Today, the nasoni--about 100 kg of cast iron is used to make one--are still produced by some iron foundries in the capital and others on the edge of Rome. New fountains are continuously being installed and there are even fountains outside the area of the Rome City Council. Fiumicino Faro and Ciampino, to name just two areas, have lots of drinking-fountains.

shell containing a frog which pours water into the shell. In the center of the basin, between the four shells, there is another round basin where eight more frogs are arranged around the rim, poised as if they are about to jump towards the jet of water in the middle. On the Celian Hill, in front of the church of S. Maria in Domnica, is the **fountain** known as the **Navicella** (little ship), which was probably designed by Sansovino and dates from the early 16th century. A jet of water rises

Sacchi, who worked on the design with the architect Marcantonio De Rossi. When it was discovered that the Acqua Acetosa spring was polluted (in the late 1950s), the fountain was abandoned for a long time. At last, this delightful, elegant Baroque fountain has been restored, but it is no longer supplied with water from **Acqua Acetosa**, just normal drinking water. But the fountain itinerary doesn't end here: there are still hundreds more to see.....

Rome and wellness

Beauty farms are the modern temples of wellbeing, with treatments to help the body as well as to find a balance between mental and physical aspects. These are genuine oases of relaxation where one can escape from the frenetic rhythms of modern life. At these 'farms', it is possible to indulge oneself in one of the most precious luxuries, that is, to take a break and to take time entirely for oneself. It is now basically taken for granted that beauty farms are favored by many and are increasingly popular. This might be because the concept of health has transformed, moving ever closer to the notions of inner tranquility, physical wellbeing and appearance. The old saying that one is 'born beautiful' has changed to one 'becomes beautiful'. It is now common to see beauty and health as linked and that looking after one's body does not only mean taking care of appearances, but also includes mental and physical aspects. The various day spas in Rome are city paradises where one can escape from the chaos of the metropolis and from stress by indulging in a wide range of treatments.

Centro Benessere Saturnia Spa
Via Aurelia Antica 415, Tel. 066642740
www.saturniaspa.com
The spa is divided into five complementary areas: hydrotherapy, beauty treatments, stress management, fitness and nutrition. Each section offers a range of treatments, all overseen by qualified staff, aimed at physical and mental wellness.

Culla del Benessere
Via della Maratona 87, Tel. 0636298573
This centre has a pleasant, Moorish feel that is the result of the delightful harmony between the furnishings, lights, steam, foods and opportunities for relaxation. It offers a genuine Moroccan Turkish bath. The wellness route starts with a herbal tea and some sweet pastries, then continues with a steam bath that, with the help of oils, essences and massages, cleanses the body. Next comes the real massage, with natural henna and essential oils, in a room lit by fragrant candles.

De Russie
Via del Babuino 9, Tel. 06328881
www.roccofortehotels.com
This luxurious oasis of peace lies in the heart of the city, between Piazza di Spagna and Piazza del Popolo.
A special touch is added by the historic secret garden with centuries-old trees, orange groves and roses. You can try a number of different treatments, including some that manipulate parts of the body and others that focus on specific problems. There are also the classic beauty treatments and those focusing on physical and mental wellness.

Exedra Boscolo Luxury Hotel
Piazza della Repubblica 47
Tel. 06489381
www.boscolohotels.com
This centre is part of a luxury hotel and is a harmonious, relaxing area. There are treatments and wellness and beauty options: hydromassage using colors, a Turkish bath, herbal teas to build strength and to cleanse, massage therapy, mud therapy, massages, pedicures, manicures and hairdressers.

Roma Cavalieri Hilton Resort & Spa
Via Cadlolo 101
Tel. 0635091
www.cavalieri-hilton.it
This centre lies in a wonderful, green Mediterranean park on the highest of the Roman hills. In a charming atmosphere, you can try a range of wellness programs, including hydromassage, a Turkish bath, sauna, calidarium & frigidarium (a walk through tanks separated by hot stones and cold stones) and beauty treatments for the body and face. A range of massages are also offered: Ayurvedic, shiatsu, physiotherapy and reflexology.

Salus per Aquam
Via Giulia 4
Tel. 066877449
Here, you can try a personal 'route' to help you re-find your wellness, using steam, lights, sounds, fragrances and holistic treatments like shiatsu, Ayurvedic massage and reflexology. There are also some special options, such as a hot stone massage, using a combination of hot stones and essential oils, or a *lushly ritual*, for a sublime manicure or pedicure.

Rome = cinema

Rome has a very special place in the hearts of film enthusiasts. Every corner of the city has been used at some time or other as a location for a famous film, from the masterpieces of Fellini, Rossellini, De Sica and Pasolini, to Hollywood's extravaganzas. Cinecittà at the peak of its success and the popular Roman appeal of actors like Anna Magnani and Alberto Sordi were flanked by a thriving vein of films portraying the vitality and humanity of the countryside around the capital. The Cinecittà studios were founded on the Tuscolana road in 1937, during the Fascist period, when Benito Mussolini wanted to make sure that his empire was backed up by the right political and cultural content in the media world. For many years the studios were the biggest in Europe and Rome, especially after the end of the Second World War, was one of the world's film capitals. Great names like Rossellini and De Sica created a "Roman School" with its headquarters in Cinecittà, which absorbed the talents that flocked to Rome during the postwar period. At the time there was an extraordinary flowering of culture in Italy's capital, which attracted national directing, acting, costume, editing, photography and dubbing talents like a magnet. Rome became not only the home of the national film industry, but also a huge natural set providing a picturesque background to stories that the industry transformed into fairy tales. A series of talented Roman actors such as Alberto Sordi, and in a later generation Carlo Verdone, made Roman sayings and the Roman dialect a mainstay of Italian comedy. The Rome film industry has always identified closely with the image of the city of Rome itself, a city which has often played the lead in big budget costume dramas, a favourite Hollywood device. The city has also been explored by other non-Roman talent: from Fellini to Pasolini, nobody could resist its charm and everyone managed to create their own poetry from the infinite stmuli offered by what is rightly called the Eternal City. The rural scene in the Roman countryside has often played a leading role on the big screen too. Here directors explored the theme of a simple peasant population faced with the social and economic changes wrought by industrialisation and the onset of consumerism. The latest generation of film makers have made an effort to renew Rome's role in the collective minds of cinema goers in the light of the sweeping social changes that have taken place. They are the heirs to a wealth of culture and are faced with the somewhat burdensome task of reconciling it with the continuous evolution of today's reality.

Rome is one of the film capitals of the world, historically intertwined with the growth of the film industry. With its unrivalled profusion of art treasures, its strategic juxtaposition with the sea and the mountains, and its abundant supply of local colour, Rome has a chameleon-like quality possessed by few other cities. Imposing historical stravanganzas and modern urban dramas, middle class family sagas and burnt out lives in shanty towns, can all be catered for. There is no open air set as big and as varied as Rome.

"If Rome didn't exist, I would have dreamt it!"

The fim industry is present in Rome as it is in no other city in Italy. No other city in Italy has been so carefully described, praised and scorned on film as Rome has. The link between the Eternal City and the seventh art is rooted in history, politics and position. Rome was one of the first Italian cities to host film production and cinemas. Long a mirage for its artistic, cultural and historical importance, Rome was further consecrated by the film industry: "If Rome didn't exist, I would have dreamt it!", declared Laurence Olivier in Stanley Kubrick's *Spartacus* (1960). Rome is one of the film industry's natural homes because it is so varied and oozes so much charm, whatever the plot; film makers say that you can set the camera up on any of its street corners and be sure of the result.

Can you reconstruct a whole city from its appearances on film? You certainly can if the city is Rome. There are some unexpected surprises, some inaccuracies, some mystification, but they are all part of the mystique of film making, they only contribute to the city's fascination. Sightseeing film buffs will immediately recognise streets and squares used in shots from hundreds of different films over the years: they will all have the pleasure of recreating their own personal route through their memories.

From Termini Station and the Pantheon to Piazza del Popolo, the "Dolce vita" and more...

Termini Station, the gateway to Rome for those who arrive in train, is a leading player and provides the backdrop for De Sica's *Stazione Termini* (1953 – Indiscretion in the UK), with the middle class couple Montgomery Clift and Jennifer Jones who meet and fall in love in the meanders of the huge station: its platforms, waiting rooms and carriages are all transformed into

TCI HIGHLIGHTS

THE CITY ON A SCOOTER – ROMAN HOLIDAY

In Rome's chaotic traffic a scooter is the only way to get around. In 1953 in William Wyler's Roman Holiday it becomes the romantic, tourist image of Rome in America. Audrey Hepburn had precious memories of the shoot; when she was asked which was her favourite city she declared: "Each city in its own way is unforgettable. But... if you're asking me which my favourite is, it has to be... Rome, yes, it's certainly Rome! I'll always remember this visit as long as I live!". The film is conditioned by its setting, the characters move around the city in characteristic vehicles all made in Italy, like Joe's Vespa. The Vespa became a runaway commercial success in the US thanks to the film. In this film Rome plays the lead, it is not merely the setting, the story is about the city, not just in it. Hepburn and Peck play in an inverted version of Cinderella on a scooter, the symbol of freedom, as they wander through the Eternal City at its most stunning on their Roman Holiday. If you happen to be in Rome try taking a scooter tour round the centre, perhaps starting in Via dei Fori Imperiali. Head towards the Colosseum and follow the contours of the Palatine; between the Circus Maximus and the Tiber lies the church of St Maria in Cosmedin, where the princess and the journalist play with the famous Bocca della Verità. Further on, past the Teatro di Marcello and the white mass of the Vittoriano, is Piazza Venezia, where Anne weaved clumsily in and out of the traffic. At Piazza della Rotonda, in front of the Pantheon, Anne and Joe meet the photographer Irving who secretly snaps the princess smoking her first cigarette. Beyond Via del Corso, in the intricate network of alleys around the Trevi Fountain, you can still hear echoes of the princess' exclamation of amazement as she turns the corner of Via della Stamperia and sees the marble wonder of Rome's, and perhaps the world's, most beautiful fountain. Going back towards the Spanish Steps that lead up to Trinità dei Monti, you can imagine the penniless Anne enjoying an icecream and being given a carnation by a gallant flower seller. Joe Bradley lives in Via Margutta, at N°51, a building which is still home to artists and painters, here the journalist and the princess pass a chaste night together. Lastly, going on to Piazza del Popolo and then along the Tiber embankment to Castel Sant'Angelo, you come to the Sant'Angelo bridge where a houseboat was the scene of a wild party at the end of which the two sweethearts fall into the river and finally kiss.

symbols of a sentimental journey. Fellini also uses this setting for the arrival of his characters over the years: in 1952 the newly-weds on their honeymoon in the *Lo sceicco bianco* (The White Sheik) and in 1986, Marcello Mastroianni and Giulietta Masina playing two elderly entertainers in Ginger and Fred, a bitter look at old age and the vulgarity of television. *Roman Holiday* (1953) by Wyler, consecrate Piazza della Rotonda, the square in front of the Pantheon, as the essence of romance. Just a stone's throw away, on the other side of Via del Corso, down a couple of narrow winding streets, is one of Rome's architectural marvels and a metaphorical shrine in the history of the cinema, the Trevi Fountain. It owes most of its fame to the famous scene from Fellini's *La dolce vita* (1960), when an exuberant Anita Ekberg takes a moonlight dip, coaxing a world-weary, but fascinated, Marcello Mastroianni to follow her example. Fellini shot a myth in the history of the cinema when he concocted this marvellous mixture of beauty and magic suspended in the enchanted aura of a dream. The Trevi Fountain was no novice to the big screen, it had been used by the Lumière brothers in 1896 and was one of the romantic discoveries Audrey Hepburn made during her *Roman Holiday*. But everything following Fellini's masterpiece, an eloquent snapshot of an entire era, was mere imitation, parody or repetition. Back tracking to Via del Corso and turning right as far as Via dei Condotti brings us to the Spanish Steps. More echoes of *Roman Holiday* on the Steps themselves, and in stark contrast the claustrophobic *L'Assedio* (1998), a complicated love story shot by Bertolucci in a flat over the entrance to the underground. The square was also used as a location from one of the scenes in Anthony Minghella's *The Talented Mr. Ripley* (1999), a glossy film version of Patricia Highsmith's novel of the same name, set in a rather conventional portrait of Italy in the 1950s. Via Margutta, home to Rome's artists and painters, also appears in *Roman Holiday*. A small stone plaque on N°110 states simply that:

"This was Giulietta Masina and Federico Fellini's Roman home". Piazza del Popolo, with its twin churches, is full of famous cafés and bars traditionally visited by people from the world of cinema and television. In *La dolce vita* Marcello Mastroianni and his lover Anouk Aimée stop off there during the night and pick up a prostitute as a joke, reversing their car away into the dark.

From stylish Villa Borghese to chic Via Veneto

From the breath taking view of Rome over Piazza del Popolo from the Pincio Gardens it is a short walk over the Muro Torto bridge to Villa Borghese, Rome's most stylish park. In De Sica's Rossellini-inspired *Sciuscià* (1946) – universally acclaimed as the third masterpiece of neorealism after *Roma città aperta* (1945) and *Paisà* (1946), by Rossellini himself – the leading characters, two young shoeshine boys, are having their first riding lesson in the park's stunning Piazza di Siena arena. In *Roma* (1972) Fellini also uses Piazza di Siena as the backdrop to his sarcastic portrayal of a would-be Roman playboy trying to chat up a foreign girl. From one of the park gates on Piazzale Brasile Via Vittorio Veneto, called simply Via Veneto by the Romans, runs down to Palazzo Barberini. This is another part of Rome that became world famous with Fellini's masterpiece *La dolce vita* (1960). Strange but true: Fellini reconstructed the whole street, complete with its pavement cafés and tables, at Cinecittà, and the lively social and cultural environment described so graphically in the film was in reality rather more low key. At the time Via Veneto was far from

being the trendy thouroughfare lined with designer boutiques and five star hotels it is today, it was rather the hangout of penniless writers who camped out at its café tables, a cosmopolitan, picturesque assortment of humanity that became a myth thanks to the cinema.

From Piazza Navona to the Vatican

In the episode dedicated to Mara in De Sica's *Ieri, Oggi, Domani* (1963) Sophia Loren lives in a top floor flat with a stunning view over Piazza Navona, this is the setting where the ravishing Sophia makes her lover Marcello Mastroianni howl with an unforgettable striptease and perturbs a shy young seminarist who lives in the building opposite with his grumpy grandmother. In *The Talented Mr. Ripley* (1999) Freddie, an old friend of Dickie, cuts across the Piazza in his red sports car. Crossing the Tiber over the majestic Umberto I bridge brings us to the Palazzo di Giustizia (the courts), built with trials and tribulations between 1880 and 1911 and known to the Romans as the "Palazzaccio" because of its unfortunate beginnings. It provides the backdrop for several films on the theme of justice, including the sombre *The Trial* (1962) by Orson Welles, based on Franz Kafka's novel.

Following the Prati section of the Tiber embankment towards the Vatican brings us straight to Castel Sant'Angelo. In Pasolini's stunning debut, *Accattone* (The Scrounger, 1961), his anti-hero dives into the river off the Sant'Angelo bridge for a dare, the young bride in *Lo sceicco bianco* also ends up in the water under the bridge in a clumsy suicide attempt, as does Princess Ann with Joe the reporter in *Roman Holiday*. From here the imposing Via della Conciliazione leads to St Peter's and its famous square, the centre of Christianity and symbol of the capital. Bernini's colonnade and Michelangelo's dome are both instantly recognisable images of Rome and are widely used as such by both the cinema and television. For example in *La dolce vita*, Fellini's opening scene is an aerial shot of the dome and the square packed with pilgrims; later on Anita Ekberg rushes up to the summit of the dome, hotly pursued by a horde of paparazzi and Marcello Mastroianni: in reality the scene was shot in a studio, with the actors playing against a backdrop. The Vatican has always fascinated the film industry, both Italian and foreign directors have explored its political workings on several occasions, generally in a rather suspicious fashion, without ever managing to achieve a true, or even realistic, portrait of what goes on behind the austere walls of the world's smallest state. This is undoubtedly in part due to that reserve that only permits access to officially approved film crews (the first footage, of Leo XIII, actually goes back to 1898), so film makers have always had to make do with reconstructions and occasionally unfortunate attempts to interpret the Pope and his world, often verging on the grotesque and with a whiff of the pot boiler. Two examples are

Sophia Loren with the shy young seminarist caught in her toils in the Mara episode of *Ieri, Oggi, Domani*. An Oscar in 1963 for the best foreign film, the story is woven around the style and sheer good looks of Sophia Loren and Marcello Mastroianni in sparkling comic form. The flat where Mara, the exclusive call girl, receives her clients overlooks the magnificent Piazza Navona. The striptease she does for a lustfully howling Mastroianni was repeated by the same couple with a hefty dose of irony thirty-one years later in Prêt-à-Porter by Robert Altman.

Fellini's *Roma*, where a mummified pope presides over an ecclesiastical fashion show, and *The Godfather - Part III* (1990) directed by Francis Ford Coppola, with the Mafia involved in a melodramatic assassination of the pope.

The Tiber Embankment, Trastevere and the Ghetto

Following the river north from the Vatican De Sica's father and son in *Ladri di biciclette* (1948 - *Bicycle Thieves* in the UK) start their search for the stolen bicycle level with the Foro Italico, under the Duca d'Aosta bridge, a search that will take them to the Augusta embankment and downstream to a trattoria next to the Ripetta Walk. Trastevere, Rome's popular heart, overflowing with artists and tourists hunting for local color, makes frequent appearances in Roman films. Fellini makes what comes close to being a documentary in his *Roma*, an impassioned declaration of nostalgic love for a magical city that was gradually losing its charm: the director from Romagna with honorary Roman citizenship describes Trastevere's "festa de' noantri", the fountain in Piazza Trilussa, the alleyways, a polic charge against the hippies in St Maria in Trastevere, the stalls selling watermelon and roast pork, with the American writer Gore Vidal, another Roman by adoption, defining Rome as the "city of illusions". Level with Isola Tiberina stands the district called the Ghetto, sometimes used to provide footage of Rome's quaint streets and sometimes used more dramatically as the home of Rome's Jewish community. The imaginary Hotel Imperial in Piazza Mattei was where an eccentric countess, Ingrid Bergman, taught a very young Liza Minnelli good manners in *Nina* (1976), Vincent Minnelli's last film. And it was here, in Palazzo Costaguti, that the second murder in *The Talented Mr Ripley* takes place.

The ruins of Ancient Rome

The Flavian Amphitheatre, or Colosseum, the universally recognised symbol of Rome, made its film debut in the Lumière brothers' documentaries. Hollywood's films set in ancient Rome made during the fifties and sixties use it regularly as a

setting for fights between gladiators. As in *Quo Vadis?* (1951) by Mervyn LeRoy and *Spartacus* by Kubrick. The famous arena was rebuilt in cardboard in the Hollywood or Cinecittà studios on the basis of debatable, not to mention improbable, historical criteria, but the most accurate and daring reconstruction was undoubtedly Ridley Scott's brand new Colosseum, completely rebuilt on the computer for *Gladiator* (2000) and used on the film's Maltese set. It is also curious how films, especially Italian films, often use the Colosseum as a background rather than a setting. The Colosseum appears in Rossellini's *Paisà* (1946): the Roman episode starts and finishes in its shadow with a fleeing German panzer and an American soldier saying a final farewell to his Roman "Signorina". The Forum also appears in dozens of historical films,

naturally in the guise of more or less accurate reconstructions of how it must have looked at the time of Imperial Rome. In the disturbing nocturnal finale of *Roma* Fellini has a bunch of mute bikers roar straight through the silent monuments of the forum, a metaphor of the modern barbarian hordes devouring civilisation. The *Circus Maximus* instantly brings to mind the famous chariot races in Wyler's *Ben Hur* (1959), where the stuntmen's daring and dexterity still defy description today. In fact the scenes were shot at Cinecittà and one of the assistant directors in charge of the second film unit was a certain Sergio Leone... The Baths of Caracalla, the most sumptuous baths built during the Roman Empire, provide settings for two of Fellini's films. In the dreamy *Le notti di Cabiria* (1957 *Cabiria* in the UK) the heroine Giulietta Masina sees a procession of young pilgrims wending their way to the sanctuary of Divino Amore, something that gives her a renewed purpose in life and gives her back her smile. In *La dolce vita* the baths are the scene of the nightclub where Anita Ekberg launches into a frenetic dance with an American actor. The road that runs past the Terme di Caracalla leads on to the Appian Way, the ancient Roman road that led to Capua and on to Naples. Marcus Vinicius's legions march along it on their way back to Rome in LeRoy's *Quo Vadis?* and at the end of Kubrick's *Spartacus* the rebels are crucified in their thousands along it: however both scenes were shot in studio reconstructions. Further down the same road the candid prostitute Cabiria (Giulietta Masina) in *Le notti di Cabiria* plys her trade near Cecilia Metella's tomb, as does the main character's naive girlfriend in Pasolini's *Accattone* (1961).

The suburbs and the "borgata"

By "borgata" the Romans meant a squalid area on the outskirts of the city that had been drowned in cement by unscrupulous development. Unsightly blocks of flats were flanked by makeshift shanty towns in corrugated iron, scrap and the odd brick. The toothless, starving Capannelle (Carlo Pisacane) from Mario Monicelli's *La banda dei soliti ignoti* (1958) lives in a hovel huddling under a railway embankment in the Nomentana area, the district where all the characters live. This is the tragicomic story of five poor devils who catch wind of a prospective coup from a jailbird, go to lessons in safe-breaking with a

safebreaker who is even more hopeless than they are and then try to raid Rome's pawn bank in vain. A classic Italian comedy inspired by the French thriller *Rififi* (1955) by Jules Dassin, the film can boast a cast that includes Vittorio Gassman (in his first comic role), Marcello Mastroianni, Totò and Claudia Cardinale; it is famous for its rhythm and humour. The splendid scene of the coup was shot in a flat in Via delle Tre Cannelle, near Piazza Venezia, which can still be seen today, while the tram stop where the shabby gang catch the tram back home at dawn is at Porta Metronia, next to the Baths of Caracalla.

These were the years when Pasolini was living in Pietralata; he was a teacher and poet from Friuli who was to become the minstrel of the "borgata" and its "ragazzi di vita". And Pasolini set his first film, *Accattone*, in Pietralata and the Prenestino district, in Via Fanfulla da Lodi at Pigneto, with some scenes on the Appian Way and the Sant'Angelo bridge. *Accattone* became the symbol of lumpenproletarian youth in all its apparently amoral idleness, doomed to an almost sacrificial death: having filched some salami the protagonist escapes on a motorbike and is involved in a traffic accident on the Testaccio bridge. "I'm dandy now!" are his last words as he dies on the cobbles between two other thieves.

In 1985 in the parish church of St Maria Mediatrice in Via Cori, in the Prenestino district, Don Giulio, the character played by Nanni Moretti in his *La Messa è Finita*

TCI HIGHLIGHTS

THE ROME FILM FESTIVAL

Inaugurated on October 13, 2006, the Rome Film Festival has the ambitious aim of becoming Italy's second film festival next to Venice's world famous yearly appointment. The Film Festival is organised by the Music Foundation for Rome and is supported by a large number of institutions, including the Rome City Council. Its headquarters are in the Parco della Musica Auditorium, designed by Renzo Piano, with four cinemas. However numerous other areas and historical reference points (Via Veneto, Cinecittà) are involved in the event with meetings, viewings, exhibitions, concerts and nostalgic events crowding its nine day calendar... The idea of the festival is to involve the whole city in a huge cinema party, dedicated to both festival-goers and the film-loving public as a whole.

Info: Tel. 0645496767 – 0645496776, www.romacinemafest.org

(*The Mass is Ended*), is caught in a generational dilemma that defies solution in this film shot in Rome and Ventotene. Today the whole area has been demolished and Pigneto and Prenestino are trendy residential areas, with nightclubs and art galleries.

Further north, beyond the Montesacro garden city, the Tufello area is home to the protagonists of *Ladri di biciclette*, De Sica's neorealist masterpiece. Antonio, the billsticker protagonist, lives in a council house in the Val Melaina "borgata". The key scene shows Antonio, who was not a professional actor and in real life was unemployed, pasteing up a poster advertising the film Gilda, when his precious bicycle is stolen, this takes place under the high walls in Via Francesco Crispi, close to Villa Medici. The search for the bicycle takes him to Rome's flea market, which in those days was held in Piazza Vittorio, just south of Termini Station, and in the poignant final Antonio in desperation tries to steal another bicycle at the Olympic Stadium.

From Eur to the Sea

Via Cristoforo Colombo, the main road that runs south out of Rome down to the coast at Ostia, Fregene and Fiumicino, cuts through Eur, the district purpose built for the Universal Roman Exhibition, which had been scheduled for 1942. During the war the area languished as a more or less abandoned building site, only to be developed from the fifties onwards. Fellini used it as an open air studio on several occasions, relishing its ascetic, suspended atmosphere, with its almost timeless quality and empty spaces that left him plenty of room to arrange his "toys", the props he used to flesh his dreams out on film. *La dolce vita* opens with a helicopter transporting a statue of Christ which flies over half-finished buildings and a terrace with a swimming pool; this is where Steiner (Alain Cuny) lives, the intellectual who commits suicide and who is the friend of the journalist Marcello (Marcello Mastroianni): the two meet at dawn in the church of St Peter and St Paul, and in Eur Steiner's wife, still unaware of the tragedy, is assaulted by the paparazzi. As it heads towards Ostia Antica the

Via Cristoforo Colombo goes under the Ring Road, the motorway that runs all the way round Rome. Again it is Federico Fellini, in *Roma*, who first describes the almost surreal Dantesque ring of noise, cars hooting, incredible vehicles, rain, roaring engines and eery ladies of the night, all from a reconstruction at Cinecittà. In *Caro diario* (1993 - aka *Dear Diary*) Nanni Moretti winds his Vespa ride up in the field where Pasolini was murdered. In Fregene, which was already a popular holiday resort with the party leaders and would-be actresses of the Fascist regime and later became a favourite spot for Rome's film elite, Fellini (again) uses the pinewoods for his ironic *Sceicco bianco* filmset, a visionary recognition of provincial nobodies who suddenly discover the gilded, false world of the capital and the film industry.

The director from Romagna films the final sequences of *La dolce vita* on the beach of neighbouring Passoscuro, and returns once more to the sea and the pinewoods to make *Giulietta degli spiriti* (1965 - *Juliet of the Spirits* in the USA), dedicated to the existential, sentimental and religious crisis of a middle class Roman matron. Lastly the beach at Fregene is the scene of the sacrifice of the old philosopher and his friends' subsequent banquet with his flesh at the end of Fellini's controversial *Satyricon* (1969).

The Roman Countryside, from Ben Hur to Diabolik, and Via Fellini

Fellini used shots of Castel Gandolfo, Castel di Leva and Acilia for his *Le notti di Cabiria*, and the countryside around Marino and Cerveteri as well as the area around the Acqua Felice Aqueduct for *Il bidone* (1955 - *The Swindlers* in the UK), a crude, realistic look at the squalid undergrowth of small time Roman swindlers with a stunning Broderick Crawford in the guise of a professional confidence trickster. In 1959 some of the sea scenes in Wyler's *Ben Hur* were shot at the Lido Marechiaro beach club in Anzio and in Nettuno. The Lido Marechiaro beach club also provided Pasolini with his setting for his version of the Greek tragedy *Medea* (1969), with Maria Callas.

The spirit of Rome

Rome, like Florence and Venice, is quite unique. In the Eternal City everyday life is impregnated with history. The city's streets and squares are pervaded with immense charm, art and monumentality. But the city also has another, more secretive side to it, less well-known than the one visited on classic tourist itineraries and just as exciting and picturesque. In fact, other side of Rome has many different faces: the peaceful charm of the Protestant Cemetery, the Giardino degli Aranci (or Parco Savello) and the characterful older districts of the city. There follows a description of some of the lesser-known places in Rome, unusual places off the beaten track with a character of their own. You won't find an atmosphere like this anywhere else. Within the context of a city which has traditionally placed the emphasis on the lighter, more carefree side of life, such places are pervaded with a sense of intimacy that makes Rome quite unique.

The Casina delle Civette

In the context of Villa Torlonia, the Casina delle Civette (Little House of the Owls), built in 1839 in a highly original style, is a fine example of Roman eclecticism. Its name comes from the recurring owl motif (and other nocturnal bird species). The exterior of the house is more reminiscent of buildings north of the Alps but the imaginative and fairytale-like architecture, the exuberance of picturesque features such as little towers and covered balconies framed by decorated columns and small pillars, and the sheer caprice of certain details such as the merlons on the cornice of the roof and the elaborate window frames give it the air of a house fit for fairies. This impression is reinforced by the lovely climbing roses which frame the doorways facing the park. Another interesting detail is that many of the windows contain elaborate patterns of colored glass. The interior is now a museum of windows created by Cesare Picchiarini between 1910 and 1925, complete with preparatory drawings, sketches and cartoons, most of which are from the archive of Giuliani, a traditional Roman glazier's firm.

Villa Torlonia, which originally belonged to the Pamphilj family, was sold in 1797 by the Colonna to Giovanni Torlonia. The first restructuring phase was entrusted to the architect Valadier, but Giovanni's son Alessandro made many more alterations to the building. Between 1835 and 1840, the original villa complex was enlarged, magnificent new extensions were built and furnishings were added. Giovan Battista Caretti erected the white monumental gateway on Via Nomentana and the

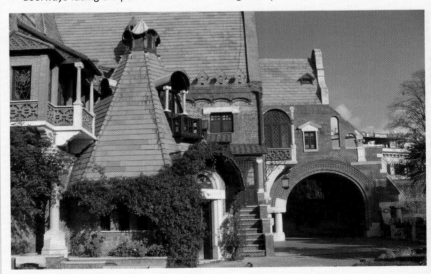

The Casina delle Civette at Villa Torlonia.

fake ruins shrouded in vegetation which merely add to the charm. The nearby Temple of Saturn, decorated with low reliefs on the tympanum and the shrines, is equally picturesque. The creepers climbing up the columns and the vegetation sprouting from the top of the gateway and the cracks in the walls make it look like something out of a set for an adventure film about the discovery of Inca temples in the jungle. During the same period, Giuseppe Jappelli created an English-style garden with original buildings, including a Swiss Chalet. At the beginning of the 20th century, this was converted into the Casina delle Civette, with the addition of the Villino Medievale and the Villino Rosso. The garden of the villa, where palm-trees add a touch of exotica, is planted with cedars of Lebanon, Himalayan and African cedars, magnolias, and, amongst the many other species of palm, the rare blue and Californian palms.

The Ghetto

Almost opposite the footbridge of Ponte Fabricio, where it is not unusual to meet a musician entertaining passers-by, are the synagogue and the beginning of Via del Portico d'Ottavia, once the "gate" of the Ghetto. This district has a very special atmosphere all of its own. The houses here are picturesque and slightly run down, reminiscent of the Rome of films made in the fifties. Under the plaster, which is worn away in places, between the creepers climbing up the walls, you can still see traces of old decoration and inscriptions in Latin. The impression of being in a very old district is reinforced by the cobbled paving, and the slightly uneven surface, which is never quite flat. Walking around the districts of Sant'Angelo and Sant'Eustachio, near Piazza Costaguti, you will discover a more intimate side of Rome with a human dimension. Rome on a smaller scale, still crowded but without the chaos and the stress and the noise. The sounds of the city seem to be muffled in these old streets. If you peep through the windows, you will see what the houses look like inside, old-fashioned and quite different from

modern Roman homes. If you look upwards you will see only a narrow strip of sky and the background noise isn't the noise of a city, but the sound of days gone by: people talking, the occasional sound of a car or motorcycle, and shop-keepers doing business with their customers. This district with its brick buildings is really like a page out of the past, with its workshops, shops, bars and other small venues, presumably much as they were 50 years ago. We recommend you visit the area in the evening or at sunset, when the alleyways and the squares are illuminated by the yellow light of the street lamps. Near the Portico d'Ottavia is an interesting archeological site and, right next to it, a typical *osteria*. If you continue along the street towards the heart of the Jewish district, you will

A typical taverna in the Ghetto district

come to one of the many famous pastry shops in the area and lots of other shops and little restaurants with tables outside, surrounded by hedges made of plants in pots. Via del Portico d'Ottavia is crossed by Via della Reginella, a good example of the real, straightforward side of Rome, full of craft workshops and places restoring antique furniture. The road ends in a little square in a hollow containing the Fontana delle Tartarughe, surrounded by tall buildings. Their windows, small compared to modern windows, cast a warm, colorful glow onto the old ivy-covered walls. Beyond the street corners, some of the narrow alleyways are cul-de-sacs, others are spanned by arches. Between Piazza Costaguti and Piazza delle Cinque Scole there is an amazing variety of buildings. They have little windows with rounded arches, cornices decorated with low reliefs of various kinds. They blend well with one another because they share the same warm colors, mainly brick red.

Turning back towards Portico d'Ottavia, on the wall of the synagogue, there is a moving inscription in memory of the victims of the Holocaust and, on another plaque, the names of victims of the Fosse Ardeatine.

Around Palazzo del Grillo

The area around Palazzo del Grillo, next to the Forum of Augustus, is a fascinating corner of Rome. Its narrow streets paved with uneven cobbles are illuminated by old-fashioned wrought-iron street-lamps. Walking around near the palazzo, many of the houses are covered with creepers, decorated with flowers and plants in terracotta pots, sitting by doorways, on window-ledges and hanging from the balconies. The doors and windows of the palazzi are decorated with a wonderful variety of cornices with architraves or pointed, barrel-vaulted or rounded arches. Often, even the cornices of the roofs are decorated with capitals, columns, and low reliefs. Many of the houses here have characteristic wrought-iron doors (often featuring a lion's head). The atmosphere is one of days gone by with tall, colorful buildings packed close to each other. On the top of the buildings there is often a terrace packed with flower-pots and potted plants, a picturesque part of the city scene. The people who live here go calmly about their daily business. Boxes of fruit and vegetables and other goods are piled high outside the shops. The doorways lead inside to the flights of steps and alleyways of private residential quarters. This district, only a stone's throw from the busy Via dei Fori Imperiali, is quiet and peaceful. To the left of the Monument to Victor Emmanuel II (called the Altare della Patria in Italian), in the area of Trajan's Markets, Trajan's Column and the church of the Santissimo Nome di Maria, a flight of steps leads up to the Torre delle Milizie and the palms and trees of the garden of Villa

Via Baccina, near Palazzo del Grillo, with the Forum of Augustus in the background.

Aldobrandini. At the top of the steps, the road slopes down to the right. Here you can see the typical houses of this area, several storeys high with tall, narrow windows. On the right is a lovely brick house with intersecting arches above the window. On the opposite side of the street are two houses which look identical, but one of them has been restored. Here you can perceive how closely past and present are linked. Further on, taking the street that slopes downhill on the left, we come to the fine building that once housed the printing-press of the Congregazione di Propaganda Fide, which published its first text in 1629.

On the right, between the buildings, you can see the remains of Trajan's Markets and, in the distance, the Monument to Victor Emmanuel II. At the bottom of the hill is the yellow rear facade of Palazzo del Grillo. An archway in the palazzo leads into the small and very picturesque square of the same name. On the left is a palazzo with decorations above the windows and on the cornice. There's a cozy little restaurant on the ground floor with an ivy-covered veranda. Above the veranda is a large wrought-iron balcony full of potted plants. On the right of the square, Via di Campo Carleo is the start of a panoramic walk overlooking the ruins of Trajan's Markets and the Forum of Augustus, the Forum of Nerva and the Forum of Peace. At the start of the walk, there are marvelous views, on various levels, across to the Monument to Victor Emmanuel II, the bell tower of Palazzo Senatorio, the ruins of the Roman Forum, the dome of the church of SS. Luca e Martina and the trees on the Palatine Hill. On the right-hand side of the square is an imposing wall of large stone blocks, part of the beautiful building known as the Casa dei Cavalieri di Rodi, ancient seat of the Knights of St John. The very elegant Palazzo del Grillo (17C) used to belong to the marquis of the same name and has now been converted into private apartments. There are decorated cornices above all the windows: lion's heads and shells or masks are recurring themes in the decoration of the main doorway and the cornice below the roof. The palazzo also incorporates a brick tower with decoration on the top. From the square, we walk up Via degli Ibernesi, a street with plenty of atmosphere. After a bend, the road slopes downhill again. In the middle of the street, just before a short flight of steps is a *nasone* (or drinking fountain, see page 119). Left of the steps, in Via Baccina, where the area of Rome called Suburra begins, a creeper suspended from a wire has created a bridge over the road. Opposite the street market in Via Baccina is Via del Garofano, which slopes downhill at first and then climbs again with lovely views all the way

along of the many terraces decorated with plants and flowers on tops of the buildings below. Retracing our steps, past the steps of Via degli Ibernesi, an archway in the imposing wall in Piazza del Grillo has lovely views down over the magnificent ruins of the Forum of Nerva. We turn down left into Via Tor de' Conti with its many fine buildings. No. 5 is a small antique furniture shop where craftsmen still restore furniture and picture frames. At the end of the street, on the right, is a marvelous view down over the ruins of the Forum of Peace, whereas, opposite, is the Torre de' Conti, a brick building on a base of alternating layers of small white and black stones.

The old Suburra area

In the narrow streets of the area known as Suburra you see a relaxed, domestic side of Rome. Here, flower-pots crowd the balconies, washing is hung out to dry and there is a gentle background buzz. You really have the impression of being in an old *borgo* with its old palazzi of various colors, their doors and windows all decorated in different ways. Down the cobbled side-streets are successions of buildings, differing in terms of architectural style, but sharing a days-gone-by atmosphere. The peeling plaster on the facades blends harmoniously with the decoration on the windows.
At the end of Via Baccina, opposite the *fora*, is the little square of the church of Madonna dei Monti. This small, quiet square on a slight slope has a fountain in the middle. A few cafés with tables outside, on verandas with potted plants, overlook the square. Grass grows in-between the cobbles, adding to the charm. Two small streets lead off the square between the buildings overlooking it. On the wall of one of the buildings on the right, with windows with barrel vaults, a creeper has grown right up to the little roof-top terrace with its collection of plants.

Via degli Zingari, in the old Suburra district.

On the right, there is one of Rome's typical drinking-fountains and the narrow Via Leonina, with a medieval appearance and lots of little shops. One of them, in a brick building with rounded arches above the windows and decorated with more little arches, sells home-made chocolate.

Looking to the left along a street dotted with potted plants, in the opposite direction to the Colosseum, there is a view of the many houses scattered about the hillside: tall, narrow and painted different colors. Parallel to it, Via degli Zingari has a few bars with tables outside defying the unevenness of the cobbles. Continuing uphill, where the street narrows, there is an ivy-covered wall on the left, while, on the right, the window-ledges of the venerable old palazzi are decorated with flower pots. Looking back from here, we can see Via Baccina stretching away between its green walls.

Here the road drops downhill again and, on the right, is a small picturesque street of abandoned buildings overgrown with creepers. Next to a shop where they restore antique furniture, at No. 36, is a bookshop which is also a tea-room and a wine-bar, a place with a real, bohemian atmosphere. Not far away, Via dei Capocci is secluded and silent, with its old-fashioned lamps on the walls, potted plants outside the front doors, shops and old craft workshops.

Via dei Fori Imperiali

If you can close your ears to the din of the traffic, a walk along Via dei Fori Imperiali is like walking through the history of Rome, past the monuments of the Eternal City. Facing the Roman Forum you are higher than the level of the archeological site. As a result, you not only have excellent views of the ruins, but also of the massive Colosseum, the startling white of the "wedding cake", and the lovely domes, bell towers and towers standing out against the skyline. It's as if all this wealth of historical delight has been placed on different levels deliberately to enhance the views. From here we can see ancient buildings stretching up towards the trees on the Capitoline and Palatine Hills. Near the viewpoint is a colorful and very attractive stall surrounded by fruit boxes, decorated with bunches of grapes which only sells fruit.

Viewing the Roman Forum and the Imperial Fora from the Capitoline Hill

A road climbs up from Piazza della Consolazione towards the Capitoline Hill. On either side of it are high walls, partly stone and partly covered with plaster, hung with wrought-iron street-lamps. Above the walls, among the buildings which cover the Capitoline Hill, you can see trees, bushes, small expanses of ivy, all kinds of unexpected vegetation (there is even grass sprouting from the roof of the nearby church of S. Maria della Consolazione!). Just before you reach the viewpoint, the road passes under a large brick archway, after which the view opens out over the *fora*. Here, high above the archeological site, you can

The Roman and Imperial Fora from Via dei Fori Imperiali.

The view over the Roman and Imperial Fora from the Capitoline Hill.

look out across the Basilica Julia and the Arch of Septimius Severus in the foreground with the other ruins stretching out into the distance, to the Roman Forum, the church of SS. Cosma e Damiano, S. Maria Antiqua, S. Francesca Romana with its tall bell tower. In the distance, on the horizon, are the arches of the Colosseum and, with luck, the sun shining through them. To the right, above the roofs of the city, the green Palatine Hill, where the trees mingle with the arches of the ancient buildings. The view from here is breathtaking, the silence thought-provoking. Seen from here, these ancient ruins with their fallen and broken columns are a stunning sight. The view stretches away towards the high arches of the Basilica of Maxentius (or Constantine). Between its columns you can see Via Cavour climbing up the Esquiline Hill and, to the left, the church of S. Lorenzo in Miranda and, behind the arch of Septimius Severus, the dome of SS. Luca e Martina, against a background of the Torre delle Milizie, trees, domes, roofs and green roof-top terraces. Behind the viewpoint are the great palaces of the Capitoline Hill and, dotted around everywhere, amongst ruins and houses, umbrella pines,

palm-trees and slender cypresses. Directly below the viewpoint is the old, uneven Roman road, paved with large stones, still in use today after 2,000 years. The white arch of Septimius Severus shines in the sun. Despite the fact that it bears obvious marks of the passing of time, it has retained its dignified monumental character. Then, looking to the right, the Palatine Hill, its trees intermingled with the arches of the buildings on its slopes and the ancient brick walls, is simply begging to be explored. This is the perfect spot to rest and contemplate the ruins.

The Aventine Hill

Leaving the traffic of Via del Circo Massimo behind, suddenly, on the Aventine Hill, you are surrounded by silent green avenues where the only sounds are the occasional passing car and birdsong. The chaos of the city lies lower down, apparently far away. The only people walking about here seem to be kindly priests (in fact many monasteries were founded here in medieval times and there are still a number of churches) who, when you ask the way, offer answers in several languages. Via di S. Sabina passes Piazza S. Pietro d'Illiria on the right, with the church

The magnificent view from the Giardino degli Aranci.

of S. Sabina and a delightful fountain where water pours out of a moustachioed face into the basin below. Next to it is the entrance to Parco Savello (better known as Giardino degli Aranci – Orangerie – because of its many citrus trees). You access the garden through a porch which was once part of Villa Balestra in Via Flaminia and which was brought here and incorporated in the walls.

The park is surrounded by a high brick wall which looks very like an ancient wall, being covered with ivy and topped with grass. The park is spacious, simple and kept meticulously tidy. It consists of a square divided into two by a gravel path which intersects with another in the middle, forming a cross. In the center of the garden is a fountain. Citrus trees in elaborately decorated terracotta vases set on marble bases line the edges of the gravel paths forming the cross in the center.

The foliage of tall umbrella pines planted around the four green squares provides shelter for the citrus trees planted in the middle, where the grass is kept short. The citrus trees planted in orderly rows and the pines surrounding them form a lovely peaceful setting. The viewpoint at the far end of the park, high above the city (here it feels as high as the top of the dome of St Peter's) is utterly unique. To the right stands the white form of the Monument to Victor Emmanuel II and, behind it, the bell tower of the Capitoline Hill and the Torre delle Milizie. To the left, many domes mark the skyline (note the dome of the synagogue among the tree-tops), the Tiber stretches out lazily like a snake, edged with trees and, opposite, is the huge dome of St Peter's, dominating everything else.

The dome is right on the line of the horizon as if holding the sky and the earth together. From here, you can see for miles, beyond the city, to the hills and the countryside which lie outside Rome.

If we continue along Via di S. Sabina, we come to a small square surrounded by a white wall. Beyond it, among the trees, is the lovely church of S. Anselmo. On the right is the monumental doorway of the seat of the Order of the Knights of St John. Stop for a moment and look through the keyhole of the door.

At the end of a long, straight gravel path with bushes on either side, in the center of the view, is the dome of St Peter's, seemingly suspended between earth and sky.

Between the Giardino degli Aranci and the square of the Knights of St John is another small garden, right below the bell tower with two-light windows belonging to the church of S. Alessio.

The Esquiline Hill

The earliest evidence for occupation of the Oppian Hill refers to some of the most luxurious houses of the Late Republican period. The first monument to be built in the area was the Porticus Liviae, which Augustus built to honor his wife. Subsequently, the hill was incorporated within the perimeter of Nero's huge Domus Aurea (Golden House), which stretched from the Palatine Hill as far as the Esquiline Hill. One of the most representative sectors of the Domus Aurea still lies on the eastern side of the hill. After Nero's death, many areas were turned over to public use by the Flavian emperors, who built large buildings such as the Flavian Amphitheater (better known as the Colosseum) and the Baths of Titus. The last two were built close to the pavilion of the Domus Aurea, in a complex built on at least two levels: a lower level with rooms with barrel-vaulted ceilings and an upper level with raised floors with underground heating known as *suspensurae*. The buildings, which seem to date from various periods, probably belonged to the main part of the baths complex, and were probably re-used and extended several times in the Late Classical period. The hill's Classical vocation was later accentuated by the building of the monumental Baths of Trajan, which had better exposure to the sun.

The complex, which covered an area of approximately 1 km², had a large walled garden. The baths building had rooms arranged symmetrically on either side of the main complex. The water supply came from a huge cistern (Cisterna delle Sette Sale) with a capacity of 8 million liters of water.

Today, the Esquiline Hill is seldom visited. Tourists tend to be more attracted by the nearby archeological area of the Colosseum and the fora. However, it is one of the city's many public parks. The entrance to the park is a gateway supported by square columns opposite Via Labicana. Climbing up Viale della Domus Aurea lined with tall, slender cypresses, ruins appear on the left in the vegetation. The whole park is criss-crossed by little paths and there are a number of fountains. On the right there are several viewpoints looking onto Via Labicana and the archeological site below. If we climb up further to the top of the hill, the noise of the city gradually disappears and is replaced by a silence and a tranquillity which we don't expect to find in the middle of a city. Here, the vegetation opens out in the form of vast meadows shaded by palms and umbrella pines, with beautiful views over the ancient ruins through the branches.

The park is surprisingly large and, with the Parco Traiano next door, offers plenty of scope for peaceful walks. The view from the top of the hill is unforgettable.

The Protestant Cemetery

When, in the 18th century, new ecclesiastical laws of the Papal States forbade the burial of non-Catholics in consecrated ground, Protestants used to be buried in an area with a bad reputation next to the Muro Torto. In the 1720s, under pressure from James Stuart III, the Old Pretender, who had been granted asylum by the Pope, a more dignified place was found for Protestant burials near the Pyramid of Cestius. After 1822, burials were no longer permitted in the old part of the cemetery and another

One of the ancient ruins on the Oppian Hill.

The inscription on the tomb of poet John Keats.

site was found in the area by the Aurelian walls. This is how the cemetery reached its present configuration and, in 1898, a small chapel was added. In 1918, the cemetery, widely known as the Protestant Cemetery although it contains the graves of Jews and other non-Christians, was declared a "Monumental Area of National Interest". Today, in a lovely setting of ornamental shrubs, flowers and fruit trees, shaded by tall umbrella pines and towering cypresses, the cemetery is a treasure-trove of delightful funerary monuments reflecting 19th-century taste, with Classical and Romantic influences. There are all kinds of funerary monuments and tombs here: small delicately decorated temples, elaborate creations in marble and travertine with white marble busts and sculptures surrounded by low hedges, mosaics, columns, crosses, friezes in low relief, small arches crowned

with flowering creepers, and touching inscriptions. Some particularly worthy of note include the "Angel of Grief", the poetic statue of "Psyche removing her mortal remains" and the touching epitaph on the tomb of the poet John Keats ("Here lies one whose name was writ in water"). The cemetery, defined by Oscar Wilde as "the holiest place in Rome", contains the remains of Italians and foreigners alike: great artists, philosophers, writers, musicians, archeologists and diplomats, including Gramsci, Gadda and Goethe's only son. It is difficult to imagine anywhere else in the city that is so peaceful, romantic and mysterious. The cemetery is a delight to visit because of its old-fashioned beauty, and because, between its bushes and flower-beds, it conceals secret, enchanted places. There is a marked contrast between the white of the tombs and the vivid colors of the luxuriant vegetation. The place is so quiet that you can hear birds singing. It's a place for contemplation, and watching the numerous cats which roam among the tombstones. It's difficult to tear yourself away. When you get outside, and look back at the trees which tower above the cemetery walls, it seems like a secret, magical oasis of peace in this busy city. Not long before he drowned and was buried here, Percy Bysshe Shelley wrote: "It might make one in love with death to think that one might be buried in so sweet a place".

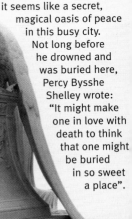

The "Angel of Grief" in Rome's Protestant Cemetery.

The Monastery Garden
of S. Croce in Gerusalemme

The monastery garden is situated inside the ruins of the Anfiteatro Castrense built by the Emperor Heliogabalus in the 3rd century as an Imperial theater for *venationes* (that is, hunting spectacles involving soldiers and wild beasts). It's the only one of its kind in Rome, apart from the Colosseum. Later, it was incorporated by Aurelian into his walls for defensive purposes. It then fell into decline and was turned into a garden in the 9th century when a

HORTUS CONCLUSUS – THE SYMBOLISM

In the early Middle Ages, gardens in monasteries were very small, while cloisters were built according to very precise symbolism to represent Paradise. Inside these walled gardens we find the flowers which symbolize the Virgin Mary together with other plants which symbolize aspects of Paradise. The well or cistern in the center symbolizes Christ, and represents the Host, the symbol of love, communion and regeneration. The four paths symbolize the rivers mentioned in the Bible. Fruit trees symbolize the Tree of Life and the Tree of Knowledge. Laurel symbolizes eternity, because it is an evergreen, and chastity because its leaves never wither. The palm is the symbol of martyrdom. The olive tree is the symbol of peace between God and Man.

Myrtle symbolizes the Virgin Mary, especially her purity and humility, because of its delicate white flowers. The cypress symbolizes mourning and grief. The cypress is also associated with the Virgin Mary, Christ and the Church because it grows upwards towards Heaven. The cross on which Jesus was crucified is supposed to have been made with cypress wood, and since the church of S. Croce owns some fragments of the Cross, this tree is of particular significance. The vine is attributed to Christ, and symbolizes the Eucharist, Christ's blood and his Passion. Lily of the valley symbolizes the Coming of the Savior and his Incarnation because it flowers during Advent. It is also associated with the purity and innocence of the Madonna. The tulip symbolizes the sin of vanity, because its beauty recalls the transience of earthly goods. The lily symbolizes chastity and purity, attributes of the Madonna, and always features in depictions of the Annunciation. The iris is another flower associated with the Virgin Mary and sometimes features instead of the lily in the Annunciation. The rose and its thorns are symbolic of the torment suffered by the martyrs. The church of S. Croce has two thorns which, which along with the climbing roses in the garden, symbolize the agony suffered by Christ. The Virgin Mary is referred to as "the rose without thorns" because she was not touched by Original Sin, and, before the Fall of Man, the rose had no thorns. The violet symbolizes modesty and humility. The lemon is attributed to the Virgin since it is a powerful antidote to poison. For this reason, and because it grows under the sun's rays, it signifies salvation. It is also the symbol of faithfulness in love, because it produces fruit throughout the year. The orange tree with its white blossom symbolizes chastity and purity in marriage and is traditionally worn by the bride. The pomegranate depicted in the hand of the Christ-child is the symbol of the Resurrection. Held in the hand of the Madonna, it symbolizes her chastity. It also represents the Church, which is able to unify many peoples and cultures in one faith. The strawberry symbolizes Paradise. Its three-lobed leaves symbolize the Trinity, while its tiny white flowers allude to innocence and humility. Its color is reminiscent of the blood of Christ, and hence the Passion. The fig tree sometimes represents the Tree of Good and Evil but it also symbolizes indulgence because Judas hung himself from a fig-tree. In Ancient Rome, on the other hand, the fig-tree had a positive association and symbolized fertility and well-being.

monastery was annexed to the church of S. Croce. In 16th century prints, the area already features in its current format. This charming place, unknown to many Romans, is included in the itinerary which starts at the Basilica of St John Lateran and leads past the Aurelian walls to the Anfiteatro Castrense. Now, the garden is organized as it was originally, with the same vegetables, flowers, fruit and herbs. There are even guided tours of the garden, which combines esthetics with the symbolic meanings of the plants (see box: insert). The flowers, medicinal plants, fruit-trees and vegetables are arranged in the

with vegetables, either in lines or concentric circles, following the shape of the theater. On the right of the fountain, covered with a luxuriant laurel hedge, is a small citrus plantation with old trees from the original garden. This citrus plantation is mirrored by another on the left, creating a sort of ante-chamber planted with the original vegetable species: two varieties of peas and broad beans, replaced in summer by eggplant, tiny tomatoes, green beans and basil. The secret of successful vegetable gardening is all about knowing how to combine the growing of pulses, vegetables and salads in an

The monastery garden of S. Croce in Gerusalemme, with the statues of St John Lateran in the background.

shape of a cross, a clear reference to the Benedictine motto *Ora et labora* (Pray and Work). Vines (ancient Roman varieties) and white climbing roses trained on high pergolas provide shade throughout the garden. Beneath them grow wild strawberries, violets, blue agapanthus, megasea and vittadinia. The little paths are edged with ancient stones found in the garden: pieces of stone and marble lie side by side next to ordinary bricks in a logical re-use of old material. In the center of the garden, the large, low, round basin covered with tufa and a soft layer of moss is used for watering the garden. The cross-shaped structure of the garden where the cultivated areas are situated are planted

intelligent "collaborative" way. Against the walls at the far end of the garden, where it's cooler and shadier, there are blackberries, apples, radishes, tarragon and chives. In addition to citrus fruit, there are other fruit trees (figs, persimmons, pomegranates, kiwi fruits and an olive tree). Patches of color are provided by stocks, lilies, lilies of the valley, daffodils, roses, narcissus, tulips and a few calicanthus and camelia bushes. The Cistercian monks of the monastery look after the garden. Thanks to their work, the place stays alive, changing continuously with the seasons, following the natural cycles of the plants.

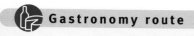
The flavors of Rome: typical local dishes and international cuisine

It's a well-known fact that you eat well in Rome. Roman cuisine must be one of the oldest, and is steeped in ancient traditions. Tourists who visit Rome soon discover how tasty food is here, and enthuse wildly about classics such as *bucatini all'amatriciana*, *rigatoni co' la pajata* and *facioli co' le cotiche*. Traditional Roman recipes are the legacy of centuries of culinary activity, yet another example of the city's close links with the past. Rome is rightly proud of its status as a world metropolis in the field of gastronomy, with an offering that delights the palates of gourmets who come here from every corner of the globe.

The next section follows the cultural routes of the Heritage section of this guide, and suggests places where you can get to grips with the gastronomic side of Rome, replenish your energy and delight your taste-buds, as you work your way from one sight to another.

Route 1

On your way around the monuments described in the section on the Holy City, you can have your first taste of Rome's magnificent food and wine. But Rome also offers a wide range of specialties from other regions of Italy and also a good selection of international cuisine. You may begin with a delicious breakfast at the **Bar Bella Napoli**, at 246 Corso Vittorio Emanuele II. This is one of the area's most popular bars. Not only does it serve great coffee: it also serves delightful sweets and cakes from the south of Italy such as *cannoli*, *cassate* and ice-cream. We also recommend their savory southern Italian specialties for a quick snack. Close to the Bar Bella Napoli is the **Pizzeria Montecarlo** (13 Vicolo Savelli, Tel. 066861877, www.sevoinapizzadillo.com), famous for its exquisite pizzas and traditional *primi piatti* (rice, pasta or soup dishes). Not far away, located in one of Rome's most beautiful

and characteristic districts, between Campo dei Fiori and San Pietro, at 129a Via dei Banchi Vecchi (parallel to Corso Vittorio Emanuele II), is **Ristorante Il Pagliaccio** (Tel. 0668809595, www.ristoranteil pagliaccio.it). This elegant venue serves traditional cuisine with a creative touch, and is in the medium-high price-range. Its cuisine is well worth trying. The restaurant consists of two pleasant rooms with a small lounge for aperitifs or after-dinner drinks, and an impressive wine-cellar on the ground floor with about 150 Italian wines. Close by is **Salumeria di Via dei Banchi Vecchi**, with an old-fashioned white marble counter. In winter, they sell fresh ricotta made that morning and their own salamis and hams. If we continue along Via del Pellegrino, at 22 Campo de' Fiori we find **Forno Campo de' Fiori** (Tel. 0668806662, www.fornocampo defiori.com). This baker's has an excellent reputation locally. You can

TCI HIGHLIGHTS

CODA ALLA VACCINARA

This dish was conceived in the trattorias around a Roman slaughterhouse where the workers used to collect the parts of meat that could not be sold.
The fat is removed from the tail, which is then cooked in a meat and tomato sauce with lots of herbs and sultanas, pine-nuts and bitter chocolate.
Tiny pieces of chopped celery are added at the end.

TRIPPA ALLA ROMANA

This is one of Roman cuisine's most flavorsome dishes.
The recipe involves cooking the tripe for a long time. (Tripe is a cow's stomach cut into thin strips). Its wonderful flavor is the result of cooking the boiled tripe for a shorter time in a sauce made with celery, carrots, onions and tomatoes.
Just before serving, mint, and grated pecorino and parmesan cheese are added.

buy not only cakes, pizzas by the slice and home-made pizzas, but also Rome's famous *pizza bianca*.
The bakery opened during the Renaissance, and has been providing delights for Roman palates ever since, although it no longer sells bread. Another address worth noting in the Campo de' Fiori area is 74/75 Piazza della Cancelleria. **Ristorante Ditirambo** (Tel. 066871626, www.ristoranteditirambo.com) serves tasty traditional Italian cuisine and first-class salamis, hams and cheeses. This charming venue, divided into two small dining-rooms, is half-way between a French bistrot and an old-fashioned Roman *osteria*. It serves pasta (including that typical Roman specialty *tonnarelli a cacio e pepe* and the ubiquitous *fettuccine*), home-made bread and desserts. It also has an impressive wine-list, all very reasonably priced. At 21 Via dei Giubbonari is the **Antico Forno Roscioli** (Tel. 066875287), a very trendy place (and rather pricey as a result), popular with actors, celebrities and other famous personalities. It has been doing business for 30 years. As well as having an excellent range of Italian and foreign wines, it has an impressive choice of cheeses, hams and salamis from Lazio, as well as pasta and desserts made on the premises and dishes requiring a great deal of

preparation. On the same street, the perfect place for a delicious breakfast is **Bar Bernasconi** (16 Piazza Cairoli Benedetto, Tel. 0668806264), which has a historic bakery churning out cakes and ice-cream, some based on Jewish recipes. Try their freshly-made *cornetti* or cakes in the morning or their delicious savory nibbles at lunch-time. Next to Ristorante Roscioli is the **Filettaro di S. Barbara** (88 Largo dei Librari, Tel. 066864018), where you can taste their excellent fried fillet of cod, and they have tables outside where you can enjoy your food and Rome's mild climate. **Ristorante Cul de Sac** (73 Piazza Pasquino, Tel. 0668801094), opposite the famous statue of Pasquino, is a historic venue that is very popular with Romans and tourists alike. It has a charming ambience with wooden tables and wall-to-wall bottles. The cuisine here is imaginative, but does not neglect the classics of the Roman tradition, such as *trippa* (tripe) and *coda alla vaccinara* (oxtail). Try their excellent range of cheeses, hams and salamis, accompanied by sweet and spicy sauces. Medium price-range.
At the **Bar Latteria**, at 4 Vicolo del Gallo, they serve delicious *maritozzi* with cream. 56 Piazza del Paradiso is **Josephine's Bakery** (Tel. 066871065), a jolly place for a cup of tea, serving home-made cakes. Behind St Peter's,

TCI HIGHLIGHTS

THE SPECIALTIES OF THE ROMAN CUISINE

The *antipasti* in Roman cuisine are for whetting your appetite for the *primo piatto*. So they tend to be a selection of savory tastes of temptation rather than full-size dishes. *Bruschetta alla romana* - Bruschetta is well-known: a slice of firm bread toasted or baked in the oven, rubbed hard with garlic and served with a drizzle of extra virgin olive oil. *Crostini alle alici* – Slices of bread with mozzarella are baked in the oven until golden, then spread with a sauce made with milk, butter and finely chopped anchovy fillets. *Panzarella* – Slices of stale bread are soaked in water and are then rubbed with very ripe tomatoes. Tomatoes are then placed on top of the slices of bread and seasoned with salt, extra-virgin olive oil, vinegar and basil.

Gnocchi alla romana – The traditional recipe for *gnocchi alla romana* uses potatoes to make the gnocchi, but nowadays, in international cuisine, the name refers to small round slices of semolina that have been cooked in milk and added to egg yolks and cheese. The circles of semolina are then laid in an oven-proof dish, sprinkled with butter and grated cheese, baked in a hot oven and served piping hot. *Rigatoni co' la Pajata* –

at 43/45 Via Mengarini, is **Ristorante Le Tre Zucche**, formal and sophisticated, which serves simple, excellent cuisine, and the hospitality is exceptional. North of St Peter's, in the Piazzale Mazzini area, is **Bar Antonini** in Via Sabotino (Tel. 0637517845-063724354), with a traditional ambience. It has delicious local *pasticcini*, excellent ice-cream, and delicious savories to have with drinks. If you fancy looking down on Rome from Monte Mario, do stop at the **Bar Zodiaco** (Tel. 0635496640), at 90 Viale Parco Mellini, in a lovely setting: very romantic, especially at night when the city lights add to this already delightful city.

ITINERARIES

Route 2

Near Via del Corso, it's worth stopping at the **Palazzetto** in Vicolo del Bottino (http://www.wineacademyroma.com/it/it-ristorante.htm) This small palazzo houses a café with a terrace overlooking the Spanish Steps. It is very popular in summer at Happy Hour. The palazzo was built in the 16th century and was rebuilt in 1898. In 1998, the film producer Bertolucci chose it as the setting for his film *L'Assedio (The Siege)*, set in springtime in the historic center of Rome. The palace has been lovingly restored to its former glory by exposing original materials and beautiful architectural details. On the ground floor, in the center of the beautiful circular staircase with a wrought-iron banister, is a 19th-century polychrome marble floor. The dishes served in the restaurant in the palace are a compromise between traditional and modern cuisine, and it's fairly expensive. The chef uses fresh, genuine ingredients which vary according to the season and what is available. The home-made pasta and bread are delicious, and, for wine lovers, there are more than 400 wines to choose from. The Palazzetto also organizes interesting tasting courses,

One of the most typical dishes of Roman cuisine. The gut of a young calf is chopped up fine and cooked with oil, garlic, parsley, white wine, tomatoes and chili pepper, then served with *rigatoni* (a type of pasta). The *pajata* can also be cooked in the oven with potatoes, a lot of olive oil, salt, fennel, garlic and rosemary. This dish is sometimes served as a main course.

Fagioli con le cotiche – Boiled beans are added to boiled pork skin. They are mixed in a pot and cooked gently with lard, ham fat, garlic, parsley and tomato sauce.
Fritto misto alla romana – This dish belongs to Italy's great tradition of fried dishes and includes calf's brains, liver, artichokes, courgettes, ricotta, apples, pears, and slices of bread dipped in milk. There is another version which consists of slices of lean meat, lamb cutlets and vegetables which have been boiled, and dipped in a batter of water, flour and oil. *Saltimbocca alla romana* – This Roman dish has rightfully won a place in international cuisine. Thin slices of veal are fixed to a slice of cooked ham and a sage leaf with a toothpick. They are then cooked with butter and a little white wine.

which are sometimes held in English and French. But people who really want to taste traditional Roman cuisine should go to the **Trattoria Campana** (18, Vicolo della Campana, Tel. 066867820), which has the claim to fame of being Rome's oldest restaurant. It has very simple, old-fashioned decor, a comfortable atmosphere and great character. It is in the medium price-range.

Route 3

Another recommendation near Via del Corso, at 42 Piazza di Pietra, is the **Bar Salotto 42** (Tel. 066785804), where you can enjoy books and coffee simultaneously. Located opposite the Temple of Hadrian, the venue is a mixture of old and new. With its walls lined with bookshelves and cosmopolitan atmosphere, Salotto 42 is not only a bookshop but also a lounge bar serving Scandinavian food. The store, selling CDs, jewelry, watches and cufflinks, also has information about art and cultural events. Book and film presentations are held here in a musical setting. Another place worth stopping is the **Caffettiera** at 61 Via Margutta, housed in a former painter's studio. You can still see the lovely Art-Nouveau glass ceiling and the large room which used to be the artist's studio. Here the food is based mainly on Neapolitan cuisine.

Another is the **Atelier Canova Tadolini** (150/a/b Via del Babuino, Tel. 0632110702), where they serve coffee, tea, hot chocolate and wine, and which has plaster casts of some of Canova's works.

Route 4

When you explore the area between the Torre delle Milizie and the Trevi Fountain, you simply must stop at the fashionable **Ristorante F.I.S.H.** (which stands for Fine International Seafood House, at 16 Via dei Serpenti, Tel. 0647824962). The name says it all. In fact, here, the menu is entirely fish-orientated. It's an international restaurant and sushi-bar based on international cuisine, with a minimalist ambience and obvious marine decor. So be prepared for a mega-fish experience, both raw and cooked. There are three menus to choose from: Mediterranean, Oriental and Oceania. Some dishes hail from the Mediterranean tradition and others from Sushi New Generation cuisine, which means traditional sushi and sashimi dishes with innovative ingredients and new recipes. It has a good wine-list with Italian and international labels. Good price-quality ratio. The fish in this trendy venue is always extremely fresh, so it's worth paying a bit more. Another must is the **Enoteca Trimani Wine Bar**

TCI HIGHLIGHTS

CARCIOFI ALLA GIUDIA

This dish is of Jewish origin and is yet another indication of the numerous influences in Roman cuisine. The recipe involves removing the stalk and tougher outside leaves of

the artichokes. The softer, more edible parts of the artichoke are then cooked in oil before being fried, once again with boiling oil. As always, various different forms of this recipe have evolved, with some of the most common being listed here: *carciofi alla matticella*, typical of Velletri, named after the bundle of dry sticks over which they used to be cooked; *carciofi alla romana*, which are stuffed with the tender part of their own stalks mixed with mint, salt and pepper and then cooked in water and olive oil, and another recipe with peas called *carciofi con i piselli*.

(37/b Via Cernaia, Tel. 064469630), certainly a benchmark in Rome when it comes to quality wines. It's a brightly-lit venue with pale wood furnishings, a long counter and shelves full of bottles of wine and spirits. It has paper napkins but high-quality cutlery, and the restaurant has an interesting, wide-ranging menu with classic *primi piatti* (rice, soups and pasta dishes), beef from Argentina, swordfish, *crostini*, quiches and an interesting selection of hams, salamis and cheeses from Italy and further afield, in the middling price-range.

Route 5

The historic heart of Rome has some of Rome's most treasured venues. They include the restaurant **La Sora Lella** (16 Via Ponte 4 Capi, Tel. 066861601, www.soralella.com), on Isola Tiberina, where the traditions of Roman trattorias blend with modern influences. Sora Lella was Elena Fabrizi, sister of a famous actor called Aldo Fabrizi. Today, the restaurant (three charming dining-rooms on two floors) is run by the next generation of the same family. They serve typical Lazio cuisine with imaginative touches which still reflect the great Roman culinary tradition. The desserts are home-made and it has a vast range of wines and cheeses from the region. The menu, of very high quality, changes according to the season and enables you to taste what's available locally at a medium-high price. In addition to their famous *fettuccine* (home-made of course) and the classic *tonnarelli*, you can sample wonderful *carciofi alla giudia, baccalà alla romana in guazzetto* and local *abbacchio*. Another very typical restaurant at the lower end of the price-range is the **Antica Osteria da Giovanni** (41/a Via della Lungara, Tel. 066861514). The Roman Ghetto is famous for its cake shops, which sell bread and cakes made on the premises. Wonderful smells of candied fruit and almonds waft down the streets nearby. In Via del Portico d'Ottavia you will find **Forno del Ghetto**, an old bakery specializing in Jewish cakes, frequented as much by Romans as by tourists, and the **La Dolce Roma** cake-shop (at 20), which specializes in Austrian cakes but also makes traditional Roman specialties. Right next to the old

ABBACCHIO

Traditional *abbacchio* (the Roman name for lamb), one of the most typical dishes of Roman cuisine, is really a lamb stew made with the leg and shoulders of a young lamb, but one version can also be baked in the oven. *Abbacchio alla cacciatora* is made with garlic, rosemary, white wine, anchovies and chili pepper. The name *abbacchio a scottadito* (meaning "burn your fingers") involves cooking lamb cutlets on the grill and turning them over several times. While they are cooking, the cutlets are repeatedly basted using a sprig of rosemary dipped in a marinade of oil, salt and pepper. *Abbacchio brodettato*, a typical Easter lunch dish, is covered with a sauce which gives it an unusual flavor. The recipe involves sealing the lamb in a pan with oil, salt, pepper, and chopped onion and ham. Afterwards it is dusted with flour, sprinkled with white wine, and covered with hot water until the liquid turns into a thick sauce. When it is cooked, egg yolks, lemon and chopped herbs are mixed together and poured over the lamb. *Braciolette d'abbacchio fritte panate* – This is another recipe for lamb cutlets. First the cutlets are tossed in a mixture of eggs, salt, pepper and breadcrumbs, then they are fried in very hot oil.

Portico is the **Osteria da Gigetto**, a treasure-trove of Roman cuisine, where you can sample *carciofi alla giudia* prepared according to the traditional recipe. Close by is the **Trattoria Sora Margherita**, which you enter by a small door on Piazza delle Cinque Scole. The atmosphere is warm and friendly and you can eat real Roman food at a reasonable price. The walls are covered with newspaper cuttings and the chef often comes out to chat to her customers. First comes a large carafe of wine and a generous helping of *tonnarelli a cacio e pepe*. And then, as red stains begin to cover the paper tablecloth, a plate of *carciofo alla giudia* with crispy leaves, and finally the ubiquitous lamb. Here, the customers are regulars. Slightly further away, in the Testaccio district, at 29 Via Mastro Giorgio, is one of Rome's historic restaurants, **Felice** (Tel. 065746800), with a sophisticated, charming ambience. Dishes served here include *bucatini cacio e pepe* (prepared by the chef at table), *bucatini alla amatriciana* and *bucatini alla carbonara*. They also do very good tripe, melt-in-your-mouth *coda alla vaccinara* (oxtail) and *abbachio*, in other words, the best of classic Roman cuisine at a reasonable price. Another venue in the same area, at 30 Via Monte Testaccio, is the famous **Ristorante Checchino dal 1887** (Tel. 065746318, www.checchino-dal-1887.com), with barrel vaulting, located under Monte dei Cocci. Their

traditional menu includes classics like *insalata di zampi*, *rigatoni con la pajata*, *coda alla vaccinara*, *cicoria di campo*, matured *pecorino romano* and *torta di ricotta*. In Viale di Porta Ardeatina, **Casa del Jazz** (Tel. 067008370, www.casajazz.it) is a magnificent villa next to the Aurelian walls of Porta Latina. Having been rescued from the clutches of organized crime, it has been transformed into a restaurant and café with a jazz auditorium. The ambience is friendly and its three dining-rooms are always decorated with flower- and fruit-arrangements to give it a Mediterranean flavor. The menu is a delightful contrast of the products of sea and land. Freshly-caught fish are displayed on the counter in the middle of the dining-room, where you can choose your fish and watch it being cooked (their sushi and sashimi dishes are divine). In the Portuense area, at 20 Via Pian Due Torri, is the **Pasticceria Cecere** (Tel. 0655285868), a stronghold of Roman tradition, with quality products ranging from sweet to savory.

Route 6

When you visit the St John Lateran area, **Passion Chocolate** is a great place for chocolate *aficionados* (116 Via S. Giovanni in Laterano, Tel. 3395871406). Right opposite the little church of S. Clemente, close to the Colosseum, this little shop sells chocolate galore, handmade

TCI HIGHLIGHTS

ROME'S JEWISH TRADITION

The Jewish community in Rome dates back to as early as the 1st century BC. From 1556 until the end of the Papal States in 1870, Jews were restricted to living in a small area of the city that came to be known as the Ghetto, between Campo dei Fiori and Isola Tiberina, around Via del Portico d'Ottavia. Even today, it is an area full of character, where Jewish families still live,

with food shops and restaurants which observe Jewish customs and rituals. There are several Jewish bakeries, which sell unleavened bread and sweets with a particular flavor: small tarts with candied fruit and sultanas, *bombe* and *ciambelle* (doughnuts),

chocolates, chocolate bars made from particular *crus* of cocoa and all sorts of other delights including fruit and vegetables filled with ice-cream. But the shop also sells hand-made boxes to wrap them in, picture-frames and candles, and even a selection of wines and liqueurs which go splendidly with chocolate.
Here the wrappings are almost as extraordinary as the chocolates, thanks to the owner's passion for wicker baskets and dried flowers.
She also holds tastings of chocolate, wines and a fabulous home-made chocolate liqueur. All in all, this is a chocolate-lovers' paradise and a wonderful place to pick up a gift.
On the same street, 59/A, is the **Osteria Isidoro** (Tel. 067008266), a quiet place for a meal, where there are 40 different *primi piatti* on the menu (anyone who can eat them all gets a free lunch!) and other Roman specialties, including lamb kebabs, all at a reasonable price. A few steps away from the Colosseum, on the corner of Via Celimontana (21/B) and Via Marco Aurelio (34/A), is **Il Pentagrappolo** (Tel. 067096301, www.ilpentagrappolo.com), a wine and music bar, with an intimate ambience, low lights, and piano music in the background. Here you can try their quality menu of traditional Roman cuisine and taste top-quality Italian and French wines.
Ideal for a pre-dinner drink.
It also organizes evenings with live music, wine and food evenings and events with special themes, when you can buy wines, spirits and gourmet specialties.

Route 7

In the area between Isola Tiberina and the Janiculum there are plenty of good eating places. In Viale Trastevere, **Moroni** serves delicious pizzas, *supplì* and *filetti di Baccalà* (medium-high price-range). In Via del Moro, in the lovely area of Trastevere, the **Enoteca Ferrara** (Tel. 0658333920, www.enotecaferrara.it) is in a 15th-century palazzo, with excellent food and wines (medium-high price-range). In 2003, it won Italy's "Oscar" of wine as best Enoteca. It sells wines, and is also a café and restaurant. The chef here adds an imaginative touch to traditional dishes which are served with excellent wines. Another place in the heart of Trastevere, at 41/a Via della Lungara, is the **Antica Osteria Da Giovanni** (Tel. 066861514), where they serve the best of Roman cuisine at a fair price.
At 24 Piazza S. Cecilia is the **Pizzeria Roma Sparita** (Tel. 065800757), where classic pizza is baked in a wood oven. The menu includes dishes based on what is available during the season at a fairly low price. Another good pizzeria is **Gatta Mangiona** (30-30/a-32 Via F. Ozanam, Tel. 065346702), at Monte Verde, near Villa Pamphili. The pizza here is thick, soft and fragrant, and the chef uses top-quality

almond cakes, cinnamon biscuits, *pizzarelle* made with honey, and especially *torta ricotta* (cheesecakes) made with ricotta, flavored with either chocolate or cherries.

OTHER SPECIALTIES

Bucatini all'amatriciana – This sauce gets its name from the town of Amatrice, in the Province of Rieti. The dish is made by taking bucatini or spaghetti (fairly similar tyres of pasta) and serving them with a sauce made with lard, pork cheek, white wine, tomatoes, pecorino and chili pepper. *Pasta a cacio e pepe* – Once the pasta is cooked, exactly the right amount of the hot pasta water is conserved to make a creamy sauce with pecorino cheese and freshly-ground black pepper.
Spaghetti alla carbonara is possibly a modern version of an old-fashioned dish called "*spaghetti alla sagiovannara*". Spaghetti is tossed in a sauce made with butter, cheese, egg yolks, pepper and either bacon or pork cheek.

ingredients. For example, pizza made with DOP *buffalo mozzarella* (medium price-range). Those with a sweet tooth should not miss the **Gelateria San Crispino** (Tel. 066793924, www.ilgelatodisancrispino.com) by the Trevi Fountain, perhaps one of Rome's best *gelaterie* (Italian ice-cream parlor). Artisan skills and top-quality ingredients, which must be in season, are the order of the day.

Route 8

At Villa Borghese, the **Art Cafè** (Via del Galopattoio) is located in the Galleria Nazionale d'Arte Moderna (Modern Art Gallery). It's very popular as a night venue and much frequented by people from the fashion world and theater artistes (consequently it is fairly expensive). It has a sophisticated restaurant, a disco that continues well into the early hours of the morning, and stages fashion shows and shows films, but its main attraction is its lovely location. Another recommendation in the beautiful setting of Villa Borghese is the **Casina Valadier**, which has incredible views over the city. The restaurant serves Italian food with different menus and prices in different parts of the villa. There's a cafè which is great for breakfast and there are

wine-tastings of Italian and international wines. In the garden, in the late morning, the café service is followed by a buffet lunch. At the Vineria in the Sala Romana, you can taste wines accompanied by hot and cold nibbles, salamis and hams and cheeses, typical specialties from all over Italy and abroad. The belevedere terrace on the first floor is a lovely place to spend the afternoon or evening, or you can dine *à la carte* in one of the dining-rooms. The Sala Impero, with its beautiful semi-circular terrace facing Villa Borghese, acts as a dining-room in winter.
Finally, you can book dinner in the Sala Crociera, which has a terrace at each corner, and fantastic views over Rome. Here again, the amazing location justifies the expense.
At the Galleria Nazionale d'Arte Moderna, inside Villa Borghese, the **Caffè delle Arti** (Via delle Belle Arti, Tel. 0632651236, www.caffedellearti-roma.it), is not only a café but also serves Mediterranean and international cuisine on its lovely terrace. Not far away, at 35 Piazzale di Ponte Milvio, the **Caffetteria del Gianfornaio** (Quartiere Flaminio, Tel. 063333472) serves delicious baked specialties and is the ideal place for a snack.

TCI HIGHLIGHTS

BACCALÀ ALLA ROMANA

These are pieces of cod rolled in egg and breadcrumbs and fried in a pan with onions, garlic, capers, sultanas and pine-nuts. Anchovies, pepper, lemon juice and chopped parsley are added before serving. The recipe for *Baccalà in umido* involves boiling the cod, covered with very thinly-sliced onions, on a base of butter and breadcrumbs. When it has boiled, the cod is covered with a sauce made with oil, anchovies and tomatoes. Finally, it is garnished with salt, pepper and chopped parsley. To make *Baccalà in guazzetto*, fillets of cod are coated with flour and fried quickly in a pan. Then they are cooked in a tomato sauce flavored with anchovies, raisins and pine-nuts.
Another cod recipe is *filetti di baccalà fritti*: the skin and bones are removed from the fillets which are left to soak in water. After a period of soaking, they are then cut into strips and coated with a batter made with water, flour, fresh yeast and salt. The fillets are then fried in extra-virgin olive oil until golden.

The Tiber: history, legend, archeology and wildlife

The fundamental role played by rivers in the founding of cities and the development of trade and cultural exchange is well-documented, as is the importance of the Tiber in the history of Rome, described by many Classical writers. Over the centuries, the Tiber became the main commercial, military and economic thoroughfare of the city of Rome. All kinds of materials and goods were brought here from every corner of the known world. Because of the vital importance of the Tiber, Rome created a large-scale, far-reaching network to manage and maintain the river and the port areas along its course, that important stretch of the river which linked Rome to the trading capitals of the Mediterranean. Roman rulers undertook drainage and land reclamation projects, building a complex system of canals, which constituted one of the first massive transformations of the substrata of the city. The building of the huge sewer called the Cloaca Maxima, *receptaculum omnium purgamentorum urbis* (the "main collector of the city's sewerage", as Livy describes it), is one of the first examples of the large infrastructures built with the aim of improving hygiene and the environment, a practice which later spread throughout the Empire. Augustus, Claudius and Trajan are just three of the emperors who undertook work on the Tiber which, together with its constant maintenance, shows how vital the river was to the Romans in their everyday life. With the fall of the Empire and Rome's subsequent decline, the river was used much less, for light local traffic and small-scale craft production. However, when Rome rose again to new splendor, the city began once more to look after its river. The Tiber has always been mentioned by historians and poets. They describe battles fought on the river, festivals held on its banks, the frenzied activity of its ports, the boats which followed the flow of its current, its islands and the hydraulic engineering projects which were undertaken to improve the flow of this important navigable thoroughfare, confirming the longstanding, close, dynamic relationship between the city and its river.

THE TIBER WITHIN THE CITY...

Now it is the river's turn to introduce visitors to centuries of Roman history from an unusual and fascinating standpoint, offering a different and charming way of getting to know the city. For information and bookings please contact the Compagnia di Navigazione Ponte Sant'Angelo, Vicolo Margana 11/B, Roma (www.battellidiroma.it, Booking Office Tel. 0668301585, Customer Service: Tel. 066789361).

Cruise with audio-guide

SERVICE OPERATES: THROUGHOUT THE YEAR FROM WEDNESDAY TO SUNDAY

SAILING SCHEDULE: FROM MARCH 15 TO NOVEMBER 15, FOUR CRUISES A DAY, DEPARTING AT 11.00 AM, 12.30 PM, 4.00 PM AND 5.30 PM. FROM NOVEMBER 16 TO MARCH 14, 2 CRUISES A DAY, DEPARTING AT 11.00 AM AND 4.00 PM.

TICKETS: FULL-PRICE € 12; OVER 65 € 8; KIDS AGED BETWEEN 6 AND 12 € 5; KIDS AGED BETWEEN 0 AND 6 FREE. DISABLED PASSENGERS PAY THE SAME RATES, ACCORDING TO AGE, AND MAY BE ACCOMPANIED BY ONE PERSON FREE.

POINT OF DEPARTURE: CALATA DEGLI ANGUILLARA (OPPOSITE ISOLA TIBERINA)

The cruise follows the Tiber from Castel Sant'Angelo towards Isola Tiberina and as far the bridge of Ponte Risorgimento, providing unusual views of Rome. The itinerary touches on 2,750 years of Roman history with a commentary in 6 languages (Italian, English, French, German, Spanish and Japanese). The service operates throughout the year, except in particularly bad weather, or when the boats need servicing. You are advised to be at the jetty at least 15 minutes prior to departure. The cruise lasts 1hr 10mins. With regard to disabled passengers, regrettably wheel-chairs cannot be wheeled on board but passengers may be lifted from wheelchairs into the boat. Please contact the Customer Service of Compagnia di Navigazione Ponte Sant'Angelo for further information.

Cruise with dinner on board

SERVICE OPERATES: ALL YEAR

SAILING SCHEDULE: FROM MARCH 15 TO NOVEMBER 15 FROM THURSDAY TO SATURDAY. FROM NOVEMBER 16 TO MARCH 14: ON FRIDAY AND SATURDAY. DEPARTURE: 9.00 PM.

TICKETS: FULL-PRICE € 53 (DRINKS NOT INCLUDED).

POINT OF DEPARTURE: PONTE SANT'ANGELO

The splendid view of the Vatican from Ponte S. Angelo.

An unusual way to spend an evening, on board one of the finest boats in the fleet. Traditional tasty Roman cuisine, a relaxed, elegant ambience and soft background music combine to create a perfect romantic, unforgettable evening, watching the magical charm of Rome illuminated at night. On request, the boat can also be hired during the week for private events (for quotations and bookings please call 0697745414). You are advised to be at the jetty at least 15 minutes prior to departure. Disabled passengers are most welcome. Disabled passengers who require special assistance should contact the Customer Service of Compagnia di Navigazione Ponte Sant'Angelo for advice.

Cruise with wine-bar on board

SERVICE OPERATES: THROUGHOUT THE YEAR

SAILING SCHEDULE: FROM THURSDAY TO SATURDAY. DEPARTURE: 9.00 PM.

TICKETS: FULL-PRICE € 30

POINT OF DEPARTURE: PONTE SANT'ANGELO

At the wine-bar, you may choose from a selection of cheeses, hams and salamis to enjoy with a glass of wine, and a dessert, as you watch Rome illuminated from the boat. You are advised to be at the jetty at least 15 minutes prior to departure. The cruise lasts 2hrs 15mins. Disabled passengers are most welcome. To reach the point of departure, disabled passengers with wheel-chairs should access the boat at the Molo di Calata degli Anguillara (opposite Isola

Tiberina). Please contact the Customer Service of Compagnia di Navigazione Ponte Sant'Angelo for further information.

Cruise to Ostia Antica

SERVICE OPERATES: THROUGHOUT THE YEAR

SAILING SCHEDULE: FROM FRIDAY TO SUNDAY. THERE IS ONLY ONE CRUISE PER DAY, DEPARTING AT 09.15 AM FROM PONTE MARCONI, AND ARRIVING AT OSTIA ANTICA AT 11.30 AM. THERE ARE TWO HOURS FOR THE PASSENGERS TO VISIT THE SITE. THEN THE BOAT DEPARTS FROM OSTIA ANTICA AT 1.30 PM AND ARRIVES BACK AT PONTE MARCONI AT 4.00 PM.

TICKETS: FULL-PRICE (ONE-WAY) € 12; OVER 65 (ONE-WAY) € 7; KIDS AGED BETWEEN 6 AND 12 (ONE-WAY) € 6; KIDS AGED BETWEEN 0 AND 6 FREE. DISABLED PASSENGERS PAY THE SAME RATES, BASED ON AGE, BUT MAY BE ACCOMPANIED BY ONE PERSON FREE. PRICES REFER TO A ONE-WAY TRIP ONLY. FOR RETURN TICKETS, THERE IS A SUPPLEMENTARY CHARGE OF € 1 PER PERSON.

POINT OF DEPARTURE: PONTE MARCONI

This cruise to the archeological site of Ostia Antica to visit the Roman ruins offers various sightings of wildlife in the countryside just outside Rome. The cruise may also be booked for other days of the week for private groups. Those interested should send an e-mail to a.pica@battellidiroma.it. For groups of at least 50 people it is also possible to book lunch on board. Those interested should call 0697745414 or send an e-mail to: a.pica@battellidiroma.it. You are advised to be at the jetty at least 15 minutes prior to departure. The cruise lasts 2 hrs 20 h. Disabled passengers may access the boat at the jetty of Ponte Marconi. At Ostia Antica, the company which organizes the cruise does not have permission to use gangways and therefore disabled passengers must be lifted on and off the boat with the assistance of the personnel on board.

THE TIBER BEYOND ROME...

This cruise offers you the chance to sail along the Tiber beyond the section of the river within the city boundary to the Riserva Naturale Regionale Tevere Farfa, a nature reserve situated NE of Rome in the territory of the towns of Nazzano, Torrita Tiberina and Montopoli in Sabina. The cruise is an excellent way of enabling people to enjoy the river in an environmentally-friendly way, on boats with electric motors powered by solar panels. On the cruises our passengers can admire the river environment, a wetland that is particularly rich in terms of wildlife and inhabited by many species of flora and fauna. Because the engine is electrically powered, we can sail silently past reed-beds and woods and observe many bird species: herons, coots, moorhens, water rail, mallard, greater-crested grebe. With luck, there may also be sightings of wild boar, coypu, fox and porcupine. The length of the cruises varies. This affects the likelihood of seeing certain species, such as buzzard, or the rarer osprey and peregrine falcon. The longer tours include a stop so that you can enjoy a walk in the nature reserve. The cruises operate between March and December and can be booked for private groups of at least 12 people, even on weekdays. We recommend you bring comfortable clothing, hiking shoes and binoculars. For further information and bookings please call Tel. 3381714070; www.teverefarfa.it.

Wildlife cruises

DURATION: 5 HRS

ITINERARY: DEPARTURE FROM NAZZANO (OR TORRITA TIBERINA FOR GROUPS ARRIVING BY BUS) TOWARDS S. ORESTE, ROUND TRIP.

TICKETS: FULL-PRICE € 35. SNACKS AVAILABLE ON BOARD.

POINT OF DEPARTURE: JETTIES AT NAZZANO AND TORRITA TIBERINA

Nazzano - Torrita Tiberina

DURATION: 2 HRS

ITINERARY: DEPARTURE FROM JETTY AT NAZZANO – CRUISE ON THE TIBER – STOP AT JETTY AT TORRITA TIBERINA – RETURN TO JETTY AT NAZZANO

TICKETS: FULL-PRICE € 10

WILDLIFE CRUISES OPERATE: ON SATURDAY AND SUNDAY FROM 9.00 AM. BOOKING RECOMMENDED.

Tevere - Farfa

DURATION: 40 MINS

ITINERARY: SHORT CRUISE ON THE TIBER

TICKETS: FULL-PRICE € 6

POINTS OF DEPARTURE: FROM THE JETTY AT NAZZANO OR THE JETTY AT TORRITA TIBERINA (ONLY FOR GROUPS ARRIVING BY BUS) WITH FREE TIME IN THE RESERVE. PARTICIPANTS WILL BE GIVEN FREE INFORMATION ABOUT THE NATURE RESERVE. PICNICS ARE PERMITTED IN THE ORGANIZED PICNIC AREAS. A NEARBY RESTAURANT HAS A SPECIAL ARRANGEMENT WITH THE TORRITA TIBERINA RESERVE (TOURIST MENU € 20: TO BOOK PLEASE CALL 076530287)

SAILING SCHEDULE: SATURDAY AND SUNDAY, FROM 11.00 AM TO 7.00 PM. BOOKING RECOMMENDED.

DIRECTIONS FOR REACHING THE JETTIES AT NAZZANO: TO REACH NAZZANO FROM ROME, TAKE THE A1DIR ROME-FLORENCE HIGHWAY IN THE DIRECTION OF FLORENCE AND EXIT AT FIANO ROMANO. CONTINUE NORTH TOWARDS NAZZANO ON THE VIA TIBERINA (FOLLOWING SIGNS FOR FIANO ROMANO AND NAZZANO). NAZZANO IS SITUATED ABOUT 20 KM NORTH OF THE HIGHWAY

View of Ponte Fabricio, Isola Tiberina, at sunset.

EXIT. WHEN YOU REACH NAZZANO, THE JETTY IS EASY TO FIND. (THE DRIVE TO NAZZANO FROM THE CENTER OF ROME TAKES ABOUT 40 MINUTES). YOU CAN ALSO REACH THE AREA BY TAKING THE SAME A1 HIGHWAY AND LEAVING IT AT THE PONZANO ROMANO - SORATTE EXIT. THE TORRITA TIBERINA JETTY CAN ALSO BE REACHED BY TRAIN. THE STATION OF POGGIO MIRTETO IS ONLY 200M FROM THE JETTY. A RAILWAY CONNECTS THE ROME STATIONS OF FIUMICINO AIRPORT, OSTIENSE AND TIBURTINA TO ORTE (FURTHER NORTH). STARTING AT TIBURTINA STATION, THE TRAIN JOURNEY TO POGGIO MIRTETO TAKES ABOUT 45 MINUTES.

The underground wonders of Rome

During its more than 2,700 years of history, Rome has accumulated an artistic cultural heritage which has no equal anywhere. Often, the best-known images of the city of its most spectacular and famous monuments, like the Colosseum or the Pantheon, Rome's heritage also has a more unusual, lesser-known side, in the precious pa of history preserved underneath the city. Wells, aqueducts, catacombs and prisons are some of the underground sights of the city. There are also parts of ancient vil mithraeums, crypts, *titoli* (house-churches), necropolises, nymphaeums and temples wh as the ground level has gradually risen, have become buried and largely forgotten. This tle-known, secret subterranean treasure, which has been preserved underground, hid from normal tourist itineraries, offers you the chance to experience something quite di ent: a fascinating journey probing into the deeper parts of the Eternal City. Below describe some of the many possible itineraries in the underground heart of Rome.

PRYING INTO ANCIENT CEMETERIES

Catacombs Ad Decimum

These catacombs, discovered by chance in 1905 when the land in a vineyard subsided, is in an excellent state of preservation and is one of the most important examples of Christian archeology. Dated to between the late 3rd century and the late 4th or early 5th century, the complex contains many tombs. Some of them have been damaged but others have been perfectly preserved with fine inscriptions and traces of frescoes.

Catacombs of Generosa

These fascinating catacombs near the old Via Portuense were discovered by chance in 1868 under a vineyard. It is full of religious mementos from the Classical period and is an unusual shape because of the lie of the land. The complex lies under an early-Christian basilica built by Pope Damasus in the 4th century and consists of narrow tunnels with tombs on either side, decorated with paintings typical of Christian funerary art.

Catacombs of Priscilla

The catacombs of Priscilla consist of three levels of burials and extend for a total length of 13km. They are situated between Via Salaria and Via Nomentana, in an area with many catacomb complexes. The *cubicula* and lunettes of the catacombs, famous because they contain the tombs of many martyrs, are richly decorated with Christian paintings dating from the 2nd, 3rd and 4th centuries.

There is a depiction of the Virgin Mary holding the Child on her lap which is thought to be one of the oldest of its kind in the Western world. The fact that the morphology of the land resembles a quarry suggests that it was a re-use of a former quarry.

Jewish catacombs under the Randamini vineyard (Appia Antica)

These catacombs near the Appian Way, discovered in the late 19th century, date from the Roman Imperial period. They probably occupy the site of a former pagan burial ground. Unlike Christian cemeteries, kokim, formerly tombs of eastern origin, are decorated with beautiful paintings featuring themes from Judaism and pagan cults. These catacombs are the only ones belonging to the Jewish community, whose presence in Rome is documented from the 2nd century BC.

Colombarium of Pomponius Hylas

The park by Via di Porta Latina contains many tombs from the Roman period including an excellently preserved

Spiral staircase at Villa Medici.

A speleologist explores a Roman aqueduct dating from the Imperial period.

contains a necropolis where about 150 tombs have been found. The necropolis contains funerary monuments, some of which are two storeys high, and many of which are richly decorated inside with paintings, stuccoes and mosaics. There are marble inscriptions on the front of the tombs with the names of the deceased, the conditions under which the tombs could be used and, often, their dimensions. Terracotta reliefs were placed next to the inscriptions indicating the trade of the deceased during their lifetime. They mainly seem to refer to a business class of merchants and freedmen.

Necropolis at Ostia

The cemetery was found in 1918 not far from the church of S. Paolo. It is part of a tomb complex which extends for 350m used from the 2nd-1st century BC until the 4th or 5th century AD. The necropolis, famous for the fact that it is supposed to contain the tomb of the Apostle Paul, is very important from a historical point of view since it documents the transition from the funerary practice of cremation to inhumation. The burials include colombariums, multiple tombs where cinerary urns were stored, individual burials and noble burials, some of which still bear traces of decoration.

Pyramid of Cestius

The pyramid, 37m high and built with a cement infill covered with marble slabs, is based on Egyptian models brought to Rome after the conquest of Egypt (30BC). In the 3rd century it was incorporated into the Aurelian walls. A small door on the west side, added when the pyramid was discovered in the 17th century, leads into the passageway leading to the burial chamber. The walls are covered with plaster and painted with panels depicting candelabra and female figures.

colombarium discovered in 1831. The rectangular tomb is partly dug out of the rock and shows a high degree of complexity both in its architectural features and the fine decoration of stuccoes and paintings. In the center of the apse is a small shrine on a platform framed by two small columns. These support a frieze and a tympanum, built of bricks and covered with plaster.

Hypogeum in Via Livenza

The hypogeum was discovered in 1923 during building work in Via Livenza and Via Po, 250m from the Aurelian Walls. It is part of the cemetery of Via Salaria. A side-lane leads off from Via Salaria Vetus and runs close to the walls. Apart from a few private houses and a kiln associated with the requirements of the cemetery, all the buildings found in this area are tombs. The hypogeum (an underground chamber) is quite large and situated in an area that was used exclusively for burials. However, although its precise function has yet to be established, the hypogeum itself was never used as a burial place.

Necropolis at Porto

The Isola Sacra is an artificial island once called the *insula portus* or *portuensis* (harbor island). The northern part of it

Tombs in Via Latina

These famous burial chambers are decorated with white and polychrome stuccoes dating from

151

the 2nd century. They depict animals, centaurs, mythological scenes, naiads, sea monsters and hippocampuses (the latter are some of the finest and best-preserved). The tombs are situated in one of the prettiest parts of the Roman countryside, dominated by the aqueducts of Acqua Claudia and Acqua Marcia, in view of the medieval Tor Fiscale and about 3km from Porta Latina, and should not be missed.

The underground vaults of the church of SS. Cosma e Damiano

The church is dedicated to Cosma and Damian, the brothers who were doctors, martyred during Diocletian's persecution of the Christians (303 AD). It was built during the papacy of Felix IV (526-530 AD) and incorporates part of the Bibliotheca Pacis, used to display a plan of Rome, the Forma Urbis Romae, and of the Temple of Romulus, given to the Church by the Emperor Theodoric. In

Mithraeum at S. Prisca on the Aventine Hill.

THE MYSTERIES OF ANCIENT PLACES OF WORSHIP

Mithraeum of Circus Maximus

The mithraeum (a sanctuary dedicated to the god Mithras) was discovered in the 1930s. It is a large building dating from the 2nd century, and was altered several times. The ground floor was converted into a mithraeum in the 3rd century. This is one of the largest cult sites dedicated to Mithras in Rome. A magnificent marble relief depicts the ceremony of the *taurobolium* (during which a bull was sacrificed), following the example of Mithras who, accompanied by Cautes and Cautopates (Persian gods), Sol and Luna, is depicted in the act of raising his dagger to slay the bull.

addition to the imposing Classical structures, such as the large round temple which overlooks the Via Sacra with its beautiful bronze door, it is possible to visit the earlier church, where part of the pre-Cosmatesque floor is preserved. The beautiful mosaic in the apse, dedicated to the saints after whom the church is named (526-530 AD), is a masterpiece of early-Christian art. Near the cloister, it's worth pausing to look at the 18th-century Neapolitan crib.

Under the church of S. Crisogono

Below the church are the remains of one of the oldest *tituli* (house-churches) in Trastevere, together with the *titulus* of Callixtus and the *titulus* of Cecilia. The early Christian basilica, discovered in 1908, has a single nave and differs from other churches dating from the Roman period because, at the sides of the apse, are two areas which were used respectively as a baptistery and a *secretarium* (or auditorium). The three arches at one side once formed the entrance and the far end of the church was closed off by the facade of a 3rd-century Roman house, which is still well preserved.

Under the church of S. Lorenzo in Lucina

A corridor runs along the side of the sacristy and down to the earlier part of the church. Here, below the nave and middle of the upper church is a fine black and white mosaic floor with typical geometric designs from the 2nd century. The wall of the apse rests on a straight wall from an earlier period painted with broad sections of frescoes depicting plant motifs.

HOUSES AND MUCH MORE...

Roman houses under Ss. Giovanni e Paolo

The Roman houses on the Celian Hill are a splendid example of three 2nd-century houses which were converted into a porticoed building with a workshop looking onto the street. This alteration took place in the first half of the 3rd century. In the 4th century, the structure became a noble residence (the splendid decoration dates from this period). Later in the 4th century, the building was altered again following the martyrdom of Sts John and Paul, when the *confessio*, a rectangular niche with a raised platform decorated with paintings with Christian themes, was added. Then, in the 5th century, the magnificent basilica was built.

The Roman insula of Ara Coeli

Of the numerous buildings discovered on the slopes of the Capitoline Hill when the area was being isolated (1931-1942), one of the largest and most remarkable is an *insula* (a house with several floors). On the ground floor there were shops overlooking the courtyard surrounded by a portico with pillars. A balcony with travertine slabs leads to the rented flats,

each of which has several rooms illuminated by rectangular windows. The rooms become smaller in the higher storeys.

Under the church of S. Nicola in Carcere

The facade of the church is perfectly aligned and incorporated into one of the three temples of the Forum Holitorium. In fact, under the church, you can see the podiums of the temples and part of the colonnades of narrow columns which separated them. The base of the Temple of Juno has a series of small roofed cells arranged along the longer sides of the temple. When these small cells were first discovered, some thought that it might have been a prison. However, it seems more likely that these were money-changers' shops used by the many merchants who frequented the temples of the Forum Holitorium.

Vicus Caprarius - Città dell'Acqua

The archeological site of Città dell'Acqua, in the marvellous setting of the Vergine Aqueduct, gives you the chance to admire a complex of buildings dating from the Imperial Roman period. It was discovered between 1999 and 2001. On the site, which has an area of about 400m², you can visit an ancient Roman *insula*, which was transformed into a fine noble residence in the 2nd century. The house is divided into two separate units which must once have covered an area of more than 2,000 m². Note the imposing walls of the *castellum acquae* (distribution tank) of the Vergine Aqueduct, which still contains water. A museum has been added to the archeological site. It contains some fine polychrome marble mosaics, as well as statues and architectural fragments made of Luni marble.

Excubitorium of the Seventh Cohort

Discovered in 1865-1866 about 8m below the modern street level, the walls of the dormitory complex were covered in graffiti mentioning the Seventh Cohort of the fire brigade, whose job it was to supervise the 9th and 10th regions of the city.

Fountain of Anna Perenna

On the slopes of the Parioli Hills, about 10m below ground, there is a fountain dedicated to Anna Perenna, an Archaic Roman goddess, whose name appears on the inscriptions on the monument. It was found by chance in 1999 during construction work. The numerous finds made in the cistern behind the fountain are associated with the use of the springs here. Exactly what this place was used for remains a mystery, but it seems likely that the fountain was used for magical or religious purposes.

Horti Sallustiani (Gardens of Sallust)

The monumental complex of the Horti Sallustiani is one of the most imposing buildings in Imperial Rome. It is what remains of the huge park in Ancient Rome which once divided the Quirinal Hill from the Pincian Hill. Created by the historian Sallust, the villa was one of the most luxurious in Ancient Rome. It lies 10m below ground level and comprises an impressive central hall covered with a dome, with other rooms arranged around it. Formerly, the villa occupied much of the Quirinal Hill.

Latrine in Via Garibaldi

This Ancient Roman latrine, discovered in 1963, has a splendid mosaic floor with geometric motifs and frescoed walls, making it quite unique. The bottom of the water channel is paved with Roman bricks, while the sides are faced with *cocciopesto* (or *opus signinum*). On the left side of the far wall there is a lintel, suggesting that there was once a door (now walled up) leading into another room that has not yet been excavated.

Sun-dial of Augustus

The *horologium solarium* was built by the Emperor Augustus in the Campus Martius after the conquest of Egypt. For this occasion, the obelisk of the pharaoh Psammeticus II was brought here and erected so that it cast a shadow onto the vast horizontal quadrant (thought to have measured 150m x 70m). The quadrant was originally paved with white marble. Bronze lines and letters were set into the marble to mark the hours and the seasons.Part of this vast paved area can still be seen in the basement of a private house.

Underground district of Trevi

This large Roman complex was found in 1969, more than 7m below ground and is one of the city's best-kept secrets. The district, which covers an area of about 1,600m², includes an *insula* with *tabernae* (shops), a *domus* (house) and

Jewish catacombs on the Appian Way.

a building with an apse. You can also admire sections of a Roman road, a fountain, and a splendid floor in *opus sectile* (geometric patterns made with polychrome marble).

Under the church of S. Clemente

The archeological complex of S. Clemente is situated in the valley between the Oppian Hill and the Celian Hill. The first church of S. Clemente, now underground, was created in the second half of the 4th century in a Roman house dating from the 3rd century. In turn, the Roman house stood above an earlier building surrounded by walls in tufa, with a travertine cornice. A narrow passageway only 80cm wide separates this area from an *insula* where a mithraeum was built in the 3rd century.

Under the basilica of S. Giovanni in Laterano

This underground environment conserves memories of the early history of Christianity and the complex succession of building and town-planning schemes executed in the area of the church of St John Lateran. It includes the remains of various structures and three ancient building complexes: a noble house dating from some time in the 1st century with some very magnificent frescoes, the "new" barracks for the soldiers of the Imperial horse-guard, which were subsequently destroyed by Constantine, and a 3rd-century Roman house built on a trapezoidal plan with a large central courtyard.

Under the basilica of S. Maria Maggiore

Under the famous basilica of S. Maria Maggiore, there are some wonderful Roman remains, including the ruins of an interesting bath complex where you can see frescoes, a number of shrines and *suspensurae* (the raised floors built to enable hot air to circulate underneath-the ancient form of underground heating). There is also a remarkable fresco which is actually a farming calendar. Originally, it depicted scenes of the tasks carried out in the countryside in the various seasons of the year. However, only a part of the original cycle, which was 35m long, survives.

 TCI HIGHLIGHTS

For information about opening hours, guided tours and what to wear, we suggest you consult the Roma Sotterranea website (www.romasotterranea.it, Tel. 3473811874). For information about Vicus Caprarius - Città dell'Acqua, consult the website of the archeological association Archeodomani (archeodomani@yahoo.it, Tel. 3397786192).

Under Villa Adriana, Tivoli

The villa, described in detail on page 105, offers an extensive network of underground routes, which were conceived as service corridors for the servants. Some of them are still unexplored.

described in detail on page 105

SPELEOLOGICAL EXPEDITIONS

Etruscan aqueducts at Formello

A recent exploratory campaign has brought to light some interesting features, including water pipes which have been functioning for 2,500 years, a tufa dam built to create a water distribution tank and a tufa brick quarry. For this unforgettable experience, you are advised to wear rubber boots. The administration provides protective helmets and lights.

Caffarella tufa quarry

Below the wonders of Rome there is a maze of tunnels stretching for kilometers. They are the indelible marks left by intensive activity over the centuries to extract tufa and pozzolana to build the temples, houses, palaces and churches of the Eternal City. This not-to-be-missed experience combines archeology and speleology.

Underground emissary of Lago di Nemi

The itinerary involves walking through a water-channel underground, enabling you to appreciate the digging techniques of the *fossores* 2,000 years after the event. The entrance is located on the edge of Lake Nemi, where the water-channel enters the soft lava, continuing into the heart of the hill. Here, the hard basalt rock was cut using an innovative technique which, even in the 6th century, made it possible to build structures of this size using concentric cuts. You are advised to wear comfortable clothing, rubber boots and to take a torch. The organization which maintains the site provides protective helmets.

PASQUINO, CHAMPION OF FREE SPEECH

There was once a tailor called Pasquino whose tongue was even sharper than his needle. His biting criticism of the vices and injustices practised by those in authority (including His Holiness the Pope) made him a real celebrity in 15th-century Rome, which, at that time, had come under the rule of the Papal States. Pasquino's shop overlooked the square which now bears his name. In the middle of it was a marble bust which was used as a shoe-scraper. After the tailor died, (in about 1500), the bust was placed on a pedestal close to the rear facade of Palazzo Orsini (now Palazzo Braschi) on the orders of Cardinal Oliviero Carafa, who lived there at that time. Following Pasquino's example and reviving a tradition dating back to Ancient times, when poets and aspiring poets used to attach their verses to statues, walls and pillars, people (who always remained anonymous) began to use it for affixing satires, sarcastic comments, witty epigrams and songs criticizing the corruption and arrogance of those in power, which became known as *pasquinate* (pasquinades). In the 16th century, Pietro Aretino (the pseudonym of the writer, poet and playwright Francesco Accolti – 1492-1556) was obliged to flee Rome because of the pasquinades he had written criticizing the election of the new Pope. In the 18th century, crimes of opinion were severely punished by the Law. This custom, which later spread to other statues of Classical date, only came to an end with the end of the rule of the papacy, when Rome was annexed to the rest of Italy. Pasquino represents the spirit of the people of Rome, which, before it existed in the form of a "talking statue", existed in the witticism and shrewd irony of poets such as Horace, Martial, Juvenal, Ovid and Catullus, in the satire, in the *animus* of the people of Ancient Rome. The Roman people were skeptical to the point of cynicism, having witnessed and been the victims of misdeeds of papal power. They had been deceived and disillusioned by the very power whom, they had hoped, would redeem their spiritual and material poverty. They ran a considerable risk, but did not fail to use the only weapons they had: irony, jokes and ridicule. The forerunner of the Free Press, Pasquino is the mocking voice of the people, its revenge for the acts of repression exercized by papal power. Pasquino is not a revolutionary but his words bite, injure, admonish, criticize, libel and desecrate, slander, make secrets public and ridicule those in power along with their vices. For 400 years, Pasquino was the "press of the opposition" to the papacy. Adrian IV, the English pope who would not tolerate being criticized by a mere statue, ordered it to be thrown into the Tiber. But one of his more enlightened advisors managed to dissuade him from carrying out his threat, saying that, if he had Pasquino drowned, his voice would be heard even more loudly through the frogs who lived at the bottom of the river. That, because the people were able to let off steam through Pasquino, they did not resort to other potentially more dangerous forms of protest. Some popes attempted to keep Pasquino quiet by placing an armed guard, but had to abandon the idea because the unpopular decision resulted in Pasquinos springing up all over the city. For 400 years Pasquino wrote a parallel story that was often close to the "official" version, but which revealed its innermost secrets. Pasquino is the voice of the man on the street, of the alleyways, the shops, the clergy and the drawing-rooms of the aristocracy. The people who wrote the pasquinades might be students, men of letters, or the servants of cardinals or other members of the clergy. Some even acted "under protection" on behalf of important people. But anonymity was almost always assured to avoid getting into trouble with the Law. Some paid for their pasquinades with their lives, or were condemned to other sentences but this did not silence Pasquino, even when guards were placed to keep watch over him.

Soon, Pasquino found an interlocutor in Marforio, a bearded river-god, whose statue now stands in the Musei Capitolini: the two began to talk to each other, producing a repartee worthy of the finest modern political cartoonists. Other talking statues include Facchino, a small fountain in the form of a statue of a man pouring water out of a barrel. He wears the clothes typically worn by the stevedores (*facchini*) of the city, hence his name. The statue, which dates from the second half of the 16th century, stands in Via Lata and, according to popular tradition, was inspired by the traditional water-seller, the man who used to collect water from public fountains and sell it for a modest sum, delivering it from door to door. Another statue, situated in a corner of Palazzetto Venezia in Piazza S. Marco, is known as Madama Lucrezia. This enormous female bust 3 meters high came from a temple dedicated to Isis. Her nickname is that of a noble-woman who lived during the 15th century. Tradition tells that the woman, who had fallen in love with the King of Naples, who was already married, came to Rome to try to obtain a divorce for the king from the Pope. But her attempt failed and, the following year, the king died. The hostility of his successor forced the woman to return to Rome, where she lived in the square where the statue now stands. In Piazza Vidoni, next to the left-hand wall of the church of S. Andrea della Valle, not far from Piazza Navona, stands the statue of Abate (Abbot) Luigi. A short epitaph engraved on the base reads: "*Fui dell'antica Roma un cittadino /ora abate Luigi ognun mi chiama / conquistai con Marforio e con Pasquino nelle satire urbane eterna fama / ebbi offese, disgrazie e sepoltura ma qui vita novella e alfin sicura*". (I was a citizen of Ancient Rome/ now everyone calls me Abbot Luigi/ I earned eternal fame along with Marforio and Pasquino writing urban satires/ I received rebuke, misfortune and a

decent burial but now lead a new, fairly secure life.) The statue depicts a man dressed in a toga of the Late Roman period. His nickname was probably inspired by the sacristan of the nearby church of the Sudario who, according to popular tradition, closely resembled the figure in the sculpture. "Il Babuino" (that is, "baboon") stands in front of the church of S. Attanasio dei Greci, in the central Via del Babuino. The name of the statue, placed here as part of a decorative fountain, refers to the grinning face of the sculpture, which the passage of time has rendered even more grotesque. This collection of talking statues is referred to as "*Il congresso degli arguti*" (the conference of the witty). Lastly, we would like to mention another very famous work which didn't "talk" but, in its own way, issued cutting judgements. Under the porch of the church of Santa Maria in Cosmedin is a large marble disk (thought to be a man-hole cover dating from Ancient Roman times carved with the mask of a river-god), known as the Bocca della Verità (literally, Mouth of Truth). It was placed here in 1632 having been situated for centuries in the outer wall of the church. In the Middle Ages, its mouth was purported to have oracular powers, and it was used for testing whether people were telling the truth or not when placed before Divine Judgement. If the accused told a lie with his/her hand in the mouth of the disk, it would be "bitten off". It is said that the tribunes used to "assist" Divine Judgement when they were convinced of the guilt of the accused. Today, anyone who wishes to subject themselves to Divine Judgement may still do so by placing their hand in the "Bocca".

The statue of Pasquino represents the Romans' right to freedom of speech.

The whole world has passed through Rome. As a result, the local gastronomy is incredibly composite yet highly diversified, with an astonishing spectrum of food and wine, where typical local dishes may be found next to exotic flavors and smells. Something that distinguishes local cuisine and which is common to every dish is Athe down-to-earth, genuine tastes of the Roman Campagna, from its famous pecorino cheese to the equally well-known wines of the Castelli Romani, and very good quality olive oil. When it comes to cakes and sweet things,

	PASTA		OIL
	HAMS AND SALAMI		WINE
	CHEESE		CAKES

Food

the local gastronomy is consistent with the Roman custom of giving priority to the most flavorsome, pleasurable aspects of life and always reflects the Romans' deeply ingrained culture of la "buona tavola" (good eating).

Highlights

- A traditional flavor: pecorino romano.
- The excellent wines of the Castelli Romani.
- The gold of Sabina, centuries of producing good-quality olive oil.
- Authentic, genuine flavors at festivals with a gastronomic focus.

Inside

Rome, from the Campagna Romana to global status

Rome is an extraordinary historical, political and artistic capital, but in terms of cuisine, it is a city-province. Indeed, the province is "Roman" in the original, broader sense. It comprises the coastal strip between Civitavecchia and Anzio and the hills inland, the Monti della Tolfa and Cerveteri and the Castelli Romani with its wines and *trattorie*, the Apennines with its sheep farms, where cheese is still produced on site, and the industrious atmosphere of the countryside around Rome with its vegetables and fruit. As a result, even the simplest venues offer food and wine from across the province; in other words, "Roman" products and "provincial" cuisine, continuing an age-old link between city and countryside. *Pecorino romano*, *caciotta genuina romana* and *ricotta genuina romana* (one of Lazio's oldest cheeses) and *carciofo romanesco* IGD all come from areas near the city; while *abbacchio alla cacciatora* (lamb chasseur), *pajata* and *coda alla vaccinara* (stewed intestines and oxtail), *fritto misto alla romana*, *saltimbocca* (veal rolls with ham and sage) and *carciofi alla giudía* (Sephardic-style artichokes) are fundamentally Roman but use products from further afield. Discovering the temples of Roman cuisine is part of understanding the city's rustic, flavorsome, colorful soul, which can still be found by wandering aimlessly without any specific restaurants to try. The infinite number of eating places on each side of the Tiber form an arch,

Scene in the Castelli Romani.

starting at "Checchino dal 1887", the cradle of *coda alla vaccinara* (it began as an *osteria* in a converted abattoir), and ending at Caffè "Greco" in Via Condotti, with its busts and mementos of Casanova, Goethe and Wagner. In the streets between are the stalls of Campo de' Fiori, the noise and tastes of the Piazza delle Cappelle markets near the Pantheon and Piazza S. Cosimato in Trastevere, and the interesting Ghetto area (see further on).

There are many options when it comes to day-trips out of the city. The Castelli Romani area is top of this list. Not only is the landscape lovely, but very varied, and full of picturesque villages and magnificent views. Take the Alban Hills, with its vineyards and olive-groves, lakes (Albano, Nemi), green woodland and chestnut forests. And, of course, there are plenty of *osterie*. Castelli Romani wines are famous, with nine having DOC labels. The extra-virgin olive oil produced here— either golden yellow or pale green, with a fruity taste—is also excellent. The wide range of local products include *porchetta* (suckling pig) from Ariccia, *pane casareccio* (home-made

bread) from Genzano (and Lariano), minute strawberries from Nemi and *salame cotto*. The tasty cuisine, based on fresh or free-range products, focuses on Roman recipes: pan-fried endive, beans cooked with pork skin, cabbage soup, broccoli cooked in different ways, suckling pig and freshly-picked raw broad beans, not to mention *pecorino* cheese and the local white wine. We would like to make some more suggestions for day-trips. The first is to Ostia and Anzio, to explore the remains of the vast city which was once Rome's port and to experience the delightful fish cuisine of a place which has been a holiday resort since the time of Nero. Then Tivoli, where the delightful gardens of the Villa d'Este, the Aniene waterfall in the Villa Gregoriana park, and the largest of the Imperial Roman villas, Hadrian's Villa, are the highlights. If you go on to the Monti Simbruini area, at Subiaco you can visit the monastery and convent founded by St Benedict: the Sacro Speco and S. Scolastica (named after his sister), the former built daringly over a precipice. Here you can taste the strong flavors of the local mountain cuisine: mushrooms and game, local trout, *caciotta* cheese and cured meats. The northern part of the province, the Monti Sabatini, Lake Bracciano and Trevignano Romano area, has a broad range of country and lake-side cuisine using vegetables, sausages and lake fish. Bracciano and the countryside sloping towards the coast and Cerveteri is prime ham country (*prosciutto romano*) and produces good wines, such as Cerveteri DOC. In the countryside they grow olives, vines and artichokes, and wild boar is a common on menus. Civitavecchia is renowned for its fried fish dishes. Inland, among the Monti della Tolfa, once a mining area, the air is different and so is the food: cured meats, meat from Maremma cattle and chestnuts from the woods on the inland-facing slopes.

PASTA

The cuisine of the Province of Rome is not only ancient but extremely varied. Some of the recipes are traditionally associated with the Etruscans while other eating habits were inherited from the Romans, like eating pasta with pulses, especially chickpeas and beans. Yet, Roman cuisine has inherited more from the common people than from the upper echelons . Hence the popularity of some dishes that are eaten all over Italy: *bucatini all'amatriciana, spaghetti alla carbonara* and *spaghetti alla carrettiera*, which, according to tradition, originated in the Abruzzo and Umbria respectively. Other strong inflences on the cuisine came from the Roman countryside, the areas of Sabina and the Ciociaria (the area around Anagni). But also the eating habits of the south: home-made pasta, sometimes produced using very old techniques. The infinite varieties of *fettuccine* come from the Ciociaria area. It is impossible to draw up a complete list of the sauces which accompany pasta in this region. Here are some of the most famous: *pajata* (a suckling calf's intestines), served with *rigatoni*, *gricia* (which originated in Norcia and was imported from Umbria); the terribly simple *ajo e ojo* (aglio e olio in Italian, namely garlic and olive oil), often a good excuse for a late-night *spaghettata* with friends, and *cacio e pepe* (cacio cheese and pepper), again a very old recipe.

Some of the recipes of Lazio date back to Ancient Roman times.

FOOD

Bucatini

They are rather like large spaghetti pierced (bucati) by a hole. They are served throughout central Italy but are certainly an undisputed hallmark of Roman cuisine. They go well with thick, very flavorsome sauces, like the classic—and nowadays internationally-known—amatriciana, but also carbonara (see p. 145 of the Itineraries section) or more flavorsome sauces made with vegetables such as broccoli, perhaps sautéed in olive oil and garlic.

Cuzzi di Roviano

This fresh pasta is made with a mixture of wheat, buck wheat and maize flour, water and eggs. The shape is similar to that of strozzapreti.

Fettucce and Fettuccine

The size of these pasta ribbons varies from area to area. Fettucce and fettuccine are some of the best-known forms of home-made pasta. The pasta, made of wheat flour and eggs, is rolled flat and cut into long strips. The width varies from 5 to 12mm in the case of fettucce. Sauces served with fettuccine range from the simple and very old butter and cheese (it must be parmesan or pecorino, or, if you live in Rieti, ricotta), perhaps with fresh black pepper, to sauces made with fish and seafood (on the coast), the classic tomato and basil sauce with chilli or sauces made with vegetables and served with grated pecorino cheese.

Frascarelli (Frascatelli)

Frascarelli are typical of simple cuisine and originated in the Province of Rieti and in Umbria, however they are also common in Rome. They are made with hard flour, water and salt dough which is broken into small pieces and used in soups or served with sauce. The classic accompaniment is a tomato sauce, with grated pecorino.

Gnocchi

Lazio cuisine has many different recipes for gnocchi. *Gnocchi alla romana* are made with milk and semolina, cut into squares, placed in a baking tin with knobs of butter and generous helpings of parmesan and baked in the oven. Another type of gnocchi to be found in Rome but which originated in other provinces of Lazio are gnocchi ricci, typical of the province of Rieti. They are made with flour, eggs and warm water. They are oval in shape and are obtained by rubbing the thumb and index finger together.

The Province of Rieti is also where the gnocchi de lu contadino (peasant's gnocchi) originated. This very humble dish is made with wheat flour and salted water, without any potatoes. Other Rieti specialties include gnocchi di castagne, made with potatoes and chestnut flour and gnocchitti de pulenta (small gnocchi made with polenta), which are made with a mixture of maize and wheat flour, salt and warm water, and are smaller than potato gnocchi.

Maltagliati (Fregnacce)

As in other areas of central Italy, in Rome, maltagliati (or fregnacce) are irregularly-shaped lozenges of pasta made with wheat flour and water. The flat layer of pasta, which must not be rolled too thin, is rolled up and then cut diagonally. Maltagliati, traditionally the fare of poor farming folk, are usually served with light sauces (containing no meat).

Quadrucci

Quadrucci are made with egg pasta and are to be found in various parts of Italy.

TCI HIGHLIGHTS

BUCATINI ALL'AMATRICIANA

Bucatini certainly don't require much introduction. With their distinctive hole in the middle, *bucatini* served with an amatriciana sauce is a famous Italian dish. Ironically, this champion of Lazio cuisine seems to have originated in Abruzzo. The small town of Amatrice (Province of Rieti), which gave its name to this tasty sauce, once belonged to the Province of L'Aquila. Pork cheek, tomato, onion and plenty of grated pecorino are the main ingredients of an amatriciana sauce, but, as often happens with great dishes of country cooking, there are various theories about where bucatini come from. Some say they come from the simple cuisine of the shepherds of the Apennines, who used to make a version of the famous sauce without tomatoes, while others maintain that the sauce we know today was invented by a chef from Amatrice who added tomatoes to the recipe. And no-one seems to agree about the amount of onion or the type of tomato that should be used. As far as onions are concerned, the people from Amatrice don't use them at all, even though many great chefs include them in their recipes. With regard to tomatoes, some recommend San Marzano tomatoes, while others favor the Casalino variety, typi-

cally used in the Roman suburbs.

RECIPE:

400g bucatini,
150g pork cheek (or bacon),
3 ripe tomatoes,
1 red chilli pepper
40 g of grated pecorino cheese

Cut the pork cheek into slices and then into cubes, put into a casserole dish and reduce the fat by adding a little water. Then remove the cubes of cheek, and add the tomatoes to the fat, having removed the skins and seeds and cut them into pieces. Sprinkle a little chilli into the "pan" to add flavor and add a little salt and pepper. Cook for 10 minutes. Then put the cubes of cheek back into the pan and heat through. Cook the *bucatini* in salted water and once cooked *al dente*, drain and add to the sauce with grated pecorino cheese. Mix well and serve hot.

In Rome they are served with a sauce made with peas fried with the cheek of a pig (guanciale).

Strozzapreti

Strozzapreti are common throughout the region. They are rather like large spaghetti that has been made by hand. The dough consists simply of flour and water. They are normally served with

These typical tonnarelli can also be made by hand.

thick sauces, or sometimes with a porcini mushroom sauce.

Tonnarelli

This is another type of hand-made spaghetti. It is also made with flour and water. It is commonly found throughout the region.

CIVITAVECCHIA

Pastificio di Pierantonio Margherita
Via S. Leonardo 19,
Tel. 076632013
This artisan pasta made in this pasta house can be said to represent the best of Roman cuisine: fettuccine, tagliatelle, gnocchi di patate and various kinds of filled pasta. They also make green pasta using spinach, although that needs to be ordered in advance.

ROME

Cellini
Viale Odescalchi 39/41 Tel. 065131443
A delicatessen with a vast range of fresh pasta in its most classic forms: from typical gnocchi di semolino to tortellini.

Fratelli Marinaro
Via Val Padana 55, Tel. 068120209
www.marinaropasta.com
This artisan workshop makes everything from quadrucci to strozzapreti, traditional gnocchi, gnocchi alla romana, tagliatelle and lasagne and specializes in a huge range of pasta shapes. Don't miss their ravioli filled with lemon zest, saffron and ricotta or the more traditional ravioli filled with red chicory and speck or pumpkin.

Gatti & Antonelli
Nemorense, Via Nemorense 211
Tel. 0686218044
Here they sell fettuccine, quadrucci and filled pasta like tortellini, ravioli and cannelloni filled with ricotta and spinach of the highest quality.

La Bontà di Galizia Valentina
Via Andrea Doria
Tel. 0639729023
This workshop makes fresh and dried artisan pasta. Their home-made pasta includes fettuccine, tortellini and gnocchi di patate.

Pastificio F.lli Fiorentini
Via di Prataporci 20, Tel. 062072464
This artisan pasta workshop makes not only the great classics but also typical Lazio pasta shapes like gnocchi di semolino, strozzapreti and stringozzi.

TIVOLI

Pasta all'Uovo Marcello
Via Arnaldo Parmegiani 3/A
Tel. 0774312266
This shop sells artisan fresh pasta like fettuccine, and regional specialties of filled pasta.

VELLETRI

Pastificio Gabrielli Franca
Via Appia Vecchia 4
Tel. 069631034
This artisan pasta workshop has plenty of imagination. It makes ravioli with ricotta and spinach, artichokes or mushrooms, and gnocchi di patate with beetroot or nettles. They put wonderful sauces in their lasagne: bolognese, porcini mushrooms, salmon and peas.

FOOD

Rome's gastronomic tradition is still flavorsome and rustic, based on the products of shepherds and *butteri* (cattle herdsmen on horseback). When Romans sit down to eat, they enjoy the tasting flavors of the land. They regard eating and sharing jolly conversation as an essential part of daily life. Roman cuisine favors the simple, genuine products of the countryside, certain spices (cinnamon, cloves, chilli pepper) and strong flavors (garlic, onion, basil, rosemary) which give its many recipes a distinctive flavor. Numerous hams, salamis and sausages are made in Lazio and are often used as ingredients for *primi piatti* and main courses, resulting in ingenious, delicate combinations: *farricello* (a special type of spelt) cooked with the skin of a ham, and the ever-popular *bucatini all'amatriciana* flavored with pork cheek fried until it becomes crunchy; *prosciutto crudo* from the mountains served with figs, and omelets made with tomatoes, onions and *guanciale* (pork cheek).

The corallina sausage contains hand-cut lard.

Corallina romana

This pork sausage from the Rome area is made with lean cuts (usually the shoulder) which are removed from the bone, trimmed and minced to a fairly large grain. The meat is mixed with strips of hand-cut lard, seasoned with ground pepper and whole peppercorns, salt and garlic which has been crushed and left to marinate in wine for a day. The mixture is put into natural gut, tied off and left to dry for a day in a room heated by a brazier. The salami is then taken to a ventilated place where it is hung up to mature for 2 or 3 months.

Guanciale dei Monti Lepini al Maiale Nero

Many products are made with meat from the black pigs of the Monti Lepini, including this one made with pork cheek. This typical salami of the Rome area is triangular and very flavorsome. It is marinated in Cesanese wine with herbs and spices.

Lardo Stagionato al Maiale Nero

This Roman specialty is made from cuts of pork belly and loin. Matured for between 90 and 120 days.

Pancetta di Suino

This bacon is produced throughout the region in various versions: *tesa* (stretched out flat) seasoned with spices and pork skin, and the finer *arrotolata* (rolled) version which is smoked.

Pancetta Tesa Stagionata alle Erbe al Maiale Nero

This bacon is made in Rome and in Carpineto Romano with pork from the black pigs of the Monti Lepini. It is rectangular and comes in two versions: classic or flavored.

Porchetta di Ariccia

This specialty from Ariccia, which is found all over the Castelli Romani, is made with pork meat from animals weighing between 70kg and 80kg. The meat is seasoned with salt, pepper, garlic, rosemary, wild fennel seed and other spices which vary from one producer to another. It is then rolled up and tied with string, and is run through long-ways with a spit. Finally it is cooked slowly, preferably in a wood-fired oven, for about 3 hours.

Salamis come in different shapes and sizes according to the part of the gut used.

Chilli and garlic are used to flavor many sausages and salamis.

Prosciutto dei Monti Lepini al Maiale Nero

This ham, produced in Rome and in Carpineto Romano, has a very tasty, garlicky flavor. Matured for at least 24 months.

Salame Cotto

Made from top-quality lean pork meat (from the leg) and belly fat.
The meat is seasoned, put into twisted gut and boiled for 15 minutes. It is made in the area of the Castelli Romani during the winter months and should be eaten hot.

Salsiccia dei Monti Lepini al Maiale Nero

This aromatized salami is made in Rome and in Carpineto Romano. It has a strong, slightly lemony flavor.

Spianata romana

Also known as mortadella romana, this salami is found all over Lazio.
It is made with lean cuts of pork (shoulder and trimmings) which are minced very finely with cubes of hand-cut fat from the throat of the pig. The mixture is seasoned with ground pepper, salt and crushed garlic that has been marinated in wine. It is then stuffed into gut from the large intestine.
Tied off into salamis of medium size, these are then pressed for 7 days in special containers or between planks of wood to give them their characteristic flat shape.
Once they have been pressed, the salamis are transferred to a ventilated environment to mature.
When cut, the long slices are a dark red color dotted with obvious lumps of fat.

Zampetti

This typical cured meat from Monterotondo is made from pig's trotters. Once they have been cooked, cut into strips and salted, they are ready for eating.

ALBANO LAZIALE

Macelleria Flavio Mancini
Via Marconi 18
Tel. 069324766
Artisan production of local pork specialties: porchetta, coppa di testa, small fat sausages, fresh and dried sausages, salame cotto, prosciutto di montagna, pancetta, guanciale and loin.

ARICCIA

Dentico Porchette
Via Vallericcia 118, Tel. 069340485
The main product made here is porchetta di Ariccia and freshly-made sausages, but they also make guanciale (pork cheek) and coppa di testa.
La Casa della Porchetta
Vicolo dei Rovi 2,
Tel. 069343436
Only home-made products are sold here: porchetta di Ariccia, prosciutto, freshly-made sausages, matured sausages and coppa.

CASTEL GANDOLFO

Norcineria La Villetta
Via Appia Nuova 28
Tel. 069325513
Artisan production of typical pork specialties: porchetta, freshly-made and dried sausages, pancetta and coralline.

GENZANO DI ROMA

Norcineria Gastronomia F.lli Azzocchi
Corso Don Giovanni Minzoni 45/47
Tel. 069396553
This shop makes its own pork specialties: porchetta, guanciale and prosciutto, small dried and freshly-made sausages; also local cheeses.

FOOD

TCI HIGHLIGHTS

Products with the DOP and IGP labels

Protecting food production is the first step to safeguarding a heritage which is not only of economic significance, but also, and more importantly, of cultural importance. It is an act which confirms and aims to preserve the quality of a product. The DOP and IGP labels protect a product's environment, the human input and its quality. Products carrying the DOP (Protected Designation of Origin) label are products which, first, must comply with a strict set of production regulations, based on the local tradition, which specify what raw materials must be used and how they are processed. Secondly, they must be produced in a particular geographical area, although the "typical production area" may extend beyond the territory of a town and refer to a whole region. Products carrying the IGP (Protected Geographic Indication) label are protected in a similar way to DOP products (in terms of complying with production regulations and the particular area in which it may be produced) but the processing and packaging may be conducted in a wider area. The IGP label is the form of protection most often applied to fruit and vegetable products and their derivatives.

MARINO

Norcineria Bernabei Vitaliano
Corso Vittoria Colonna 13
Tel. 069387897
Artisan production of meats and pork products: prosciutto, sausages made with meat and liver flavored with orange, porchetta, normal and smoked pancetta, loin and salame cotto.

ROME

Antica Norcineria Viola
Piazza Campo de' Fiori 43
Tel. 0668806114
From the great salami-making tradition of Norcia in Umbria, this butcher makes various specialties from the region, and Roman specialties such as soppressata and guanciale.

Gastronomia Salumeria Emilio Volpetti
Via Marmorata 47, Tel. 065742352
www.volpettinternetcom
As well as many regional specialties, this delicatessen sells cheese, salamis, hams, olive oil from all over Italy, 40 kinds of bread and salt cod. Also freshly-made dishes and a good range of wines.

La Tradizione
Via Cipro 8, Tel. 0639720349,
www.latradizione.it
This shop offers a wide range of top quality specialties from Lazio including

Roman delicacies like matured guanciale, cacio fiore, pecorino, coppiette and porchetta di Ariccia.

Re Caviale di Alessandro Massari
Via Montello 26, Tel. 063720243
www.recaviale.it, www.ercoli1928.it
This delicatessen in the heart of Rome sells a vast range of hams and salamis from all over Italy, and, as the name suggests, caviar.
But also pecorino romano and ewe's milk ricotta, schiacciata, salamella appassita and pane casereccio di Genzano.

SUBIACO

Antica Norcineria Sant'Andrea
Largo Camporesi 4, Tel. 077485387
Specialties from the local area and the rest of Italy, including prosciutto, pancetta, guanciale, wild boar sausages, coppa di testa and coppiette. Cheeses include pecorino and caciotta made with goat's or ewe's milk, mozzarella del Ferentino and Frusinate, pane casereccio and pasta.

VELLETRI

Salumeria Pietro Marinelli
Viale G. Oberdan 26, Tel. 069627287
This artisan pork-butcher makes its own hams and salamis: coppiette, porchetta, prosciutto, aromatized guanciale, loin, and freshly-made and dried sausages.

CHEESE

Like Rome itself, pecorino romano is thousands of years old! It is mentioned in the works of Pliny, Galeno, and Varro, and in *De Re Rustica* where Columella describes how pecorino cheese was made in the 1st century BC, using a method that is very close to the one used in modern dairies. Shepherds with their flocks are often depicted in old prints of the Roman countryside, wandering among the villas and aqueducts. Fortunately, even today, despite the encroaching metropolis, you don't have to go very far to find the dairies where this famous cheese is produced or vestiges of the ancient beauty immortalized in the words and paintings of the writers and painters of the Romantic period: fields and meadows, patches of broom and oak-forests, set in landscape which has seen a whole sequence of historical events.

Fresh ricotta cheese (which is also made with cow's milk) also has a very long tradition, whereas ricotta romana has a denser, more grainy consistency. It is used in many traditional recipes, in fillings for fresh pasta, or mixed with vegetables to make them lighter, but also for making desserts and tarts.

Classic dishes of Lazio cuisine include spaghetti a cacio e pepe, gnocchi di semolino gratinati in forno (semolina squares baked in the oven), pecorino con le fave (peorino cheese with fresh broad beans), spaghetti all'amatriciana (spaghetti with tomatoes, bacon, chilli and fresh basil): the simple dishes of country people. Gastronomically speaking, the city has not contributed a great deal, but, over the centuries, it has welcomed people from various cultures and has absorbed something from each.

FOOD

Burrata di Bufala.

This cheese from Fiumicino made with raw buffalo's milk is stuffed with cream and pieces of mozzarella.

Caciocavallo di Bufala (Plain or Smoked)

This stretched-curd cheese from Fiumicino is made with buffalo's milk. Straw is used to smoke the cheese.

Caciocavallo Vaccino (Plain or Smoked)

This stretched-curd cow's milk cheese is made throughout the region and is matured for between 30 days and 6 months.

Cacio Fiore

This soft cheese from Anguillara Sabazia made with raw ewe's milk was described by the Roman agronomist Columella in the 1st century AD.

Caciotta di Bufala

Made in Fiumicino and Itri (in the province of Latina) with buffalo's milk, this cheese may be soft or hard depending on how long it is matured, while the taste ranges from mild to fairly strong.

Caciotta di Mucca

This cheese is made throughout the region. The soft cheese is made as *primo sale* (the term used to describe fresh soft cheeses sold in basket-like plastic containers) and hard cheeses, in the case of the matured version, for between 30 days and 6 months.

Caciotta Genuina Romana

Typical of the Agro Romano (as the countryside around Rome is called), this is a fresh or semi-matured cheese made with whole ewe's milk. This round cheese has a slight crust when matured and a whitish-yellow body with sparse eyes and weighs 1-2.5kg. It has a distinctive flavor and a mild taste with a hint of acidity. When the caciotta genuina romana is removed from the brine, it is matured for 15 to 90 days. It is in the process of being awarded the DOP quality label.

Caciotta Mista Ovi-Vaccina del Lazio

This cheese, made with raw or semi-cooked cow's and ewe's milk, which sometimes contains flavorings, is produced throughout the region. Matured for a maximum of 30 days.

Caseus Romae

This semi-hard cheese is made with pasteurized ewe's milk. It meets the regional specifications for Lazio pecorino which were drawn up with the aim of promoting the role of the Campagna Romana (Roman countryside). It is in the process of being awarded the DOP label.

Formaggio di Capra

Made in Castel Madama by traditional goat farmers, this fresh goat's milk cheese has 11% fat and no added salt. The white cheeses are round and weigh about 250g. They should be eaten soon after purchase and keep for 2 or 3 days.

Pecorino Romano DOP

With good reason, pecorino romano DOP is regarded as the heir of the cheese eaten by Roman legionaries and emperors. This hard cheese is made between October and July with whole, fresh pasteurized ewe's milk from free range sheep. The cheeses are round with flat edges, have a diameter of 25-35cm and weigh 2- 3.5kg. The maturing process lasts for at least 5 months in the case of table cheese, and at least 8 months in the case of cheese for grating. It has a thin crust, is ivory- or straw-colored, and is sometimes coated with a special neutral or black protective layer. When cut, the body is compact or has a few eyes, and the color ranges from white to a lighter or darker straw color. Its characteristic smell is due to the fact that a starter culture called *scotta innesto*, prepared daily by the cheese-maker according to a traditional recipe, is added to the milk. The table cheese has a fairly strong aromatic flavor which becomes strong, and pleasantly intense when the cheese is matured for longer. The consortium's trade-mark applied to the cheeses is protected by the DOP label. It depicts the stylized head of a sheep (to distinguish it from pecorino cheese made in Sardinia and Tuscany).

Pressato a Mano

This soft cheese made with raw ewe's milk is a typical product of the Province of Rome. Its name refers to the fact that it is shaped and processed by hand. It has a mild flavor and a milky, smoky aftertaste.

Provola di Bufala (Plain and Smoked)

This stretched-curd cheese is matured for a maximum of a week, and is typical of the south of the region. Its flavor ranges from

Bread, cheese and young, freshly picked broad beans.

Typical rural scene in the Roman countryside.

mild to medium-strong and the flavor is stronger if matured for a longer time.

Provola di Vacca (Plain and Smoked)

Produced throughout the region, this stretched-curd cheese is matured for more than 30 days and up to 6 months. Recently it has been sold as a fresh cheese in the *primo sale* version.

Ricotta Romana DOP

This is one of Lazio's oldest cheeses and can be distinguished from similar products by its granular texture and strong taste. It is made between November and June using whole whey from ewe's milk from sheep fed exclusively on fresh grass. It is obtained by letting the cream rise to the surface, having heated the whey to a temperature of 80-90°C/176-194°F, after which it is put into containers shaped like a truncated cone. It weighs between 0.5kg and 2 kg. It should be eaten fresh, without any maturing. The body is an intense white color, and is compact and soft. It has a mild, full-bodied flavor and a slightly acidic taste. The production area is the Agro Romano (as the countryside around Rome is called) and the plain traversed by the lower reaches of the Tiber, most of which now lies in the Province of Rome.

ANGUILLARA SABAZIA

I Due Laghi

Le Cerque, Tel. 0699607059
www.iduelaghi.it
This dairy makes and sells cheeses made of goat's and mixed goat's and ewe's milk,

fresh, semi-mature and matured primo fiore, aromatized cheeses and ricotta made with goat's milk.

ROME

Avenati

Via Milano 44, Tel. 064882681
The shop sells various Italian cheeses, including the following regional cheeses: pecorino romano and ricotta romana, primo sale and fior di latte.

Casa dei Latticini Micocci

Via Collina 14, Tel. 064741784
A broad selection of Italian and foreign cheeses: buffalo mozzarella, ricotta made with ewe's milk, low-fat yoghurt, pecorino romano and pecorino di Campagnano, caciocavallo, and ricotta della Sabina made with cow's and ewe's milk.

Cooperativa Agricola Stella

Via Garigliano 68, Tel. 068542681
This cooperative runs a farm and a dairy, and offers a wide range of typical Lazio cheeses, salamis and cured meats. Cheeses sold here include mozzarella and rosina made from Ciociaria buffalo's milk, pecorino, ricotta and scamorza.

Mozzarellamania Food

Piazza dell'Ara Coeli 14, Tel. 066783780
The shop sells Italian cheeses including regional specialties such as pecorino, ricotta romana and caciotta. You can also buy olive oil from the Sabina hills.

Lopez Giuseppe

Via di Boccea 472, Tel. 066144724
This dairy makes and sells typical local cheeses such as pecorino, ricotta and various types of caciotta made with ewe's milk.

FOOD

OIL

In a land which has every right to be called historic in terms of olive oil, the sheer variety of areas used for olive cultivation and the number of varieties ensures excellent growth potential. The figures suggest olive cultivation is spreading, the quantities produced are high and the industry is increasingly specialized. With regard to quality, the olive oil produced near Rome is delicately poised between the refined fluidity of northern Italy and the robust, flavorsome oil from the south. Numerous cultivated varieties and clones have been selected from the indigenous varieties, which grow in different kinds of soil and thrive in various amounts of sun. As such, many types of oil are produced here. In addition to those described below, other olive-growing areas in the Province of Rome include the Colli di Tivoli, northeast of Rome in the Aniene Valley; the slopes of the Monti Tiburtini, Monti Prenestini and Monti Ruffi, where olive-groves are often at a considerable altitude; and Castelli Romani, the "classic" olive-growing area around the Monti Albani, where food is only cooked with local oil. It varies from golden yellow to pale green, has a fruity taste and is slightly bitter when the oil has just been pressed.

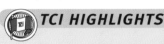

TCI HIGHLIGHTS

WHERE TO TASTE ...

...**Sabina olive oil:**
Marcellina: COSAR, Via della Stazione 172, Tel. 0774424163
Montelibretti: Azienda Agricola Tre Colli, Via Carolano 20, Tel. 0744608080
...**Soratte olive oil:**
Capena: L'Antica Macina, Via Provinciale, Tel. 069074173
Sant'Oreste: Agrisirole Soratte, Follonica, Tel. 0761578301 - 0761579516

Olio Extravergine d'Oliva Sabina DOP

Sabina is the area between the Tiber, the mountain ranges of the Monti Sabini, the Monti Lucretili and the Monti Cornicolani, and a large part of the Turano valley to the east. Some also include the Rieti Valley and the end of the Salto Valley. The DOP label which recognises and protects "Sabina gold" was the first to be awarded in Italy. The area is a combination of lovely landscape – wild and bare, with wooded areas higher up, but covered with maquis, vines and olives which stretch down to the Roman countryside – and landscape associated with history and art. The castles perched on the hill-tops and the medieval hill-towns are the living proof of its past. The cuisine of the area is simple and complex at the same time. In a sense, all its flavors are concentrated in the oil. In the Sabina area between the provinces of Rieti and Rome, new olive groves reflecting modern systems of olive cultivation alternate with the old, some of which are centuries old. According to tradition, Canneto Sabino, in the heart of Sabina, has the oldest olive-tree in Europe (2,000 years old, with a circumference of 7m and about 14m high). Sabina extra-virgin olive oil DOP has a maximum acidity of 0.7%, is yellow with hints of green, with a smooth, fruity, uniform smell and a taste which is slightly aromatic when the oil has just been pressed. It must be made with healthy olives when they are beginning to change color and production must not exceed 6,500kg per hectare in specialized olive groves with a maximum oil yield of 25%. The oil is made from the Leccino, Frantoio, Carboncella, Rosciola, Procanico and

Salviana olives. The result is a well-balanced, high-quality oil, suitable for fresh salads, sauces and boiled fish. Three other denominations from the area, Castelli Romani, Colli Viterbesi and Tuscia are soon expected to receive DOP certification.

Olio Monovarietale Extravergine di Carboncella

This olive oil is produced in the provinces of Rieti and Rome using only Carboncella olives (also called Carbognola, Carbona, Marsella, Ritornella and Oliva tonda), which are indigenous to Lazio but also common in other regions. The oil is a golden greenish-yellow with a medium-strong fruity flavor.

Olio Monovarietale Extravergine di Itrana

The production area comprises the areas of Nerola (Rome), Fondi (Latina) and Itri (Latina). Obtained from the Itrana cultivar, it is green verging on opaque yellow, with a mature fruity smell and a smooth, delicate taste with bitter, spicy undertones.

Olio Monovarietale Extravergine di Salviana

This oil produced in the Sabina area is made from the cultivar Salviana. It is a

clear, yellow oil with a medium fruity taste with bitter and spicy undertones.

Olio Monovarietale Extravergine di Sirole

Another area devoted to olive-oil production in the Province of Rome is Soratte, situated below the homonymous mountain. This area is called the Bassa Sabina, and its boundaries are the lakes of Bracciano and Martignano and the Tiber. The main cultivar grown here is the indigenous Sirole variety. The area of production lies mainly in the municipality of Sant'Oreste. The color varies from yellow to pale green, it has a slightly fruity smell and an aromatic taste, with bitter and spicy undertones when it has just been pressed.

 TCI HIGHLIGHTS

MUCH MORE THAN BREAD...

Oil-tasting should always involve bread, which, in the province of Rome, is made in many ways. The ancient tradition of baking bread possibly began here with the Latins, who made focaccia, and has continued to the present. This is confirmed by the old-sounding names of some of the bread still sold today, suggesting the past is linked to the present in an uninterrupted sequence. The *ciriola romana* is the most common Roman bread. It is a small, long puffy loaf with very white dough.

Pane casereccio, found across the region, is still made in the traditional way. One of the most famous and popular versions of it, *Pane casereccio di Genzano* IGP, was the first bread in Italy to attain IGP status. It must be made entirely on the premises and has the advantage of exceptionally pure air and water. Wheat flour is mixed with water, salt and natural yeast. The loaves (0.5-2kg) are dusted with bran and laid on layers of canvas in wooden boxes. They are baked at a high temperature, preferably in a wood oven. This gives the bread a thick brown, slightly bitter crust, which protects the white, spongey dough. The addition of bran also highlights this contrast, making the crust darker and crunchier. Genzano bread is ideal for *bruschetta*. *Pane di Lariano*, a poor relative of the more famous bread from Genzano, is made with white and wholemeal flour. The loaves can be long or round, weigh 1-2kg and are baked in ovens fired with chestnut branches. *Pane scuffiato di Velletri* is named after the special process used to make it, which creates a hollow space in each loaf. As a result, it is often filled with local delicacies to create a snack. Another well-known and popular bread is *Pane di Vicovaro*. Romans have always associated the town of Vicovaro with bread. Once upon a time, nearly all the inhabitants were involved in bread-baking, and would take their wares to the city each morning to sell while still hot. The bread made here has an unusual aroma as broom is used to heat the ovens. The *pizza bianca* made in Rome is an offshoot of the many types of *focaccia* made here, and the city's inhabitants still regard it as a sort of ritual. It is has a delicious, fragrant aroma and is usually 2-3cm thick. It used to be used for ascertaining the temperature of an oven, since it changes color very quickly. Wheat flour is mixed with water, sea salt, natural yeast, malt and olive oil. It is left to rise for four hours and then rolled out to the size of the tin, sprinkled with salt and drizzled with oil. It is left to rise again briefly before being baked.

FOOD

From the myth of the Castelli Romani to the Vineyards of the Etruscans

The Castelli Romani, described by travelers throughout history, is still one of the most interesting wine tourism areas in Italy, but they are also proof that wine-making in the province is rapidly evolving. Impressively located between hills, the plain and mountains, the wineries of this area represent a tradition over 2,000 years old. The natural setting and its artistic connotations are well-known, and it is all the pre-requisites for becoming popular haunts of wine tourism. Vine-cultivation in the province is divided into two main areas: the Castelli Romani, in the Alban Hills, traditionally the stronghold of the sector, and the Sabina Hills, near the Tiber, divided between the provinces of Rome and Rieti. The Province of Rome is famous for white wine: Malvasia and Trebbiano vines dominate but indigenous red grape varietals can also do well. The pride of local wine-production is Frascati, one of Italy's top 20 DOC wines. Here the quality is always high. With regard to how vines are trained, increasingly, vines trained on wires between poles are replacing the old-style overhead canopied vines, a legacy of when quantity was key. This itself is proof of the efforts made by wine-producers in recent years to improve their products. In fact, wine-production in the province is growing rapidly. Farmers are trying to improve things by matching products with the environments best suited to them. The production structure is dominated by wine cooperatives and consortiums, while private enterprise plays a limited role.

The Castelli Romani

Beyond the gates of Rome is the gay world of the Castelli Romani, dotted with villas, gardens and *trattorie*, where wine-making has long shaped the landscape. The hills southeast of Rome, which comprise the Alban Hills and the Tuscolan Hills but are always referred to as the Castelli Romani, are the most important wine-growing areas in the region and one of the main attractions for wine tourism in Lazio. These hills are what remains of the region's ancient volcano. Its craters have become lakes and its deposits have resulted in fertile land. Vines have been grown here since ancient times, an activity spurred on by the demands of the wine market in Rome. It is a civilized land with a long history, dotted with medieval towns, villas, vines and woods, a natural choice for the excursions of city-dwellers. White grapes tend to prevail, mainly Malvasia and Trebbiano, but there are several varietals of each. Then there are Bellone, Bombino, Greco and other local grape varietals. Cesanese and Sangiovese are the most common red grape varietals. The whole area is covered by the Castelli Romani DOC label, which includes the best of its wine-production.

Castelli Romani DOC

In the Castelli Romani area, vine cultivation goes back hundreds of years. The DOC wines produced here, divided into Bianco, Rosso and Rosato, do it credit. The ideal climate, favored by several lakes with their own micro-climates, and land rich in potassium and phosphorous play an important part in the high quality of the wines. The white wine, made with Malvasia and Trebbiano grapes, is the color of straw, has a fruity bouquet and an intense, fresh, harmonious taste. An ideal wine to drink with fish or desserts. The red, ruby in color, has a persistent winey bouquet and a fresh, rounded taste, while the rosé has a harmonious taste

Vineyards in the Castelli Romani.

and a fruity bouquet. Both wines are delicious with local meat dishes.

Cerveteri DOC

This wine is also produced in the form of Bianco, Rosso and Rosato. The white wine is a straw-yellow color with a delicate bouquet and a full, dry, harmonious taste. It comes Frizzante (fizzy) or Amabile (medium dry) and is excellent with sea and fresh-water fish, artichokes, salamis and cured meats, and *primi piatti* made with mushrooms or truffles. Red Cerveteri is a ruby red wine with lots of flavor and body, while the rosé has a delicate, harmonious flavor and a fruity bouquet.

Colli Albani DOC

Made with Malvasia and Trebbiano grapes, wines from the Alban Hills are straw-yellow, with a delicate bouquet and a fruity taste. The area also produces a Spumante which, under the Novello and Superiore labels, is a wine that can be drunk throughout the meal.

Colli della Sabina DOC

This DOC label shared between the provinces of Rome and Rieti applies to Bianco, Rosso and Rosato wines. The white wine is a straw-yellow color, has a delicate bouquet and can be drunk throughout a meal or goes well with fish. The red wine is a bright ruby-red, with an intense bouquet and a rounded flavor which varies from dry to medium-dry. It is a wine that can be drunk throughout a meal, as is the rosé, which has a delicate fruity bouquet and a fresh taste which varies from dry to medium-dry.

Traditional songs to accompany good wine.

Colli Lanuvini DOC

Wine-production here dates back to the Etruscans and then the Latins. The area, situated in the southwest of the Alban Hills, has a warm, dry climate which is compensated by the altitude of the vineyards (300-400m asl). The wine produced here is straw-yellow, with a delicate bouquet and a fruity flavor. It is best drunk with fish or vegetables dishes.

Frascati DOC

Frascati, one of the Castelli Romani area's best-known and most popular wines, is produced from grapes grown on land of volcanic origin. It is straw-yellow and has a delicate bouquet. It is very tasty and has a mild, smooth taste. It goes well with many local Roman specialties.

FOOD

 ## TCI HIGHLIGHTS

Outside the province..

Although the wines mentioned here are not from the Province of Rome, they deserve a mention as they are common in the province. The first is the Est! Est!! Est!!! DOC from Montefiascone. The volcanic land around Lake Bolsena is ideal for vine-cultivation. It is the champion of the wines from the Province of Viterbo, including the Colli Etruschi Viterbesi DOC wines. It is a white wine with a variable straw-yellow color, and a delicate, slightly aromatic bouquet. It has a mild, smooth taste and can be drunk throughout a meal. Another excellent wine is Orvieto DOC, produced in 5 municipalities in the Province of Viterbo, and especially at Castiglione in Teverina. This famous white is mainly made with Trebbiano grapes but also includes Verdello, Grechetto and Canaiolo Bianco. It is straw-yellow, has a delicate bouquet and a dry taste with a slightly bitter after-taste. It can be medium-dry, medium-sweet or sweet. It may be drunk throughout a meal or with fish. The sweeter versions are ideal with dessert.

TCI HIGHLIGHTS

WINE CATEGORIES

Three labels define Italian wines according to quality. IGT (Typical Geographic Indication) guarantees vine cultivation according to certain regulations. DOC (Controlled Origin Denomination) indicates conformity to regulations for a given area of origin, and production and maturation procedures. The top label is DOCG (Guaranteed and Controlled Origin Denomination); there are around 20 DOCG wines in Italy, 6 in Tuscany. VDT is for table wine with an alcohol content of at least 10%.

Genazzano DOC

Genazzano DOC wines are white or red. The white wine has a delicate bouquet, a fresh, harmonious taste, and goes well with carciofi alla giudia, fried fillet of baccalà (cod) and baked fresh-water fish. The red wine from this area, which has a fragrant, fruity bouquet, and a fresh, vigorous taste, goes well with salamis and cured meats, chicken and the traditional porchetta di Ariccia (suckling pig).

Marino DOC

The wine made in Marino is straw-yellow, has a delicate bouquet and a fruity taste. It goes well with traditional local dishes.

Montecompatri-Colonna or Montecompatri or Colonna DOC

This white wine is made from typical grape varietals of the area. It is straw-yellow in color, has a bouquet with slight hints of fruitiness and goes well with *primi piatti*, omelettes and baked fish.

Velletri DOC

This DOC label applies to a white and a red wine. The first is made with the Malvasia and Trebbiano, and goes well with soups and vegetable omelettes. The

red wine goes well with regional meat dishes, like coda alla vaccinara, porchetta di Ariccia and fegatelli di maiale.

Zagarolo DOC

The white wine produced in this municipality is reminiscent, in terms of its taste and smell, of the wines made nearby in Frascati and the Alban Hills. Dry or medium-dry, it is made with Malvasia and Trebbiano grapes, grape varietals which have been common in the Province of Rome since the time of Pliny. It is straw-yellow in color, with a winey bouquet and a dry, fresh taste with a hint of bitterness. It is recommended with fish, fried artichokes and broccoli strascicati (fried in olive oil with garlic and chilli pepper).

CERVETERI

Cantina Sociale Cooperativa di Cerveteri
km 42,7 Via Aurelia, Tel. 06994441
- ● Cerveteri Rosso Secco Vigna Grande - DOC
- ○ Cerveteri Bianco Vigna Grande - DOC

FRASCATI

Casale Marchese
Via di Vermicino 68, Tel. 069408932
www.casalemarchese.it
- ● Casale Marchese Rosso - IGT
- ● Marchese dei Cavalieri - VDT
- ○ Frascati Superiore - DOC

GROTTAFERRATA

Castel de Paolis
Via Val de Paolis, Tel. 069413648
www.casteldepaolis.it
- ● Quattro Mori Lazio - IGT

- ○ Frascati Superiore
  Campo Vecchio - DOC
- ○ Selve Vecchie Lazio - IGT
- ○ Vigna Adriana Lazio Bianco - IGT
- ○ Frascati Superiore
  Cannellino - DOC

WINE LEGEND

Wines are listed with symbols which indicate their type
- ● red
- ○ white
- ● rosé
- ◐ sweet or dessert

MARINO

Di Mauro Paola - Colle Picchioni
Frattocchie, Via di Colle Picchione 46
Tel. 0693546329
- ● Colle Picchioni Perlaia
  Lazio Rosso - IGT
- ● Colle Picchioni Vigna
  del Vassallo Lazio Rosso - IGT
- ○ Marino Coste Rotonde - DOC
- ○ Marino Donna Paola - DOC
- ○ Le Vignole Lazio Bianco - IGT

MONTE PORZIO CATONE

Costantini Pietro - Villa Simone
Via Frascati-Colonna 29, Tel. 069449717
www.pierocostantini.it
- ● La Torraccia - VDT
- ○ Frascati Cannellino
  Vigneto Torricella - DOC
- ○ Frascati Superiore
  Villa Simone - DOC

ROME

Conte Zandotti
Via Colle Mattia 8
Tel. 0620609000
www.cantinecontezandotti.it
- ○ Frascati Cannellino - DOC
- ○ Frascati Superiore - DOC
- ○ Rumon Malvasia
  del Lazio - IGT

VELLETRI

Colle di Maggio
Via Fienili,
Tel. 0696453072
- ● Porticato Rosso Lazio - IGT
- ● Tulino Rosso Lazio - IGT
- ○ Porticato Bianco Lazio - IGT
- ○ Tulino Bianco Lazio - IGT

FOOD

 TCI HIGHLIGHTS

SAMBUCA ROMANA

The famous liqueur Sambuca Romana is made with star aniseed, alcohol, water, an infusion of herbs, elderberries and coriander. It has an alcohol content of 40% and a sugar-concentration of 38%. Renowned and popular throughout Italy, Sambuca Molinari is a sweet liqueur that is transparent or white, with an alcohol content that varies from 40%-43%. It is available in a white version, which is sometimes aromatized with coffee, and a black version aromatized with chocolate. The secret of Sambuca is the essential oils which are obtained by distilling star aniseeds infused in pure alcohol. These are added to a concentrate of sugar and aromas. The recipe is very old, and many say that it was the Arabs who introduced it to the Mediterranean area. The town where it was first tasted was Civitavecchia, in Lazio, where ships from the East used to moor. The crews introduced local sailors to this liqueur. In 1945, in Civitavecchia, Angelo Molinari began to produce Sambuca on an industrial scale. It is drunk as a digestive and should be drunk cold. Often a coffee bean is placed in the bottom of the glass of white Sambuca. Often used in confectionery, it is also a common ingredient in cocktails.

The Province of Rome has a split personality gastronomically speaking. First there is Rome, with its incredibly complex history and the modern city, which is no less varied; beyond is the countryside, stretching from the Tyrrhenian Sea to the mountains of the Apennines, with its traditional farming landscape, much of which is devoted to grazing. Like all cosmopolitan cities, in addition to the more common sorts of cakes found all over Italy and imported foreign specialties, the capital has its own specialties, ranging from maritozzi, cakes made with flour, eggs, butter and salt, served plain or with cream, to the torta di ricotta (cheesecake) based on an old Jewish recipe. In other words, the capital offers a broad range of local, Italian and foreign varieties of biscuits, cakes and confectionery.

Biscotti della Sposa

They make many different kinds of biscuits in Lazio. These are typical of Marino, where they are traditionally eaten at weddings. Once they were presented wrapped in a hand-embroidered linen handkerchief by the mother of the bride to the wedding guests.

Biscotti and Ciambelle all'Uovo

These biscuits from Genzano di Roma resemble sponge fingers and the doughnuts are also baked in the oven.

Bussolani

These biscuits from Genzano di Roma contain honey and hazelnuts and are rather like tozzetti di pasta frolla.

Cacione

This typical product of Civitella San Paolo has a tradition which is centuries old. The outer part is made with flour, eggs, sugar, wine and oil, and the filling is made of pumpkin boiled in wine, sugar, cinnamon, vanilla flavoring, kermes and other dessert liqueurs, grated orange and lemon zest, cocoa powder, walnuts and hazelnuts. It is baked in the oven.

Ciambelle al vino or Ciammellette or Risichelle

Common throughout the provinces of Rome, Frosinone and Latina, these provide a classic end to a meal. Flour, yeast, olive oil and sugar are mixed together to form a dough which is shaped into rings. These are soaked in white wine and dipped in sugar prior to being baked in the oven at 200°C/392°F for about 30 minutes.

Ciambelle da Sposa

Produced throughout the region, these biscuits were traditionally made for weddings.

Crostata di ricotta

Sheep rearing has always been a tradition of the Campagna Romana. As a result, ricotta is much used in the local cuisine and forms the basis of many recipes, including cake recipes. This dairy product,

Delicious cheesecake made with ricotta.

combined with honey, fruit and aromatic substances, was used in Ancient Rome and still survives today in the crostata di ricotta or cheesecake, which has now spread beyond its original territory. The recipe involves a short pastry base, which is filled with a mixture of ricotta—ideally made from ewe's milk, since it contains more fat and is damper than ricotta made from cow's milk—sugar, eggs and flavorants, especially cinnamon. There are many variations on this basic theme, including the addition of sultanas, candied peel or seasonal products such as figs or chestnuts. A traditional recipe of

Rome's Jewish community adds sour cherries or chocolate.

Fave dei Morti
Round biscuits made with flour and toasted almonds.

Ferratelle
These biscuits are made throughout the region with flour, eggs, sugar, lemon, liqueur, butter and vanilla flavoring.

Maritozzi
The earliest form of maritozzo was a simple cake which bakers and housewives used to make with leavened dough. Originally they were larger than they are now, a sort of loaf made with flour, eggs, honey, butter and salt. The maritozzo was a good luck gift given by a fiancé to his bride-to-be on the first Friday in March, corresponding roughly to our modern tradition of celebrating St Valentine's Day. For that occasion, the surface of the cake was decorated with icing sugar depicting two hearts with arrows, and it sometimes contained a ring or a small gold object. This is a clue to the origin of the name, a humorous rendering of the Italian word for husband, *marito*. During Lent, maritozzi were made according to a slightly different recipe: they were smaller, darker and were cooked for longer, and sultanas, pine-nuts and candied peel were added to the dough. They were called *Er santo maritozzo*, or *Quaresimale* ("the Lent cake"), and, in the past, were the only cakes that were compatible with the strict diet recommended during Lent. Now that Lent is no longer followed so rigidly, the cake has become a common sight in coffee bars, and is served plain or filled with cream or whipped cream, and, more rarely, in the version traditionally made for Lent.

Mostaccioli
These dry biscuits from Cerveteri are diamond-shaped and contain walnuts and hazelnuts.

Murzelli
This Christmas specialty comes from Genazzano but, at Christmas it is common throughout the Province of Rome. These diamond-shaped biscuits are made with honey, hazelnuts and wheat flour, and baked in a medium-hot oven.

Pangiallo di Genazzano
This traditional round, golden honey-flavored cake made at Christmas is common throughout the Province of Rome.

Pizza dolce di Civitavecchia
This typical sweet Easter pizza is made with flour, sugar, bread dough, ricotta, butter, cinnamon, eggs, natural yeast, milk, aniseed, vermouth and kermes. After it has been left to rise for a long time, the top of the cake is brushed with beaten egg. It is then placed in a baking tin and cooked in a hot oven.

Pupazza Frascatana
This local specialty from Frascati is a strange hangover from an ancient cult involving a fertility goddess with three breasts, two of which provide milk and the third wine! (in honor of the local wine industry and the local legend which says that babies born in Frascati are not only fed on milk). These large biscuits have only a few ingredients (honey, flour, water, extra-virgin olive oil and orange essence). Normally they are about 25cm long, but on really important festivals bakers produce even bigger versions.

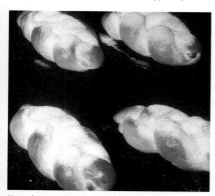

Nowadays maritozzi are associated with Lent.

FOOD

The pupazza frascatana: typical biscuits from Frascati.

Subiachini

As you might have guessed, these cakes come from the town of Subiaco, where all the cake-shops and baker's sell them. The dough consists of chopped almonds, egg whites, sugar and honey. The mixture is poured onto rice paper, baked in the oven, and then cut into diamond shapes. The final touch is a layer of lemon icing.

Torteno di Pasqua

These ring-shaped cakes are flavored with aniseed and liqueur, left to rise for a long time and then baked in wood ovens. Common in the provinces of Frosinone, Latina and Rome.

Tozzetti di Pasta Frolla

These diamond-shaped biscuits from Genzano di Roma are flavored with almonds or plain chocolate.

FRASCATI

Pasticceria Purificato
Piazza del Mercato 4, Tel. 069420282
Artisan production of the traditional cakes of the Castelli Romani: pupazze frascatane, ricotta cheesecakes and ciambelle al vino.

Cherry jam is often used in pastry-making.

ROCCA PRIORA

Sognatesori
Via degli Anemoni 44, Tel. 069405006, www.biscotti.it
This artisan company specializes in making biscuits, cakes and chocolate, using only top-quality ingredients.

ROME

Antica Biscotteria Cipriani
Via Carlo Botta 19, Tel. 0670453930
A small shop with a workshop attached which makes local specialties.

Confetteria Moriondo e Gariglio
Via del Piè di Marmo 21/22
Tel. 066990856
A shop with a long history selling its own chocolate and Easter eggs, pralines,

There are many different recipes for ciambelle, one of which includes wine.

chocolate logs and a wide range of fruit cakes and other typical local specialties, including beautiful red boxes of its own chocolates.

Giolitti
Via Uffici del Vicario 40, Tel. 066991243
www.giolitti.it
This shop opposite Montecitorio offers a wide range of cakes, ice-cream cakes, and 40 different flavors of soft ice-cream, all kinds of dainty biscuits and enormous cakes. Traditional cakes sold here include the ciavatta, made with puff-pastry with a ricotta or lemon filling and dry ring-shaped biscuits flavored with wine.

Regoli
Via dello Statuto 60, Tel. 064872812
This small shop sells crostata al limone and maritozzi filled with cream.

Food and Wine Festivals

APRIL

➤ First week after Easter
SAGRA DEL CARCIOFO ROMANESCO
Ladispoli
For further information:
Tel. 06992311
(www.comune.ladispoli.roma.it)
A week devoted to artichokes, either raw, or cooked in many different ways. As well as games, music and eating, the festival involves a parade of allegorical floats and the free distribution of *mammole*, or artichokes without thorns. The festival ends with a concert, followed by a fireworks display.

MAY

➤ May/June
SAGRA DELLA TELLINA
Fiumicino
For further information:
Tel. 066504061
The festival is all about tasting this tiny and very tasty clam which is typical and quite common off this section of the Lazio coast.
The day ends with a fireworks display over the sea.

JUNE

➤ First Sunday in June
SAGRA DELLE FRAGOLE E DEI FIORI
Nemi
For further information:
Tel. 069365011-069365012
Nemi is renowned for its strawberries and flowers. For this festival, it is bedecked with flowers while events in the squares revive ancient local traditions. The women wear local costume and distribute free flowers and strawberries. In the year 2000, Nemi entered the Guiness Book of Records for having made the largest bowl of strawberries in the world, using a ton of fruit!

➤ First weekend of June
SAGRA DEL PESCE
Fiumicino
For further information:
Tel. 066504061
In the square where the fish market is held, an enormous quantity of fish is fried in traditional giant frying-pans and distributed free.

➤ First or second Sunday in June
SAGRA DELLE CERASE
Palombara Sabina
For further information:
Tel. 0774636427 0774636462
(www.comune.palombara sabina.rm.it)
Palombara is famous as a producer and exporter of *cerase* or cherries. This festival is a celebration of cherries. There are stalls and stands selling cherries and other typical local specialties, as well as games, dancing and other kinds of entertainment. There is a procession of local people dressed in typical 19th-century costume in the morning and, in the afternoon, a parade of allegorical floats decorated with flowers, leaves and, of course, cherries. For the occasion, exhibitions of paintings and antiques are organized in Castello Savelli.

AUGUST

➤ First weekend of August
SAGRA DEL POLLO RUSPANTE
Fiumicino
Info: Tel. 066504061
This festival held in the little farming town of Tagliarella celebrates free range chickens. Delicious spit-roast chickens are distributed free and other events are held through the day.

➤ Last weekend of August
SAGRA DELL'UVA E DEL VINO DEI COLLI CERITI
Cerveteri
Info Tel. 0689630238
(www.comune.cerveteri.rm.it)
The festivities include a parade of allegorical floats and the distribution of grapes and wine. Other entertainments: wine exhibitions, folk music and evening concerts.

SEPTEMBER

➤ First weekend of September
SAGRA DELLA PORCHETTA
Ariccia
Info Tel. 0694549045
Ariccia honors its most famous son, roast pork, which was a favorite with the Emperor Nero. This festival is a celebration of tradition, history, tasting and entertainment, and focuses on the locally-made, succulent roast pork, complete with scrumptious crackling. There is music, folk-dancing and an amazing fireworks display. The artisans who make the porchetta are all from Ariccia and guard their secret jealously. The highlight is the allegorical float parade, when buns filled with porchetta are given to onlookers.

➤ Mid September
FESTA DEL PANE CASARECCIO
Genzano di Roma
For further information:
Tel. 0693711357 - 0693711359
For the traditional Pane Casareccio festival, local bakers make a giant bruschetta by slicing up long loaves of bread until it is more than 1km long and weighs more than 2,000kg. The giant bruschetta is then handed out to the people. There is also an event called "Mani in Pasta" (a competitive workshop for kids where they learn about making bread), as well as musical entertainment and exhibitions on various themes.

➤ Last or second-last Sunday in September
SAGRA DEL PIZZUTELLO
Tivoli
For further information:
Tel. 0774453342
This festival, which started in 1933 and is devoted to Pizzutello, the typical curved table grapes grown along the Aniene, is a celebration of the local grape varietal.

➤ Last or second-last Sunday in September
BENVENUTA VENDEMMIA
Frascati, Velletri, Cerveteri
Info Tel. 068604694
(www.mtvlazio.com)
This event shows how a bottle of wine is produced, from picking the grapes to tasting the must, and enables the public to taste wine drawn straight from the barrel. Every winery offers tastings and local specialties in a corner devoted to locally produced foods. The event is also staged simultaneously in Colonna, Zagarolo, Grottaferrata, Torrimpietra, Albano and Ardea.

FOOD

	CERAMICS
	FABRICS AND EMBROIDERY
	BOATS
	GOLDSMITHERY
	FASHION

Local craft products are the outward manifestation of the extraordinary cultural wealth of Rome and its province, and express very well the many facets of Roman life. In this sphere, you may admire the art of gold- and silversmiths who still work to commission, patronized by a wealthy secular and religious clientele, and the thousand-year-old tradition of producing beautiful ceramics. One of the capitals of the world, Rome is part of the international scenario of top fashion and worldly living. As well as the classy downtown shops, the boutiques, and old-fashioned tailors' with a long tradition, there are many markets;

some large, some small, held in the streets and squares, where you can find absolutely anything. They're worth seeing, too, partly because of the local folklore which they sometimes attract.

Highligts

- Folklore, and all kinds of goods on sale at city markets.
- Jewelry, gold- and silverware of the finest quality.
- The glamour of the boutiques and Rome's old-fashioned tailor's shops.
- Top-quality merchandise in Rome's classy window displays.

Inside

Over the course of the centuries two distinct tiers of craftwork have developed in and around Rome. The first tier consists of the refined, noble work constantly been carried out in the Eternal City as it was embellished by successive forms of governments, from the Roman Republic to the Empire and on through papal rule, the kingdom of Italy and a republic once again. The churches, buildings, monuments and gardens that make Rome such an enchantment are the tangible expression of artistic ability displayed by an unbroken succession of great artists, continually renewed by new arrivals, summoned to Rome by powerful rulers determined to leave their mark on the city. The second tier were the craftsmen working in the Roman countryside, who were born and grew up in a rural setting, almost always considered secondary to the important work of farming and mainly concerned with solving the problem which arose in day to day life. The former type of craftwork is still healthily active today, rarely noticed or used by common consumers because its practitioners are all busily engaged in carrying out commissions, just as they were in the past. As far as the second type of craftsman is concerned, there has recently, especially over the last decade, been an increasing desire for hand-made objects. City dwellers have rediscovered the village craftsman and this has caused a general upsurge in trade, with the countryside dipping deeply into the treasure trove of its traditions.

Metals

Ladles, pots, pans and cake tins were all once upon a time hand-made in copper by craftsmen who in turn were teachers, handing on their trade to their apprentices who then set up shop themselves. The advent of aluminum and steel almost wiped this trade out, it has only been revitalized over the last few years as consumers became exasperated with the excessive standardization of industrial products. Customers became more and more interested in the decorative value of objects rather than their mere functionality. This encouraged craftsmen to branch out into a wider assortment of products, such as fireplace objects, ornaments, vases, boxes, paperweights, ashtrays, clothes hooks and so on that were either based on tradition or the creative impulse of the individual craftsmen.

The resurgence of coppersmiths was accompanied by a similar trend for blacksmiths all around the region, with quality products concentrating in and around the town of Tivoli.

Gold

Unlike many other areas, the region of Lazio has always had two distinct, separate markets. One was mainly centered on Rome and supplied the clergy, the nobility and those in power, while the other was more provincial and satisfied those popular cravings for jewelry, amply demonstrated by 19th century artwork, centered on beautiful, but gaudy, coral necklaces, large drop earrings, garish and elegant at the same time, massively chunky gold chains and rings loaded with outsize "sparklers". The craftsmen in the first category have continued to prosper to this day, some discreetly in the background, others evolving into international designer labels. The others have almost disappeared, replaced by a new generation of goldsmiths who have mixed creativity with technical know-how to produce wonderful imitations of antique jewelry, winning over the Italian middle classes in order to launch out on the international market. Most of these, obviously, are in Rome itself, but there are also some provincial centers of excellence, particularly towards the Alban Hills in the towns of Albano Laziale, Ariccia and Mentana.

Ceramics

To the ancient Romans terracotta was more or less the equivalent of modernday plastic: easily molded and adaptable to a variety of commercial uses, perfect to store and transport everything from oil to wine, from grain to spices, on board a ship as on a market stall or in peoples' homes. They were simple, functional objects, produced merely to meet a specific need or solve a given problem.

This style of production has continued uninterrupted down the centuries and can still be found today with vases and amphorae painted in red earth motifs; these have gradually been joined by other terracotta objects such as ashtrays, tiles, statues for the Christmas presepe (meaning crib, this refers to the Italian tradition of creating a nativity scene under the Christmas tree), and exotic masks. But long before the Roman civilization dominated the world, the Etruscans were already producing far more sophisticated pottery, where the aesthetic value of the object was of far greater importance than its practicality or functionality. It is no coincidence therefore that today the area still produces artistic pottery. Sometimes these pieces are replicas of precious Etruscan pieces, but often they are modern pieces which owe little or nothing to the past. There is also a good selection of rustic pottery that is eminently suitable for everyday use: pots, mugs, colanders, terrines and vases that combine an excellent level of workmanship with very reasonable prices.

Wood

A wander round Rome's streets and alleys soon reveals how many artists' studios and laboratories there are dedicated to the restoration of antiques, a thriving market considering Rome's centuries-old history and all the furniture, picture frames and ornaments accumulated in the cellars and attics of the Eternal City's noble palazzos. Woodworking is not confined to the capital alone, but extends throughout the whole region, which is dotted with towns and villages that can be said to specialize in this field. Lazio's craftsmen are the direct descendants of a tradition of woodworking that once produced a whole series of useful, or simply attractive, objects. Objects that range from wooden flutes to the umbrellas that used to be used by shepherds, to mortar bowls and kitchen equipment to rustic furniture, through a whole gamut of chests, benches, chairs and tables in Classical style. Indeed, the list is almost endless. With time the different parts of the region have specialized in specific ranges of products, so if you are looking for country style furniture head towards the Alban Hills and the towns of Genzano di Roma and Zagarolo. Carpineto Romano is the place to go for ornaments such as shepherd's umbrellas, pipes, tubs and a large range of containers for several use made by old-fashioned coopers, still active in the Alban Hills.

ROME

Bottega Mortet
Via dei Portoghesi 18, Tel. 066861629
Metal engraving
Fondiarte Roma
Via di Cervara 133
Tel. 062294939
Metalworking
Ilaria Miani
Via degli Orti di Alibert 13/A
Tel. 066861366
Woodworking
Nicola Arduini
Via degli Specchi 12, Tel. 0668805537
Wrought ironwork

MARKETS

A mong the many magic moments that Rome has to offer, an experience not to be missed is undoubtedly a visit to one of the colorful, noisy markets that throng the streets. This is the real Rome where you can find a film star haggling over a loaf of bread with her favorite baker in the thick Roman dialect and stallholders compete to see who can cry the virtues of their wares loudest. Roman markets are a microcosm of the city's special cultural atmosphere, where one of the world's capital cities is encapsulated in a village square. There is a bit of everything here, from great bargains to (very!) dubious buys. Rummage through the stalls for designer label clothes or marvelous antiques, but careful of the famous Roman "patacche" (rip offs), and try not to miss the fabulous local food. In markets, tourists can rub shoulders with local people and get a firsthand taste of that warmth that is such a feature of Roman folklore while enjoying a stroll through the heart of Rome.

CAMPAGNANO DI ROMA

The Campagnano Stalls
Last Sunday of each month from September to May.
250 stalls crammed into the village's historical center selling furniture, pottery, porcelain, silver, marble, jewelry, books, prints, paintings, coins and postcards. There are also some unusual items such as gramophones, old radios, jukeboxes, old navigational and flight instruments. Part of the market is dedicated to organic food, much of which is produced locally. In short, the range of goods is wonderful.
For further information:
Tel. 069044263, www.mostre.it

ROME

Campo de' Fiori
From Monday through Saturday
The Campo de' Fiori market is held in the morning in the square of the same name, spilling out into the surrounding streets. Many stalls sell fresh fruit, vegetables, fish and flowers. The square also has several shops dedicated to food, as well as some wine bars and cafés, it is a great place to spend a morning sitting reading a book at one of the little tables on the pavement outside.
For further information:
Tel. 06488991 - 0636004399 - www.romaturismo.it

The Via Margutta Art Shows
October-November/April-May
During the exhibition paintings by Italian and international artists make a colorful splash along the pavements of one of the most Bohemian streets in Rome.
For further information:
Tel. 068123340

Christmas Market
From 1 December to 6 January
Splendid Piazza Navona crowded with dozens of stalls selling Christmas decorations, toys, presents and candies. The star of the show is the "Befana", the ugly old lady who brings Italian children treats on her broomstick on January 6. Street artists who perform for passers-by provide entertainment. Rome's historical downtown glows with Christmas lights and almost all the churches boast nativity scences (known as *presepi*, these are often elaborate

The colorful market at Campo de'Fiori.

models that recreate that night) on a vast scale. Piazza Navona was built on the ruins of Domitian's stadium and maintains its original oval shape, a masterpiece of Baroque architecture not to be missed on any account.
For further information:
Tel. 06488991 - 0636004399 - www.romaturismo.it

The Flower Market
Tuesdays
A wholesale flower market in Via Trionfale that is also open to the general public, a great opportunity for those with green fingers to pick up bargains while still being spoilt for choice.
For further information:
Tel. 06488991 - 0636004399 - www.romaturismo.it

The Porta Portese market in the 1950s.

The Print Market
From Monday through Saturday
Held every morning except Sunday in Largo della Fontanella di Borghese, book and old print enthusiasts can spend many happy hours browsing here. A good place to buy books and old magazines.
For further information:
Tel. . 06488991 - 0636004399 - www.romaturismo.it

The Via Sannio Market
From Monday through Saturday
Via Sannio 8.00 am –1.00 pm Monday to Friday; 8.00 am –6.00 pm Saturdays. One of the 1970's most famous markets for clothes, today it is a happy hunting ground for rummaging through the piles of new and secondhand clothes in search of something swanky on the cheap.

For further information:
Tel. 06488991 - 0636004399 - www.romaturismo.it

Antiques Exhibition
September-October/April-May
The exhibition is held in Via de' Coronari and gives visitors a chance to admire the treasures the streets antique dealers have tucked away.
For further information:
Tel. 06488991, www.aptroma.com

Porta Portese
Every Sunday
The Porta Portese market is a truly entertaining way of spending a morning, a huge sea of stalls where it is possible to find just about everything. Founded in the 1930s the market takes its name from the ancient Porta Portuensis (still standing), one of the gates in the Aurelian walls. This vast market, a constant source of amusement and surprises, is still a good place to pick up a bargain for those who have the patience to sift through its stalls and seek out those hidden gems. Porta Portese is one of Rome's most attractive, folksy markets, with its endless stalls selling shoes, new and used clothes, kitchen accessories, antiques, sheets, towels, plants, CDs, and just about anything you care to mention. It certainly deserves a visit but buyers beware! You need a good eye to spot anything precious in the midst of the piles of junk that stalls are laden with. It is also a good idea to take a map to navigate your way through the maze of alleys and streets in Trastevere. Lastly you will need an efficient alarm clock because the market is open from 5.30am to 2.00pm, but it's the early bird who catches the worm.
For further information:
Tel. 06488991 - 0636004399 - www.romaturismo.it

SHOPPING

FASHION

Before plunging into intensive shopping in Italy's capital it is important to remember that Rome is not like other European capitals. Shopping, like everything else, is something to be savoured slowly, Roman-style. Romans intersperse their shopping forays with leisurely pauses for a coffee or a glass of wine and a snack. The Eternal City certainly has something for everyone: fashion lovers will head straight for Via del Babuino and the surrounding area, non plus ultra for high level purchases, lovers of vintage fashion will make a beeline for Via del Governo Vecchio or the Monti area, looking for that unique item, ideally made to measure. Although furniture shops are scattered all over Rome, the best buys can be found in the intricate maze of alleys leading from Via Cavour to the Forum, where there are still a certain number of craftsmen at work. If time is no object you could do worse than browse around the capital's historic bookshops or enjoy the elegant herbalists' with their traditions going straight back to the medieval monasteries, explore the old-fashioned workshops of the Suburra area or the shops in the Ghetto, where the wares are displayed outside on stalls on the sidewalk.

CASTEL ROMANO - OUTLET

McArthur Glen Factory Outlet Center
Via del Ponte di Piscina Cupa 51
Tel. 065050050, www.mcarthurglen.it
The Castel Romano center has over 90 shops selling top designer label clothes, shoes and accessories from last season's collections at prices reduced by 30 to 70%.

POMEZIA - OUTLET

Timberland Factory Outlet
Via Orvieto 36, Tel. 0691602237
Shoes and casual clothes for men, women and children by this well-known label. Discounts on items from the current season's collections, end of line goods and samples.

ROME - OUTLET

Balloon Stock
Via Terenzio 12/14, Tel. 0668806404
www.balloon.it - www.blunauta.it
Between Castel St Angelo and Piazza Risorgimento, great discounts on last season's fashion items from underwear to jumpers, cashmere to jackets and shirts.

Bulgari Outlet
Via Aurelia 1052, Tel. 066617071
Previous seasons' items and jewelry from sample sets all with the famous Bulgari label. Discounts on accessories such as leather goods, handbags, watches, scarves, glasses and perfumes.

Factory Outlet Store
Via T. Inghirami 70, Tel. 067847521
On the Via Appia Nuova, easily reached on the subway A line (Colli Albani stop), outlet for men and women's fashion, shoes and accessories: new collections at roughly half price.

Firmastock
Via delle Carrozze 18, Tel. 0669200371
Between Piazza di Spagna and Via del Corso, a small shop with a very interesting collection of labels and prices including well-known stars like Valentino, Ferrè, Armani, Cavalli and Max Mara.

Outlet Empresa
Via Campo Marzio 9/A-10, Tel. 066794093
Right downtown, tucked between Piazza Navona and Montecitorio, a shop with a great range of mainly menswear, including shoes.

Quadrifoglio Outlet
Via delle Colonnelle 10, Tel. 066784917
A stone's throw from the Pantheon, fashion at great discount prices for kids and teens.

Regola 33 Outlet
Via di S. Paolo alla Regola 33
Tel. 0668136245
Just off Campo de'Fiori all the best labels in women's fashion: Armani, Dolce & Gabbana, Fendi, Gai Mattiolo, Prada, Roberto Cavalli, Versace, Ferrè and Miu Miu.

ROME - BOUTIQUES

Angelo Di Nepi
Via dei Giubbonari 28, Tel. 066893006
Via Florida 20, Tel. 066877489

Via del Babuino 147, Tel. 0636004299
Via Frattina 2, Tel. 066786568
Via Cola di Rienzo 267, Tel. 063224800
www.angelodinepi.it
A great range of boutiques scattered around Rome, all with the distinctive ancient Roman mosaic floors and imposing crystal chandeliers. Wide choice of elegant, sophisticated clothes cut to bring out the best in materials like tweed, shantung silk and crushed velvets.

Bomba
Via dell'Oca 39/41, Tel. 063203020
One of Rome's hottest shopping spots: fashions to die for in the store windows and a bespoke dress making service with silks and pashminas as well as a performance space for musical and theatrical events.

Degli Effetti
Piazza Capranica 75/79/93
Tel. 066793630-066791650-066790202
www.deglieffetti.com
Three boutiques all on the same square with minimal-chic design, the place to find the trendiest labels in town.

Josephine de Huertas
Via del Governo Vecchio 68
Tel. 066876586
www.josephinedehuertas.com
The Roman vintage kingdom: colorful, provocative clothes.

Laura Urbinati
Via dei Banchi Vecchi 50/A
Tel. 0668136478
www.lauraurbinati.com
Bikinis in a thousand colors, slinky dresses and sophisticated accessories for that dream holiday.

Le Gallinelle
Via del Boschetto 76, Tel. 064881017
www.legallinelle.it
Super chic vintage in an erstwhile butcher's shop, haunt of actors and eccentrics.

ROME - TAILORS

Battistoni
Via dei Condotti 57/61, Tel. 066976111
One of Rome's temples of classical, elegant fashion. Film stars and tycoons both head to Battistoni to stock up on their impeccable hand sewn suits in superb materials. An enchanted store with all the fascination of past times.

Davide Cenci
Via Campo Marzio 1/7,
Tel. 066990681
Bespoke suits and a selection of prestigious label designs.

Sorelle Fontana
Via Fontanella Borghese 67/71
Tel. 0668135406

Shopping in Via dei Condotti.

When the three Fontana sisters Zoe, Micol and Giovanna designed Linda Christian's fabulous wedding dress for her marriage to Tyrone Power, this Roman dressmaker shot to international fame and is now a must for those in the know. The boutique still exerts a powerful spell and is the place to go for a fairy tale evening dress to match an enchanted evening.

Tombolini
Via della Maddalena 31/38
Tel. 0669200342, www.tombolini.it
Impeccable suits, overcoats in soft cashmere and elegant leather accessories.

ROME - TRENDS

Arsenale
Via del Governo Vecchio 64,
Tel. 066861380
Along the city's most Bohemian street, an eccentric, creative workshop that has the right clothes for every occasion: swirling skirts, soft scarves and naturally very original accessories.

Miss Sixty
Via del Corso 510, Tel. 063219374
www.misssixty.com
An eccentric, colorful space. Young, trendy and a touch kitsch, the place to go for casual, sexy gear.

SHOPPING

Rome has always been a melting-pot of cultural and social events.
As a result, there is a particular fervor for traditional popular festivals and other events at every social level, ranging from noisy, crowded events such as the traditional *palio* to the restrained mysticism of sacred music. *Palios* are held at Allumiere, Canale Monteranno and Castel Madama. At Easter, in Rome, there is the Stations of the Cross, and Velletri holds a Corsa dell'Anello (a jousting competition). These enthralling festivals in and around Rome originated in ancient popular traditions or are based on ancient customs and religious practices that have been going

on for centuries. There are also all types of musical events, meaning there is something for everyone. Indeed, what better way to spend a lovely Roman summer's night than listening to your favorite music in a spectacular setting.

Highlights

- The cultural fervor of Rome expressed in festivals with dramatic settings.
- The special dimension of concerts held against a backdrop of artistic splendor.
- The infectious excitement of the traditional *palios*.
- The colors of Gerano's Infiorata festival.

Inside

MUSIC

Does all music lead to Rome? Well, it certainly seems a tall order to find some style of music that has not prospered on the banks of the Tiber. Rome's magnetism still attracts a wide range of events, now as it did in the past, flowing with all the weight of history towards the capital along its fabled roads. Over the centuries musical development separated into two distinct streams: the formal variety reserved for the aristocracy and the papal court and the popular music passed down through the generations in the oral tradition. From the 15th century onwards Rome played a central role in the development of music in Europe, a role it still plays today, and which is liked to its innate cultural liveliness. Throughout history Rome has nurtured and propagated a vast heritage of musical achievement: for example Rome was one of the cradles of the Gregorian chant, a primary source of European music. As such, the Eternal City can be seen as being by an attractive and driving force in the fertile panorama of European and international musical culture.

CAVE, GENAZZANO, ZAGAROLO

Stradarolo
Last weekend in September
More than 150 musicians, dancers and performers throng the streets and squares of these three medieval villages in a kaleidoscope of concerts and shows.
Info: Tel. 0774550060, www.dizona.com

FRASCATI

Frammenti
First week in September
A festival held in the magic scenario of the villages clustered on the slopes of the Alban Hills just outside Rome: fragments ...of art, ideas, languages and expressive forms that communicate with each other, and coalesce in the framework of the evening festival to stimulate a movement of ideas, a workshop that transforms the stunning grounds of Villa Sciarra into a "cultural territory". A programme packed with proposals from the fields of art, cinema, theatre, literature and music.
Info: Tel. 0774550060, www.dizona.com

ROME

Accademia Nazionale di Santa Cecilia
The St Cecilia Academy is one of the most prestigious musical institutes in the world, besides being home to Italy's largest symphony orchestra. The honor roll of academics associated with the academy resounds with famous names in Italian music, including Paganini, Verdi and Rossini. The sweeping repertoire of the Academy's concerts has been graced with some of the greatest soloists of all time and prestigious conductors such as Strauss, Stravinsky and Toscanini. The Academy's top level teaching and coaching activities also deserve an honorable mention, resting as they do in the capable hands of a team of distinguished musicians divided into their various disciplines. The Academy's great tradition is encapsulated in its huge library and media resource center with its manuscripts and documents, photographs, original scores, audio and video footage and the largest ethno-musicological archive in Italy. Another precious heritage is its collection of approximately 300 instruments.
The Academy's concerts are held in Rome's new Auditorium.
Info: Tel. 0668801044, www.santacecilia.it

The Rome Auditorium
The "Parco della Musica" Auditorium, the largest concert venue in Europe, was designed by Renzo Piano, and is one of the pivots of cultural life in the capital. It is home to Santa Cecilia's orchestra and also hosts a wealth of rock and jazz concerts and events. Info: www.musicaperroma.it

Reading room of the library at the Conservatorio di S. Cecilia.

TCI HIGHLIGHTS

OTHER IMPORTANT CLASSICAL MUSIC SEASONS:

Accademia Filarmonica Romana, Tel. 063201752, www.accademiafilarmonicaromana.com
Istituzione Universitaria dei Concerti, Tel. 063610051, www.concertiiuc.it
Università di Tor Vergata, Tel. 0639372000, http://romasinfonietta.uniroma2.it
Oratorio del Gonfalone, Tel. 066875952

Concerto del I Maggio
1 May
A plethora of well-known groups and solo singers are the life and soul of this traditional concert (workers' day).
Info: Tel. 06488991, www.aptroma.com

Estate Romana -
The Roman Summer Festival
From June to September
The festival hosts many events against the breath-taking backdrop of Rome's magnificent architecture, lighting up the long summer evenings, including concerts, theatre and films.
Info: Tel. 06488991, www.aptroma.com

Festival Internazionale di Musica e Arte Sacra
Mid November
A festival of music in Rome's three patriarchal basilicas proposing music from musical literature throughout the ages.
For further information: Tel. 066869187 www.festivalmusicaeartesacra.net

Il Mare di Roma
From June to September
Rome's three most popular seaside resorts, Ostia, Fiumicino and Fregene, host 24 km of hot cultural events, concerts and theatre cooled by sea breezes.
For further information:
Tel. 06488991, www.aptroma.com

Natale in Vaticano
Mid December
The traditional appointment with the Christmas charity concert held in the Paul VI Auditorium. St Peter's Square is decorated with a spectacular Christmas tree and nativity scene.
Info: Tel. 06488991, www.aptroma.com

Roma incontra il Mondo
Late June-September
In the splendid setting of Villa Ada, it involves musicians from four continents.
Info: Tel. 064180369, www.villada.org

Roma Jazz Festival
Mid October-Mid November
Rome becomes a giant stage for some of the jazz world's top artists. An array of events celebrating cross-pollination between the arts.
For further information:
Tel. 0656305015, www.romajazzfestival.it

San Silvestro
31 December/1 January
Rome traditionally celebrates New Year's Eve with fireworks displays and rock concerts in the main squares (the subway stays open). New Year's day is always celebrated with a classical music concert in the square in front of the Quirinale.
For further information:
Tel. 06488991, www.aptroma.com

Teatro dell'Opera
The Rome Opera House organizes concerts, ballets and operas in various prestigious venues, one of the most striking being its summer season in the imposing setting of the Roman ruins at the Baths of Caracalla.
Info: Tel. 0648160219, www.opera.roma.it

ROVIANO

Tributo a...
Last weekend in August
Each year Roviano organizes a tribute to a nationally or internationally famous singer or group with large numbers of musical talents taking part. The event is linked to a themed exhibition, an arts and crafts market, a tempting array of stalls selling local foods, and places to eat and drink.
For further information:
Tel. 0774550060, www.dizona.com

SUBIACO

Rock Blues Festival
Second week in August
Summer days dedicated to rock, blues, folk music and other alternative sounds with the live participation of numerous talented musicians and groups.
Info: Tel. 0774550060, www.dizona.com

EVENTS

FOLKLORE

The large number of festivals in and around Rome, some centuries-old, some recent, show the healthy vitality of a local culture firmly rooted in local religious, popular and historical tradition. The host of events celebrated in the spring and summer months with their ritual offerings of the earth's produce and decorations in flowers and fruits (for example the numerous flower shows celebrated at Corpus Christi), are all expressions of the creative potential of Roman culture with ancient roots in pre-Christian nature rites subsequently adapted to Christianity. Fire and water are two other primary elements in a large number of ceremonies, both during the summer and in other seasons, they are held to have considerable powers of purification. Another extremely common ritual is that of sharing food or eating together, a habit that reaffirms and maintains the antique desire of the Roman people to gather together as an act of mutual recognition and celebration of their common culture.

ALLUMIERE

Palio delle Contrade
The weekend after 15 August
This festival echoes a popular tradition that goes back to the 16th century and sees the small town's six districts, or *contrade*, in friendly competition to win the prize, or *palio*. Celebrations start on Saturday evening when music and dance enliven each district and form the backdrop to a meal which is offered by the inhabitants of Allumiere to visitors from other places in a sign of friendship. On Sunday the festival opens with a long procession of people in 16th-century outfits, complete with the traditional *sbandieratori*, or banner throwers, and more than 200 participants. The main event of the festival is scheduled after the procession, the *palio*, the competition for the prize, hotly contested between the six districts of Bianca, Burò, Ghetto, Nona, Polveriera and Sant'Antonio. The race is held with donkeys rather than horses, as a homage to these animals who were traditionally used to pull the *alum* (which gave the little town its name) carts. The *palio* is held in three heats, each one run with a different donkey. At the end of the heats the district that has won the most points overall is declared the winner and holds a large party with singing and dancing in their streets.
For further information:
Tel. 0766966743 - www.allumiere.org

CANALE MONTERANO

Palio delle contrade
The Sunday closest to 24 August
The *palio*, is held in two distinct phases,

with a procession in historical costume followed by the "bigonzo race".
Six historic village districts compete for the *palio*: Carraiola, Casenove, Castagno, Centro, Montevirginio and Stigliano. During the first phase the procession wends its way through the streets of the village with each district, or *contrada* represented by roughly a hundred participants all dressed in 16th-century costumes: kings, queens, musicians, archers, banner holders and soldiers on horseback.
The race starts after the procession: the teams representing the six districts have four porters each, they have to run a race carrying the *bigonzi* (wooden barrels used in the grape harvest) on stretchers. The race course covers a stretch of 130 m along the High Street and the barrel and stretcher together must weigh at least 45 kg. The winning district is awarded a silk banner (the *palio*, or prize) and a rotating trophy, a bronze sculpture that the district keeps for a year.
For further information:
Tel. 0699674373

CASTEL MADAMA

Palio Madama Margarita
Second Sunday in July
This *palio* is held in honor of Margaret of Austria, who was given the village castle by her father, Emperor Charles V. The competition is in historical costume and involves the four districts of the little town: Empolitano, Santa Maria della Vittoria, Castelluccio and Borgo. There are five parts to the *palio*: decorations,

the procession, a "Saracen" tilting competition, a flag race and a race, the last three, on horseback, are held in the village stadium. The decorations are judged the evening before the other events, with points are awarded for the district which has managed to decorate its streets in the most attractive and colorful way. The festival proper starts on Sunday morning with a procession made up of about 50 participants from each district in 16th-century costume.

The afternoon is dedicated to the competitions on horseback: the "Saracen" tilting involves hitting the shield of a puppet on a revolving pole squarely with a lance and avoiding being hit by the puppet's outstretched arm as it rotates from the blow; the flag race is run in pairs and its aim is to snatch the adversary's flag (raised on a special pole) as you race round the track and then cross the finishing line first; the race is simply a question of speed, the first to cross the finishing line after five laps of the track. The district that manages to score the greatest number of points at the end of the five competitions wins the title of "Rione Margarita".

The festival attracts thousands of visitors who can also browse through the numerous stalls selling typical local produce which are set up for the occasion.

For further information: Tel. 077445001
www.comunedicastelmadama.it

Another attraction is the enormous frying pan set up on the seafront to cook a huge quantity of fried fish. Stalls selling a variety of goods and tasty food also line the streets for the occasion.

For further information:
Tel. 076625348

GERANO

The Madonna del Cuore Flower Show

The first Sunday following 25 April
An *infiorata* is actually far more than a flower show; the evening after the picture of Our Lady has been taken down from the altar the streets of the town are carpeted with wonderful patterns in flowers, patiently filled in to cover chalk drawings, this is in fact the oldest *infiorata* in Italy. The next morning the portrait of Our Lady is carried in solemn procession by the representatives of the Madonna del Cuore Confraternity, the event organizers, over the carpet of flowers laid down in Piazza della Vittoria. In the past the flower pictures were destroyed immediately after the procession but nowadays it is left intact until the evening when swarms of children lend a willing hand in the *sciarrata*, or destruction of the flowers. The small town of Genzano di Roma also holds an equally charming and famous *infiorata* to celebrate Corpus Christi.

For further information: Tel. 0774798002
www.comunedigerano.it

CIVITAVECCHIA

Palio Marinaro - The Sea Prize

The first Sunday before 15 August
Held on the stretch of water in front of the imposing Forte Michelangelo, the representatives of the town's various districts challenge each other to the so-called Saracen Struggle, in reality a sort of boat race. This is a pageant in historical costume which acts out an attempt by the Saracens, to invade Civitavecchia, which was successfully repelled in the year 800 AD. The amateur actors taking part are all dressed in historical outfits but use real fire and arrows. There are also various competitions for boats and a sailing regatta that the various districts of the town compete in to win the prize banner.

Genzano, a carpet of flowers.

MONTELIBRETTI

Festa della Primavera
First Sunday in June
During the traditional spring festival the four districts of this little town transform it into a Renaissance masterpiece with imposing structures and scenes and 400 participants who recreate life in those days. Events are backed up by an exhibition of local produce offering tastes of the local oil, wine and sweets. In the afternoon the districts challenge each other to a relay race and a ring joust; here a mounted competitor tries to gather as many different-sized rings as possible on his lance. In the evening the winning district receives its prize and the festival continues with music and other entertainment.
For further information:
Tel. 0774600018

ROME

Festa de' noantri
Second half of July
The "Festa de' noantri" (us others) lasts nine days and opens on the Saturday after July 16 for the celebration of the Madonna del Carmine. This is a centuries-old festival that became particularly important in Rome from 1535 onwards. In 1505 a wooden statue of Our Lady was found at the mouth of the Tiber by some Corsican fishermen who brought it upriver to Rome. The statue was given to the Carmelite friars of the church of S.Crisogono, in Trastevere, because it had been found in a wooden case with the stem of the Carmelite friars on it. The inhabitants of Trastevere held a huge festival, which has been repeated every year since then. The statue that is carried in procession today is actually a copy of the original, carved in 1730 and kept in the church of S. Agata. On the Madonna del Carmine feast day the statue is richly decorated by the sisters of the St Mary at Carmine Confraternity and carried in procession. Then it is carried from the church of S. Agata to the Basilica of S. Crisogono where it is left on display for nine days. During the days of the festival the area of Trastevere is a riot of games, stalls, music, dance and happenings. At midnight of the last Sunday of the festival a large fireworks display is held on the slopes of the Aventine Hill. On Monday morning the procession wends its way back to its place of origin. The nine-day party held between the two processions, known as the Festa de' noantri, was celebrated for the first time in 1927; its name in Roman dialect is an expression of pride of the inhabitants of the area of Trastevere.
For further information:
Tel. 0669601202 - 0669601480 - www.romaprimomunicipio.it

Via Crucis
Good Friday
The Stations of the Cross are an antique rite that consists of a procession of people praying in front of the 14 stations of the Cross showing the 14 main stages of Christ's Passion. The individual crosses are known as stations because the priest and the faithful stop for a period of time in front of each one. Every year this ritual is repeated in numerous Italian cities, but obviously Rome has a special significance, with a solemn character that would be impossible to imitate elsewhere. It is the Pope himself who leads the huge crowd of the faithful along the 14 Stations of the Cross strung out between the Colosseum and the Palatine Hill. Here he gives the

 TCI HIGHLIGHTS

ESSENTIAL DIARY DATES ARE HERITAGE WEEK:
(all Rome's state and municipally run museums are open free of charge), the foundation of Rome (celebrates the anniversary of the foundation of Rome in 753 BC with special free tours of Rome's archaeological sites and municipally run museums) and the Notte Bianca (shows, shops and clubs open all night – Tel. 060606, www.lanottebianca.it)
For further information:
Tel. 06488991, www.aptroma.com

participants his blessing from the terrace of the Temple of Venus. The Via Crucis is also known as Calvary after the hill where Christ was crucified.
For further information: Tel. 06488991 - 0636004399 - www.romaturismo.it

SANT'ORESTE

Festa della Madonna di Maggio
Last Sunday in May
During the festival a painting of the Madonna (a copy of the *Madonna delle Stoffe* by Carlo Dolci painted in 1814) is placed on a special triumphal float and carried in procession by the "May Porters" to the hermitage of S. Silvestro on the slopes of Monte Soratte. When the procession arrives the local farmers light a large number of reed torches they have carefully prepared over the preceding months, which light up the whole mountain and can be seen from miles away. The end of the festival is marked by a stunning fireworks display. An extremely picturesque scenario.
For further information:
Tel. 0761579895 - www.prolocosantoreste.com

Festival celebrations at Monte Soratte at night.

SUBIACO

Festa tra Medioevo e Futuro/
Festival of the Medieval and the Future
From mid-December to 6 January
For three weeks over the Christmas period, Subiaco turns the clock back and the old crafts district of the town hosts a series of events, which bring to life the medieval past of the town and its products.
During the 16th century the old part of the town the festival is held in had become the town's commercial hub thanks to its numerous blacksmiths, coppersmiths, carpenters, ceramics workers, bakers and pasta producers. During the festival these ancient workshops are reopened and used to exhibit craftwork and typical Christmas goods. The festival also schedules food and wine tasting aimed at rediscovering traditional country recipes with their local sweets and cakes and the produce of the farms along the Aniene Valley.
There are also shows with actors in historical costume and concerts of medieval music.
For further information:
Tel. 0774822800

VELLETRI

Corsa dell'Anello
The Sunday following 17 January
The festival is held on the feast of St Anthony Abbot and is organized by the University of Mule and Cart Drivers, a guild going back to the ancient medieval universities.
In the morning the banner image of the saint is put up for auction and whoever makes the successful bid has the right to keep it until next year's auction. In the afternoon the key event of the festival takes place: the ring race.
This horseback competition involves managing to use a 30cm long wooden dagger to hook and remove a ring placed on a 2m tall support.
The riders gallop at their targets full tilt and are allowed several attempts. The winner is the horseman who has collected the most rings at the end of the race. Naturally the festival attracts a large number of stalls selling craftwork and food and wine, a number of folk groups also give performances.
For further information:
Tel. 069630896 - www.oltreroma.it

THE A-Z OF WHAT YOU NEED TO KNOW

GETTING TO

By plane

Rome has two airports: Leonardo da Vinci – Fiumicino and G.B. Pastine – Ciampino. The former, located 32 km from the city, is where most national and international flights land, while the latter, located 15 km from the city center, is mainly used for charter flights.

AEROPORTO FIUMICINO
Via dell'Aeroporto di Fiumicino, Tel. 0665951, www.adr.it.

AEROPORTO CIAMPINO, Via Appia Nuova 1651, Tel. 06794941, www.adr.it

TO AND FROM FIUMICINO AIRPORT

CAR – Take the motorway to EUR (exit 30 on the GRA – the main motorway that goes right around Rome, linking the motorway to the various SS roads that actually lead into the center) and, after the Magliana viaduct, take Via C. Colombo following the signs for the "centro".

TRAIN – Leonardo Express to Termini station, with trains every 30 minutes.
Metropolitano FMI train to Tiburtina station (Trastevere,

Ostiense, Tuscolana stops) with trains every 15 minutes (Sundays and holidays, every 30 minutes).

BUS – Terravision Shuttle to Termini station, Tel. 067130531, www.terravision.it
Schiaffini Travel Shuttle to Termini station www.schiaffini.com
Contral to Tiburtina station (runs at night), EUR-Magliana stop on metro line B and the Lepanto stop on metro line A, www.contralspa.it

TAXI – In addition to the taxis at arrivals, both airports have a shuttle service that can be booked (24 or 48 hours in advance): Airport Connection Service, Tel. 06333832212, www.airportconnection.it; Platinum Services, Tel. 0697843186; Airport Shuttle, Tel. 0642013469-064740451-0642014507, www.airportshuttle.it

TO AND FROM CIAMPINO AIRPORT

BUS – Terravision Shuttle to Termini station, Tel. 067130531, www.terravision.it
Schiaffini Travel Shuttle to

Termini station (runs at night), Anagnina stop on metro line A and Ciampino train station (runs every 20 minutes; from the bus stop, you can take the metro to Termini).

By train

TERMINI STATION, Piazza dei Cinquecento, Call Center Trenitalia 892021, www.romatermini.it.
The station, which is where most Intercity and Eurostar trains arrive, is the hub of the city transport system (this is where the two metro lines meet); on the piazza in front of the station, aside from the taxis, there are numerous stops for the local transport buses.

TIBURTINA STATION, Piazza della Stazione Tiburtina, Call Center Trenitalia 892021, www.trenitalia.com.
The station is on metro line B and bus routes 492, 649, and 40N. It has a 24 hour supermarket.

By car

The main motorway, called an Autostrada, is the A1. Coming from the north, take the Roma

TRANSPORT

Public Transport

METRO LINES, Tel. 0657531, www.metroroma.it; operating 5.30am to 23.30pm (Saturdays 0.30am).

BUS AND TRAM
The public transport services operate in the stations of: Termini, Trastevere, Ostiense, Tuscolana, Flaminio and Tiburtina.
Atac, Via Volturno 59, www.atac.roma.it
Trambus, Via Prenestina 45, Tel. 0646951, www.trambus.com
CoTral, Via Carducci 2, www.cotralspa.it

Car hire

Avis, Tel. 06452108391, www.avisautonoleggio.it
Fiumicino Tel. 0665011531
Ciampino Tel. 0679340195
Termini station Tel. 064814373
Hertz, www.hertz.it
Fiumicino Tel. 0665011553
Ciampino Tel. 0679340616

Termini station Tel. 064740389
Europcar, www.europcar.it
Fiumicino Tel. 0665010879
Ciampino Tel. 0679340387
Termini station Tel. 064882854
Maggiore National, www.maggiore.it
Fiumicino Tel. 0665010678 - 0665011508
Ciampino Tel. 0679340368
Termini station Tel. 064880049 - 064883715

MOTORBIKE AND SCOOTER RENTAL
New Scooter for Rent, Via IV Novembre 96 a/b, Tel. 066790300
Roma in Scooter, Corso Vittorio Emanuele II 204, Tel. 066876922
Scooters for Rent, Via della Purificazione 84, Tel. 064885485
Happy Rent, Via Farini 3, Tel. 064818185
Treno e Scooter, Termini station, Via Marsala, Tel. 0648905823

CONTACTS

BIKE RENTAL
Bici & Baci, Via del Viminale 5, Tel. 064828443
Happy Rent, Via Farini 3, Tel. 064818185
Treno e Scooter, Termini station, Via Marsala, Tel. 0648905823

GUIDED TOURS AND ASSOCIATIONS
Sindacato Nazionale delle Guide Turistiche, Via S. Maria alle Fornaci 8/d, Tel. 066390409, www.centroguideroma.it
Centro Guide CAST, Via Cavour 184, Tel. 064825698 - 064880848, www.cast-turismo.it
Guide di Roma e Vaticano, Via L. Gadola 3, Tel. 0662304101, www.guideroma.com
Cooperativa Sociale Il Sogno, Viale Regina Margherita 192, Tel. 0685301758, www.romeguide.it - There are numerous interesting tours, including the

Nord exit off the A1 and you get onto the SS4 Salaria road; coming from the south, take the Roma Sud exit off the A1 and you get onto the GRA (motorway around Rome) at exit 19 or Est (A24). To get to the main parts of the city from the GRA, use the following exits:

Vatican, Prati, Castel S. Angelo: 1 SS1 Aurelia

Foro Italico, Piazza del Popolo, Villa Borghese, Piazza di Spagna: 3 SS2 Cassia and 6 SS3 Flaminia

Villa Ada, Villa Borghese, Via Veneto: 8 SS4 Salaria

Porta Pia, Termini station: 11 SP Nomentana

S. Lorenzo: 13 SS5 Tiburtina

Termini station, S. Maria Maggiore: 16 SP Prenestina and 18 SS6 Casilina

S. Giovanni in Laterano: 21 SS215 Tuscolana and 23 SS7 Appia

EUR, S. Paolo fuori le Mura, Testaccio, Colosseum, Trastevere: 26 SS148 Pontina and 27 Via Colombo

By bus

Eurojet, Tel. 064747703, www.eurojetviaggi.it
Eurolines, www.eurolines.it

CLIMATE

The climate is temperate, typically Mediterranean and definitely enviable. The summers are often quite hot, but spring and autumn are characterized by good weather and the winters are not too harsh.

Planetarium, the municipal Astronomy Museum, the Rome Ghost Tour and a walk in the Ponte district through the mysterious history of Ancient Rome.

Eur, Salone delle Fontane, Via Ciro il Grande 10, Tel. 0644340160, www.romaeur.it – A tour of the Eur area.

Zètema Progetto Cultura, Via Attilio Benigni 55/59, Tel. 06820771, www.zetema.it – guided tours of the city as well as of the Etruscan necropolises of Cerveteri and Tarquinia.

110 Open, Tel. 0646952252 – open-top bus tours with multilingual guides and audio-guides; stop&go options where you can get on and off at the scheduled stops throughout the day.

Archeobus, www.trambus.com/servizi turistici.htm – tours,

with multilingual guides, of the archeological sites of Appia Antica.

Air and balloon tours

Cityfly, Tel. 0688333, www.cityfly.com – 20 minute aerial tours of the city at 450 m that give you a bird's-eye view of the city.

Hot-air balloon, Tel. 0632111511, www.aerophile.it – at 150 m, this is a thrilling way to discover Rome. Special flights can be booked: Art flights, with art historians, "Wings on your Feet", for people in wheelchairs, and a flying aperitif.

WEBSITE OF ROME

www.romaturismo.it
www.comune.roma.it
www.abcroma.it
www.romeguide.it
www.inroma.to
www.enjoyrome.com
www.dizona.com

Inside

Tourist information

Hotels and restaurants

At night

Museums and monuments

EMERGENCY NUMBERS

112	Military Police (Carabinieri)
113	State Police (Polizia)
115	Fire Department
117	Financial Police
118	Medical Emergencies
1515	Fire-watch
803116	Road Assistance

ALBANO LAZIALE

📋 c/o IAT Frascati
Piazza Marconi 1,
Tel. 069420331

Hotels

Miralago ★★★ ★
Via dei Cappuccini 12
Tel. 069321018
www.hotelmiralagorist.it
45 rooms
Credit cards: American Express, Diners Club, Visa, Mastercard, Bancomat
Located in a quiet area and immersed in the green Castelli Romani Park, the hotel offers cozy charming rooms and a restaurant serving local food. During summer, you can dine in the garden. Internet point for residents.

Restaurants

Antica Abbazia ❢ ★
Via S. Filippo Neri 19
Tel. 069323187
Closed Mondays
Credit cards: American Express, Diners Club, Visa, Mastercard, Bancomat
The two indoor restaurants and, during summer, an outside garden restaurant serve typical Italian food including home-made desserts.

Museums, Monuments and Churches

Musei Civici di Albano
Viale Risorgimento 3
Tel. 069323490-069325759
www.museicivicialbano.it
Mondays, Tuesdays, Fridays, Sundays 9.00-13.00; Wednesdays, Thursdays 9.00-13.00, 16.00-19.00; Saturdays 8.00-14.00

ANZIO

📋 Ufficio Informazioni Turistiche
Piazza Pia 19, Tel. 069845147

Hotels

G.H. dei Cesari ★★★★
Via Mantova 3, Tel. 06987901
www.hoteldeicesari.com
72 rooms
Large seafront hotel with private parking. Residents can enjoy hotel facilities such as sauna, swimming pool, fitness club and restaurant. The restaurant is open to non-residents.

Lido Garda ★★★ ★
Piazza Caboto 8, Tel. 069870354
www.lidogarda.com
42 rooms
A short distance from the ferry-boats to the Pontine Islands, this 1970s' hotel offers a swimming

pool and a restaurant serving seafood specialties.

Restaurants

Alceste al Buon Gusto ❢❢
Piazzale S. Antonio 6
Tel. 069846744
Closed Tuesdays
Typical seafood restaurant with two beach-front terraces.

Flora ❢❢
Via Flora 9, Tel. 069846001
www.ristoranteflora.it
Closed Tuesdays (except in summer)
Local and classic cuisine.
Credit cards: American Express, Diners Club, Visa, Mastercard, Bancomat
Restaurant with private rooms During summer you can dine in the garden; its cuisine includes daily fresh seafood and meat specialties.

Boccuccia ❢ ★
Lavinio Stazione, Via Nettunense km 31,5, Tel. 069870567
www.ristoranteboccuccia.it
Closed Tuesdays
Credit cards: American Express, Diners Club, Visa
Noted for its spacious indoor and outdoor spaces, (during summer, you can enjoy dining in the garden under a lovely gazebo), the restaurant serves local food including seafood, meat and pizza cooked in a wood-oven.

Museums, Monuments and Churches

Museo Civico Archeologico
Via di Villa Adele 2
Tel. 0698499479-0698499411-3284117535
www.comune.anzio.roma.it
Mondays-Fridays 9.00-13.00, 15.00-18.00; Saturdays and holidays: 10.30-12.30, 16.00-18.00

Museo dello Sbarco di Anzio
Via di Villa Adele 1, Tel. 069845147
Tuesdays, Thursdays , Saturdays, Sundays 10.00-12.30, 16.00-18.00 (in summer 17.00-19.00)

ARICCIA

📋 c/o IAT Frascati
Piazza Marconi 1,
Tel. 069420331

Hotels

Villa Aricia ★★★ �␣
Via Villini 4/6 (Appia Nuova)
Tel. 069321161
www.hotelvillaricia.com
63 rooms
Credit cards: American Express, Diners Club, Visa, Mastercard, Bancomat
In a large park, this 19th-century

hotel has been completely refurbished. Its restaurant offers typical, local dishes (including the excellent porchetta).

CAPRANICA PRENESTINA

Museo Civico Naturalistico dei Monti Prenestini
Piazza Aristide Frezza 5
Tel. 069584031 – 069584126,
www.comunecapranica.it
The museum opening hours vary according to the season.

CASTEL GANDOLFO

📋 c/o IAT Frascati
Piazza Marconi 1,
Tel. 069420331

Hotels

Castelvecchio ★★★★ ⅟
Viale Pio XI 23, Tel. 069360308
www.hotelcastelvecchio.com
48 rooms
Credit cards: American Express, Diners Club, Visa, Mastercard, Bancomat
Close to the Papal gardens, this stylish art nouveau palace faces the Albano lake. Furnished with taste, the hotel has a restaurant as well. In its roof-terrace residents can enjoy the solarium with swimming pool.

Restaurants

Antico Ristorante Pagnanelli ❢❢ ★
Via A. Gramsci 4, Tel. 069360004
www.pagnanelli.it
Closed Tuesdays
Credit cards: American Express, Diners Club, Visa, Mastercard, Bancomat
Regional tradition and fine cuisine characterize this warm and cozy restaurant with a magnificent lake view. Its wine cellar has been built into the lava rock and offers around two thousand different wine labels. Wide selection of olive oils, cheeses, and salami.

CERVETERI

📋 Associazione Artemide
Piazza A. Moro 1,
Tel. 0699552637

Restaurants

Vladimiro ai Bastioni ❢❢
Via Agillina 25/27, Tel. 069953061
Open evenings, except Sundays
Closed Wednesdays
Credit cards: Visa, Mastercard, Bancomat
A restaurant located in the historic center serves Mediterranean food.

Sora Lella ¶
Castello di Ceri 6, Tel. 0699207292
Closed Wednesdays
Credit cards: Visa, Bancomat
Fully immersed in the natural inland, this restaurant has a terrace facing the ancient town walls. It serves home-made, local produce.

Rural Lodgins

Casale di Gricciano
Gricciano Quota 177,
Via di Gricciano 16, Tel. 069941358
www.casaledigricciano.com
Closed January
Credit cards: American Express, Diners Club, Visa
Set in the hills, residents can enjoy a real holiday in the countryside as well as at historic Etruscan sites and the beach of "Campo di Mare". Among the farmhouse facilities are swimming pool, restaurant and bicycle rental. The area is renowned worldwide for its artichokes, fruits, olive oils and wines.

CIVITAVECCHIA

> ☑ **IAT**
> *Viale Giuseppe Garibaldi*
> *42, Tel. 076625348*

Hotels

De la Ville **** ♿
Viale della Repubblica 4
Tel. 0766580507
www.roseshotels.it
45 rooms
Credit cards: American Express, Diners Club, Visa, Mastercard
The hotel, built in the second half of the 19th century, is not far from the rail station and the port. It offers some private rooms built in the old original spa. The hotel restaurant serves seafood specialties.

Sunbay Park Hotel **** ♿
Via Aurelia Sud km 67,5
Tel. 076622801
www.sunbayparkhotel.it
58 rooms
Credit cards: American Express, Diners Club, Visa, Mastercard, Bancomat
The hotel has a small private port, swimming pools, private parking, tennis and squash courts, fitness club and a restaurant serving mainly seafood dishes.

Restaurants

L'Angoletto ¶¶
Via P. Guglielmotti 2 corner Viale della Vittoria 19, Tel. 076632825
www.angoletto.com
Closed Sunday evenings and Mondays
Credit cards: American Express, Diners Club, Visa, Mastercard

The restaurant offers typical food including local seafood specialties, home-made pastas and desserts.

Scaletta ¶¶
Lungoporto Gramsci 65
Tel. 076624334
Closed Tuesdays
Credit cards: American Express, Diners Club, Visa, Mastercard
The restaurant is located close to the port within the Sangallo walls. You can enjoy its wide range of fine local products including cheeses, salami and oils. The restaurant's specialties are seafood and home-made desserts.

FIUMICINO

> ☑ **c/o IAT Civitavecchia**
> *Viale Giuseppe Garibaldi 42,*
> *Tel. 076625348*

Hotels

Hilton Rome Airport **** ♿
Via A. Ferrarin 2, Tel. 0665258
www.hilton.com
517 rooms
Credit cards: American Express, Diners Club, Visa, Mastercard, Bancomat, JCB
Not far from the airport, this large and modern hotel offers state-of-the-art technologies and facilities including private parking, sauna, swimming pool, tennis courts, fitness club and solarium.

Mach 2 *** ♿
Via Portuense 2465, Tel. 066507149
www.hotelmach2.it
40 rooms
Credit cards: American Express, Diners Club, Visa, Mastercard, Bancomat
Just 2 km from the airport, this welcoming modern hotel is located near the sea, the river and the pinewood. It has private parking and a seafood restaurant.

Restaurants

Al Porticciolo-Pascucci ¶¶
Viale Traiano 85, Tel. 0665029204
www.alporticciolo.com
Closed Sunday evenings and Mondays (in July and Agust open all the evenings)
Credit cards: American Express, Diners Club, Visa, Mastercard, Bancomat
A cozy restaurant divided in two rooms serving a seafood menu.

Perla ¶
Via di Torre Clementina 214
Tel. 066505038
Closed Tuesdays
A seafood restaurant.

Marina ¶
Via Torre Clementina 140
Tel. 0665047360

Closed Thursdays
Credit cards: American Express, Diners Club, Visa, Mastercard, Bancomat
A picturesque restaurant located in the port area. Cozy and welcoming it serves seafood specialties and has terracotta flooring and wooden walls.

Rural Lodgins

Borghetto di Roma ♿
Tragliatella, Via di Cadutella 36
Tel. 0630859089
www.borghettodiroma.it
Closed a period in November
Credit cards: Bancomat
Just a few kilometers away from the seaside, this 20th-century farmhouse is set in the hills and has a swimming pool. Its food and produce come from the farm itself. Residents can enjoy walks and horse riding.

Casale Doria Pamphilj ♿ ★
Testa di Lepre, Via O. Occioni
Tel. 066689590
www.doriapamphilj.it
Open mid March-October and December
Credit cards: American Express, Visa, Mastercard, Bancomat
Immersed it the Roman countryside, the farmhouse is located in the bright tall old granary and offers its residents cozy rooms built in the granary with original ceilings and terracotta flooring.

FRASCATI

> ☑ **IAT**
> *Piazza Marconi 1*
> *Tel. 069420331*

Hotels

Cacciani *** ♿
Via Diaz 13/15, Tel. 069401991
www.cacciani.it
21 rooms
Credit cards: American Express, Diners Club, Visa
Located in the heart of Frascati, the hotel offers a terrace view of Rome. Its restaurant serves local food and home-made desserts. Some of the rooms are quite big and located in an old building.

Colonna *** ♿
Piazza del Gesù 12, Tel. 0694018088
www.hotelcolonna.it
20 rooms
Credit cards: American Express, Diners Club, Visa, Mastercard
Recently built with great attention to detail, the hotel has state-of-the art facilities. Its continental and Italian buffet breakfast is served in a magnificent and unusual frescoed room.

Eden Tuscolano ** ♿ ★
Via Tuscolana 15
Tel. 069408589
www.edentuscolano.it
36 rooms
Credit cards: American Express, Diners Club, Visa, Mastercard, Bancomat
A 1920s villa surrounded by a park. The hotel is welcoming and has numerous facilities. It has easy access to Rome. Its restaurant serves both local and Italian cuisine.

Restaurants
Zarazà ↑
Viale Regina Margherita 45
Tel. 069422053
Closed Mondays (Oct to May also Sunday evenings)
Credit cards: American Express, Visa
From the awesome restaurant terrace, you can enjoy a panoramic view of Rome and the Tiburtina Valley. In one of its cozy rooms, guests can admire a "sperone" stone fireplace, a stone that can only be found in this area. The cuisine specializes in local food and home-made desserts.

Museums, Monuments and Churches
Scuderie Aldobrandini - Museo Tuscolano ★
Piazza Marconi 6
Tel. 069417195
www.hochfeiler.it/scuderiealdobran dini
Tuesdays-Fridays 10.00-18.00; Saturdays, Sundays 10.00-19.00

GENZANO DI ROMA

> ℹ️ *c/o IAT Frascati*
> *Piazza Marconi 1,*
> *Tel. 069420331*

Hotels
G.H. Primus ****
Via G. Pellegrino 12, Tel. 069364932
www.grandhotelprimus.it
92 rooms
Credit cards: American Express, Diners Club, Visa, Mastercard
The hotel offers rooms with balconies, a roof restaurant serving local food, private parking and a swimming pool.

Villa Robinia **
Via F.lli Rosselli 19
Tel. 069398617
www.hotelvillarobinia.it
30 rooms
Credit cards: American Express, Diners Club, Visa, Mastercard, Bancomat
Beautifully set among centuries-old trees, the hotel is ideal for

guests looking for a relaxing stay. The restaurant serves local cuisine prepared with local produce.

Restaurants
Enoteca La Grotta ↑↑
Via Italo Balardi 31
Tel. 069364224
Closed Wednesdays
Credit cards: American Express, Diners Club, Visa, Mastercard, Bancomat
Set in a 17th-century setting, the restaurant has an outdoor area for summer. The cuisine uses local produce and the menu varies according to season and availability. Good selection of wines and distilled spirits.

La Scuderia ↑ ★
Piazza Sforza Cesarini 1
Tel. 069390521
Closed Mondays
Credit cards: American Express, Diners Club, Visa, Mastercard, Bancomat, JCB
Located in the former stables of the 17th-century Sforza Cesarini palace, the restaurant offers local food and a good range of wines and distilled spirits.

Rural Lodgins
Agropolis ♿
Landi, Via S. Gennaro 2
Tel. 069370335
www.agropolisagriturismo.net
Open June-September, weekends and holidays
Credit cards: Visa, Mastercard, Bancomat
Set it the Roman Castles Park, the hotel is only 30 km away from Rome and a short walk away from the railway station. Rome is 45 mins by train. The farmhouse offers a panoramic view of the Circeo, the Pontine Islands and the Lepini Mountains. Residents can use the surrounding wide green areas to practice sport or simply to relax. Facilities include a swimming pool and restaurant.

Tre Palme ♿
Landi, prima strada Muti 73
Tel. 069370286
www.trepalmeagriturismo.it
Open March-October
Set among vineyards and olive trees and surrounded by the Roman Castles Park, this nice and relaxing farmhouse is immersed in cultivated fields and furnished mainly with wood. Swimming pool.

GROTTAFERRATA

> ℹ️ *c/o IAT Frascati*
> *Piazza Marconi 1,*
> *Tel. 069420331*

Hotels
G.H. Villa Fiorio **** ♿
Viale Dusmet 28, Tel. 0694548007
www.villafiorio.it
24 rooms
A beautiful Patrician villa immersed in a green park. The inside of the villa has wonderful furnishings. Facilities include private parking, a swimming pool and restaurant.

Park Hotel Villa Grazioli **** ♿
Via U. Pavoni 19
Tel. 069454001
www.villagrazioli.com
62 rooms
Credit cards: American Express, Diners Club, Visa, Mastercard
Magnificent 19th-centrury villa surrounded by a beautiful park; frescoed rooms, stylish guestrooms, private parking, a swimming pool and restaurant.

Verdeborgo *** ♿
Via Anagnina 10
Tel. 06945404
info@hotelverdeborgo.com
www.hotelverdeborgo.it
18 rooms
Credit cards: American Express, Visa, Mastercard, Bancomat
An art deco-style farmhouse surrounded by an age-old park. It offers rooms with wonderful wooden furnishings, terracotta flooring and frescoed ceilings in the common areas.

Restaurants
Cavola d'Oro ↑↑
Via Anagnina 35, Tel. 0694315755
www.lacavoladoro.com
Closed Mondays
Credit cards: American Express, Visa, Bancomat
Ancient Roman-style restaurant with a garden restaurant used in summer. It serves traditional dishes including pizza rustica, meat and seafood specialties.

Nando ↑↑
Via Roma 4, Tel. 069459989
www.ristorantenando.it
Closed Mondays
Credit cards: American Express, Diners Club, Visa, Mastercard, Bancomat, JCB
A fresh, youthful environment which combines local and sophisticated cuisine. The restaurant has two lovely welcoming rural rooms with wooden beams and ceilings. It offers a sophisticated selection of wines and distilled spirits.

Taverna dello Spuntino ↑↑
Via Cicerone 22, Tel. 069459366
www.tavernadellospuntino.com
Credit cards: Visa, Mastercard, Bancomat
Set in a cellar cut into volcanic

rock, this picturesque '60s restaurant offers sophisticated regional cuisine.

La Briciola ⸙
Via G. D'Annunzio 12
Tel. 069459338
Closed Sunday evenings and Mondays
Near the Abbey of S. Nilo, the restaurant offers traditional dishes including seafood specialties.

LADISPOLI

📖 **Pro Loco**
Piazza Della Vittoria 11
Tel. 069913049

Hotels

La Posta Vecchia ★★★★★
Palo Laziale, Tel. 069949501
www.lapostavecchia.com
19 rooms
Credit cards: American Express, Diners Club, Visa, Mastercard, Bancomat
With a view on the Tyrrhenian Sea, this splendid hotel – embellished with wonderful furnishings – was built in the 1600s by Prince Odescalchi. Surrounded by a beautiful garden, residents can admire archeological findings from the glorious Roman Empire. All rooms and suites face either the sea or the park. Facilities include a restaurant, parking, swimming pool.

Villa Margherita ★★★
Via Duca degli Abruzzi 147
Tel. 0699221155, www.bluhotels.it
95 rooms
Credit cards: American Express, Diners Club, Visa, Mastercard, Bancomat
Facing the sea, this hotel has a restaurant and a swimming pool.

Restaurants

Sora Olga ⸙⸙
Via Odescalchi 99, Tel. 0699222006
Closed Wednesday in winter
Credit cards: American Express, Diners Club, Visa, Mastercard, Bancomat
In a welcoming 20th-century building, the hotel offers a simple menu with seafood specialties, pizza and a selection of olive oils.

MARINO

📖 **c/o IAT Frascati**
Piazza Marconi 1,
Tel. 069420331

Restaurants

La Credenza ⸙⸙
Via Cola di Rienzo 4, Tel. 069385105
Closed Sundays and Monday midday
Located in the city center, this

picturesque restaurant with barrel vaults and stone decorations, specializes in local dishes and offers a selection of regional oils, salami and cheese.

Cantina Colonna ⸙
Via G. Carissimi 32, Tel. 0693660386
Open evenings except Saturdays and Sundays
Closed Wednesdays
Credit cards: American Express, Visa, Mastercard, Bancomat
Picturesque restaurant set in the Roman Castles Park specializing in local dishes.

Rural Lodgins

Dormi in Economia
Frattocchie, Via dei Glicini 25
Tel. 0693546776
www.dormineconomia.it
Closed November and January
Comfortable B&B surrounded by vineyards and olive trees. Located near Castelgandolfo, residents can enjoy hiking and walking in the surroundings of the Castelgandolfo and Nemi lakes.

MONTE PORZIO CATONE

📖 **c/o IAT Frascati**
Piazza Marconi 1,
Tel. 069420331

Hotels

Villa Vecchia ★★★★ ♿
Via Frascati 49, Tel. 0694340096
www.villavecchia.it
92 rooms
Credit cards: American Express, Diners Club, Visa, Mastercard
Set in the hills and surrounded by centuries-old olive trees, this 16th-century hotel combines modern comfort and a taste of the past. Facilities include private parking, a sauna, swimming pool, fitness club and restaurant.

Restaurants

I Tinelloni ⸙
Via dei Tinelloni 10
Tel. 069447071
www.itinelloni.com
Closed Wednesdays
Credit cards: American Express, Diners Club, Visa, Mastercard, Bancomat
A welcoming restaurant offering outdoor table service in summer. Its traditional and local cuisine specializes in grilled vegetables, high-quality salami, spaghetti all'amatriciana (spaghetti with bacon and tomato sauce), coda alla vaccinara (Roman oxtail skew), stewed innards with artichokes and home-made desserts.

NEMI

📖 **c/o IAT Frascati**
Piazza Marconi 1,
Tel. 069420331

Hotels

Diana Park Hotel ★★★★
Via Nemorense 44, Tel. 069364041
www.hoteldiana.com
30 rooms
Credit cards: American Express, Diners Club, Visa, Bancomat
Modern hotel with garden, terrace private parking, restaurant with view of the lake where you can try traditional local dishes.

Museums, Monuments and Churches

Museo delle Navi Romane
Via di Diana 15, Tel. 069398040
www.archeologia.beniculturali.it
Mondays-Saturdays 09.00-19.00;
Sundays 09.00-13.00

OSTIA ANTICA

Museums, Monuments and Churches

Museo Ostiense
Viale dei Romagnoli 717
Tel. 0656358099-0656352830
www.itnw.roma.it/ostia/scavi
January, February, November and December: Tuesdays-Sundays 9.00-16.30. March: Tuesdays-Sundays 9.00-17.30. Summertime (last Sun in Mar-last Sun in Oct): Tuesdays-Sundays 9.00-13.30, 14.15-18.30. Last Sunday in October-end October: Tuesdays-Sundays 9.00-17.30

PALESTRINA

📖 **c/o IAT Subiaco**
Via Cadorna 59,
Tel. 0774822013

Hotels

Stella ★★★
Piazzale della Liberazione 3
Tel. 069538172, www.hotelstella.it
28 rooms
Credit cards: American Express, Diners Club, Visa, Mastercard, Bancomat
Set in the city center, the hotel is classical and comfortable at the same time. Its restaurant is open also to non-residents.

Rural Lodgins

Le Colline
Via Colle Pastino 20, Tel. 069575670
www.agriturismobiolecolline.com
Closed end-August-mid September
Farmhouse surrounded by ancient ruins located in the Roman countryside, right below the first

Apennine mountains. Residents can not only enjoy the wonderful countryside but also oriental practices like shiatsu, Ayurvedic massages and iridology. Trips to Rome, Tivoli, Subiaco, Frascati, Fiuggi and Ciociaria, as well as walks into the Alban Hill Nature Park and the wood valleys of the Simbruini Mts. Bike rental, swimming pool and restaurant.

Museums, Monuments and Churches

Museo Nazionale Archeologico Prenestino
Via Barberini 22, Tel. 069538100
www.archeologia.beniculturali.it/p ages/atlante/S66.html
January-February, November March-October 9.00-17.00; September 9.00-17.30; April 9.00-18.00; May 9.00-18.30; June-Agust 9.00-19.30

ROME

i **APT Roma**
Via Parigi 11, Tel. 06488991
www.romaturismo.it
Leonardo da Vinci Airport Fiumicino, Terminal B
Tel. 0665956074
i **Enjoy Rome**
Via Marghera 8a
Tel. 064451843-064450734
www.enjoyrome.com
i **Ufficio Informazioni Comune di Roma**
Stazione Termini, binario 4
Tel. 0648906300
i **Ufficio Pellegrini e Turisti**
Piazza S. Pietro
Tel. 06884466
i **Punti Informazione Turistica**
Open all year 9.00-18.00
Castel S. Angelo: Piazza Pia
Fontana di Trevi:
Via Minghetti
Piazza Navona:
Piazza Cinque Lune
S. Giovanni in Laterano:
Piazza S. Giovanni
S. Maria maggiore:
Via dell'Olmata
Stazione Termini:
Galleria Gommata and Piazza dei Cinquecento
Trastevere: Piazza Sonnino
Via dei Fori Imperiali:
Piazza Tempio della Pace
Via Nazionale:
Palazzo delle Esposizioni

Hotels

Aldrovandi Palace ***** &
Via U. Aldrovandi 15, Tel. 063223993
www.aldrovandi.com
121 rooms

Credit cards: American Express, Diners Club, Visa, Mastercard
Large hotel with every facility and comfort located just at a short walk from the Villa Borghese Park and the old city center. The hotel offers a wonderful private garden with a swimming pool, fitness club and restaurant.

Bernini Bristol ***** ★
Piazza Barberini 23, Tel. 06488931
www.berninibristol.com
127 rooms
Credit cards: American Express, Diners Club, Visa, Mastercard
Built in 1870 and rebuilt in 1939, the hotel combines the tradition and the splendor of those years. Set in the city center, it offers large rooms furnished with old tapestries and antiques. Rooms and suites (with hydromassage) all having stylish and classy furnishings. Fitness club and restaurant.

De Russie ***** &
Via del Babuino 9, Tel. 06328881
www.roccofortehotels.com
125 rooms
Credit cards: American Express, Visa, Mastercard
In the heart of Rome, this early 19th-century building has stylish and classy furnishings. Its rooms and suites offer every comfort and most of them face the Secret Garden created in the 1700s by the architect Valadier. Facilities include a restaurant, wellness center with swimming pool, sauna and fitness club.

G.H. De La Minerve ***** &
Piazza della Minerva 69
Tel. 06695201
www.hotel-invest.com
135 rooms
Credit cards: American Express, Diners Club, Visa, Mastercard, Bancomat
Located in a 17th-century palace, the hotel's atmosphere is elegant and sophisticated at the same time. Facilities include a swimming pool and the restaurant serves Mediterranean cuisine. The roof garden is open in the evening (June to September).

G.H. Parco dei Principi ***** &
Via Frescobaldi 5, Tel. 06854421
www.parcodeiprincipi.com
180 rooms
Credit car ds: American Express, Diners Club, Visa, Mastercard, Bancomat
Close to the Villa Borghese gardens, the hotel is an oasis of peace and elegance immersed in a park with a swimming pool. Residents can enjoy three restaurants, a fitness club, sauna and a gym.

St. Regis Grand Hotel ***** &
Via Vittorio Emanuele Orlando 3
Tel. 0647091
www.stregis.com/grandrome
161 rooms
Credit cards: American Express, Diners Club, Visa, Mastercard
Magnificent 19th-century building located in one of the most elegant and beautiful parts of Rome. The hotel rooms are refined with antique furnishings. Sauna, fitness club and restaurant.

The Westin Excelsior ***** &
Via Vittorio Veneto 125
Tel. 0647081
www.westin.com/excelsiorrome
319 rooms
Credit cards: American Express, Diners Club, Visa, Mastercard
A short walk away from the Villa Borghese gardens and immersed in the legendary charm of Via Veneto, the hotel is embellished with old furnishings and golden decoration. Restaurant, piano bar, sauna, swimming pool and fitness clubs.

Aleph ***** &
Via S. Basilio 15, Tel. 06422901
www.boscolohotels.com
96 rooms
Credit cards: American Express, Diners Club, Visa, Mastercard, Bancomat
A wonderful mix of luxury, sophisticated design and modern technology, the hotel has comfortable rooms – some with private balconies – a sauna, fitness club, steam room, reading area, wine bar, roof garden and restaurant.

Aran Park Hotel **** &
Via R. Forster 24, Tel. 06510721
www.aranhotels.com
324 rooms
Credit cards: American Express, Diners Club, Visa, Mastercard
Out of town but only 15 mins from the city center and 30 mins from the airport. The hotel is immersed in a huge park and offers bright rooms with marbled bathrooms. Roof garden restaurant serving regional food. Lounge bar and a fitness club.

Art **** &
Via Margutta 56, Tel. 06328711
www.hotelart.it
46 rooms
Credit cards: American Express, Diners Club, Visa, Mastercard, Bancomat
Located nearby art galleries and antiques shops, the hotel is a restored old boarding school in which residents can admire bronze busts, serigraphies and architectural works from Bernini, Borromini and Le Corbusier, and poems hung on walls. The

bedrooms are high-tech and the modern comforts are perfectly combined with handmade headboards in Florentine Leather. Sauna and fitness center.

Artemide ★★★★ &
Via Nazionale 22, Tel. 06489911
www.hotelartemide.it
85 rooms
Credit cards: American Express, Diners Club, Visa, Mastercard
19ᵗʰ-century palace with briar-root furnishings and travertine bathrooms. Its bar/restaurant serves regional cuisine.

Atahotel Villa Pamphili ★★★★ & ★
Via della Nocetta 105, Tel. 066602
www.hotelvillapamphili.com
247 rooms
Credit cards: American Express, Diners Club, Visa, Mastercard, Bancomat, JCB
All rooms have balconies with a view of the "Doria Pamphilj" park. The hotel facilities include a restaurant, free shuttle service to and from the town center and Fiumicino airport, swimming pool, tennis courts and fitness club.

Atlante Star ★★★★ ★
Via Vitelleschi 34, Tel. 066873233
www.atlantehotels.com
61 rooms
Credit cards: American Express, Diners Club, Visa, Mastercard
A sophisticated 1920s hotel with stylish and comfortable bedrooms. Its bathrooms are made of marble and have spa bathtubs. Roof garden and three restaurants.

Barberini ★★★★ &
Via Rasella 3, Tel. 064814993
www.hotelbarberini.com
35 rooms
A late 19ᵗʰ-century hotel embellished with precious marble, rooms with classy furnishings and state-of-the art technology. Internet access, American bar, roof garden with panoramic view and restaurant.

Best Western Hotel President ★★★★ &
Via Emanuele Filiberto 173 Tel. 06770121
www.rosciolihotels.com
192 rooms
Credit cards: American Express, Diners Club, Visa, Mastercard
Located nearby San Giovanni in Laterano, the hotel offers every comfort. The restaurant serves both local and international cuisine.

Beverly Hills ★★★★ ★
Largo B. Marcello 220 Tel. 068542141
www.hotelbeverly.com
183 rooms

The hotel has rooms with classical wooden furnishings, cozy common areas, a restaurant serving both Italian and local cuisine, fitness club and Internet access.

Capo d'Africa ★★★★ &
Via Capo d'Africa 54, Tel. 06772801
www.hotelcapodafrica.com
65 rooms
Credit cards: American Express, Diners Club, Visa, Mastercard
Just a short walk away from the Colosseum, the hotel has rooms varying in furnishings and styles, balconies with panoramic views and a small restaurant. Facilities include Internet access and a fitness club.

Columbus ★★★★ &
Via della Conciliazione 33 Tel. 066865435
www.hotelcolumbus.net
92 rooms
Credit cards: American Express, Diners Club, Visa, Mastercard
A very comfortable and stylish hotel built inside the 15ᵗʰ-century Palazzo della Rovere, very close to the Vatican City. Garden restaurant.

Degli Aranci ★★★★ &
Via B. Oriani 11, Tel. 068070202
www.hoteldegliaranci.com
54 rooms
Credit cards: American Express, Diners Club, Visa, Mastercard, Bancomat
Just behind Villa Borghese, an art nouveau hotel with rooms offering all comforts (some baths with hydromassage) and a garden restaurant on the terrace.

Dei Consoli ★★★★ &
Via Varrone 2/D, Tel. 0668892972
www.hoteldeiconsoli.com
28 rooms
Credit cards: American Express, Diners Club, Visa, Mastercard, Bancomat, JCB
Located between the Vatican and Piazza di Spagna, a late 19ᵗʰ-century palace full of an atmosphere of bygone times, elegant bedrooms with marbled bathrooms and Spanish porcelain.

Delle Nazioni ★★★★ & ★
Via Poli 7, Tel. 066792441
www.remarhotels.com/nazioni
83 rooms
Credit cards: American Express, Diners Club, Visa
Just a short walk from Piazza Fontana, the hotel is a palace immersed in bygone charm with amazing halls and elegant and comfortable bedrooms.

Empire Palace Hotel ★★★★ &
Via Aureliana 39, Tel. 06421281
www.empirepalacehotel.com
110 rooms

Credit cards: American Express, Diners Club, Visa, Mastercard
Prestigious building that once belonged to the Mocenigos (in 1870), a noble family from Venice. Its facade, arcades and wall decorations still maintain some architectural traits typical of Venetian palaces. Also restaurant.

Farnese ★★★★ ★
Via A. Farnese 30, Tel. 063212553
www.hotelfarnese.com
23 rooms
Credit cards: American Express, Diners Club, Visa, Mastercard, Bancomat
An early 20ᵗʰ-century Patrician villa located between Piazza del Popolo and the Vatican City. Furnished with antiques and extremely classy, it has an amazing roof terrace.

Giulio Cesare ★★★★
Via degli Scipioni 287 Tel. 063210751
www.hotelgiuliocesare.com
90 rooms
Credit cards: American Express, Diners Club, Visa
A 20ᵗʰ-century hotel with a small private garden that combines 19ᵗʰ-century antique furnishings and modern facilities.

Gladiatori ★★★★
Via Labicana 125, Tel. 0677591380
www.hotelgladiatori.it
17 rooms
Credit cards: American Express, Diners Club, Visa, Mastercard
A small but exclusive hotel just a short walk away from the Collosseum and ruins from Imperial Rome, it offers soothing and welcoming bedrooms. Also roof garden restaurant.

Holiday Inn Rome West ★★★★ &
Via Aurelia km 8.4, Tel. 0666411200
www.alliancealberghi.com/ rome-west-hi
237 rooms
Credit cards: American Express, Diners Club, Visa
Immersed in the green, the hotel provides a shuttle service to the Marcello theatre and Fiumicino airport. It has a restaurant serving regional cuisine, a garden with an evening piano bar, swimming pool and fitness club.

Imperiale ★★★★
Via Vittorio Veneto 24 Tel. 064826351
www.hotelimperialeroma.it
95 rooms
Credit cards: American Express, Diners Club, Visa, Mastercard, Bancomat
Located in a suggestive 17ᵗʰ-century building, the hotel prides itself on comfort.

Jolly Hotel Leonardo da Vinci **** ⚀ ★
Via dei Gracchi 324, Tel. 06328481
www.jollyhotels.it
256 rooms
Credit cards: American Express, Visa, Bancomat
Right in the center, the hotel has rooms and bedrooms with every modern comfort. Also restaurant.

Jolly Hotel Midas **** ⚀ ★
Via Aurelia 800, Tel. 06663961
www.jollyhotels.com
344 rooms
Credit cards: American Express, Diners Club, Visa, Mastercard, Bancomat, JCB
Close to Fiumicino airport, this modern and classy hotel has a restaurant, piano bar, swimming pool and a free shuttle service to the town center.

Jolly Hotel Villa Carpegna **** ★
Via Pio IV 6, Tel. 06393731
www.jollyhotels.it
201 rooms
Credit cards: American Express, Diners Club, Visa, Mastercard
Set in a green and quiet area, the hotel has comfortable rooms, a restaurant, Internet access, swimming pool and fitness club.

Jolly Hotel Vittorio Veneto **** ⚀ ★
Corso d'Italia 1, Tel. 0684951
www.jollyhotels.com
201 rooms
Credit cards: American Express, Visa, Mastercard, Bancomat
A modern and functional hotel against the backdrop of the Villa Borghese gardens. Its restaurant organizes interesting events themed with different gastronomic specialties. Also evening piano bar.

Locanda Cairoli **** ⚀ ★
Piazza B. Cairoli 2
Tel. 0668809278
www.locandacairoli.it
13 rooms
Credit cards: American Express, Diners Club, Visa, Mastercard, Bancomat
Set in the Campo de' Fiori area, this small but very pretty hotel offers customized service to meet all clients' needs.

Locarno **** ⚀
Via della Penna 22, Tel. 063610841
www.hotellocarno.com
66 rooms
Credit cards: American Express, Diners Club, Visa, Mastercard
An art nouveau style palace with antique furnishings, fireplace in the common areas and comfortable bedrooms with wooden floors. Internet access, terrace, garden and restaurant.

Marcella Royal **** ⚀
Via FlaVia 106, Tel. 0642014591
www.marcelloroyalhotel.com
86 rooms
Credit cards: American Express, Diners Club, Visa, Mastercard
An Umbertinian hotel with pretty and comfortable bedrooms. Solarium and roof garden with panoramic view of the city.

Mascagni **** ★
Via V. E. Orlando 90
Tel. 0648904040
www.hotelmascagni.com
40 rooms
Credit cards: American Express, Diners Club, Visa, Mastercard, Bancomat
In a street located between Villa Borghese, Via Veneto and the Quirinale, the hotel was first built in the early 20th century and now has state-of-the-art comforts and facilities.

Mecenate Palace Hotel **** ⚀
Via Carlo Alberto 3, Tel. 0644702024
www.mecenatepalace.com
62 rooms
Credit cards: American Express, Diners Club, Visa, Mastercard
A charming building in the Renaissance style, refurbished and comfortly furnished in the romantic atmosphere of the late 1800; roof garden with view on the town.

Meliá Roma Aurelia Antica **** ⚀ ★
Via degli Aldobrandeschi 223
Tel. 0666544, www.solmelia.com
270 rooms
Credit cards: American Express, Diners Club, Visa, Mastercard, Bancomat, JCB
Just 15 mins from Fiumicino airport, an elegant and classy hotel with state-of-the-art comforts. Swimming pool and shuttle service to the center.

Memphis **** ★
Via degli Avignonesi 36
Tel. 06485849
www.remarhotels.com/memphis
17 rooms
Credit cards: American Express, Diners Club, Visa, Mastercard
Close to Via Tritone, this small hotel has good facilities and cozy bedrooms.

Napoleon **** ★
Piazza Vittorio Emanuele 105
Tel. 064467264, www.napoleon.it
75 rooms
Credit cards: American Express, Diners Club, Visa, Mastercard, Bancomat
Halfway between the Colosseum and the Termini railway station, the hotel has stylish rooms and a restaurant.

Nazionale **** ⚀
Piazza Montecitorio 131
Tel. 06695001
www.nazionaleroma.it
95 rooms
Credit cards: American Express, Diners Club, Visa
Behind a 18th-century facade with a view on Piazza Montecitorio, the hotel has elegant and classy bedrooms. The restaurant offers traditional Italian cuisine.

Novotel Roma la Rustica **** ⚀ ★
Via A. Noale 291
Tel. 06227661
www.accorhotels.com/italia
149 rooms
Credit cards: American Express, Diners Club, Visa, Mastercard, Bancomat
In a strategic location, the hotel has comfortable rooms with double-glazing windows, Internet access, an American bar, swimming pool, and shuttle service to and from Termini railway station.

Oxford **** ★
Via Boncompagni 89
Tel. 064203601
www.hoteloxford.com
56 rooms
Credit cards: American Express, Diners Club, Visa, Mastercard, Bancomat
A short walk from Via Veneto – built inside a 19th-century palace, the hotel has rooms with classical wooden furnishings, a restaurant serving traditional Italian cuisine and a bar.

Palace **** ⚀
Via Vittorio Veneto 70
Tel. 06478719
www.boscolohotels.com
94 rooms
Credit cards: American Express, Diners Club, Visa, Mastercard, Bancomat
An old art deco building with a beautifully frescoed hall. The restaurant specializes in local cuisine. Swimming pool.

Park Hotel dei Massimi **** ⚀
Largo Vincenzo Ambrosio 9
Tel. 0635347200
www.massimiparkhotel.it
85 rooms
Credit cards: American Express, Diners Club, Visa, Mastercard, Bancomat
A short walk from the Vatican, the hotel offers intimate and cozy rooms. Also restaurant.

Piranesi **** ★
Via del Babuino 196, Tel. 06328041
www.hotelpiranesi.com
32 rooms
Credit cards: American Express, Diners Club, Visa, Mastercard, Bancomat

Built inside the Palazzo Nainer, designed and developed by the architect Valadier at the end of the 18th century, the hotel has rooms with flourished balconies and hidden gardens. Panoramic roof garden and wellness center with sauna and gym.

Ponte Sisto **** &
Via dei Pettinari 64
Tel. 06686310
www.hotelpontesisto.it
103 rooms
Credit cards: American Express, Diners Club, Visa, Mastercard
Built in a 18th-century building in the heart of Renaissance and baroque Rome, the hotel has very comfortable bedrooms, Internet access and a panoramic restaurant.

Quality Hotel Nova Domus **** & ★
Via G. Savonarola 38
Tel. 06399511
www.novadomushotel.it
116 rooms
Credit cards: American Express, Diners Club, Visa, Mastercard, Bancomat
Only five mins away from the Vatican Museums, the hotel has comfortable rooms with double-glazed windows. Its panoramic restaurant serves local and classical Italian dishes.

Quirinale **** &
Via Nazionale 7, Tel. 064707
www.hotelquirinale.it
208 rooms
Credit cards: American Express, Diners Club, Visa, Mastercard
A mid 19th-century palace with Imperial-style antique furniture. The rooms are sophisticated and with luxurious furnishings. The rooms are extremely classy and the restaurant serves seasonal produce.

Raphael **** &
Largo Febo 2, Tel. 06682831
www.raphaelhotel.com
55 rooms
Credit cards: American Express, Diners Club, Visa, Mastercard
In the heart of Rome, the hotel has a wonderful facade and amazing antique furniture. Roof garden with a suggestive view of Rome, restaurant and fitness club.

Ripa Hotel **** &
Via degli Orti di Trastevere 1
Tel. 0658611, www.ripahotel.com
170 rooms
Credit cards: American Express, Diners Club, Visa, Bancomat
In the heart of Trastevere, the hotel is famous for its '70s design. The hotel suites vary in furniture and style and the lofts have a futuristic flavor. In the evening, guests can choose between the piano bar with jazz music and the restaurant.

Sofitel Roma **** ★
Via Lombardia 47, Tel. 06478021
www.accorhotels.com/italia
113 rooms
Credit cards: American Express, Diners Club, Visa, Mastercard
With a view of the Villa Borghese gardens, the hotel has an Imperial neoclassical style and extremely comfortable bedrooms, Internet access, a panoramic terrace and restaurant.

Starhotels Michelangelo **** & ★
Via della Stazione S. Pietro 14
Tel. 06398739
www.starhotels.com
179 rooms
Credit cards: American Express, Diners Club, Visa, Mastercard
Near St Peter's Square and just a few minutes away from the most suggestive historical and artistic area of Rome. The hotel has comfortable rooms and a restaurant with regional and international cuisine.

Turner **** ★
Via Nomentana 29, Tel. 0644250077
www.hotelturner.it
52 rooms
Credit cards: American Express, Diners Club, Visa, Mastercard, Bancomat
Near Porta Pia, this welcoming and sophisticated hotel – with fine, golden decorations and precious furniture – has superior rooms with hydromassage.

Victoria **** ★
Via Campania 41
Tel. 06423701
www.hotelvictoriaroma.com
110 rooms
Credit cards: American Express, Diners Club, Visa, Mastercard
Just a short walk from Via Veneto and the Villa Borghese park – in late 19th-century palace – the hotel has carpeted and wooded rooms and original '70s or Imperial style furnishings. Also restaurant.

Visconti Palace **** &
Via F. Cesi 37, Tel. 063684
www.viscontipalace.com
247 rooms
Credit cards: American Express, Diners Club, Visa, Mastercard
Located in the city center, the hotel has very comfortable rooms, a fitness club and outdoor patio.

Accademia *** & ★
Piazza Accademia di S. Luca 74
Tel. 0669922603
www.travelroma.com
82 rooms
Credit cards: American Express,

Diners Club, Visa, Mastercard, Bancomat
Near the Trevi Fountain – in an old palace – this welcoming hotel has rooms with a good range of facilities.

Adventure *** ★
Via Palestro 88, Tel. 064469026
www.hoteladventure.it
23 rooms
Credit cards: American Express, Diners Club, Visa, Mastercard, Bancomat, JCB
This hotel in a late 19th-century palace is a short walk from the Termini railway station and has a breakfast room rich in fine and golden decorations and crystals.

Amalia ***
Via Germanico 66, Tel. 0639723356
www.hotelamalia.com
30 rooms
Credit cards: American Express, Diners Club, Visa, Mastercard, Bancomat
A short walk from the Vatican City – in a late 19th-century building – the hotel has high-quality rooms at good rates.

Arcangelo *** ★
Via Boezio 15, Tel. 066874143
www.hotelarcangeloroma.it
33 rooms
Credit cards: American Express, Diners Club, Visa, Mastercard, Bancomat
Located in a peaceful and classy street, the hotel combines stylish furnishings, functionality and comfortable bedrooms and bathrooms. Lovely roof garden with a view of St Peter's Dome.

Astrid *** &
Largo A. Sarti 4, Tel. 063236371
www.hotelastrid.com
48 rooms
Credit cards: American Express, Diners Club, Visa, Mastercard, Bancomat
A '30s palace combining modern comforts and a breathtaking view of the Tiber River and St Peter's.

Best Western Hotel Spring House *** & ★
Via Mocenigo 7
Tel. 0639720948
www.bestwestern.it/springhouse_rm
51 rooms
Credit cards: American Express, Diners Club, Visa, Mastercard
Near St Peter's and the Vatican Museums, the hotel is functional and nicely structured.

Best Western Hotel Villafranca *** &
Via Villafranca 9, Tel. 064440364
www.hotelvillafrancaroma.com
94 rooms
Credit cards: American Express,

Diners Club, Visa, Mastercard, Bancomat
In the neighbourhood of the Termini railway station hospitality is given in a palace of late 1800, having large and functional rooms; restaurant, bar service 24 hours.

Carlo Magno *** &
Via Sacco Pastore 13
Tel. 068603982
www.carlomagnohotel.com
55 rooms
Credit cards: American Express, Diners Club, Visa, Mastercard, Bancomat
The hotel stands out for its common welcoming area and the hall. The breakfast room is bright, very pretty and with English-style decorations and furniture. The bedrooms are comfortable and it has a lovely roof garden.

Cesàri *** & ★
Via di Pietra 89/A, Tel. 066749701
www.albergocesari.it
47 rooms
Credit cards: American Express, Diners Club, Visa, Mastercard, Bancomat, JCB
In the very heart of Rome – between the Trevi Fountain and the Pantheon – the hotel is proud of its long tradition of hospitality (it first obtained a license in 1787) and has well furnished rooms with a range of comforts.

Comfort Inn Bolivar *** ★
Via della Cordonata 6
Tel. 066791614
www.bolivarhotel.it
35 rooms
Credit cards: American Express, Diners Club, Visa, Mastercard, Bancomat
Set in the old city center, near the major monuments, this old palace has welcoming, modern rooms and panoramic views from both the terrace and the roof garden.

Contilia *** &
Via Principe Amedeo 81
Tel. 064466875
www.hotelcontilia.com
41 rooms
Credit cards: American Express, Diners Club, Visa, Mastercard, Bancomat
In the heart of the old center, this old palace has a cozy atmosphere and a high-quality service.

Corot *** & ★
Via Marghera 15/17
Tel. 0644700900
www.hotelcorot.net
28 rooms
Credit cards: American Express, Diners Club, Visa, Mastercard, Bancomat
Near the Termini railway station, the hotel offers comfortable rooms

differing in style and furniture and double-glazed windows.

Del Corso *** &
Via del Corso 79, Tel. 0636006041
www.hoteldelcorsoroma.com
18 rooms
Credit cards: American Express, Visa, Mastercard
Between Piazza di Spagna and Piazza del Popolo, the hotel has comfortable rooms and suites, and a panoramic roof garden.

Delle Muse *** & ★
Via T. Salvini 18 , Tel. 068088333
www.hoteldellemuse.com
60 rooms
Credit cards: American Express, Diners Club, Visa, Mastercard, Bancomat
A quiet and relaxing '30s villa with a large garden used as a restaurant in summer.

Domus Sessoriana *** & ★
Piazza di S. Croce in Gerusalemme 10, Tel. 0670615
www.domussessoriana.it
65 rooms
Credit cards: American Express, Diners Club, Visa, Mastercard, Bancomat
This unique hotel was once a Roman residence and then a basilica of genuine historical and artistic interest. The rooms, with terracotta flooring and classical furniture, are located in a wing of the adjacent monastery. The hotel floors can be reached by a see-through elevator from which guests can admire famous 19th-century pictures. Terrace with panoramic view of the city.

Eurogarden *** ★
salita Castel Giubileo 197
Tel. 068852751
www.eurogarden.net
48 rooms
Credit cards: American Express, Diners Club, Visa, Mastercard, Bancomat
Just 8 km from the center and immersed in a park, this bungalow offers independent rooms with cherry- or walnut-tree furniture. Some rooms have a romantic flavor thanks to their cane furniture. Swimming pool.

Fenix *** &
Viale Gorizia 5, Tel. 068540741
www.fenixhotel.it
73 rooms
Credit cards: American Express, Diners Club, Visa, Mastercard
A small palace surrounded by the Villa Torlonia and Villa Paganini gardens offering nicely furnished rooms and cozy common areas with parlors and private sitting rooms. Facilities include a garden and restaurant.

Fontana *** ★
Piazza di Trevi 96, Tel. 066786113
www.hotelfontana-trevi.com
25 rooms
A 16th-century palace opposite the Trevi Fountain with comfortable rooms that all have individual styles and furnishings. Panoramic terrace.

Garda *** & ★
Via Lombardia 30, Tel. 064882480
www.hotelgardaroma.it
30 rooms
Credit cards: American Express, Diners Club, Visa, Mastercard, Bancomat
In a very exclusive tourist area – near Via Veneto, Piazza di Spagna and Via dei Condotti – this hotel is in an elegant early 20th-century palace.

Internazionale *** ★
Via Sistina 79, Tel. 066793047
www.hotelinternazionale.com
42 rooms
Credit cards: American Express, Visa, Mastercard, Bancomat
A few meters from Trinità dei Monti stairs, in an ancient monastery structure, of which some ruins are still visible, comfortable rooms with different furniture (several antiques) are offered; panoramic terrace.

La Giocca *** &
Via Salaria 1223, Tel. 068804411
www.lagiocca.it
88 rooms
Credit cards: American Express, Diners Club, Visa, Mastercard, Bancomat
A comfortable '70s hotel with a restaurant serving local dishes. Swimming pool.

Mariano *** ★
Piazza M. Fanti 19
Tel. 064466147
www.hotelmariano.com
33 rooms
Credit cards: American Express, Diners Club, Visa, Mastercard, Bancomat
Located between the S. Maria Maggiore and Termini railway stations, this hotel has amazingly large corridors and rooms with modern furniture.

Mercure Roma
Corso Trieste *** & ★
Via Gradisca 29, Tel. 06852021
www.accorhotels.com/italia
97 rooms
Credit cards: American Express, Diners Club, Visa, Mastercard
Near Villa Torlonia, the hotel has comfortable rooms with sound reducing windows, an American bar, Internet access, sauna and fitness club.

Mercure Roma
Piazza Bologna *** ⚥ ★
Via Reggio di Calabria 54
Tel. 067001874
www.accorhotels.com/italia
113 rooms
Credit cards: American Express, Diners Club, Visa, Mastercard, Bancomat
Near the Tiburtina railway station, a '50s building with comfortable rooms and sound reducing windows.

Mozart *** ⚥ ★
Via dei Greci 23/B, Tel. 0636001915
www.hotelmozart.com
56 rooms
Credit cards: American Express, Diners Club, Visa
This 18th-century palace between Piazza del Popolo and Trinità dei Monti has lovely rooms (some with balconies overlooking the city), Internet and a roof garden with a bar.

Patria *** ★
Via Torino 36, Tel. 064880756
www.nih.it/hotelpatria
49 rooms
Credit cards: American Express, Diners Club, Visa, Mastercard, Bancomat
A welcoming building from the '40s with very comfortable rooms.

Portoghesi ***
Via dei Portoghesi 1
Tel. 066864231
www.hotelportoghesiroma.com
27 rooms
Credit cards: Visa, Mastercard
Baroque-like palace located in the old center a short distance from Piazza di Spagna and Piazza Navona. It has 19th-century furnishings and a roof garden with a magnificent view of Rome.

Rimini *** ★
Via Marghera 17, Tel. 064461991
www.hotelrimini.it
37 rooms
Credit cards: American Express, Diners Club, Visa, Mastercard
A welcoming 19th-century palace with classical, comfortable rooms. Restaurant.

Santa Costanza *** ⚥ ★
Viale XXI Aprile 4
Tel. 068600602
www.hotelsantacostanza.it
70 rooms
Credit cards: American Express, Diners Club, Visa, Mastercard
In a quiet area and with easy access to the center, this mid 20th-century hotel has lovely rooms with sound reducing windows and wooden floors.

Santa Maria *** ⚥
Vicolo del Piede 2, Tel. 065894626
www.hotelsantamaria.info
18 rooms
Credit cards: American Express, Diners Club, Visa, Mastercard, Bancomat
A short walk from Piazza S. Maria in Trastevere, the hotel has bright rooms – some with iron headboards – and a suggestive breakfast room with a wooden ceiling. It has an internal patio, free Internet access and bike rental.

Sant'Anselmo *** ★
Piazza S. Anselmo 2, Tel. 065745174
www.aventinohotels.com
34 rooms
Credit cards: American Express, Diners Club, Visa, Mastercard
On the Aventino River and in a peaceful area, the hotel offers welcoming bedrooms, classy common areas and a lovely indoor garden with a bar.

Teatro di Pompeo ***
Largo del Pallaro 8
Tel. 0668300170
hotel.teatrodipompeo@tiscali.it
www.hotelteatrodipompeo.it
13 rooms
Credit cards: American Express, Diners Club, Visa, Mastercard, Bancomat
Built on the ancient Roman Pompeius Theatre, the hotel has comfortable rooms and common areas with antique furniture.

Teatropace33 *** ★
Via del Teatro Pace 33
Tel. 066879075
www.hotelteatropace.com
23 rooms
Credit cards: American Express, Diners Club, Visa, Mastercard, Bancomat
The hotel offers classy and very comfortable rooms with bathrooms in Siena marble. The beautiful spiral staircases are notable.

Tritone *** ★
Via del Tritone 210, Tel. 0669922575
www.travelroma.com
43 rooms
Credit cards: American Express, Diners Club, Visa, Bancomat
In the city center, a comfortable hotel with a panoramic roof garden.

Villa del Parco *** ⚥ ★
Via Nomentana 110
Tel. 0644237773
www.noh.it/hotelvilladelparco
29 rooms
Credit cards: American Express, Diners Club, Visa, Mastercard, Bancomat
An art nouveau villa with a private home feel. It has comfortable rooms with classical furnishings and English-style common areas. Garden.

Villa Florence *** ⚥
Via Nomentana 28, Tel. 064403036
www.hotelvillaflorence.it
34 rooms
Credit cards: American Express, Diners Club, Visa, Mastercard, Bancomat, JCB
An art nouveau villa that has maintained its wonderful original structure. It has comfortable rooms and, in the garden, guests can admire some Roman ruins. Private parking.

Zone Hotel *** ⚥
Via Alfredo Fusco 118
Tel. 0635404111
www.groupevaladier.com
56 rooms
Credit cards: American Express, Diners Club, Visa, Mastercard, Bancomat
Immersed in the peaceful green of Monte Mario, the hotel has comfortable rooms and a good range of facilities.

Casa Domitilla ** ⚥
Via delle Sette Chiese 280
Tel. 065133956, www.domitilla.it
66 rooms
Close to the Appian Way and some early-Christian tombs, this '70s building has easy access to the center.

Restaurants

La Pergola ⑪⑪⑪⑪⑪
Via Cadlolo 101
Tel. 0635092152
www.cavalieri-hilton.it
Open in the evening
Closed Sundays and Mondays
Credit cards: American Express, Diners Club, Visa, Mastercard, Bancomat
Located at the top of Monte Mario, more precisely on the roof, the hotel boasts the most exclusive restaurant in Rome. The view is amazing and the restaurant is a real luxury. In summer guests can also dine on the outdoor terrace.

Alberto Ciarla ⑪⑪⑪⑪
Piazza S. Cosimato 40
Tel. 065818668
www.albertociarla.com
Open in the evening
Closed Sundays
An elegant and sophisticated restaurant specializing in traditional seafood cuisine using quality ingredients.

Camponeschi ⑪⑪⑪⑪
Piazza Farnese 50, Tel. 066874927
www.ristorantecamponeschi.it
Open in the evening
Closed Sundays
Credit cards: American Express, Visa, Mastercard
A luxurious restaurant in Piazza Farnese serving innovative but

at the same time traditional Italian and regional dishes. The cellar has excellent local wines and some house produce.

George's 🍴🍴🍴
Via Marche 7, Tel. 0642084575
www.georgesristorante.it
Closed Sundays
Credit cards: American Express, Diners Club, Visa, Mastercard, Bancomat
In a 19th-century palace, this sophisticated and classy restaurant with live music serves high-quality traditional cuisine.

La Rosetta 🍴🍴🍴
Via della Rosetta 8, Tel. 066861002
www.larosetta.com
Closed Sundays
Credit cards: American Express, Diners Club, Visa, Mastercard, Bancomat, JCB
Famous for its home-made bread and desserts, it serves excellent seafood specialties.

La Terrazza 🍴🍴🍴
Via Ludovisi 49, Tel. 06478121
www.hotel-eden.it
Credit cards: American Express, Diners Club, Visa, Mastercard, JCB
On the roof of one of the most exclusive city hotels, the restaurant has a magnificent view of the city. It specializes in local and regional meat and seafood dishes.

Le Jardin du Russie 🍴🍴🍴
Via del Babuino 9, Tel. 0632888870
www.hotelderussie.it
Credit cards: American Express, Diners Club, Visa, Mastercard
This restaurant has traditional meat and seafood specialties, a good range of olive oils, cheese and salami. In summer guests can enjoy dining in the garden.

Mirabelle 🍴🍴🍴 ★
Via di Porta Pinciana 14
Tel. 0642168838
mirabelle@splendideroyal.it
www.mirabelle.it
A restaurant on the 7th floor with table service, in summer on the terrace, offering a panoramic view of Villa Borghese and Villa Medici. The classical-style restaurant is immersed in neoclassical architecture and serves meat and seafood specialties.

Quinzi e Gabrieli 🍴🍴🍴
Via delle Coppelle 5, Tel. 066879389
www.quinziegabrieli.it
Open in the evening
Closed Sundays
Credit cards: American Express, Diners Club, Visa, Mastercard, Bancomat
A small but classy restaurant near the Pantheon specializing in high-quality and fresh seafood.

Sapori del Lord Byron 🍴🍴🍴
Via G. de Notaris 5, Tel. 063220404
www.lordbyronhotel.com
Closed Sundays
A very exclusive and sophisticated restaurant with '70s art deco furnishings that serves seasonal Mediterranean dishes.

Terrazza Paradiso 🍴🍴🍴
Via dei Bastioni 1, Tel. 066873233
www.atlantehotels.com
Credit cards: American Express, Diners Club, Visa, Mastercard, Bancomat
This roof garden restaurant specializes in meat and seafood dishes. Beautiful panoramic view.

Agata e Romeo 🍴🍴🍴
Via Carlo Alberto 45, Tel. 064466115
www.agataeromeo.it
Closed Saturdays and Sundays
Credit cards: American Express, Diners Club, Visa, Mastercard, Bancomat
Just a short walk from the church of Santa Maria Maggiore, this restaurant serves local dishes using first class produce.

Al Presidente 🍴🍴🍴
Via in Arcione 95, Tel. 066797342
Closed Mondays
Credit cards: American Express, Diners Club, Visa, Mastercard, Bancomat
A restaurant close to the Quirinale specializes in local and regional meat and seafood dishes.

Asador Cafè Veneto 🍴🍴🍴 ★
Via Vittorio Veneto 118
Tel. 064827107 www.cafeveneto.it
Closed Mondays
Credit cards: American Express, Diners Club, Visa, Mastercard, Bancomat
A sophisticated restaurant with the feel and charm of Rome's old and famous coffee shops. It serves regional and Argentine specialties.

Enoteca Capranica 🍴🍴🍴
Piazza Capranica 99/100
Tel. 0669940992
www.enotecacapranica.it
In August, open evenings
Closed Saturday midday, Sundays and holidays
Credit cards: American Express, Diners Club, Visa, Mastercard, Bancomat
Halfway between the Pantheon and Montecitorio, this is one of the oldest wine bars in Rome. Its seasonal cuisine specializes in meat and seafood dishes.

Il Convivio Troiani 🍴🍴🍴
Vicolo dei Soldati 31
Tel. 06869432
www.ilconviviotroiani.com
Open in the evening
Closed Sundays

Credit cards: American Express, Diners Club, Visa, Mastercard, Bancomat
In one of the small streets surrounding Piazza Navona, this restaurant serves some of the best regional dishes.

La Penna d'Oca 🍴🍴🍴
Via della Penna 53, Tel. 063202898
Open in the evening
Closed Sundays
Credit cards: American Express, Diners Club, Visa, Mastercard, Bancomat
A beautiful art nouveau restaurant with garden table service in summer. Famous for the freshness of its seasonal produce.

L'Olimpo 🍴🍴🍴 ★
Piazza Barberini 23, Tel. 0642010469
www.berninibristol.com
Credit cards: American Express, Diners Club, Visa, Mastercard
A restaurant often visited by celebrities with a roof garden boasting a wonderful view of Rome. Sophisticated Mediterranean cuisine.

Piperno 🍴🍴🍴
Via Monte dei Cenci 9
Tel. 0668806629
www.ristorantepiperno.it
Closed Sunday evenings and Mondays
Credit cards: Diners Club, Visa, Mastercard, Bancomat
A very famous restaurant that, in summer, offers table service on a cozy and romantic square in old Rome. It serves traditional dishes.

Sabatini in Trastevere 🍴🍴🍴
Piazza di S. Maria in Trastevere 13, Tel. 065818307
Credit cards: American Express, Diners Club, Visa, Mastercard
A picturesque restaurant with antique furniture and delightful decorations. It serves traditional cuisine including meat and seafood specialties.

Shangri Là Corsetti 🍴🍴🍴
Viale Algeria 141, Tel. 065918861
www.shangrilacorsetti.it
Credit cards: American Express, Diners Club, Visa, Mastercard
Immersed in the green, this elegant and classical restaurant specializes in meat and seafood dishes, seasonal wild mushrooms and truffles and home-made desserts.

Taberna de' Gracchi 🍴🍴🍴 ★
Via dei Gracchi 266/268
Tel. 063213126
www.tabernagracchi.com
Closed Sundays and Monday midday
Credit cards: American Express, Diners Club, Visa, Mastercard, Bancomat

Lively but classy, the restaurant serves traditional cuisine specializing in grilled meat and seafood.

Al Bric ¶¶
Via del Pellegrino 51
Tel. 066879533
Open evenings (in winter also Sunday midday)
Closed Mondays in summer
In the heart of Rome and near Campo dei Fiori, this picturesque restaurant serves traditional local cuisine.

Al Grappolo d'Oro ¶¶
Via Palestro 4/10, Tel. 064941441
www.algrappolodoro.it
Closed Sundays and Saturday midday
A traditional local restaurant serving Italian food and specializing in home-made pasta and desserts.

Al Moro ¶¶
Vicolo delle Bollette 13
Tel. 066783495
Closed Sundays
Credit cards: American Express, Visa
The restaurant is open till 11.30pm and serves real traditional local dishes including some seafood specialties.

Antico Arco ¶¶
Piazzale Aurelio 7
Tel. 065815274
Open in the evening
Closed Sundays
Credit cards: American Express, Diners Club, Visa, Mastercard, Bancomat
In a historical palace opposite S. Pancrazio arch, the restaurant serves sophisticated local dishes.

Aurora 10 da Pino il Sommelier ¶¶ ★
Via Aurora 10, Tel. 064742779
www.aurora10.it
Closed Mondays
Credit cards: American Express, Diners Club, Visa
A welcoming restaurant specializing in local cuisine including grilled meat and seafood dishes.

Bros ¶¶
Via Mameli 45
Tel. 065816158
www.brosroma.com
Closed Sunday midday
Credit cards: American Express, Diners Club, Visa, Mastercard
Located in the Trastevere area, this welcoming restaurant has terracotta flooring, wrought iron lamps and stone vaults. Innovative cuisine.

Cafè Romano ¶¶
Via Borgognona 4/M
Tel. 0669981500

www.royaldemeure.com
Credit cards: American Express, Diners Club, Visa, Mastercard, Bancomat
The restaurant specializes in Mediterranean cuisine and Italian wines. Careful chosen seasonal produce.

Campana ¶¶
Vicolo della Campana 18
Tel. 066867820
Closed Mondays
Credit cards: American Express, Diners Club, Visa, Mastercard, Bancomat, JCB
In business since 1518, this restaurant is proud of being the oldest tavern in Rome and only offers local dishes.

Castello di Lunghezza ¶¶
Via Tenuta del Cavaliere 112
Tel. 0622483390
www.castellodilunghezza.com
Closed Mondays and Sunday evenings
Credit cards: American Express, Diners Club, Visa, Mastercard, Bancomat
Guests enjoy dining outside under the arches of the 12th-16th-century cellars. The restaurant is built in a cave and has lovely volcanic walls and simple furniture.

Checco er Carettiere ¶¶
Via Benedetta 10, Tel. 065800985
www.checcoercarettiere.it
Credit cards: American Express, Diners Club, Visa, Mastercard, Bancomat
A truly typical Roman restaurant where the atmosphere and the cuisine are typical of the Trastevere area. It specializes in deep-fried dishes, lamb, coda alla vaccinara (Roman oxtail skew), and seafood.

Corsetti il Galeone ¶¶
Piazza S. Cosimato 27
Tel. 065809009
Closed Mondays
Open since 1922, the restaurant room looks like an old boat and serves seafood specialties and local dishes.

Da Pancrazio ¶¶
Piazza del Biscione 92
Tel. 066861246
www.dapancrazio.com
Closed Wednesdays
Credit cards: American Express, Visa, JCB
Located in the ruins of the Pompeius theatre, the restaurant has old capitals and columns from the 1st-century BC. The restaurant remains open after 10pm and serves local dishes. Terrace table service in summer.

Delle Vittorie ¶¶ ★
Via Montesanto 64
Tel. 0637352776,

www.dellevittorie.it
Closed Sundays
A restaurant open till late specializing in local cuisine and only using fresh produce. In summer it has outdoor table service facing St Peter's dome.

Evangelista ¶¶
Via Zoccolette 11/A, Tel. 066875810
Open in the evening
Closed Sundays
Credit cards: Visa, Mastercard, Bancomat
At short walk from the Jewish ghetto and in the heart of Rome, this old restaurant serves regional cuisine and takes pride in its famous artichokes (stone cooked).

Giggetto al Portico d'Ottavia ¶¶
Via del Portico d'Ottavia 21/A
Tel. 066861105
www.giggettoalportico.com
Closed Mondays
Credit cards: American Express, Diners Club, Visa, Mastercard, Bancomat
A typical Roman trattoria serving local and Jewish specialties: deep-fried artichokes, lamb, ricotta and sour black berry cake. Also a wine bar in a cave where the atmosphere is like Ancient Rome.

Giovanni ¶¶
Via Marche 64, Tel. 064821834
Closed Friday evenings and Saturdays
Credit cards: American Express, Diners Club, Visa, Mastercard
A classical restaurant with leather chairs and sofas and terracotta flooring. It serves artichokes braised with mint, fresh seafood and home-made pasta and desserts.

Il Margutta-Vegetariani dal 1979 ¶¶
Via Margutta 118, Tel. 0632650577
www.ilmargutta.it
Credit cards: American Express, Diners Club, Visa, Mastercard, Bancomat
A vegetarian restaurant serving seasonal dishes.

La Luna d'Oro ¶¶
Via dei Greci 25, Tel. 0636001716
Closed Sundays
Credit cards: American Express, Diners Club, Visa, Mastercard, Bancomat
Just opposite the Santa Cecilia Music Academy, the restaurant is decorated with natural material only (wicker and oak wood). It proudly boasts its 'sanpietrini' (famous cube stones) on the entrance floor and a glass conservatory. Meat and seafood specialties.

La Sughereta ¶¶ ★
Via degli Aldobrandeschi 223
Tel. 0666544, www.solmelia.com

Credit cards: American Express,
Diners Club, Visa, Mastercard

A classy restaurant facing onto a
forest with terrace for table service
in summer and a garden in winter.

L'Arcangelo ¶¶
Via G.G. Belli 59-61, Tel. 063210992
*Closed Saturday midday, Sundays
and holidays*
Credit cards: American Express,
Diners Club, Visa, Mastercard,
Bancomat

An old and typical local trattoria
with wooden walls and scattered
old prints. The cuisine is both
creative and traditional.

Le Bain ¶¶
*Via delle Botteghe Oscure 32/A-33,
Tel. 066865673, www.lebain.it*
Closed Sundays
Credit cards: American Express,
Visa, Mastercard, Bancomat

A very peculiar restaurant with a
cozy and soft atmosphere. It serves
traditional meat and seafood
specialties, a range of local salami
and cheese. Also wine bar.

Le Mani in Pasta ¶¶
Via dei Genovesi 37, Tel. 065816017
Closed Mondays
Credit cards: American Express,
Diners Club, Visa, Mastercard

In the Trastevere area, the
restaurant serves Mediterranean
dishes using high-quality produce.

Le Tamerici ¶¶
*Vicolo Scavolino 79
Tel. 0669200700
www.letamerici.com*
Open in the evening
Closed Sundays
Credit cards: American Express,
Diners Club, Visa, Mastercard,
Bancomat

Near the Trevi Fountain, this refined
restaurant offers quality regional
cuisine at reasonable prices.

L'Officina dei Sapori ¶¶
*Via Flaminia 297
Tel. 0697600350
www.officinadeisapori.com*
Open in the evening
Closed Sundays
Credit cards: American Express,
Diners Club, Visa, Bancomat

Near the Auditorium, the
restaurant is open till 1am and
specializes in home-made
pasta and desserts.

Mamma Angelina ¶¶
*Viale A. Boito 65
Tel. 068608928*
Closed Wednesdays
Credit cards: American Express,
Diners Club, Visa, Mastercard

A typical Roman trattoria in an old
building in the center. It serves
traditional dishes.

Matricianella ¶¶
*Via del Leone 3, Tel. 066832100
www.matricianella.it*
Closed Sundays
Credit cards: American Express,
Diners Club, Visa, Mastercard

A short distance from Piazza
Borghese, the restaurant
offers traditional dishes and
Jewish desserts.

Myosotis ¶¶
*Piazza della Cappella 49
Tel. 066865554, www.myosotis.it*
Open in the evening
Closed Sundays
Credit cards: American Express,
Diners Club, Visa, Mastercard,
Bancomat

Set in a relaxing atmosphere, the
restaurant serves simple and
traditional cuisine using home-
made oil dressing.

Osteria del Velodromo Vecchio ¶¶
Via Genzano 139, Tel. 067886793
*Closed Sundays and Monday-
Wednesday evenings*
Credit cards: American Express,
Visa, Mastercard, Bancomat

A small restaurant frescoed with
scenes from Via Appia and Piazza
di Spagna. Authentic local cuisine
including salt and pepper
tonnarelli, tripe and saltimbocca
alla romana (veal and ham rolls).

Osteria della Frezza ¶¶
*Via della Frezza 16, Tel. 0632111482
www.gusto.it*
Credit cards: American Express,
Diners Club, Visa, Mastercard,
Bancomat

A three-floor tavern with a
mezzanine area, wine and salami
cellar and food tasting counter
offering warm dishes, salami and
cheeses.

Osteria dell'Ingegno ¶¶
*Piazza di Pietra 45, Tel. 066780662
www.osteriadellingegno.it*
Credit cards: American Express,
Diners Club, Visa, Mastercard

Open till after 10pm, the restaurant
serves Mediterranean dishes made
with seasonal produce. It offers
wine tasting in the cellar, home-
made salami, pasta and desserts.

Osteria St. Ana ¶¶
*Via della Penna 68/69
Tel. 063610291*
*Closed Saturday midday and
Sundays*
Credit cards: American Express,
Diners Club, Visa, Mastercard

A typical Roman tavern open since
1968 and serving regional dishes
and seafood specialties.

Papà Giovanni ¶¶
*Via dei Sediari 4, Tel. 0668804807
www.ristorantepapagiovanni.it*
Closed Sundays

Credit cards: American Express,
Visa, Mastercard

In a 17th-century palace, the
restaurant boasts picturesque
rooms and areas for cheese
tasting accompanied by wines
from its cellar.

Paris ¶¶
Piazza S. Calisto 7/A, Tel. 065815378
*Closed Sunday evenings and
Mondays*
Credit cards: American Express,
Diners Club, Visa, Mastercard,
Bancomat, JCB

In a 17th-century building, the
restaurant offers local traditional
cuisine and a rich selection of
wines from its cellar.

Primoli ¶¶
*Via dei Soldati 22/23
Tel. 0668135112, www.ilprimoli.it*
*Closed Saturday midday and
Sundays*
Credit cards: American Express,
Diners Club, Visa, Mastercard

A restaurant dotted with old
photos and open till after 10pm.
It serves traditional meat and
seafood dishes, home-made pasta,
bread and desserts.

Red Restaurant & Design ¶¶
*Via P. de Coubertin 30
Tel. 0680691630
www.redrestaurant.roma.it*
Credit cards: American Express,
Diners Club, Visa, Mastercard,
Bancomat

Inside the Auditorium, the
restaurant is open from 11am till
very late and offers a range
of dishes. Good selection of olive
oils, cheese and local salami.

Riparte Cafè ¶¶
*Via degli Orti di Trastevere 7
Tel. 065861816
www.riparte.com*
Closed Sundays
Credit cards: American Express,
Diners Club, Visa, Mastercard

A cozy and classy restaurant with
areas for mini exhibitions.
Mediterranean dishes. Live jazz
music in the piano bar.

Sangallo ¶¶ ★
*Vicolo della Vaccarella 11/A
Tel. 066865549
www.ristorantesangallo.com*
Open in the evening
*Closed Saturday midday and
Sundays*
Credit cards: American Express,
Diners Club, Visa, Mastercard,
Bancomat

A comfortable and classical
restaurant serving buffalo produce
and home-made pasta and
desserts.

Sanpietrino ¶¶
*Piazza Costaguti 15, Tel. 0668806471
www.ilsanpietrino.it*

Open in the evening
Closed Sunday midday
Credit cards: American Express,
Diners Club, Visa, Mastercard,
Bancomat
Built in the stables of a 16th-century
Patrician palace in the Ghetto area,
the restaurant is named after its
typical porphyry stone floor. Local
cuisine with innovative touches.

Spirito Divino ¶¶
Via dei Genovesi 31/B
Tel. 065896689
www.spiritodivino.com
Open in the evening
Closed Sundays
Credit cards: American Express,
Diners Club, Visa, Mastercard,
Bancomat
A restaurant with two rooms in a
building from the Middle Ages. The
cuisine boasts some Imperial
Roman recipes. Home-made jams
and fruit preserves.

Tram Tram ¶¶
Via dei Reti 44/46, Tel. 06490416
Closed Mondays
Credit cards: American Express,
Diners Club, Visa, Mastercard,
Bancomat
Located in S. Lorenzo, the
restaurant is furnished with tram
and train carriages. Mediterranean
cuisine.

Trattoria Monti ¶¶¶
Via S. Vito 13
Tel. 064466573
Closed Sunday evenings and
Mondays
In the Esquilino area, the
restaurant has served local
specialties for over 30 years.
Vegetarian options also available.

Vecchia America-Corsetti ¶¶
zona EUR, Piazza Marconi 32
Tel. 065911458
www.corsettivecchiaamerica.it
Closed Saturday midday
Credit cards: American Express,
Diners Club, Visa
Open till after 10pm, the restaurant
recalls the old Far West and serves
traditional cuisine specializing in
seafood and pizza.

Vecchia Roma ¶¶
Piazza Campitelli 18
Tel. 066864604
www.ristorantevecchiaroma.com
Closed Wednesdays
Credit cards: American Express,
Diners Club, Visa, Mastercard
A restaurant in an old, converted
church specializing in seafood and
vegetarian dishes. Outdoor table
service in summer.

Vinando ¶¶
Piazza Margana 23
Tel. 0669200741
www.vinando.net

Credit cards: American Express,
Visa, Mastercard, Bancomat
A 24-hour restaurant for those who
love dining and sipping good wines
and spirits. It offers over 700 wine
labels: Traditional seasonal menus;
cheese and salami selection.
Wine and distilled spirits tasting
at the bar counter.

Agustarello ¶
Via G. Branca 98
Tel. 065746585
Closed Sundays
A typical tavern in the Testaccio
area serving traditional specialties.

Ai Spaghettari ¶
Piazza S. Cosimato 58/60
Tel. 065800450
www.aispaghettari.com
Closed Mondays and Tuesday
midday
Credit cards: American Express,
Diners Club, Visa, Mastercard,
Bancomat
In the heart of Trastevere, the
restaurant is proud of its longstanding traditional local cuisine. It
offers seafood specialties,
tonnarelli, veal and ham rolls,
home-made cakes. Table service in
the garden in summer.

Da Armando al Pantheon ¶
Salita de' Crescenzi 31
Tel. 0668803034
www.armandoalpantheon.it
Credit cards: American Express,
Diners Club, Visa, Mastercard
An interesting restaurant famous
for its traditional cuisine and film
memorabilia. Traditional menu
with vegetarian options.

Da Roberto e Loretta ¶
Via Saturnia 18/24
Tel. 0677201037
www.robertoeloretta.it
Closed Mondays
Credit cards: American Express,
Visa, Bancomat
A restaurant with a classical feel,
brass chandeliers, antique
furniture and pictures of old Rome.
Local cuisine.

Da Sergio ¶
Vicolo delle Grotte 27
Tel. 066864293
Closed Sundays
Credit cards: American Express,
Diners Club, Visa, Mastercard,
Bancomat
Inside an old building and at a
short distance from Piazza Navona,
the restaurant offers traditional
local cuisine: fettuccine
all'amatriciana, gnocchi, lamb,
tripe, dried cod and home-made
desserts.

Da Vittorio ¶
Via Musco 29/31, Tel. 065408272
Closed Saturdays and Sundays
Credit cards: American Express,

Diners Club, Visa, Mastercard,
Bancomat, JCB
A restaurant offering traditional
local cuisine including home-made
desserts and a good selection of
national and regional wines.

Dal Cavalier Gino ¶
Vicolo Rosini 4, Tel. 066873434
Closed Sundays and holidays
At a short walk from Piazza del
Parlamento, the restaurant serves
traditional dishes.

Fabrizio ¶
Via S. Dorotea 15, Tel. 065806244
Closed Wednesdays in winter,
Sundays from July to September
Credit cards: American Express,
Diners Club, Visa, Mastercard,
Bancomat
Located in the Trastevere area
in a former convent, this restaurant
serves typical local dishes.

Gnegno ¶
Via Prati della Farnesina 10/12
Tel. 063336166
Closed Sundays
Credit cards: American Express,
Diners Club, Visa, Mastercard,
Bancomat
Near Ponte Milvio, this interesting,
traditional restaurant specializes
in local Roman cuisine and home-
made desserts. In summer it offers
table service in the conservatory.

La Danesina ¶
Via del Governo Vecchio 127
Tel. 066868693
Closed Mondays and Tuesday
midday
Near Piazza Navona, the restaurant
has an old trattoria feel and
serves traditional local dishes.

Le Rose ¶
Via Sacrofanese 25
Tel. 0633613050
Closed Mondays
Just outside the city, this country
house faces a river where
swimming is permitted and serves
high-quality local cuisine and
home-made desserts at reasonable
prices.

Trattoria Cadorna dal 1947 ¶
Via Cadorna 12, Tel. 064827061
Closed Saturdays and Sunday
midday
A typical restaurant with outdoor
service in summer. It specializes in
simple local cuisine.

Trattoria del Ragioniere ¶
Via G. Mercatore 7
Tel. 0624303599
Closed Sundays
A typical local restaurant
specializing in simple local cuisine.

Zampagna ¶
Via Ostiense 179, Tel. 065742306
Open on midday
Closed Sundays

A picturesque restaurant near St Paul's Basilica with a private garden, red and white check table covers and traditional cuisine.

Rural Lodgins

Cavendo Tutus ★
Via della Pisana 948/950
Tel. 0666156512
Immersed in the green of the Tenuta dei Massimi park, this quiet and relaxing hotel specializes in cyclists' needs (including repairs and rental). Also restaurant.

Lecanfore ♿
Divino Amore, Via P. Cavalloni 42,
Tel. 0671350578
www.lecanfore.it
Credit cards: Visa, Mastercard, Bancomat
Nearby the Appian Way archaeological site, this early 20th-century farmhouse sits on organically cultivated land in the Roman countryside. Swimming pool, horse riding classes, horse riding and mountain bike tours.

Rodrigo De Vivar
Ostia Antica, Piazza della Rocca 18/19, Tel. 065652535
www.rodrigodevivar.com
Credit cards: American Express, Diners Club, Visa, Mastercard, Bancomat
This farmhouse, once belonging to the Princes of Aldobrandi, enjoys a breathtaking view of the Pope Julius II della Rovere's castle and the hamlet. The farmhouse – close to the archeological site – is famous for horse breeding and horse riding. It also offers ceramics workshops, singing lessons and bicycle rental. Restaurant.

Vivai Montecaminetto
Via Sacrofanese 25
Tel. 0633615290
www.agriturismoroma.it
Open mid March-mid November; mid December-mid January
A pink farmhouse immersed in the green of an oak wood. Its balconies offer a view of the Roman countryside. Restaurant and easy access to Piazzale Flaminio.

At night

Acqua Negra
Largo del Teatro Valle 9
Tel. 0668136830
www.acquanegra.it
A minimalist restaurant, coffee house and American bar decorated with soft colors. A long bar counter links the three rooms. Clients can enjoy downtempo, new-jazz and rare-grooves music.

Akab-Cave
Via di Monte Testaccio 69
Tel. 065782390
A famous club where the greatest international rock bands have

performed. Today it is a stepping stone for emerging artists and host to short-film festivals.

Alexanderplatz
Via Ostia 9, Tel. 0639742171, www.alexanderplatzjazz.com
One of the most renowned jazz clubs in Rome where the greatest national and international artists have performed live. In summer the show moves to the Villa Celimontana gardens for the Villa Celimontana festival. For true jazz lovers.

Alpheus
Via del Commercio 36
Tel. 065747826
www.alpheus.it
A club with three bars and three large areas for concerts, music festivals and shows. The music varies each night with rock, world and Latin American music.

Baja
Lungotevere Arnaldo da Brescia - Ponte Margherita, Tel. 0632600118
A club inside the riverboat on the Tiber with a mixture of ethnic and hi-tech furniture. Famously crowded for its appetizers and drinks, if offers a menu enriched by Italian specialties that can be enjoyed while listening to lounge music. At night, the music changes into powerful ethno, dub and ethno-house rhythms.

Bar del Fico
Piazza del Fico 26/28
Tel. 066865205
Under the shadow of the tall fig tree that gave the square its name, it offers a peculiar mixture of art deco and '70s atmosphere. At night, the bar is filled many of Rome's most glamorous.

Bar dell'Anima
Via S. Maria dell'Anima 57
Tel. 0668640121
Behind Piazza Navona, the bar has a baroque atmosphere with big chandeliers, mirrors and aluminum structures. Guests can enjoy a cocktail drink while listening to lounge music.

Baretto di Ponte Milvio
Ponte Milvio
A small bar with an outdoor counter and a tropical feel. The tables are in a pedestrian area crowded by young people out for the night.

Bibamus
Via S. Maria dell'Anima 18
Tel. 066833946
A welcoming place in the center offering a mixture of wine bar and pub where customers can enjoy a good choice of draft beers, and Italian and Spanish wines in a cozy and relaxing atmosphere. Outdoor tables in summer.

Big Mama
Vicolo S. Francesco a Ripa 18, Tel. 065812551, www.bigmama.it
A famous spot in Rome, the bar is a real temple for jazz music lovers. This small and cozy bar has seen performances from the greatest American blues and jazz musicians. Restaurant.

Cafè della Scala
Via della Scala 4
Tel. 065803763
A tiny and relaxing café where customers can enjoy watching the buzz of Roman city life.

Cafè de Oriente
Via di Monte Testaccio 36
Tel. 065745019
A must for clubbers who love Latin American music and love to dance the night away to Cuban and R&B rhythms. Clubbers have a choice of 4 dance floors including the roof terrace.

Caffè Latino
Via di Monte Testaccio 96
Tel. 0657288556
Live concerts in this welcoming and cozy club playing Latin American music, soul, funky and acid-jazz.

Classico Village
Via Libetta 3, Tel. 0657288857
www.classico.it
A club built in a former factory where customers can dance, watch movies, or explore art galleries and shows. The music varies: house, garage, funk and Britpop. Outdoor club in summer.

Etò
Via Galvani 46
Tel. 065748268
A white style club with two dance floors offering a variety of music, themed events, fashion parties, brand presentations and disco music nights. A very eclectic club.

Ex Magazzini Stile 89
Via Magazzini Generali 8, Tel. 065758040
Built in a former warehouse, the club offers a restaurant, drinks, events and art expositions. Split in two floors, it alternates postmodern and ethnic style.

Fonclea
Via Crescenzio 82/A, Tel. 066896302, www.fonclea.it
One of the most famous clubs in Rome, it has two basement floors for rock concerts and large tables for table games and dinners. It proudly boasts over 50 different kinds of cocktails.

Freni e Frizioni
Via del Politeama 4/6
Tel. 0658334210
Built in a former workshop, it has fashionable vintage furnishings, superb snacks and cocktails.

Gianicolo
Piazzale Aurelio 5
Tel. 065806275
Opposite Porta S. Pancrazio, a must for cocktail-lovers. It has a room with wooden tables and walls dotted with pictures of stars and celebrities; outdoors, customers can enjoy the patio.

Gloss
Via del Monte della Farina 43
Tel. 0668135345
One of the most crowded bars in Rome with a sophisticated atmosphere. Specialties: cocktails and wines.

Il Locale
Vicolo del Fico 3, Tel. 066879075
A small, popular bar featuring emerging bands. It has draft beers, cocktails, art expositions and short films.

In Vino Veritas
Via Garibaldi 2a, Tel. 347194758o
A young and buzzing place for real wine lovers. It offers good selection of wines and some interesting dishes.

Jam Cafè
Via degli Argonauti 18
Tel. 0657287330
A '70s style café for lively nights playing house and live music.

Jonathan's Angels
Via della Fossa 16, Tel. 066893426
A club combining kitsch and naïf. Cocktails and live music.

La Maison
Vicolo dei Granari 3, Tel. 066833312
Designer sofas and chandeliers in this ethno-classical bar with live music. In summer it offers a roof terrace overlooking the EUR area.

Lettere Caffè
Via di S. Francesco a Ripa 100
Tel. 0658334379
www.letterecaffe.org
A cultural café offering live music, book presentations, reading evenings, Internet and video.

Magnolia
Piazza Campo de' Fiori 4/5
Tel. 0668309367
Cocktail bar on the most over crowded square in Rome.

Momart
Piazza 21 Aprile 19
Tel. 0686391656,
www.momartcafe.it
An ideal bar for drinks with outdoor tables.

Nazca
Via del Gazometro 40/42,
Tel. 065747638
American lounge bar with leopard-skin prints and bright red curtains where you can listen to hip hop, chill out and lounge music. Trendy.

News Cafè
Via della Stamperia 72,
Tel. 0669923473
A New York-style bar, with wooden and steel furniture, playing lounge music. It offers a long list of cocktails and has tables on the terrace.

Officine Digitali
Via Bove 36
Tel. 0699704307
An ideal place for TV lovers as it is inside the Taxi Channel studio. Guests can taste the reality show atmosphere while drinking and smiling to the cameras.

Ombre Rosse Cafè
Piazza S. Egidio 12
Tel. 065884155
In one of the most picturesque squares in Rome, the bar boasts a view of the Tiber River.

Société Lutece
Piazza di Montevecchio 17
Tel. 0668301472
In the very heart of the city, it specializes in drinks and cheese and home-made bread snacks, cocktails, wines and other deli options.

Stardust
Vicolo de' Rienzi 4
Tel. 0658320875
A bar with different offerings. It changes between tea room, appetizer bar with drinks and music bar, on a same day. A must for those who love burning the midnight oil.

Taverna del Campo
Piazza Campo de' Fiori 16
Tel. 066874402
A very fashionable bar specializing in cocktails and wine tasting. The outdoor tables are ideal for admiring the beauty of the adjacent square.

Vineria Reggio
Piazza Campo de' Fiori 15
Tel. 0668803268
A meeting place for young people offering wines and cocktails; outdoor tables and indoor wooden benches.

Museums, Monuments and Churches

Antiquarium Comunale del Celio
Via Parco del Celio 22
Tel. 067001569-0669924307
Temporarily closed

Centrale Montemartini
Viale Ostiense 106
Tel. 0639967800-065748030
www.centralemontemartini.org
Tuesdays-Sundays 9.30-19.00;
24 and 31 December: 9.00-14.00.
Closed 1 January, 1 May,
25 December

Domus Aurea
Viale della Domus Aurea 1
Tel. 0685301758
www.archeorm.arti.beni
culturali.it
Everyday 9.00-20.00.
Closed Tuesdays

Galleria Colonna ★
Via della Pilotta 17
Tel. 066784350-066794362
www.galleriacolonna.it
Saturdays 9.00-13.00 and by appointment. Closed August

Galleria Comunale d'Arte Moderna e Contemporanea - G.C.AM.C.
Via F. Crispi 24
Tel. 064742848
www.comune.roma.it/avi
Temporarily closed

Galleria Corsini
Via della Lungara 10
Tel. 0668802323
www.galleriaborghese.it
Tuesdays-Sundays 8.30-13.30

Galleria Doria Pamphilj ★
Piazza del Collegio Romano 2
Tel. 066797323
www.doriapamphilj.it
Mondays-Wednesdays, Fridays-Sundays 10.00-17.00. Closed Thursdays, 1 January, Easter, 1 May, 15 August, 25 December

Galleria e Museo Borghese
Parco di Villa Borghese,
Piazzale Museo Borghese 5
Tel. 068413979-068417645-0632810
www.galleriaborghese.it
Tuesdays-Sundays 9.00-19.00.
Entry every two hours by reservation

Galleria Nazionale d'Arte Antica - Palazzo Barberini
Via Quattro Fontane 13
Tel. 064824184-0642003669
www.galleriaborghese.it/barberini/it/
Tuesdays-Sundays and holidays 9.00-19.00

Galleria Nazionale d'Arte Moderna
Viale delle Belle Arti 131
Tel. 0632298401-06322989
www.gnam.arti.beniculturali.it
Tuesdays-Sundays 8.30-19.30

Galleria Spada
Piazza Capo di Ferro 13
Tel. 066874896-066874893
www.galleriaborghese.it
Tuesdays-Sundays 8.30-19.30

Keats-Shelley Memorial House ★
Piazza di Spagna 26
Tel. 066784235
www.Keats-Shelley-House.org
Mondays-Fridays 9.00-13.00,
15.00-18.00; Sundays 11.00-14.00,
15.00-18.00

Mausoleo delle Fosse Ardeatine
Via Ardeatina 174
Tel. 065136742
www.anfim.it
Mondays-Sundays 8.15-17.00.
Closed 1 January, Easter, 1 May,
15 August

Musei Capitolini
Piazza del Campidoglio 1
Tel. 0667102475
www.museicapitolini.org
Tuesdays-Sundays 9-20

Musei Vaticani
Viale Vaticano,
www.vatican.va
Closed Sundays (except last
Sun in the month) and
Vatican holidays

Museo Barracco
Corso Vittorio Emanuele II 166
Tel. 0668806848-066875657
www.comune.roma.it/
museobarracco

Museo Birra Peroni
Via Renato Birolli 8
Tel. 06225441
www.peroni.it
Visits by prior arrangement

**Museo della Basilica di
S. Giovanni in Laterano**
Piazza S. Giovanni in Laterano
Tel. 0669886433
Mondays-Sundays and holidays
9.00-18.00

Museo della Civiltà Romana
Piazza G. Agnelli 10
Tel. 065926135-065926041
www.comune.roma.it/
museociviltaromana
Tuesdays-Sundays 9.00-14.00.
Closed 1 January, 1 May,
25 December

Museo dell'Arte Classica
Piazzale A. Moro 5
Tel. 0649913827-960
www.uniroma1.it/musei
Mondays-Thursdays 9.00-17.00;
Fridays 9.00-14.00. Closed August

**Museo delle Antichità Etrusche
e Italiche**
Piazzale A. Moro 5
Tel. 0649913315
www.uniroma1.it/musei
Visits by request Mondays-Fridays
9.30-13.00, and guided tours

Museo delle Cere
Piazza SS. Apostoli 67
Tel. 066796482
Mondays-Sundays 9.00-20.00
(in summer 20.30). July: Fridays-
Sundays 9.00-23.00. August:
Mondays-Sundays 9.00-23.00

**Museo delle Mura Aureliane
di Roma**
Via di Porta S. Sebastiano 18
Tel. 0670475284
Tuesdays-Sundays 9.00-14.00

Museo di Porta S. Paolo
Via R. Persichetti 3
Tel. 065743193
www.itnw.roma.it/ostia/scavi
Tuesdays-Saturdays 9.00-13.30,
14.30-16.30. Open 1st and 3rd
Sunday in the month. Closed
1 January, 1 May, 25 December

**Museo di Roma -
Palazzo Braschi** ★
Piazza S. Pantaleo 10
Tel. 0667108312-0667108313
www.museodiroma.
comune.roma.it
Tuesdays-Sundays 9.00-19.00

**Museo di Roma
in Trastevere**
Piazza S. Egidio 1/b
Tel. 065816563
www.comune.roma.it/
museodiroma.trastevere
Tuesdays-Sundays 10.00-20.00.
Closed 1 January, 1 May,
25 December

**Museo Nazionale Etrusco
di Villa Giulia**
Piazzale di Villa Giulia 9
Tel. 063201951-063226571
www.beniculturali.it
Tuesdays-Sundays 8.30-19.30.
Closed 1 January, 25 December

**Museo Nazionale del Palazzo
di Venezia**
Via del Plebiscito 118
Tel. 0669994318-066780131
Tuesdays-Sundays 8.30-19.30
(last entry 18.30)

**Museo Nazionale di Castel
S. Angelo**
Lungotevere Castello 50
Tel. 066819111-0668191124
Tuesdays-Sundays 9.00-19.00.
28 June-15 August: Saturdays
20.45-00.45

**Museo Nazionale Romano -
Crypta Balbi**
Via delle Botteghe Oscure 31
Tel. 066977671-066780147
www.archeorm.arti.beniculturali.it
Tuesdays-Sundays 9-19

**Museo Nazionale Romano -
Palazzo Altemps**
Piazza S. Apollinare 44
Tel. 0639967700-06684851
www.archeorm.arti.beniculturali.it
Tuesdays-Sundays 9.00-19.45

**Museo Nazionale Romano -
Palazzo Massimo alle Terme**
Largo di Villa Peretti 1
Tel. 0648903500-0648020275
www.archeorm.arti.beniculturali.it
Tuesdays-Sundays 9.00-20.00

**Museo Nazionale Romano -
Terme di Diocleziano**
Viale E. De Nicola 79
Tel. 06477881-0639967700
www.archeorm.arti.beniculturali.it

Tuesdays-Sundays 9.00-19.30.
Closed 1 January, 25 December

Museo e Antiquarium Palatino
Piazza S. Maria Nova 53 -
Via di S. Gregorio 30
Tel. 06699841
www.archeoroma.com/Palatino/
museo_palatino.htm
Mondays-Sundays 8.30-two hours
before the sunset. Guided tours
by request. Closed 1 January and
25 December

Museo Storico dei Bersaglieri
Porta Pia - Via XX settembre
Tel. 064857223
www.esercito.difesa.it/root/musei/
museo_bersaglieri.asp
Visits by prior arrangement

Palazzo delle Esposizioni
Via Nazionale 194
Tel. 064745903 - 06489411
www.palazzoesposizioni.it
Closed for restoration.

**Sacrario delle Bandiere delle
Forze Armate**
Via dei Fori Imperiali
Tel. 0647355002
Tuesdays-Sundays 9.30-15.00

SUBIACO

📋 **IAT**
Via Cadorna 59
Tel. 0774822013

Museums, Monuments
and Churches

Monastero di S. Benedetto
Tel. 077485039

TIVOLI

📋 **IAT**
Via del Barchetto
Tel. 0774334522

Hotels

G.H. Duca d'Este ★★★★ ♿
Tivoli Terme,
Via Tiburtina Valeria 330,
Tel. 07743883
www.ducadeste.com
184 rooms
Credit cards: American Express,
Diners Club, Visa, Mastercard,
Bancomat
A large hotel with a lovely
atmosphere and a good range of
sport facilities including a
swimming pool, tennis courts,
fitness club. The restaurant serves
local dishes.

Torre S. Angelo ★★★★ ♿ ★
Via Quintilio Varo
Tel. 0774332533
www.hoteltorresangelo.it
35 rooms
Credit cards: American Express,

Diners Club, Visa, Mastercard
Set in a wonderful position, this prestigious hotel with an atmosphere of bygone times has a restaurant and a swimming pool.

Restaurants

Adriano ⏹ ♿
Villa Adriana,
Via Villa Adriana 194,
Tel. 0774382235
www.hoteladriano.it
Closed Sunday evenings in winter
Credit cards: American Express, Diners Club, Visa
In a late 19th-century palace opposite the famous Villa Adriana, the restaurant serves traditional seasonal dishes. In summer, the kitchen is open till after 10pm and offers BBQ options.

Il Grottino della Sibilla dal 1826 ⏹
Piazza Rivarola 21
Tel. 0774332606
Credit cards: American Express, Diners Club, Visa, Mastercard, Bancomat
Near villas and temples and facing a beautiful square, the restaurant offers outdoor table service in summer and specializes in local produce: cheese, salami and hams, home-made pasta and desserts, house olive oils and wines.

Rural Lodgins

La Cerra ♿
Sant'Angelo in Valle Arcese
Strada S. Gregorio km 6.8
Tel. 0774411671
Credit cards: Visa, Mastercard, Bancomat
Set on a hill in a pine wood overlooking the Roman Castles Regional Park, the hotel offers studio flats with old furnishings and wooden bungalows. Also restaurant with local produce and a swimming pool.

Museums, Monuments and Churches

Antiquarium & Museo Didattico
Villa Adriana,
Via di Villa Adriana 204,
Tel. 0774530203-0774531979
www.archeolz.arti.beniculturali.it/indexmusei.htm
Mondays-Sundays 9.00-19.00 (last entry 18.00). Closed 1 January, 1 May, 25 December

TREVIGNANO ROMANO

📑 **Comune**
Piazza Vittorio Emanuele III, 8
Tel. 069991201

Restaurants

Villa Valentina dal 1980 ⏹⏹
Via Olivetello 5
Tel. 069997647
Closed Wednesdays

Credit cards: American Express, Visa, Mastercard
A restaurant boasting a permanent picture gallery and with a garden and terrace overlooking the nearby lake. It serves both national and international dishes.

Grotta Azzurra ⏹
Piazza Vittorio Emanuele 18
Tel. 069999420
Closed Tuesdays (except hols)
Credit cards: American Express, Diners Club, Visa, Bancomat
A 19th-century building with a view on the nearby lake. Refined and seasonal cuisine. Home-made pasta and desserts.

L'Acqua delle Donne ⏹
Via dell'Acquarella 6,
Tel. 069997418
Closed Mondays
Credit cards: American Express, Diners Club, Visa, Mastercard, Bancomat
Set on Lake Bracciano, this restaurant with a terrace serves traditional local cuisine including home-made pasta, lake fish and grilled meat and dishes with local vegetables. House olive oil.

Rural Lodgins

Acquaranda
Via dello Sboccatore 8
Tel. 069985301
Open March-October by arrangement
Credit cards: Visa, Mastercard, Bancomat
A farmhouse on Lake Bracciano with its own cattle breeding, cheese and ricotta produce. Bicycle and canoe rental.

VELLETRI

📑 **c/o IAT Frascati**
Piazza Marconi 1
Tel. 069420331

Hotels

Monte Artemisio *** ♿
Via dei Laghi 253
Tel. 069631330
www.monteartemisio.it
35 rooms
Credit cards: American Express, Diners Club, Visa
In the Roman Castles Park, the hotel offers comfortable rooms, a swimming pool and a restaurant serving local specialties.

Restaurants

Benito al Bosco ⏹⏹
Contrada Morice 96,
Tel. 069633991
www.benitoalbosco.com
Closed Tuesdays
Credit cards: American Express, Diners Club, Visa, Mastercard

In a park with a swimming pool, this classy restaurant with a terrace and garden service offers local cuisine specializing in fresh seafood and local cheese. Wide range of olive oils, salami and distilled spirits.

Rural Lodgins

I Casali della Parata ♿
Via Torre di Presciano 1
Tel. 0696195154
www.casalidellaparata.it
Credit cards: Diners Club, Visa, Mastercard, Bancomat
On a hill overlooking the lowlands and the sea and in the middle of the Albani Hills, these old stone farmhouses still maintain the warm atmosphere of bygone times. Further north are the Roman Castles and the nearby lake for angling. Also BBQ, restaurant, swimming pool and horse riding.

Iacchelli ♿
Pratone, Via dei Laghi al km 15
Tel. 069633256,
www.iacchelli.com
In the heart of the Roman Castles Park, this restaurant offers restaurant service and a shop which sells local produce. Bicycle rental.

ZAGAROLO

📑 **URP**
Tel. 0695769261
www.comunedizagarolo.it

Restaurants

Tordo Matto ⏹⏹⏹
Piazza S. Martino 8
Tel. 0695200050
www.iltordomatto.com
Closed Tuesdays
Once a bakery, this nice and cozy restaurant is located in the basement of a 19th-century building. Today the place has been restructured and furnished in modern style. There are only five tables, making booking essential. The restaurant specializes in traditional yet sophisticated local dishes.

Giardino ⏹ ★
Corso Vittorio Emanuele 5
Tel. 069524015
www.ilgiardino1931.com
Closed Tuesdays
Credit cards: American Express, Diners Club, Visa, Bancomat
A 17th-century restaurant adjacent to the Rospiglioni palace. It offers rooms varying in style and furniture, and beautiful terraces. Traditional dishes creative touches. Not to miss the home-made pasta.

METRIC CONVERTIONS

DISTANCE

Kilometres/Miles

km to mi	mi to km
1 = 0.62	1 = 1.6
2 = 1.2	2 = 3.2
3 = 1.9	3 = 4.8
4 = 2.5	4 = 6.4
5 = 3.1	5 = 8.1
6 = 3.7	6 = 9.7
7 = 4.3	7 = 11.3
8 = 5.0	8 = 12.9

Meters/Feet

m to ft	ft to m
1 = 3.3	1 = 0.30
2 = 6.6	2 = 0.61
3 = 9.8	3 = 0.91
4 = 13.1	4 = 1.2
5 = 16.4	5 = 1.5
6 = 19.7	6 = 1.8
7 = 23.0	7 = 2.1
8 = 26.2	8 = 2.4

WEIGHT

Kilograms/Pounds

kg to lb	lb to kg
1 = 2.2	1 = 0.45
2 = 4.4	2 = 0.91
3 = 6.6	3 = 1.4
4 = 8.8	4 = 1.8
5 = 11.0	5 = 2.3
6 = 13.2	6 = 2.7
7 = 15.4	7 = 3.2
8 = 17.6	8 = 3.6

Grams/Ounces

g to oz	oz to g
1 = 0.04	1 = 28
2 = 0.07	2 = 57
3 = 0.11	3 = 85
4 = 0.14	4 = 114
5 = 0.18	5 = 142
6 = 0.21	6 = 170
7 = 0.25	7 = 199
8 = 0.28	8 = 227

TEMPERATURE

Fahrenheit/Celsius

F	C
0	-17.8
5	-15.0
10	-12.2
15	-9.4
20	-6.7
25	-3.9
30	-1.1
32	0
35	1.7
40	4.4
45	7.2
50	10.0
55	12.8
60	15.5
65	18.3
70	21.1
75	23.9
80	26.7
85	29.4
90	32.2
95	35.0
100	37.8

LIQUID VOLUME

Liters/U.S. Gallons

l to gal	gal to l
1 = 0.26	1 = 3.8
2 = 0.53	2 = 7.6
3 = 0.79	3 = 11.4
4 = 1.1	4 = 15.1

Liters/U.S. Gallons

l to gal	gal to l
5 = 1.3	5 = 18.9
6 = 1.6	6 = 22.7
7 = 1.8	7 = 26.5
8 = 2.1	8 = 30.3

INDEX OF NAMES

GENERAL INDEX

ROMAN EMPERORS

The emperors marked with an asterisk* do not belong to the family under which they are listed. The permanent division of the Roman Empire into the Western and Eastern Empires begins with Honorius. The names listed after Honorius refer to the emperors of the Western Empire.

Julio-Claudii (27 BC-68 AD)

Augustus	27 BC-14 AD
Tiberius	14-37
Caligula	37-41
Claudius	41-54
Nero	54-68
Galba	68-69
Otho	69
Vitellius	69

Flavians (69-96)

Vespasian	69-79
Titus	79-81
Domitian	81-96
Nerva	96-98
Trajan	98-117
Hadrian	117-138

Antonines (138-192)

Antoninus Pius	138-161
Marcus Aurelius	161-180
Commodus	180-192
Pertinax	193
Didius Julianus	193

Severians (193-235)

Septimius Severus	193-211
Caracalla	211-217
Macrinus*	217-218

Heliogabalus	218-222
Alexander Severus	222-235
Maximinus	235-238
Gordian I	238
Gordian II	238
Pupienus	238
Balbinus	238
Gordian III	238-244
Philip I	244-249
Decius	249-251
Trebonianus Gallus	251-253
Aemilian	251-253
Volusianus	251-253
Valerian	253-260
Gallienus	260-268
Claudius II	268-270
Aurelian	270-275
Tacitus	275-276
Probus	276-282
Carus	282-283
Numerian	283-284
Carinus	283-285
Diocletian	284-305
Maximian	286-305
Costantius Chlorus	305-306

Second Group of Flavians (306-363)

Constantine the Great	306-337

reigned until 324 with:

Galerius*	305-311
Maximian*	307-308
Maxentius*	307-312
Licinius	308-324
Maximinus Daia*	310-313
Constantinus II	337-361

reigned until 350 with:

Constantine II	337-340
Constans	337-350
Julian	361-363
Jovian	363-364
Valentinian I	364-375

with:

Valens	364-378
Gratian	365-383
Valentinian II	375-392
Theodosius	379-395

(Western Empire)

Honorius	395-423
Constans III	423-425
Valentinian III	425-455
Avitus	455-457
Majorian	457-461
Libius Severus	461-465
Anthemius	467-472
Olybrius	472
Glycerius	473-474
Julius Nepos	474-475
Romulus Augustulus	475-476

POPES

This chronological list, based on the Papal Yearbook published by the Vatican City, shows the name of each pope, and the first (date of consecration) and last years of his pontificate, which does not necessarily correspond to the year of his death.

St Peter, not known when he came to Rome, but martyred there in the year 64 or 67.
St Linus, 67-76.
St Anacletus or Cletus, 76-88.
St Clement, 88-97.
St Evaristus, 97-105.
St Alexander I, 105-115.
St Sixtus I, 115-125.
St Telesphorus, 125-136.
St Hyginius, 136-140.
St Pius I, 140-155.
St Anicetus, 155-166.
St Soter, 166-175.
St Eleutherius, 175-189.
St Victor I, 189-199.
St Zephrinus, 199-217.
St Callixtus I, 217-222.
[St Hippolytus, 217-235].

St Urban I, 222-230.
St Pontian, 230-235.
St Anterus, 235-236.
St Fabian, 236-250.
St Cornelius, 251-253.
[*Novatian*, 251].
St Lucius I, 253-254.
St Stephen I, 254-257.
St Sixtus II, 257-258.
St Dionysius, 259-268.
St Felix I, 269-274.
St Eutychian, 275-283.
St Caius, 283-296.
St Marcellinus, 296-304.
St Marcellus I, 308-309.
St Eusebius, April-August 309 (or 310).
St Miltiades or Melchiades, 311-314.

St Sylvester I, 314-335.
St Mark, January- October 336.
St Julius I, 337-352.
Liberius, 352-366.
[Felix II, 355-365].
St Damasus I, 366-384.
[Ursinus, 366-367].
St Siricius, 384-399.
St Anastasius I, 399-401.
St Innocent I, 401-417.
St Zozimus, 417-418.
St Boniface I, 418-422.
[Eulalius, 418-419].
St Celestine I, 422-432.
St Sixtus III, 432-440.
St Leo I the Great, 440-461.
St Hilary, 461-468.
St Simplicius, 468-483.
St Felix III (II), 483-492.

St Gelasius I, 492-496.
Anastasius II, 496-498.
St Simmacus, 498-514.
[Lawrence, 498-505].
St Hormisdas, 514-523.
St John I, 523-526.
St Felix IV (III), 526-530.
Boniface II, 530-532.
[Dioscorus, September-October 530].
John II, the first to change his name when he acceded to the papal throne, 533-535.
St Agapitus I, 535-536.
St Silverius, 536-537.
Vigilius, 537-555.
Pelagius I, 556-561.
John III, 561-574.
Benedict I, 575-579.
Pelagius II, 579-590.
St Gregory I the Great, 590-604.
Sabinian, 604-606.
Boniface III, February-November 607.
St Boniface IV, 608-615.
St Deusdedit or Adeodatus I, 615-618.
Boniface V, 619-625.
Honorius I, 625-638.
Severinus, May-August 640.
John IV, 640-642.
Theodore I, 642-649.
St Martin I, 649-655.
St Eugenius I, 654-657.
St Vitalian, 657-672.
Adeodatus II, 672-676.
Donus, 676-678.
St Agatho, 678-681.
St Leo II, 682-683.
St Benedict II, 684-685.
John V, 685-686.
Conon, 686-687.
[Theodore, 687].
[Paschal, 687].
St Sergius I, 687-701.
John VI, 701-705.
John VII, 705-707.
Sisinnius, January-February 708.
Constantine, 708-715.
St Gregory II, 715-731.
St Gregory III, 731-741.
St Zachary, 741-752.
Stephen II (III), 752-757.
St Paul I, 757-767.
[Constantine, 767-769].
[Philip, 768].
Stephen III (IV), 768-772.
Adrian I, 772-795.
St Leo III, 795-816.
Stephen IV (V), 816-817.
St Paschal I, 817-824.
Eugenius II, 824-827.
Valentine, August-September 827.
Gregory IV, 827-844.
[John, 844].
Sergius II, 844-847.

St Leo IV, 847-855.
Benedict III, 855-858.
[Anastasius, 855].
St Nicholas I, 858-867.
Adrian II, 867-872.
John VIII, 872-882.
Marinus I, 882-884.
St Adrian III, 884-885.
Stephen V (VI), 885-891.
Formosus, 891-896.
Boniface VI, April 896.
Stephen VI (VII), 896-897.
Romanus, August-November 897.
Theodore II, December 897.
John IX, 898-900.
Benedict IV, 900-903.
Leo V, July-September 903.
[Christophorus, 903-904].
Sergius III, 904-911.
Anastasius III, 911-913.
Landus, 913-914.
John X, 914-923.
Leo VI, May-December 928.
Stephen VII (VIII), 928-931.
John XI, 931-935.
Leo VII, 936-939.
Stephen VIII (IX), 939-942.
Marinus II, 942-946.
Agapitus II, 946-955.
John XII, Ottaviano, of the counts of Tusculum, 955-964.
Leo VIII, 963-965.
Benedict V, 964-966.
John XIII, 965-972.
Benedict VI, 973-974.
[Boniface VII, for the first time, 974].
Benedict VII, 974-983.
John XIV, Pietro, 983-984.
[Boniface VII, for the second time, 984-985].
John XV, 985-996.
Gregory V, Bruno, of the dukes of Carinthia, 996-999.
[John XVI, John Filagato, 997-998].
Sylvester II, Gerbert, 999-1003.
John XVII, June-November 1003.
John XVIII, 1004-1009.
Sergius IV, Pietro, 1009-1012.
Benedict VIII, Teofilatto of the counts of Tusculum, 1012-24.
[Gregory, 1012].
John XIX, Romano, of the counts of Tusculum, 1024-32.
Benedict IX, Teofilatto, of the counts of Tusculum, 1032-44.
Sylvester III, Giovanni, January-February 1045.
Benedict IX, for the second time, April-May 1045.
Gregory VI, John Gratia, 1045-46.
Clement II, Sudiger, of the lords of Morsleben and Hornburg, 1046-47.
Benedict IX, for the third time, 1047-48.

Damasus II, Poppo, July-August 1048.
St Leo IX, Bruno, of the counts of Egisheim and Dagsburg, 1049-54.
Victor II, Gebhard, of the counts of Tollenstein and Hirschberg, 1055-57.
Stephen IX (X), Frederick, of the dukes of Lorraine, 1057-58.
[Benedict X, John, 1058-59].
Nicholas II, Gerhard, 1059-61.
Alexander II, Anselm of Baggio, 1061-73.
[Honorius II, Kidult, 1061-72].
St Gregory VII, Hildebrand, 1073-85.
[Clement III, Guibert of Ravenna, 1084-1100].
Blessed Victor III, Dauferius (Desiderius), 1086-87.
Blessed Urban II, Odo de Lagery, 1088-99.
Paschal II, Ranierus, 1099-1118.
[Theoderic, 1100].
[Albert, 1102].
[Sylvester IV, Maginulfo, 1105-1111].
Gelasius II, Giovanni Caetani, 1118-19.
[Gregory VIII, Maurice Burdinus, 1118-21].
Callixtus II, Guido of Burgundy, 1119-24.
Honorius II, Lambert, 1124-30.
[Celestine II, Teobaldo Buccapecus, 1124].
Innocent II, Lorenzo Papareschi, 1130-43.
[Anacletus II, Pietro Pierleonis, 1130-38].
[Victor IV, Gregory, March-May 1138].
Celestine II, Guido, 1143-44.
Lucius II, Gerardo Caccianemici, 1144-45.
Blessed Eugenius III, Bernardo Pignatelli, 1145-59.
Anastasius IV, Corrado, 1153-54.
Adrian IV, Nicholas Breakspear, 1154-59.
Alexander III, Rolando Bandinelli, 1159-81.
[Victor IV, Ottaviano da Monticello, 1159-64].
[Paschal III, Guido da Crema, 1164-68].
[Callixtus III, John, 1168-78].
[Innocent III, Lando, 1178-80].
Lucius III, Ubaldo Allucingoli, 1181-85.
Urban III, Uberto Crivelli, 1185-87.
Gregory VIII, Alberto de Morra, October-December 1187.
Clement III, Paolo Scolari, 1187-91.
Celestine III, Giacinto Bobone, 1191-98.

Innocent III, Lothair, of the counts of Segni, 1198-1216.

Honorius III, Cencio Savelli, 1216-27.

Gregory IX, Hugo, of the counts of Segni, 1227-41.

Celestine IV, Goffredo Castiglioni, October-November 1241.

Innocent IV, Sinibaldo Fieschi, 1243-54.

Alexander IV, Rainaldo, of the counts of Ienne, 1254-61.

Urban IV, Jacques Pantaléon, 1261-64.

Clement IV, Guy Foucois, 1265-68.

Blessed Gregory X, Teobaldo Visconti, 1272-76.

Blessed Innocent V, Pietro di Tarantasia, February-June 1276.

Adrian V, Ottobono Fieschi, July-August 1276.

John XXI, Pietro di Giuliano (P. Ispano), 1276-77.

Nicholas III, Giovanni Gaetano Orsini, 1277-80.

Martin IV, Simone de Brion, 1281-85.

Honorius IV, Giacomo Sevelli, 1285-87.

Nicholas IV, Girolamo Masci, 1288-92.

St Celestine V, Pietro da Murrone, August-December 1294.

Boniface VIII, Benedetto Caetani, 1294-1303.

Blessed Benedict XI, Niccolò Boccasini, 1303-04.

Clement V, Bertrand de Got, 1305-14.

John XXII, Jacques Duèse, 1316-34.

[Nicholas V, Pietro Rainalducci, 1328-30].

Benedict XII, Jacques Fournier, 1335-42.

Clement VI, Pierre Roger, 1342-52.

Innocent VI, Etienne Aubert, 1352-62.

Blessed Urban V, Guillaume de Grimoard, 1362-70.

Gregory XI, Pierre Roger de Beaufort, 1371-78.

Urban VI, Bartolomeo Prignano, last pope who was not a cardinal, 1378-89.

Boniface IX, Pietro Tomacelli, 1389-1404.

Innocent VII, Cosma Migliorati, 1404-06.

Gregory XII, Angelo Correr, 1406-15.

Avignon Papacy, Western Schism of 1378:

[Clement VII, Roberto of the counts of Genevois, 1378-94].

[Benedict XIII, Pietro de Luna, 1394-1423].

[Clement VIII, Gil Sánchez Muñoz, 1423-29].

[Benedict XIV, Bernardo Garnier, 1425-30].

Pisan Papacy:

[Alexander V, Peter Philgaro, 1409-1410].

[John XXIII, Baldassarre Costa, 1410-1415].

Martin V, Oddone Colonna, 1417-31.

Eugenius IV, Gabriele Condulmer, 1431-47.

[Felix V, Amedeo, Duke of Savoy, 1440-49].

Nicholas V, Tommaso Parentucelli, 1447-55.

Callixtus III, Alfonso de Borja (Borgia), 1455-58.

Pius II, Enea Silvio Piccolomini, 1458-64.

Paul II, Pietro Barbo, 1464-71.

Sixtus IV, Francesco Della Rovere, 1471-84.

Innocent VIII, Giovanni Battista Cybo, 1484-92.

Alexander VI, Rodrigo de Borja (Borgia), 1492-1503.

Pius III, Francesco Todeschini Piccolomini, October 1503.

Julius II, Giuliano Della Rovere, 1503-13.

Leo X, Giovanni de' Medici, 1513-21.

Adrian VI, Adrian Florensz, 1522-23.

Clement VII, Giulio de' Medici, 1523-34.

Paul III, Alessandro Farnese, 1534-49.

Julius III, Giovanni Maria Ciocchi del Monte, 1550-55.

Marcellus II, Marcello Cervini, April-May. 1555.

Paul IV, Gian Pietro Carafa, 1555-59.

Pius IV, Giovan Angelo de' Medici, 1560-65.

St Pius V, Antonio Ghislieri, 1566-72.

Gregory XIII, Ugo Boncompagni, 1572-85.

Sixtus V, Felice Peretti, 1585-90.

Urban VII, Giambattista Castagna, September 1590.

Gregory XIV, Niccolò Sfondrati, 1590-91.

Innocent IX, Giovanni Antonio Facchinetti, November-December 1591.

Clement VIII, Ippolito Aldobrandini, 1592-1605.

Leo XI, Alessandro de' Medici, April 1605.

Paul V, Camillo Borghese, 1605-21.

Gregory XV, Alessandro Ludovisi, 1621-23.

Urban VIII, Maffeo Barberini, 1623-44.

Innocent X, Giambattista Pamphilj, 1644-55.

Alexander VII, Fabio Chigi, 1655-67.

Clement IX, Giulio Rospigliosi, 1667-69.

Clement X, Emilio Altieri, 1670-76.

Blessed Innocent XI, Benedetto Odescalchi, 1676-89.

Alexander VIII, Pietro Ottoboni, 1689-91.

Innocent XII, Antonio Pignatelli, 1691-1700.

Clement XI, Giovanni Francesco Albani, 1700-21.

Innocent XIII, Michelangelo dei Conti, 1721-24.

Benedict XIII, Pietro Francesco Orsini, 1724-30.

Clement XII, Lorenzo Corsini, 1730-40.

Benedict XIV, Prospero Lambertini, 1740-58.

Clement XIII, Carlo Rezzonico, 1758-69.

Clement XIV, Giovanni Vincenzo Antonio Ganganelli, 1769-74.

Pius VI, Giannangelo Braschi, 1775-99.

Pius VII, Barnaba Chiaramonti, 1800-1823.

Leo XII, Annibale Della Genga Sermattei, 1823-29.

Pius VIII, Francesco Saverio Castiglioni, 1829-30.

Gregory XVI, Bartolomeo Alberto Cappellari, 1831-46.

Blessed Pius IX, Giovanni Maria Mastai Ferretti, 1846-78.

Leo XIII, Vincenzo Gioacchino Pecci, 1878-1903.

St Pius X, Giuseppe Melchiorre Sarto, 1903-14.

Benedict XV, Giacomo Della Chiesa, 1914-22.

Pius XI, Achille Ratti, 1922-39.

Pius XII, Eugenio Pacelli, 1939-58.

John XXIII, Angelo Giuseppe Roncalli, 1958-63.

Paul VI, Giovanni Battista Montini, 1963-78.

John Paul I, Albino Luciani, September 1978.

John Paul II, Karol Wojtyla, 1978-2005.

Benedict XVI, Joseph Ratzinger, 2005-.

GLOSSARY

Acroterion
A sculptural figure or ornament mounted on the apex or corners of a pediment

Ambo, pl. ambones
A raised platform in an early Christian church from which parts of the service were conducted

Ambulatory
Open-air walkway flanked by columns or trees; also corridor or passageway in theater, amphitheater, or catacombs

Amphitheater
An oval or round building with tiers or seats around a central arena, used in Ancient Roman times for gladiatorial contests and spectacles

Architrave
The lowermost division of a classical entablature, resting directly on the column capitals and supporting the frieze

Atrium
The forecourt of an early Christian church, flanked or surrounded by porticoes. Also an open-air central court around which a house is built.

Attic
Topmost storey of a classical building (esp. triumphal arches)

Basilica
Rectangular-shaped building: in Roman times, used for the administration of justice; in early Christian times, used for worship, and generally with a central nave and side aisles, possibly with apse/s.

Bucrania
A form of classical decoration – heads of oxen garlanded with flowers

Calidarium
Room for hot or steam baths in a Roman bath

Campagna
The countryside around Rome

Cantoria
Choir-stalls or gallery for the choir in a church

Capital
Part which links a column to the structure above. In classical architecture, capitals were Doric, Ionian, or Corinthian

Cavea
Spectator seating of a theater or amphitheater, usually divided into sections which were assigned to different social classes

Cella
The principal chamber or enclosed part of a classical temple where the cult image was kept

Ciborium
Casket or tabernacle containing the host; also a canopy above the altar

Cippus (pl. cippi)
Sepulchral monument, sometimes in the form of an altar

Codex (pl. codices)
A manuscript book, esp. of Scriptural or Classical texts, usually on vellum

Colombarium
A building, usually underground, with niches for urns containing the ashes of the dead

Confessio
Crypt below the high altar, usually containing the relics of a saint

Cosmatesque, Cosmati work:
is a style of floor-making typical of the Medieval era in Italy, and especially of Rome and its surroundings, deriving from *Cosmati*, one of the groups of marble craftsmen who created works by taking marble from ancient Roman ruins, and arranging the fragments in geometrical decorations

Crater
An antique vessel used for mixing wine and water

Cubiculum
Cavity dug out of the rock in a catacomb where a body was laid

Dalmatic
Wide-sleeved overgarment with slit sides worn by priest or deacon

Edicola
Shrine, niche

Encaustic painting
Type of painting in which pigment is mixed with melted beeswax and resin, and the color is fixed by heat after application

Entablature
The horizontal section of a classical order that rests on the columns, usually composed of a cornice, frieze and architrave

Exedra
A large apsidal extension of the interior volume of a church; often a semi-circular open area

Forum (pl. fora)
A large flat area in an Ancient Roman town, the center of political life

Frigidarium
Room for cold baths

Gens
Family (in Roman times)

Ghibelline
Name to describe supporters of the Holy Roman Emperor in medieval history

Guelf
Name to describe supporters of the Pope in Medieval history

Iconostasis
A screen or partition separating the part of the church where the clergy officiate from the worshippers, especially in an Eastern church.

Incunabulum (pl. incunabula)
Book printed before 1501.

Mithraeum
Cult site of the Eastern god Mithras

Necropolis
Pre-Christian tombs grouped in or over a particular area, or the area itself.

Oculus
Circular opening, especially at the top of a dome

Opus sectile
A mosaic or pavement made of thin slabs of colored marble cut in geometrical shapes

Pendentive
A spherical triangle forming the transition from the circular plan of a dome to the polygonal plan of the supporting structure, often used to depict the four Evangelists esp. in an early church

Peristyle
A colonnade surrounding a building or courtyard

Pilaster
A shallow, rectangular feature projecting from a wall, with a capital and a base and architecturally treated as a column

Pluteus
Marble panel, usually decorated

Polyptych
Altar-piece consisting of a number of panels. A *diptych* has two panels; a *triptych* has three.

Pronaos
An open vestibule before the cella of a classical temple or porch in front of a church

Quadriga
A chariot drawn by four horses

Quadriporticus
A four-sided portico, often in front of a building and surrounding a central courtyard

Sacristy
Part of church where furnishings and vestments are kept, and where clergy prepare for services

Sarcophagus (pl. sarcophagi)
Stone coffin, often with relief decoration or inscription

Serliana
Round-headed archway flanked by smaller compartments, the side compartments being capped with entablatures on which the central compartment rests

Silenus
Minor woodland deity and companion of Dionysus in Ancient Greek mythology, with a horse's ears and tail

Spandrel
The triangular space between two adjoining arches

Spina
Low stone wall connecting the turning-posts at either end of a Roman circus

Stele
Upright stone bearing a monumental inscription

Tepidarium
The hot room in a Roman bath

Terme
In Ancient Rome, usually public building complexes for hot and cold baths. Already common by the 2nd century BC, the popularity of bath complexes reached its height in the Imperial period, when swimming-pools, massage rooms, gymnasiums (*palestrae*), gardens and libraries were added. The actual bath complex (*Terme*) consisted of a changing room, a warm room with a warm pool (*tepidarium*), a hot room with a hot pool (*calidarium*), a sauna and a room with pools of cold water for cold baths (*frigidarium*)

Titulus
The first house-churches or parish churches in Rome

Triclinium
Dining-room; banqueting hall

Tympanum
The triangular space at the top of the facade of a temple, often recessed and decorated with sculpture

Volute
A spiral, scroll-like ornament

PICTURE CREDITS

Notes

Notes

Notes

Hotel Piranesi
PALAZZO NAINER
ROMA

*H*otel Piranesi enjoys an enviable position for sightseeing Rome and its fascinating monuments.

*S*ince its establishment, it has been a symbol of excellent hospitality based on style and elegance.

**Via del Babbuino, 196
00187 Roma
Tel. +39 06328041
Fax +39 063610597
info@hotelpiranesi.com
www.hotelpiranesi.com**

Cul de Sac   *Winebar*

This historical Roman wine bar, formerly the location of an old "Vini e Oli" (Wines and Oil) in the early 1900s, gave origin in 1977 to the Winebar phenomenon in Rome by offering a vast selection of wines served together with an assortment of cold meats and regional cheeses from all over Italy. It is located in Piazza Pasquino, the famous Roman piazza home to one of the two "talking" statues of Rome.

The name of the place derives from its particular architectural shape (long and narrow). In fact, the wine bar's floor plan develops longitudinally with a sequence of wooden benches and fishermen's nets hanging above, creating a setting similar to the third class coaches of the trains in the '60s.

A blanket of bottles, placed on 4 rows of shelves that are 19 metres long, decorates the walls and livens the environment. The wine list, encyclopaedic and subdivided by Region of production, provides the beginner with additional information on the wine's main characteristics (production area, different types of grapes with which the wine is made, organoleptic characteristics). The list offers a selection of approximately 1500 different labels. Besides the cheeses and cold meats, homemade gastronomic specialties, which betray the multiethnic origins of the owners, are served. Among others, notable is the "Topik" (a pocket of chick peas and potatoes with raisins and pine nuts). Among the first course dishes there are soups (onions and red lentils), "pizzoccheri" from Valtellina (northern fresh pasta dish), Strozzapreti alla siciliana (fresh pasta/Sicilian recipe), and excellent homemade lasagna. Among the second course dishes, there are Brandade di baccalà (dried cod purée), tripe and "involtini alla romana" (meat rolls /Roman recipe), guinea hen with grains, grape leaf rolls with meatballs cooked in wine with potato purée. The homemade deer, partridge, pheasant and hare patés are unforgettable.

Service is quick and efficient, the waiters are kind and attentive and are especially educated in wine. They are always willing to help you in deciding which wine to select with your dish.

Opening hours: from 12.00 a.m. to 4.00 p.m. and from 6.00 p.m. to 00.30 a.m.

 CartaSi   VISA   VISA Electron **Bancomat**

Roma - P.zza Pasquino, 73 • Tel. 06 68801094
e-mail: enoteca.culdesac@virgilio.it

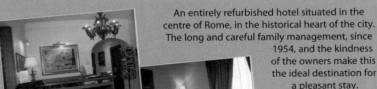